Exploring the Word of God: The Four Gospels

Matthew, Mark, Luke, and John

By J. Michael Feazell, Michael D. Morrison, Joseph Tkach, James G. Herst, Paul Kroll, Timothy D. Finlay, Dan Rogers, and others

CONTENTS

The Four Gospels

1.	Why Do We Need Four Gospels?	1
2.	Can We Trust the Gospels?	6
3.	The Search for the Real Words of Jesus	12
4.	The Gospels and Us	17
5.	How Do We Know About Jesus?	21
6.	What Jesus' Parables Reveal	26
7.	How Many Points in a Parable?	35
8.	What the Gospels Teach Us About God	40
9.	What the Gospels Teach Us About Jesus	44
10.	What the Gospels Teach Us About the Holy Spirit	49
11.	What the Gospels Teach Us About the Scriptures	51
12.	What the Gospels Teach Us About Angels and Demons	55
13.	The Gospels and the Gospel	57

Matthew

14.	Explore the Gospels: Matthew	59
15.	42 Men and Five Women: A Study of Matthew 1:1-16	62
16.	The Virgin Will Give Birth to a Son: Matthew 1:18-23	65
17.	Jesus: Tempted on Our Behalf	67
18.	Matthew 5:17-19 and the "Law"	70

19.	Matthew 5: Sermon on the Mount	78
20.	Matthew 6: Sermon on the Mount, Part 2	90
21.	Matthew 7: Sermon on the Mount, Part 3	95
22.	Matthew 9: The Purpose of Healings	99
23.	Matthew 13: Parables of the Kingdom	103
24.	Jesus Walks on the Water (Matthew 14)	108
25.	More Parables of the Kingdom	122
26.	Matthew 16: What Kind of Messiah?	129
27.	Matthew 18: Parable of the Unforgiving Servant	133
28.	Parable of Workers in the Vineyard	139
29.	The Hero Who Wouldn't (Matthew 21)	141
30.	What Matthew 24 Tells Us About "The End"	149
31.	Matthew 24:20: Why Pray Not To Flee on the Sabbath?	160
32.	Good News in an Alabaster Jar (Matthew 26)	163
33.	Sold…For Thirty Pieces of Silver	171
34.	Pilate's Wife (Matthew 27)	172

Mark

35.	Explore the Gospels: Mark	174
36.	A Lesson in Humility (Mark 1:1-8)	177
37.	A Lesson in Transition (Mark 1:1-8)	181
38.	A Lesson About Power (Mark 1:1-8)	184
39.	A Lesson About Baptism (Mark 1:9-11)	187
40.	A Lesson About Temptation (Mark 1:12-13)	191
41.	A Lesson About Fulfillment (Mark 1:14-15)	195
42.	A Lesson About Fishing (Mark 1:16-20)	199
43.	A Lesson About Authority (Mark 1:21-28)	203
44.	A Lesson About Asking (Mark 1:29-34)	206
45.	A Lesson About Priorities (Mark 1:35-39)	209
46.	A Lesson About Misperception (Mark 1:40-45)	213
47.	A Lesson About Healing (Mark 2:1-12)	218
48.	A Lesson About Assumptions (Mark 2:13-17)	223
49.	A Lesson About Old and New (Mark 2:18-22)	226
50.	A Lesson About God's Love (Mark 2:23-28)	229
51.	Does Mark 2:27-28 Command the Weekly Sabbath?	233
52.	A Lesson About Appearances (Mark 3:7-12)	237
53.	Another Lesson About Authority (Mark 3:13-19)	242

54.   A Lesson About Envy (Mark 3:20-27)   244
55.   A Lesson About Damnation (Mark 3:22-30)   247
56.   A Lesson About Hard Hearts (Mark 4:10-13)   249
57.   A Lesson About Satan (Mark 4:14-15)   252
58.   A Lesson About Seeds (Mark 4:16-20)   254
59.   A Lesson About Measurement (Mark 4:21-25)   256
60.   A Lesson About Lessons (Mark 4:30-34)   258
61.   A Lesson About Storms (Mark 4:35-41)   261
62.   Jesus Is Coming (Mark 5:1-18)   263
63.   A Lesson About Hope (Mark 5:21-43)   266
64.   A Lesson About Faith (Mark 6:1-6)   268
65.   A Lesson About Instructions (Mark 6:7-12)   270
66.   A Lesson About Guilty Consciences (Mark 6:14-29)   272
67.   Feeding 5,000 and Walking on Water (Mark 6:30-52)   274
68.   Everyone Must Die! A Study of Mark 8:27-38   278
69.   The Transfiguration: Sneak Peek at the Resurrection   282
70.   The Fig Tree and the Temple in Mark 11:12-16   285
71.   A Tasty Sandwich (Mark 11)   293

Luke

72.   Explore the Gospels: Luke   296
73.   Special Report: What You Have Heard Is True!   302
74.   Open Letter to a Wealthy Man   306
75.   Luke's Legacy to Women   312
76.   The Prominence of Women in the Gospel of Luke   316
77.   Luke's "Orderly" Account – An Examination   318
78.   Announcing the King: A Study of Luke 1:1-38   325
79.   Two Songs of Praise: A Study of Luke 1:39-80   329
80.   A Savior Is Born: A Study of Luke 2:1-21   334
81.   What Child Is This? A Study of Luke 2:22-52   339
82.   A New Look at the Good Samaritan   343
83.   Parable of the Lost Son   346
84.   The Prodigal God   353
85.   Lazarus and the Rich Man   357
86.   Lazarus and the Rich Man   362
87.   The Comma of Luke 23:43   365

John

88.	Explore the Gospel of John: "They Might Have Life"	370
89.	John 1: The Word Made Flesh	376
90.	John 2: Turning Water Into Wine	379
91.	John 3: An Odyssey of Faith	383
92.	John 4: Jesus and the Samaritan Woman	385
93.	John 4: Living Water	406
94.	John 4: True Worship	408
95.	John 6: 'Let Nothing Be Wasted'	411
96.	John 9: A Blinding Light	416
97.	John 10: Which Voice Do You Hear?	420
98.	John 10:10 – The Abundant Life	423
99.	John 11: 'Lazarus, Come Out'	425
100.	John 12: Palm Sunday	428
101.	Right Words, But the Wrong Reason – John 12:12-19	430
102.	John 13: Footwashing: A Tradition of Service	432
103.	John 14: "In His Name'	434
104.	John 19: Crowned With Thorns	437
105.	Can You Believe It? A Study of John 20:18-29	439
	About the Contributors	441
	About the Publisher	442
	Grace Communion Seminary	444

WHY DO WE NEED FOUR GOSPELS?

By Timothy D. Finlay

At the heart of Christianity is the person and work of Jesus Christ. So we would expect the Christian Scriptures to include an account of Jesus' life. But why do we have four – the Gospels according to Matthew, Mark, Luke and John? Isn't this redundant? Wouldn't one be enough?

On the contrary, our knowledge of Jesus Christ would be incomplete if we had only one Gospel. Or even if we had three Gospels but were missing one. Matthew, Mark, Luke and John each told the story from a different perspective, because each had a different audience in mind. We tend to blur these four distinctive portraits of Jesus together. But knowing how an act or saying of Jesus fits in with each author's perspective can greatly enhance our understanding of its meaning.

Here is a brief introduction to the particular message and theme of each of the four Gospels. Because of space limitations, we will usually cite locations rather than quote verses in full. But if you look up some of these verses in the New Testament, you will begin to see how each Gospel has a unique message. You will also see how all four work together to build a complete picture of the life and work of Jesus Christ.

Matthew — the bridge

Matthew's readers were mainly Jewish Christians, and he emphasized Christianity's continuity with the Hebrew Scriptures (what we call the Old Testament) and traditions. Through Matthew we are told the relationship of Jesus to the law and the Old Testament prophets. This Gospel, placed first in the New Testament, is like a bridge from Old to New. Matthew quotes from the Old Testament more frequently than any other New Testament writer.

The most sacred part of the Hebrew Bible was the Torah, the five books containing the law of Moses. Matthew likewise concentrates most of Jesus' teaching in five long discourses as the new covenant counterpart to Mosaic law.

1. (5:1-7:29) In the "Sermon on the Mount," Jesus expanded his disciples' understanding of three central topics: the law, worship and good deeds.
2. (10:1-42) Jesus called the apostles and commissioned them to speak for him, just as God had commissioned Moses and the prophets.
3. (13:1-52) In seven parables, Jesus added a new dimension to the understanding of the kingdom of God.
4. (18:1-35) Jesus outlined a code of conduct that would enable his followers to establish and maintain their new-found spiritual relationships.
5. (chapters 23-25) Jesus showed how and why the old order, with its hypocrisy, must give way to a new age of peace and justice, in which righteousness would be rewarded and evil punished.

Matthew encouraged Jewish converts to see their heritage in the context of a greater law, and their history in the light of the spiritual kingdom of God. For Matthew, Jesus' fulfillment of the Scriptures did not mean that those Scriptures had lost their significance and could therefore be discarded. Rather, for Matthew the Hebrew Scriptures gained significance through Jesus and continue to be part of the "treasure" of the scribe trained for the kingdom of heaven (see Matthew 13:52) (Daniel J. Harrington, *The Gospel of Matthew*, Sacra Pagina series, page 22).

Mark — 'This is what happened'

Mark's Gospel is fast-moving and dramatic. It reads like a series of eye-witness accounts. Because of this action-packed style, Mark's Gospel is an ideal starting point for discovering who Jesus Christ is and what he is all about.

Mark is more concerned about telling us what happened, rather than when it happened. He writes more like a journalist than a historian. He cuts to the quick, introducing Jesus to people who have perhaps heard of him but don't know him very well yet.

Verbs like "run," "shout" and "amaze" abound in this book. Mark's favorite adverb is *euthys*, meaning "immediately" or "at once" (it occurs ten times in chapter 1 alone).

Mark does not delay the action by telling us about Jesus' genealogy, or even his birth. Rather, Mark begins with the briefest survey of the ministry of John the Baptist, the baptism of Jesus and his testing in the wilderness by Satan (1:1-13). Then the action begins, and continues nonstop for 16 chapters. Event quickly follows event. On occasion, one story is interrupted to begin another, and the first story finished later.

Mark's account of the events leading up to Jesus' trial and crucifixion is especially detailed and vivid. Mark's purpose is to show that Jesus is the Son of God (1:1). When Jesus is baptized, a heavenly voice proclaims, "You are my Son" (1:11).

Jesus has the authority to forgive sin, a prerogative of God alone (2:5-12). Evil spirits recognize Jesus as the Holy One of God (1:24), the Son of God (3:11) and Son of the Most High God (5:7-8).

> In Mark's Gospel, the authority of Jesus is stressed by the manner of his teaching (1:22) and by the numerous miracles. But Mark also warns his audience that miracles could be ambiguous. After all, they lead Pharisees and Herodians to oppose Jesus (3:6); cause scribes to think of Jesus as possessed (3:22); leave people from his home-town unimpressed (6:1-3); cause Herod to imagine that Jesus is John the Baptist redivivus [resurrected] (6:14-16); and do not eliminate the disciples' misunderstanding (6:52; 8:17-21) (Ben Witherington III, *The Christology of Jesus*, page 163).

The point was, nobody in the human realm fully understands this truth. Even Peter, who rightly professes Jesus as the Christ, fails to realize Jesus' purpose: to die and after three days rise again (8:31; cf. 9:12, 31; 10:33, 45). The only human acknowledgment that Jesus is the Son of God, comes from a centurion looking at Jesus on the cross.

This, then, is the message of the Gospel of Mark – that we can fully understand who Jesus is only through his suffering, death and resurrection.

Luke — for people like us

Luke, like all the evangelists, acknowledges that Jesus was God, but he also stresses his humanity. Luke shows us that, in Jesus, God became a part of his own story, just as some producers will give themselves a small role in their own films. Except that there was nothing small about Jesus' role when he stepped into history!

Luke shows us that Jesus was a real-life person who lived in Galilee and Judea during the reigns of the Roman Emperors Augustus and Tiberius.

Like Matthew, he gives us Jesus' genealogy and an account of his birth.

But only Luke records Jesus' circumcision (2:21), his presentation at the temple (2:22-38), his growth as a child (2:40), his meeting at age 12 with the religious teachers in the temple (2:41-51) and his continued development "…in wisdom and stature, and in favor with God and men" (2:52). These details establish Jesus as a historical personality.

At the beginning of his ministry, Jesus proclaimed what his mission was all about: to bring good news to the poor, release to the captives, sight to the blind and freedom to the oppressed (4:18).

Luke shows Jesus as extremely concerned about the welfare of all people, but having special empathy for those who were despised or undervalued by society: the tax collectors, Samaritans, the poor, Gentiles. No class or group was excluded; Christ's message of salvation was for everyone. Luke seems to make a special point of highlighting Jesus' concern for women.

> Luke features the responsiveness of women (7:36-50; 8:1-3; 8:48; 10:38-42; 13:10-17; 24:1-12). Often it is not just a woman but a widow who is cited, since she represented the most vulnerable status within society (2:37; 4:25-26; 7:12; 18:3, 5; 20:47; 21:2-3). Whether in parable or by example, these women show that they are sensitive to the message of Jesus. Though on the fringes of first-century society, they are in the middle of Luke's story. Often they are paired with men (2:25-28; 4:25-27; 8:40-56; 11:31-32; 13:18-21; 15:4-10; 17:34-35; Acts 21:9-10), a feature suggesting that the Gospel is for both genders (Daniel Bock, in *Dictionary of Jesus and the Gospels*, page 506).

Many of the most poignant parables that show repentance and forgiveness of sin being offered to everyone are found only in Luke. For example, the good Samaritan (10:30-37), the great feast (14:15- 24), the prodigal son (15:11-31) and the Pharisee and the tax collector (18:9-14).

Luke shows us that God's concern extends to everyone, not just those who are 'good' or naturally inclined to religion. In Jesus Christ, God became one of us, so that he could save all of us.

John — 'And now for something completely different'

John's was the last Gospel to be written, perhaps 60 or more years after the crucifixion. Rather than tell the whole story, he selects incidents from only about three weeks of Jesus' life. But these he explores in great detail.

John wants to let us know in profound detail who Jesus Christ was, where he came from and what he came to do (8:14). He summed it up in what is perhaps the most often quoted of all Bible verses: "For God so loved the world that he gave his one and only Son, that whoever believes in him shall not perish but have eternal life" (John 3:16).

This Gospel explains God's love and his gift of eternal life, in simple, everyday language that can be understood by anyone. But don't be misled by the apparent simplicity. John's message of Jesus Christ is a deep mine, with many levels of understanding. It will repay a lifetime of study.

For example, John devotes several chapters to Jesus' last talk with his disciples (John 14-17). He explores the relationship between the Father, Son and Holy Spirit. John dwells at length on what may at first seem to be a minor incident. For example, the healing of a blind man (chapter 9), or the chance meeting of Jesus and a Samaritan woman at a well (4:1-26).

But these vignettes were chosen because they illustrated vital lessons for all who would become disciples, not only in his time, but through the ages. John helps the non-believer to believe and the believer to come to a deeper level of understanding.

Whereas Matthew, Mark and Luke show us how Jesus taught in parables, there are no parables in John. Instead, he focuses on the symbols that Jesus used to describe and explain his role as our Savior, each beginning with "I am":

...the bread of life (6:35);

...the true light (8:12);

...the door to life (10:7);

...the good shepherd (10:11);

...the resurrection (11:25);

...the way, the truth and the life (14:6);

...the true vine (15:1).

Like the other evangelists, John tells us of Jesus' miracles: he transforms water into wine (2:1-11), heals a nobleman's son (4:43-54), and a cripple (5:1-16), feeds the five thousand (6:1-14), walks on water (6:15-21), restores a blind man (9:1-41) and raises Lazarus from the dead (11:1-46).

But he doesn't call them miracles. To John, they are *signs,* and they have a purpose that goes beyond the wonder of the act itself. Each sign tells us more about the overall reason why Jesus Christ came to earth. He came not so that a few could be healed, but so that all could have life (John 10:10).

So, while the other Gospels present Jesus' message in terms of "the kingdom of God," John prefers the term "eternal life." Eternal life, although having magnificent future implications, also becomes a present reality for the believer: "Whoever hears my word and believes in him who sent me has eternal life" (5:24).

CAN WE TRUST THE GOSPELS?

Are the Gospels of Matthew, Mark, Luke and John
historically reliable documents? Has modern New Testament
scholarship undermined the historical reliability of the Gospels?
Can the Scriptures be taken seriously as historical records?

By Jim Herst

It is only fair that the historical reliability of the Bible should be tested by the same criteria that are used to test all historical documents. In his definitive work, *Introduction to Research in English Literary History,* Professor Charles Sanders explains three basic principles involved in evaluating the reliability of historical documents (p.143 ff.). They are the bibliographic test (have the original manuscripts been handed down faithfully?), the internal evidence test (what the books tell us about themselves) and the external evidence test (an examination of other sources that shed light – such as contemporary ancient literature).

Future articles in this series will evaluate the Gospels in light of internal and external evidence. In this article we will focus on the bibliographic test – how historically reliable the Gospels are in terms of manuscript witnesses to the New Testament in general.

The bibliographic test is an examination of the textual transmission by which the documents have reached us. In other words, since we do not have the original documents (called autographs), how reliable are the copies we have in regard to the number of manuscripts and the time interval between the original and the copies we have?

Let's take a closer look at what biblical scholars call manuscript attestation and time interval.

1. How many manuscripts of the Greek New Testament exist today?

There are more than 5,300 known Greek manuscripts of the New Testament. If we add over 10,000 manuscripts of the Latin Vulgate and at least 9,300 other early versions, then we have more than 24,000 manuscript copies of portions of the New Testament. No other document of antiquity even begins to approach such numbers and attestation. In comparison, Homer's Iliad comes second, with only 643 surviving manuscripts. Even then, the first complete preserved text of Homer dates from the 13th century AD.

It is no wonder that S.E. Peters observes that: "On the basis of manuscript tradition alone, the works that made up the Christians' New Testament were the most widely circulated books of antiquity" (*The Harvest of Hellenism,* p. 50).

F.J.A. Hort adds that, "in the variety and fullness of the evidence on which it rests, the text of the New Testament stands absolutely and unapproachably alone among ancient prose writings" (*The New Testament in the Original Greek,* p. 561).

Bruce Metzger, Emeritus Professor of New Testament Language and Literature at Princeton Theological Seminary, also stresses the uniqueness of New Testament textual witnesses compared with other writings of antiquity. He states: "The works of several ancient authors are preserved for us by the thinnest possible thread of transmission" (*The Text of the New Testament,* p. 34).

Dr. Metzger gives three pertinent examples: *The History of Rome,* by Vellius Paterculus, survived to modern times through only one incomplete manuscript – a manuscript that was subsequently lost in the seventeenth century after being copied by Beatus Rhenanus at Amerbach. A second example is the *Annals* of the famous historian Tacitus, the first six books of which are in a single manuscript dating from the ninth century. And the only known manuscript of the *Epistle to Diognetus,* an early Christian composition which editors usually include in the corpus of the Apostolic Fathers, perished in a fire at the municipal library in Strasbourg in 1870.

Metzger writes: "In contrast with these figures, the textual critic of the New Testament is embarrassed by the wealth of his material" (p. 34).

2. How long is the interval of time between the composition of the books of the New Testament and the dates of the earliest of our manuscripts?

The great biblical scholar Sir Frederic G. Kenyon, who was the director and principal librarian of the British Museum, and second to none in authority for issuing statements about manuscripts, concluded that:

> "besides number, the manuscripts of the New Testament differ from those of the classical authors, and this time the difference is clear again. In no other case is the interval of time between the composition of the book and the date of the earliest extant manuscripts so short as in that of the New Testament" (*Handbook to the Textual Criticism of the New Testament,* p. 4).

Dr. Kenyon goes on to explain that the books of the New Testament were written in the latter part of the first century. He points out that "… the earliest extant manuscripts, trifling scraps excepted, are of the fourth century

– say from 250 to 300 years later."

This may seem a considerable interval, but it is nothing compared with the gap that separates the great classical authors from the earliest surviving manuscripts of their works. For example, scholars believe that they have, in all essentials, an accurate text of seven plays of Sophocles. Yet the earliest substantial manuscript upon which it is based was written more than 1,400 years after the poet's death!

Writing along similar lines, F.F. Bruce, former Professor of New Testament Studies at the University of Manchester, explains that, of the 14 books of the *Histories of Tacitus* (circa A.D. 100), only four and one-half survive (*The New Testament Documents,* p.16). And his minor works (*Dialogus de Oritoribus, Agricola, Germania*) all descend from a 10th-century copy.

Bruce also points out that *The History of Thucydides* (circa 460-400 BC) comes to us from eight manuscripts, the earliest dating from circa A.D. 900 along with a few papyrus scraps from the beginning of the Christian era.

"The same is true for Herodotus," Bruce says, "Yet no classical scholar would listen to an argument that the authenticity of Herodotus or Thucydides is in doubt because the earliest manuscripts of their works which are of use to us are over 1,300 years later than the originals" (pp. 16-17).

Harold Greenlee agrees with Bruce, and states the obvious conclusion: "Since scholars accept as generally trustworthy the writings of the ancient classics—even though the earliest manuscripts were written so long after the original writings, and the number of extant manuscripts is in many cases so small – it is clear that the reliability of the text of the New Testament is assured" (*Introduction to New Testament Textual Criticism,* p. 16).

Gospel truth

As we mentioned earlier, the bibliographic test examines the quality of the textual transmission by which documents reach us. And in this context, the New Testament – including the Gospels of Matthew, Mark, Luke and John – sits right at the top of the class.

But the bibliographic test cannot establish the "inspiration" of the Gospels. It can't even demonstrate that the content of the Gospels – such as the sayings and actions of Jesus – are "historical fact." Graham Stanton, Professor of New Testament Studies at King's College, University of London, puts it well:

> No amount of historical evidence for the life and teaching of Jesus ever proves "Gospel truth." After all, some who saw and heard Jesus for themselves drew the conclusion that he was a magician and false

prophet. Proof cannot reside either in any new papyrus fragment (however early its date), or in any artifact uncovered by archaeologists. (*Gospel Truth,* 192)

Dr. Stanton then concludes:

Down through the centuries Christianity has taken many forms – and it still does today. None the less, Christians of all persuasions have always insisted that God has disclosed his purposes for humanity in the life, death, and resurrection of Jesus. So if historical reconstruction of the actions and teaching of Jesus is at odds with this central theological conviction, then "Gospel truth" is called in question. (193)

The historical reconstruction of Jesus' life and ministry is not "at odds with this central theological conviction," but it is in absolute harmony with the most fundamental tenet of the Christian faith, "... that God was reconciling the world to himself in Christ ..." (2 Corinthians 5:19).

Matthew found at Oxford!

On Christmas Eve, 1994, *The Times* (London) ran a front-page story entitled: "Oxford papyrus is 'eye-witness record of the life of Christ.'" Apparently a German Bible scholar, Carsten Thiede, had found fragments of Matthew's Gospel at Magdalen College, Oxford. The fragments had been acquired at Luxor in Egypt in 1901 by Charles B. Huleatt, a former scholar at Magdalen. Huleatt gave the fragments to his college that same year.

The first fragment contained parts of Matthew 26:7-8 on one side and parts of Matthew 26:31 on the other. The second fragment contained parts of Matthew 26:10 and of verses 32-33. The third fragment contained parts of Matthew 26:14-15 and of verses 22-23.

They were first published by the famous papyrologist, C.H. Roberts, in 1953. Roberts recognized that, because there was writing on both sides of the fragments, they had come from a codex (the predecessor of the modern book) and not from a papyrus roll.

Collaborating with other scholars of his day, Roberts dated the fragments to the late second century. However, 40 years later, *The Times* quoted Carsten Thiede as saying that the fragments might date from the middle of the first century, a date which, if confirmed, would revolutionize scholarly understanding of the origins of the Gospels.

The Times pointed its readers to Thiede's forthcoming discussion of his findings in the January 1995 issue of *Zeitschrift für Papyrologie und Epigraphie* (if any of our readers are interested in learning more about Thiede's views, this article was reprinted in Tyndale Bulletin 46 [1995], pp. 29-42).

As it turned out, there was a serious discrepancy between the sensational claims made in *The Times* and the cautious tone of the academic journal. Carsten Thiede had actually concluded: "… it may be argued that it (the Matthew papyrus) could be redated from the late second to the late first century, some time after the destruction of the Temple in Jerusalem (in A.D. 70)." However, most scholars today feel that there is no persuasive evidence in favor of a first-century dating of these Magdalen fragments.

In the words of Graham Stanton: "They are certainly not from the first century. They may well be part of the earliest surviving copy of the four Gospels brought together in one codex: our earliest witness to a momentous development within early Christianity."

Suggestions for further reading

Aland, Kurt, and Aland, Barbara, *The Text of the New Testament,* Eerdmans, revised edition, 1989.

Black, D.A., and Dockery, D.S., *New Testament Criticism and Interpretation,* Zondervan, 1991.

Brown, R.E., *The Critical Meaning of the Bible,* Chapman and Paulist Press, 1981.

Ladd, G.E., *The New Testament and Criticism,* Eerdmans, 1966.

Marshall, I. H. (ed.), *New Testament Interpretation,* Paternoster, 1977, and Eerdmans, 1978.

Metzger, Bruce, *The Text of the New Testament,* Oxford, Oxford University Press, 1964; revised edition, 1992.

Vagnay, L., and Amphoux, Christian-Bernard, *An Introduction to New Testament Textual Criticism,* Cambridge University Press, 1991.

Glossary

- AUTOGRAPH: A reference to the original manuscript of an author's work. Since we do not possess any original manuscripts of the Bible, scholars must work with later copies.

- BIBLE: From the Latin, *biblia,* the name given to the Holy Scriptures that include the Old and New Testaments. Originally the term comes from *biblos,* the center of the papyrus plant, which was used to create writing material. The written product was then referred to as a *biblos.* John Chrysostom, Bishop of Constantinople from A.D. 397 to 407, is credited with being the first person to use the plural *ta biblia* ("books") as a designation for the Old and New Testaments.

- CODEX: Ancient manuscripts of either papyrus or vellum (made from the skins of cattle or other animals) that were put into book form rather than a scroll.

- CRITICISM: From the Greek, *krino*, meaning "to judge, discriminate, decide." Not to be considered as a negative term in New Testament studies.
- GOSPEL: From the Greek *euangelion*, meaning "good news." Later designated as a book that tells the good news of the life and teaching of Jesus.
- PAPYRUS: A plant that grows in the delta area of the Nile in Egypt that was used as a writing material from the fourth century BC to the seventh century AD.
- SCROLL, ROLL: The product of pasting parchment or papyrus sheets side by side to form a long continuous strip that could be rolled up to make a scroll.
- TESTAMENT: From the Latin *testamentum*, which was used to translate the Hebrew and Greek words for "covenant." Since the time of Tertullian it has been used to designate the two main divisions of Scripture: the Old and New Testaments.
- VULGATE: The Latin version of the Bible produced by Jerome in the fourth century AD and ratified by the Council of Trent in 1546 as the official Scripture for the Roman Catholic Church.

THE SEARCH FOR
THE REAL WORDS OF JESUS

Some scholars think the Gospels attribute sayings to Jesus
he never made. The Gospel writers denied that they
put their own ideas on Jesus' lips. Who is right?

By Paul Kroll

In the 1990s, a group of scholars called the Jesus Seminar created headline news, especially in the United States. To put it simply, they questioned whether the Bible is the inspired word of God.

The seminar was composed of specialists in the New Testament Gospels. They taught at leading universities and seminaries in North America and represented every major Christian denomination and tradition. The Jesus Seminar staked out a heady goal for itself. It hoped to recover the actual words Jesus spoke, uncover what he really thought and discover which deeds recorded in the Bible he accomplished.

At its spring 1991 meeting, the Jesus Seminar concluded its first phase— six years of debating and voting on the words of Jesus. In that autumn, the seminar began its second phase, analyzing the biblical accounts of Jesus' life and deeds.

During their quest to discover the true voice of Jesus, the seminar rejected about 80 percent of his words, calling them later creations. The discarded words of Jesus included statements:

- **About his death.** Most seminar members are convinced Jesus did not predict his death as the Gospel accounts describe. Nine in 10 think "Jesus had no special foreknowledge of his death," says Robert W. Funk, the Jesus Seminar's founder.

- **On the cross.** The Gospels attribute some well-known statements to Jesus as he was dying. Among them is: "My God, My God, why have You forsaken Me?" (Matthew 27:46, New King James throughout). Such sayings were all dismissed by the seminar as the later "work of the individual evangelists."

- **During a Jewish trial.** All four Gospels describe a Jewish trial and condemnation of Jesus before his crucifixion (see, for example, Mark 14:53-65). An overwhelming majority of the Jesus Seminar (97 percent) do not think any such trial occurred. "The Jewish role in these events is a figment of Christian imagination," wrote Dr. Funk in *The Fourth R,* a publication of the seminar's Westar Institute.

- **After the resurrection.** All four Gospels end with Jesus talking with and teaching the disciples *after* his resurrection. The Jesus Seminar does not accept any after-death words of Jesus. It says Gospel "statements attributed to the risen Jesus are not admissible as evidence for the historical Jesus."

- **Not overheard by others.** On several occasions the Gospel writers report Jesus' conversations when neither they nor other humans were present. These conversations include Jesus' words during his time in the wilderness and his prayer in the Garden of Gethsemane the night of his arrest. The seminar dismisses these verbal portraits. "Words attributed to Jesus in the absence of an auditor," said the seminar, "are assumed to be the fiction of the storyteller." They "cannot be used to determine what Jesus said."

- **About founding a church.** In Matthew 16:18, Jesus reportedly said, "I will build My church." The seminar disagrees that Jesus could make such a statement. "Jesus had no intention of starting a new religion," Dr. Funk says, stating the seminar's majority position. "He had no idea that a new religion would transpire or that he would become a cult figure in it." In Dr. Funk's view, Jesus "would have been appalled by it."

- **In exalted titles.** In the Gospel of John, Jesus refers to himself in exalted "I am" statements. He says "I am the bread of life," "the light of the world," "the resurrection and the life" (John 6:48; 8:12; 11:25). Throughout John, Jesus stresses his preexistence and preeminence. "Before Abraham was, I AM," he says (John *8:58*). "I and My Father are one" (John 10:30). The Jesus Seminar does not think Jesus viewed himself this way, says Marcus Borg, a critical scholar and seminar member. "In the judgment of the seminar (and of most mainstream scholarship since the last century)," he writes, "Jesus did not speak that way." Dr. Funk says the seminar scholars almost unanimously feel that Jesus "didn't think of himself as divine."

- **About the Second Coming.** The Gospels record Jesus' insistence that he would return to set up the kingdom of God on earth (Matthew 24:29-31; Luke 21:25-27). Most seminar participants do not think Jesus expected to return. "The Jesus Seminar thinks he didn't speak of the coming of the Son of Man at all," said Dr. Borg. Almost all the Fellows (97 percent) believe Jesus did *not* expect to return or usher in a new age "either now or in the distant future," says Dr. Funk.

- **Referring to fulfilled Scriptures.** The Gospel writers have Jesus apply several Hebrew scriptures to his life and ministry (Luke 4:16-21; John 5:39-46). The Jesus Seminar rejects these as words put on the lips of Jesus. Dr. Funk says, "The Christian community culled the Hebrew Scriptures for proof that Jesus was truly the Messiah." The Gospel writers, especially Matthew, made "the event fit the prophecy."

Were Jesus' teachings changed?

The seminar believes most of Jesus' statements and teachings as reported in the Gospels are inaccurate. The Gospels are called "gilded portraits" of Jesus. This premise, the seminar points out in its *Gospel of Mark,* is "shared by all critical scholars of whatever theological persuasion."

Did the Gospel writers create their own fake Jesus narratives and statements, or did they faithfully preserve his teaching? The question is of more than casual academic interest. If the Gospel writers perpetrated a theological hoax, their Gospels would not be "gospel truth." How could they be the word of a God who does not lie? (Titus 1:2).

Suppose, as the seminar maintains, the Gospel writers created Jesus' sayings. Let us say for argument's sake the seminar has discovered the almost inaudible voice of the true "historical Jesus" amidst the cacophony of purported faked conversations and bogus narratives in the Gospels.

What are the consequences to us of a Jesus who had no concept of dying for humanity's sins; did not found his church; did not think of himself as divine? On what basis can the Christian hope of the resurrection and salvation be established?

Consider the implication of just one seminar claim—that Jesus did not announce his return to set up the kingdom of God on earth. If this claim were true, it would put the Christian hope in serious jeopardy. The Bible links the resurrection of the dead and salvation with Jesus' return (see Matthew 24:29-31; 1 Corinthians 15:51-52; 1 Thessalonians 4:13-17).

We need to know whether the Gospels are the true word of God or the fraudulent words of men. The Jesus Seminar, of course, does not think the biblical Gospels are the word of God. Dr. Borg writes in *The Fourth R,* "The gospels are human documents, not 'divine' documents." Like other Christian writings and creeds, the Gospels are "human products" and should not be "accorded divine status."

"There is a price one pays" for considering the Gospels as purely human products, admits Dr. Borg. The consequence is that "there are no divinely guaranteed formulations of truth." According to Dr. Borg, "The Gospels are seen as *the developing tradition of the early Christian community*" and "reflect the viewpoints of their authors" and "the Christian communities for which they spoke."

The Gospel writers, however, repudiate these notions. They claim to have accurately portrayed Jesus' life and teaching.

John a trustworthy witness

The writer of the Gospel of John claims he was an eyewitness of *all* the teachings and circumstances of Jesus' life that he writes about. He maintains his Gospel is a true account of Jesus' thoughts and words.

John said of himself and his Gospel: "He who has seen has testified, and his testimony is true; and he knows that he is telling the truth" (John 19:35). Again he says: "This is the disciple who testifies of these things, and wrote these things; and we know that his testimony is true" (John 21:24).

John was there when Jesus spoke and worked; he knew Jesus personally. In a letter to the church, John wrote of this Jesus "which we have heard, which we have seen with our eyes, which we have looked upon, and our hands have handled" (1 John 1:1).

John, in this same epistle, when speaking of Jesus, insists that he and the others "have seen, and bear witness, and declare to you that eternal life which was with the Father and was manifested to us" (verse 2). John maintained that he wrote a true testimony of Jesus' words and works: "That which we have seen and heard we declare to you" (verse 3).

Mark knew eyewitnesses

As a teenager, Mark may even have seen and heard Jesus. The Gospel of Mark refers to "a certain young man" who followed the arrested Christ and then fled (Mark 14:51-52). Many scholars think that this story, which plays no role in the Gospel and is not found in any other Gospel, is a cryptic reference to the author.

Mark clearly had access to Jesus' teachings through these important eyewitnesses when writing his Gospel. For this reason, we can have confidence in what Mark reported of Jesus' words, teachings and life.

The Gospel of Mark was written by an individual who may have been only a *partial* witness to Jesus' life and teachings. Should this invalidate his Gospel account? Mark was intimately associated with the apostles and eyewitnesses. He was the cousin of Barnabas, a co-worker with Paul

(Colossians 4:10) and is further identified as John Mark in Acts 12:12.

Robert H. Stein, professor of New Testament at Bethel Theological Seminary, points out that Mark "lived in Jerusalem and his home was a center of the early church." Because of this, "He was no doubt privy to much eyewitness testimony," writes Dr. Stein.

The Bible tells us Mark was closely associated with the apostle Paul in preaching the gospel message (Acts 12:25; 13:5; 15:36-39). Mark is called a fellow laborer with Paul (Philemon 24). At the end of his life, Paul instructs Timothy: "Get Mark and bring him with you, for he is useful to me for ministry" (2 Timothy 4:11). As well, a close relationship existed between the apostle Peter and Mark, evidenced by Peter's reference to him as "my son" (1 Peter 5:13).

THE GOSPELS AND US

The witnesses to Jesus' life and their associates affirm
that they correctly passed on Jesus' teachings to us.
Can we believe their testimony?
Where do we stand if we *disbelieve?*

Jesus did not write any of the Bible. Neither does the risen Christ speak directly to all the church today. We live about 2,000 years after Jesus' earthly ministry ended. We don't have tape recordings of what Jesus said. We may even lack the exact wording of his teaching.

Of course, the issue is not over *exact* words or whether the Gospels contain Jesus' precise statements. The issue is whether the Gospels give us God the Father's word as taught by Jesus and as faithfully described and applied by his authorized representatives, the apostles and their co-workers.

We cannot run and hide from our dependence on those who wrote the New testament Gospels. They are unique individuals in the history of the church. These writers saw Jesus' mighty works and heard his words, or they worked closely with people who had. Only these individuals were in a position to pass on to us the correct Jesus traditions.

Those who had been with Jesus in the flesh, such as the original apostles, said they witnessed his words and teaching. Because they saw and heard Jesus, they believed (John 20:24-29). But what about those living after the apostolic age—perhaps in our day? On what basis can we believe? Jesus said of us: "Blessed are those who have not seen and yet have believed" (verse 29).

We have not personally heard Jesus teach what is written in the Gospels. We did not experience his miracles. We did not observe his crucifixion and resurrection. Nor can we prove in a scientific sense that they occurred. We are called on to believe *without* having seen what we must believe in.

What are we to do? We must see Jesus Christ through the writings of the eyewitnesses and their associates. We have the choice of either believing or rejecting what the witnesses and their co-workers said of Jesus. If we spurn their testimony, we have no foundation or authority for what we believe as Christians. It is that simple.

Critical scholars do not accept the claims of the witnesses or Gospel writers. They want corroborating, scientific proof. Robert W. Funk, the Jesus Seminar's founder, says the Jesus Seminar's conclusions about Jesus' words are not determined "by prior religious convictions, but by the evidence."

Seminar member Marcus Borg writes, "One cannot settle historical questions by 'belief.'"

However, there is no escaping belief. All attempts at a 'scientific,' critical-historical analysis of Jesus' teachings must ultimately fail. Everyone begins with certain beliefs about what could or could not happen.

By what test can we determine whether Jesus arose from the dead? Or that the disciples talked with the risen Jesus? Or that Jesus' miracles occurred? Or that statements in the Hebrew Scriptures were fulfilled in Jesus' life? No scientific, historical or critical analysis can discover to everyone's satisfaction the yea or nay of such things.

Judging the Bible through human logic forces critical scholars into circular reasoning. They must *first* decide what they think Jesus taught or how he spoke. For example, would he talk about a climactic end of the age? Or would he predict his own death? Then the seminar analyzes the Gospels to see if they fit the portrait of Jesus it has constructed.

The Gospel writers do not ask us to enter into this spiral of intellectual uncertainty. They simply say to individuals through the ages: Put your confidence in what we have said about Jesus.

John said he knew he was telling the truth about Jesus (John 19:35). Luke said his account was an accurate one (Luke 1:1-3). Matthew and Mark also present their Gospels as faithful reflections of the teachings and work of Jesus of Nazareth. Do we have the spiritual ears to believe what they wrote— to believe God directed their witness? (2 Timothy 3:16; 2 Peter 1:20-21).

Luke used eyewitness testimony

The author of the Gospel of Luke probably was *not* an eyewitness of Jesus' life and teachings. Luke, however, puts forth strong reasons why we should consider his Gospel trustworthy. He said his Gospel is solidly based on the teachings of "those who from the beginning were eyewitnesses and ministers of the word" (Luke 1:2). Luke also claimed to have had "perfect understanding of all things from the very first" (verse 3). Because of this, Luke felt qualified to write "an orderly account" of the teachings "most surely believed" among members of the church (verses 3 and 1).

In Acts, Luke commented further on his purpose for writing his Gospel: to deal with "all that Jesus began *both to do and teach,* until the day in which He was taken up" to heaven (Acts 1:1-2, emphasis ours).

Luke was the equivalent of our modern investigative reporter. According to Acts 21:15 through 27:2, Luke spent considerable time in Judea. He had ample time and opportunity to investigate what he wrote about Jesus. Luke could have referred to various written documents and oral reports detailing the teachings and circumstances of Jesus' life. As well, he no doubt consulted witnesses and church leaders at the church in Jerusalem.

Luke traveled with Paul and would have known what Paul taught. (Notice the references to "we" and "us" in Acts 16:11-15 and 20:6-16, for example.) He was Paul's "beloved physician" (Colossians 4:14) and a fellow laborer (Philemon 24). Luke stood by Paul to the end during his final persecution at Rome, even though others fled (2 Timothy 4:11).

We should consider that Luke's Gospel was researched and written more than 1,900 years closer to Jesus' life than were the conclusions of the Jesus Seminar. Whose testimony has the advantage of proximity to apostolic times? The reader can have confidence that Luke based his Gospel on the true apostolic witness to Jesus' teachings.

Early church teachings

Clearly, the Gospel writers did not create spurious "Jesus sayings." Nevertheless some critical biblical scholars, such as the Jesus Seminar members, argue that the early church created Jesus' sayings to justify its teachings.

If this argument were valid, "We would expect to find those needs reflected and dealt with in the Gospels," writes New Testament scholar Robert Stein in *The Synoptic Problem*. This need for justification would be, he says, especially true regarding "the most important religious issues that the early church faced."

The most volatile issue would have concerned the physical circumcision of gentile converts. "If the early church was creating gospel traditions to meet its religious needs," wrote Dr. Stein, "one would expect to find something on this subject."

However, no "circumcision materials" exist in the Gospels. The four Gospels contain only a single reference to circumcision, and it doesn't deal with the controversy in the church (John 7:22-23). The lack of circumcision material in the Gospels is evidence "in favor of the view that the church tended to transmit the Jesus traditions faithfully," Dr. Stein points out.

On the other hand, the book of Acts deals with the circumcision controversy in detail. The apostles and elders even meet to decide this question (Acts 15:1-29). However, no "Jesus sayings" are cited to justify their decision that gentiles did not need to be circumcised.

A careful reading of Acts shows the church's teaching on circumcision does not rely on the sayings of Jesus. No "Jesus proof texts" are cited. The church acts in Jesus' name and by his authority, but does not invent any sayings to prove their point.

Bible scholar Thorlief Boman has observed that there are 24 speeches in the book of Acts. These account for about 300 of the 1,007 verses in Acts. In these speeches, there is only a single saying of Jesus (Acts 20:35). This lack of Jesus' sayings and stories demonstrates, says Dr. Boman, "that the church did not create sayings of Jesus and read them back upon the lips of Jesus."

In the words of British biblical scholar, George B. Caird, there is "not one shred of evidence that the early church ever concocted sayings of Jesus in order to settle any of its problems."

For further reading:

- Ben Witherington III, *The Jesus Quest: The Third Search for the Jew of Nazareth*(InterVarsity, 1995).
- Darrell Bock, "The Words of Jesus in the Gospels: Live, Jive, or Memorex?" in *Jesus Under Fire* (edited by Michael J. Wilkins and J. P. Moreland; Zondervan, 1995).
- Richard B. Hays, "The Corrected Jesus, "*First Things* 43 (May 1994): 43-48.

HOW DO WE KNOW ABOUT JESUS?

The Gospels are not the only historical record of Jesus.
Classical historians mention him, too. Or do they?

By Jim Herst

The four evangelists, Matthew, Mark, Luke and John, have given us a remarkable record of the life and work of Jesus Christ. But some people discount them as biased. They want to see evidence of Jesus from historians who were not themselves part of the Christian community.

It seems that such independent corroboration does, indeed, exist. Tantalizing scraps of evidence have come down to us in the writings of ancient historians like Josephus, Tacitus and Suetonius.

But can we trust them? Do they really reinforce the Gospels with independent, unbiased evidence of Jesus?

Christians must "fight fair." Before we set too much store by these ancient records as sources, we must ask if they are reliable. Perhaps these historians were not really saying what some Christian writers want to make them say. But does it really matter? Let's take a closer look.

The Greco-Roman sources

1) Tacitus

The first Roman historian to mention Christ is Tacitus, who wrote his last significant work, the Annals, around A.D. 115. In this treatise, Tacitus describes the great fire of Rome during the reign of Nero and the emperor's subsequent persecution of the Christians there. He states:

"Nero created scapegoats and subjected to the most refined tortures those whom the common people called 'Christians'....Their name comes from Christ, who, during the reign of Tiberius, had been executed by the procurator Pontius Pilate" (Annals 15:44).

At first glance, this is an impressive passage for the Christian apologist. But let's dig a little deeper. Where did Tacitus get his information about Jesus' execution? It is doubtful that he was quoting an official Roman document from the period because, as scholars are quick to point out, he mistakenly calls Pilate a procurator when he was actually a prefect.

Perhaps Tacitus received it from his close friend Pliny the Younger, who may well have shared the knowledge he had acquired from contact with Christians in Asia Minor. But even if this is the case, the most we can say is that Tacitus is simply repeating what Christians of his day were saying about their origins. There is not much basis here for concluding that he was presenting independent testimony about the historical figure of Jesus.

2) Suetonius

In his biography of the emperor Claudius, written around A.D. 120, Suetonius writes about the expulsion of the Jews from Rome in A.D. 49. He states: "Since the Jews were constantly causing disturbances at the instigation of Chrestus, he [Claudius] expelled them from Rome" (Claudius 25:4).

Chrestus was a popular misspelling of the Greek *Christos* (Christ). Some scholars believe that Suetonius may have used a source that understood "Chrestus" to be Jesus. But he obviously misunderstood the police records, thinking that "Chrestus" was the name of some Jewish slave who became a ringleader during the riots of A.D. 49. Suetonius' account makes for interesting reading. But, again, it is far from being an independent witness to the historical Jesus.

3) Pliny the Younger

Pliny the Younger was proconsul of Bythinia, in Asia Minor, between A.D. 111 and 113. Pliny wrote a letter to the Emperor Trajan asking for advice on how to deal with the rapid growth of the Christian community in his area. Among other things, he describes the Christian custom of holding weekly meetings to sing praises "to Christ as to a god" (Letter 10. 96).

This passage is significant, because it is the only non-Christian source that tells us that Christians treated Christ as a "god." But Pliny is merely describing an element of Christian worship. His comments say nothing about the historicity of Jesus.

4) Lucian

The Roman satirist Lucian of Samosata lived from A.D. 115-200. In *The Passing of Perigrinus,* Lucian mocks the Christian life, describing Christians as those who worship "that crucified sophist [Jesus] himself," and live "under his laws." Again, we learn only what some educated people from the second century may have heard about Jesus. Lucian is definitely not an independent source of historical knowledge concerning Jesus of Nazareth.

5) Josephus

Perhaps the most significant "witness" to the life of Jesus in ancient literature is in the writings of Joseph ben Matthias, better known as Flavius Josephus (named after his patrons, the Flavian emperors Vespasian, Titus and Domitian). Josephus lived from A.D. 37 to 100, and wrote two famous works: *The Jewish War,* which was initially drafted in Aramaic, and then translated into Greek five to ten years after the destruction of Jerusalem in A.D. 70. His second work, *Jewish Antiquities,* was completed more than a decade later. This work was much longer, and recounts Jewish history from creation to the Jewish revolt against Rome (A.D. 66-70).

Contrary to what many Christians may think, Josephus does not give us much information about Jesus. In his 28 volumes of Jewish history, there are only two passages that mention Jesus. And even these references are difficult to assess. The trouble is that Josephus' writings were preserved for posterity by Christians (the Jews disowned him as a traitor). The texts available to us today contain statements that were added later by Christian editors. This is clearly seen in the famous Testimonium Flavianum, "the testimony of Josephus," found in *Antiquities* 18:63-64. It reads as follows:

> At that time there appeared Jesus, a wise man, *if indeed someone should call him a man*. For he was a doer of startling deeds, a teacher of people who receive the truth with pleasure. And he gained a following both among many Jews and among many of Greek origin. *He was the Messiah*. And when Pilate, because of an accusation made by the leading men among us, condemned him to the cross, those who had loved him previously did not cease to do so. *For he appeared to them on the third day, living again, just as the divine prophets had spoken of these and countless other wondrous things about him*. And up until this very day the tribe of Christians, named after him, has not died out.

Scholars of Josephus have been divided over the authenticity of this entire passage, although both sides acknowledge the obvious Christian additions (marked in italics above).

On one hand, some scholars argue for the genuineness of the passage (without the italicized parts). They stress that the language and grammar are typical of Josephus' style and language.

The other school of thought argues that the passage is bogus. They point to the clear Christian redaction. But they also emphasize that there are only three Greek manuscripts of Book 18 of *The Antiquities* – the earliest dating only to the 11th century – and the text of these is often in doubt.

The other well-known passage in *Antiquities* is the reference to "James, the brother of Jesus who was called the Christ" (*Antiquities* 20:200). Scholars generally agree that this is authentic Josephus. They do so for several reasons: First, this narrative is found in the major Greek manuscript tradition of *Antiquities* without variation. Second, Christian editors would not refer to James as "the brother of Jesus." Instead, they would use the reverential phrase, "the brother of the Lord" (see, for example, Paul's description of James in Galatians 1:19).

Third, the famous fourth-century church historian Eusebius also quotes this passage in his *Ecclesiastical History* (2.23.22). Interestingly, Eusebius does not quote the Testimonium Flavianum.

How do we know about Jesus?

The most we can say, then, is that Josephus is our only independent source of information about the historical Jesus. And, as we have seen, only one of his brief references to Jesus is generally recognized by the scholarly community.

So let's ask again the questions we posed at the beginning. Do these passages provide any real basis for a knowledge of Jesus as a historical figure? I think you will agree that the answer is "No." More importantly, should we use these passages as a primary means by which we bolster our faith in Jesus of Nazareth? Again, I hope you would agree that the answer is an emphatic "No!"

Our faith in Jesus Christ is not based on a few brief texts in the writings of Jewish and Greco-Roman historians – however fascinating they may be. How do we know about Jesus? Primarily through the most reliable witnesses, the Gospels – the great theological histories of Matthew, Mark, Luke and John.

Some Christians may be disappointed that all the substantial evidence for Jesus comes from Christian sources. If you are disappointed, here are a couple of questions you might want to consider:

First, why would Jesus leave any traces on the pages of secular history? He was virtually unknown – an traveling teacher who enjoyed limited popularity within a small community in a remote province on the eastern edge of the Roman empire. In the words of John P. Meier, professor of New Testament at the Catholic University of America in Washington D.C.: "Jesus was a marginal Jew leading a marginal movement in a marginal province of a vast Roman empire. The wonder is that any learned Jew or pagan would have known or referred to him at all in the first or second centuries" (*A Marginal Jew,* p. 56).

Second, does the fact that our evidence for Jesus comes from Christian sources mean that the evidence is too biased to be trusted? New Testament scholar Dr. R.T. France, former principal of Wycliffe Hall, Oxford University, gives us an excellent answer:

> The Gospel writers tell us about Jesus because they think he is worth telling about, and they want others to follow him as well. But what worthwhile history or biography has ever been written by people

who have no personal interest in what they write? Why should a 'bias' in favor of the subject render the history unreliable? Surely those who had been captivated by Jesus might be expected to take pains to pass on truth about him (*Jesus 2000,* p. 15).

Matthew, Mark, Luke and John certainly passed on the truth about Jesus. But each did so in his own unique way.

WHAT JESUS' PARABLES REVEAL

About one third of Jesus Christ's recorded teachings
are in the form of parables. What do they mean?

By Norman Shoaf

The good Samaritan. The pearl of great price. Counting the cost. The good shepherd. New wine in old wineskins. The prodigal son. Sheep and goats. Who hasn't heard of at least a couple of these? Jesus' New Testament parables are among the most powerful ideas in Western civilization!

These lessons are at the core of Christ's teaching. Nearly 2,000 years after Jesus gave them, his parables still sparkle with simple yet sublime insights about life—and startling yet comforting revelations about God's kingdom. But what, exactly, are parables? And what did Jesus intend that we learn from his parables?

Understand the genre

First, let's understand that the Bible consists of different types of writing. As we read and study the Bible, we should recognize each type of genre, or in other words, literary style. You wouldn't read a recipe for lasagna as you would a suicide note. A court summons is no comic strip. Subway graffiti does not a thank-you card make. A love letter is not an encyclopedia article. They are different types of writing, produced by different authors for different audiences. They also invite different responses.

Were parables used to hide the truth?

Mark 4:10-12 is one of the most difficult passages in the New Testament. These verses, with parallels in Matthew 13:10-15 and Luke 8:9-10, indicate that Jesus wanted to *hide* truth as well as reveal it. Mark 4 opens, "He taught them [a crowd] many things by parables" (verse 2). The chapter then relates the parable of the sower (verses 3-8).

Jesus' disciples didn't get the point. "When he was alone, the Twelve and the others around him asked him about the parables. He told them, 'The secret of the kingdom of God has been given to you. But to those on the outside everything is said in parables so that, "they may be ever seeing but never perceiving, and ever hearing but never understanding; otherwise they might turn and be forgiven"'" (verses 10-12). Here Jesus quoted Isaiah 6:9-10.

Is the kingdom of God a secret, given only to a chosen few? Did Jesus tell his parables, which seem so simple, so accessible and so timeless, to keep outsiders from understanding the truth? Does God not want to forgive sinners?

No one can come to Christ unless first drawn by God the Father (John 6:44). Yet God does not want "anyone to perish, but everyone to come to repentance" (2 Peter 3:9). In fact, God "commands all people everywhere to repent" (Acts 17:30). The explanation of the parable has in fact been published in the Bible, so that everyone can read it.

Jesus directed the story of the sower to each listener "who has ears to hear" (Mark 4:9). Jesus' message demands that we respond. "This is the one I esteem," God says, "he who is humble and contrite in spirit, and trembles at my word" (Isaiah 66:2). But not everyone approaches the truth of God in the same manner.

Jesus intended that people understand the parable of the sower. After all, he went right on to explain it (Mark 4:14-20). Different people respond differently when confronted with the truth. Some of the sown seed (representing the Word of God) is eaten by birds (snatched away by Satan). Some falls on shallow soil and fails to survive in the hot sun (hearers not rooted in the truth). Some is choked by thorns (cares of this life). But some of the seed falls on good soil and produces a crop (hearers who accept God's truth and produces spiritual fruit).

The International Standard Bible Encyclopedia says: "Jesus' teaching confronted people with radical demands, and not all were willing to comply. Some followed Him in discipleship, but others were actually driven further from the Kingdom.... It is not intellectual but volitional blindness and deafness that is in view" (vol. 3, page 657).

Jesus' listeners saw salvation personified in Jesus, the Son of God. They heard the most important message ever preached. Yet most didn't understand—they failed to believe and become converted! Matthew 13 includes this episode at the point when Jesus began to concentrate on private teaching of his disciples, rather than public preaching. John 12:40 quotes Isaiah 6:10 at this same point.

Jesus' message was not well received by hard-hearted people. What kind of heart do you have to hear the Savior of the world?

Many types of writing make up the Bible. Parables, or parabolic passages, concentrated in the Gospels, are one of those genres. The Bible also contains legal codes, such as those you can read in the books of Moses. You will find poetry in the psalms and elsewhere. There are also prophecies, histories, hymns, letters and speeches in the Bible. There are allegories, metaphors, similes, epics, riddles and wise sayings. Bible students call yet other sections didactic, apocalyptic and eschatological. They are all inspired by God. They are "God-breathed" and "useful for teaching, rebuking, correcting and training in righteousness, so that those who belong to God may be thoroughly equipped for every good work" (2 Timothy 3:16-17).

But we need to see these different literary genres—parables included—for what they are, in their contexts. We need to learn as much as we can about who wrote them, and why, and to whom. Legal codes and delicate poetry are different. Sweeping epics are not science texts. Letters may whisper personal details about their writers even as they defy being used to nail down historical or prophetic dates. Metaphors aren't meant literally. Failure to understand the literary style can lead to misunderstanding and misinterpretation. How, then, should we look at Jesus' parables?

The background to Jesus' parables

Jesus' parables have been called "heavenly stories with earthly meanings," or "earthly stories with heavenly meanings." But there is more to them than that. Both the Hebrew word *masal* and the Greek *parabole* are broadly used of proverbs, allegories, riddles, illustrations and stories. They can refer to any striking speech formulated to stimulate thought.

Interpreter C.H. Dodd, in his 1935 classic *Parables of the Kingdom,* defined a parable as "a metaphor or simile drawn from nature or common life, arresting the hearer by its vividness or strangeness, and leaving the mind in sufficient doubt about its precise application to tease it into active thought" (page 16). *The International Standard Bible Encyclopedia* states that parables are "almost always formulated to reveal and illustrate the kingdom of God" (vol. 3, page 656).

Parables are present, but not common, in the Old Testament. Perhaps the parable that most closely resembles Jesus' parables is Nathan's story of the pet lamb, which moved King David to repent (2 Samuel 12:1-13). Judges 9:8-15 and 2 Kings 14:9 symbolize kings and nations as talking plants and a wild beast; these passages are more like fables.

Was Jesus thinking of Ezekiel 17:22-24 when he told the parable of the mustard seed (Mark 4:30-32 and parallel passages)? His parable of the wicked tenants (Mark 12:1-9) echoes Isaiah 5:1-7 (the song of the vineyard). Jesus' parables often referred to nature to picture the spectacular growth of God's kingdom from a small beginning.

Outside the Gospels, the Greek *parabole* appears in the New Testament only in Hebrews 9:9, where the New King James Version says the tabernacle (verse 8) and sacrifices were "symbolic" for the present time, and in Hebrews

11:19, which says that Abraham, "figuratively speaking," received Isaac back from death after proving he was willing to sacrifice his son.

Jesus' teaching was unique

Early rabbis included parables in their writings. These parables began or ended with, and explained, Old Testament texts. Jesus' use of parables differed markedly. "The NT parables," notes *The International Standard Bible Encyclopedia,* "almost never function in this way [to explain Old Testament passages]: Jesus came not to exegete Scripture, but to reveal the new age of God's kingdom" (ibid.).

Thus, as we saw above, Jesus Christ's "nature parables" (for example, the mustard seed) showed how God's kingdom would start small but become all-encompassing. The kingdom's present aspects would seem unspectacular, its ultimate realization amazing.

His "discovery parables" (the hidden treasure, Matthew 13:44; or the pearl of great price, verses 45-46) show that God's kingdom is so valuable we can happily abandon all else for it. His "contrast parables" (the rich man and Lazarus, Luke 16:19-31; or the Pharisee and the tax collector, Luke 18:9-14) illuminate how much God loves even the lost and dispossessed and welcomes them into fellowship with him.

The "a fortiori parables"—those that ask "How much more…" (the friend at midnight, Luke 11:5-8; or the persistent widow, Luke 18:1-8)—show how much God can be trusted to act righteously. If even humans won't act in certain evil ways, Jesus asked, "How much more will your Father in heaven give…?" (Luke 11:13).

"The parables focus on God and his kingdom and in doing so reveal what kind of God he is, by what principles he works, and what he expects of humanity," comments the *Baker Encyclopedia of the Bible* (vol. 2, page 1609).

Jesus' use of parables was so masterful, and the kingdom-centered message of his parables so revolutionary, that no other New Testament personality tried to copy this aspect of his teaching. The uniqueness of Jesus' parables bolsters their place at the core of our Savior's message for humanity.

Even critics as extreme as those who make up the Jesus Seminar, who discard much of the Gospels as fabrications by early Christians, believe that in the simple, moving and transcendently beautiful messages of the parables we come as close to the historical Jesus as we are likely to get.

Parables in the Synoptic Gospels

When reading the four Gospels, you have probably noticed similarities in the accounts by Matthew, Mark and Luke. Their books are called the

Synoptic Gospels—meaning "from the same perspective." On the other hand, John's Gospel is obviously written from a different perspective. The authors of these books probably used some of the same source material for their accounts. For example, Luke, in the introduction to his account, freely states he used several sources for his research.

	Matthew	Mark	Luke
Lamp on a Stand	5:14-15	4:21-22	8:16-17; 11:33
Wise and Foolish	7:24-27		6:47-49
New and Old Cloth	9:16	2:21	5:36
New Wine	9:17	2:22	5:37-38
The Sower	13:3-8	4:3-8	8:5-8
Wheat and Weeds	13:24-30		
Mustard Seed	13:31-32	4:30-32	13:18-19
Leaven (Yeast)	13:33		13:20-21
Hidden Treasure	13:34		
Pearl of Great Price	13:45-46		
Fish in the Net	13:47-50		
Lost Sheep	18:12-14		15:4-7
Unmerciful Man	18:23-35		
Vineyard Workers	20:1-16		
Two Sons	21:28-32		
Wicked Tenants	21:33-41	12:1-9	20:9-16
Wedding Banquet	22:2-14		
Fig Tree	24:32-34	13:28-30	21:29-32
The Thief	24:43		12:39
Householder		13:32-37	
Ten Virgins	25:1-13		
Talents/ Minas	25:14-30		19:11-27
Sheep and Goats	25:31-46		
Growing Seed		4:26-29	
Two Debtors			7:41-43

Good Samaritan	10:30-37
Friend at Midnight	11:5-8
Rich Fool	12:16-21
Watchful Servants	12:35-40
Faithful Servant	12:42-48
Barren Fig Tree	13:6-9
Places of Honor	14:7-14
Great Banquet	14:16-24
Counting the Cost	14:28-33
Lost Coin	15:8-10
Lost Son	15:11-32
Shrewd Manager	16:1-9
Lazarus and Rich	16:19-31
Unworthy Servants	17:7-10
Persistent Widow	18:1-8
Pharisee Praying	18:9-14

Hearing Jesus' message

Jesus was a master storyteller. His parables contain striking images, dramatic action and bold character development, all built around universal themes that have touched people for two millennia. Yet the parables offer minimal detail. Often Jesus provided no clear explanations for the stories, leaving them open to multiple interpretations through the ages. So how can we know what the parables of Jesus mean? Some interpreters make the mistake of reading more into some parables than Jesus ever intended. In the other ditch are those who fail to catch what some parables clearly emphasize.

Until this century, most interpreters *allegorized* the parables. This means they looked for symbolic significance in as many details in the stories as possible. Augustine (A.D. 354-430), an early church father, explained the parable of the good Samaritan (Luke 10:30-37) in this way:

The man going down from Jerusalem pictured Adam leaving the peaceful place that was Eden. The robbers who beat him were the devil and his demons, who persuaded Adam to sin. The priest and the Levite (the Law and the Prophets) offered the victim no help, but the Samaritan (Christ) rescued him, pouring oil and wine (comfort and exhortation) onto the man's wounds. The donkey on which the Samaritan, or Christ, placed the man symbolized the church: the apostle Paul was the innkeeper. This is going too far, reading

31

into the parable far more detail than Jesus intended (Paul was not even a Christian yet!)

By contrast, many modern interpreters have abandoned the allegorical approach. They try to reject the temptation to read their own ideas into the parables, which they believe has led to centuries of abuse of Jesus' message. These interpreters believe that each parable has only one main point. Others argue that a parable might make up to three main points, one for each of the main characters in the story.

This was the case, they point out, with parables in classical Greek literature, and this is how Jesus' listeners, in the culture of his day, would have looked at his parables. This view sees the parable of the good Samaritan simply as an exhortation to imitate the Samaritan's outgoing concern for his neighbor. This interpretation seems consistent with the explanation Jesus himself gave for this parable (verse 37).

The story of the rich man and Lazarus (Luke 16:19-31) is another example. It's hard to wrench from this parable exact details about the afterlife. Jesus was drawing on images from Jewish and Egyptian folklore, which his listeners would have realized, to show the gulf between arrogant people in this world and those who by humble submission to God come to be in the kingdom of God.

Many modern Bible students try not to over-interpret the parables. Nevertheless, they believe Jesus gave some details not just to add spice to his stories, but to make important points.

"Parables" in John

The Gospel of John does not contain the word *parable*. But John 10:6, following verses 1-5, Jesus' metaphor of the Good Shepherd, and John 16:25, 29, following verses 20-24, about the woman in travail, translate as "figure" the Greek *paroimia,* meaning "wise saying" or "riddle."

More than once, the Greek translation of the Old Testament uses *paroimia* for the Hebrew *masal.* The Good Shepherd and the woman in travail are similar to the shorter parables in Matthew, Mark and Luke. A.M. Hunter, author of *According to John,* identifies the following "parables" in the book of John:

Blowing Wind	3:8
Bridegroom's Attendant	3:29
Fields Ripe for Harvest	4:35-38
Father and Son	5:19-20
The Slave and the Son	8:35

Good Shepherd	10:1-5
Twelve Hours of Daylight	11:9-10
Kernel of Wheat	12:24
Walking in the Light	12:35
Preparing a Place	14:2-4
The Vine and the Branches	15:1-8
Woman in Travail	16:20-24

None of these "parables" takes the same form as the longer parables in Matthew, Mark and Luke. Yet Jesus' unique style of teaching is still apparent. Thus these "parables" help establish the historical continuity between the fourth Gospel and the Synoptic Gospels.

Let the parables speak to you

If we want to understand God's Word, we need to let the parables speak to our day with vigor and importance. "Parables require their hearers to pass judgment on the events of the story and having done so to realize that they must make a similar judgment in their own lives," states the *Baker Encyclopedia of the Bible* (vol. 2, page 1609).

How can you judge your own life by hearing the messages of Jesus' parables? Study each parable thoroughly, laying aside any preconceived idea of what you think it says—or that you would like it to say. Look at the context in which you find the parable. Doing so may offer clues about its meaning. (But understand that the Gospels often record Jesus' parables without telling exactly when he gave them, or to whom, or why.)

Take note of the "rule of end stress." The climax—and point—of most parables comes at the end. Look for principles that reveal what God is like, what his kingdom is all about, how he wants to relate to humanity—and how he expects us to respond to him.

What does the parable tell you about your relationship with God and Christ? The answers you find to this question are the most important points of truth in the Bible, for, as Jesus said. "This is eternal life: that they may know you, the only true God, and Jesus Christ, whom you have sent" (John 17:3).

How does God want a citizen of his kingdom to behave? All of Jesus' parables contain parts of the answer to this question, for the present and future realities of the kingdom of God are what Christ's life, work, message, death, resurrection and High Priesthood are all about.

What is your attitude toward that kingdom? "Again," Jesus said in a parable, "the kingdom of heaven is like a merchant looking for fine pearls.

When he found one of great value, he went away and sold everything he had and bought it" (Matthew 13:45-46).

HOW MANY POINTS IN A PARABLE?

Book review: *Interpreting the Parables* by Craig L. Blomberg. 1990. Downers Grove, Illinois: InterVarsity Press. 334 pages.

Scholars have often proclaimed that each of Jesus' parables makes only one main point. Classic analyses by Adolf Jülicher, C.H. Dodd, Joachim Jeremias and Robert Stein decry the overly allegorical approaches of medieval commentators, who saw spiritual significance in every detail.

But scholars do not agree on what the *main* point of each parable is. Several points often vie for priority. Some scholars try to generalize the lesson so much that the parable teaches little at all. Some focus on what the parables say about God; others focus on the kingdom of God or on his disciples or his church.

Craig Blomberg (Ph.D. from Aberdeen, now a professor at Denver Seminary) responds to the problem of parable interpretation. In the first half of his book, he surveys ancient and contemporary approaches, effectively challenges the prevailing consensus and offers a moderate approach. In the second half, he applies his principles to Jesus' 36 parables, giving helpful summaries of different scholars' views on each parable and concisely summarizing the parables' teaching.

Problems of the consensus

In the introduction, he summarizes "the scholarly consensus" (pages 15-19): "Modern scholarship has…rejected allegorical interpretation."

A major reason is that no consensus could be reached on what each of the details represented. For example, the prodigal son's robe was variously interpreted as

> standing for sinlessness, spiritual gifts, the imputation of Christ's righteousness, or the sanctity of the soul. Clearly all of these views recognized that the father gave the robe to the prodigal to indicate his restoration to the family. But it was impossible to agree on how to match the robe with one particular aspect of a new Christian's relationship with his heavenly Father. Presumably the lesson to be learned is that the robe is not meant to be allegorized.

But the one-point approach also has weaknesses. Scholars who strenuously object to allegory admit that Jesus' audiences would have understood some of the major features to correspond to facets of the real world. And scholars who stress "only one main point" nevertheless manage to combine two or more points into some of their summary sentences.

"The parables as they appear in the Gospels do have a few undeniable allegorical elements." (Blomberg writes "as they appear in the Gospels" because some scholars recognize allegorical elements but claim that they are developments of the early church rather than being authentic words of Jesus. Allegory, some say, is an inferior form of rhetoric and would therefore not be used by Jesus.)

Allegorical features

Blomberg then presents his own approach, gathering supporting evidence from a variety of scholars. (The book has copious footnotes, which increases its usefulness.) Part of the debate is semantic, concerning the definition of allegory:

> Several scholars with cross-disciplinary expertise in Western literature and biblical studies…affirm that most of the major narrative parables of Jesus are, by every standard literary definition of the word, genuine allegories…. A parable may be an allegory even if [all] its constituent elements do not involve separate metaphors, so long as the overall point of the parable transcends its literal meaning (e.g., the story is about the kingdom of God rather than just, say, farming, fishing or banqueting). (pages 42-43)

> A mixture of parable and allegory was both common and well-liked in ancient Judaism…. 'Standard metaphors' (most notably the king standing for God)…were so frequently used by the rabbis that Jesus' audiences almost certainly would have interpreted them in fairly conventional ways. (page 37)

> The parables regularly contain not only common, down-to-earth portraits of Jewish village life but also 'extravagant' and unrealistic features which point to more than one level of meaning…. Although these features appear implausible as descriptions of normal events, they make excellent sense when interpreted allegorically. (pages 45-46)

> The parables…are much more allegorical than is usually acknowledged…. Given proper definition the parables may and ought to be termed allegories, but…this in no way requires a return to the more arbitrary exegesis which often characterized past generations. (pages 20, 23)

Blomberg, though accepting parables as allegorical, cautions against allegorizing every detail. He provides a much-needed control, noting that most parables contain three main characters or groups of characters.

Each parable makes one main point per main character — usually two or three in each case — and these main characters are the most likely elements within the parable to stand for something other than themselves, thus giving the parable its allegorical nature.

As another reasonable control, he says "all allegorical interpretation must result in that which would have been intelligible to a first-century…audience" (page 163).

The frequent use of contrasting characters suggests that Jesus originally intended in many of his parables both a message for his enemies and one for his disciples. (page 88)

Each parable looks slightly different depending on which character a given member of its audience identifies with…. The parts of a particular parable most likely to be invested with allegorical import are the two or three main characters which regularly appear as images of God, his faithful followers and the rebellious in need of repentance. (pages 148-149)

Rabbinic parables

Most of us have little background in first-century Judaism. We will therefore find the description of Jewish parables instructive (pages 59-65):

Rabbinic parables almost always begin with an introductory formula which parallels those found in the Gospels…. Often the logic…argues that 'if such-and-such is true with men, how much more so with God.'… The length and structure of the rabbinic parables also resemble those of the parables of Jesus….

The parables of Jesus and the rabbis further share common topics and imagery…. 'Judah the Prince used to cite this parable: To what is the matter like? To a king who possessed a vineyard which he handed over to a tenant…. R. Meir illustrated it by a parable. To what is the matter like? To a king who prepared a banquet and invited guests.'… "The rabbis interpreted their parables in a variety of ways, but almost always with some allegorical element.

Parables "lead the reader unwittingly along until he acknowledges the validity of the vehicle (picture-part) of the parable and is therefore forced to side with the story-teller concerning the tenor (spiritual truth) involved as well." The classic example of this is Nathan's parable to David, containing obvious allegorical elements. (We are not addressing in this review whether Jesus' parables made spiritual truths clearer or hidden. Even his disciples did not understand many of the things he taught in the plainest of language.) Jesus' parables were unlike the rabbis' in at least two major ways:

The vast majority of the rabbinic parables staunchly reinforce conventional Jewish values, serving primarily to exegete Scripture. They thus stand in marked contrast to Jesus' often "subversive" counterparts, which almost never refer back to God's written word, but gain their force from the personal authority of Christ.... The parables of Jesus further distinguish themselves by their consistent reference to the kingdom of God. (pages 66-67)

Limited allegorical interpretations

The second half of this book comments on the meanings of each of Jesus' parables, surveying previous interpretations and cautiously seeking concise statements on the parable's major points. We would disagree with a few of his specific interpretations, but I think we can agree with most of his analyses.

I encourage you to read the book yourselves; here I will simply point out that Blomberg's review of the history of the interpretation of many of the parables supports his three-point thesis:

Much of the time scholarly skepticism stems from pitting against one another different interpretations of a parable, when in fact those interpretations each complement one another.... No need remains for choosing one of the lessons at the expense of the others. (page 211)

Once we do not restrict a parable to making only one main point, we can see that the parable addresses both of these issues.... It seems unnecessary to choose between these. Each by itself seems somewhat truncated and together they yield good sense.... Several commentators...fail to admit that their encapsulation of the parable's one main point actually combines two independent thoughts. (pages 232, 246, 265)

Debates about which of these principles was the original point of the parable are futile once it is seen that all were intended from the outset. Jeremias, in fact, makes three very similar points in his exposition without acknowledging that they are distinct lessons. (page 243)

Often the history of interpretation of a given parable discloses that three complementary themes have vied for acceptance as the main point of the story. In no instance has any reason emerged for jettisoning any of these themes, except for the arbitrary assertion that parables make only one point. (page 252)

Conclusion

After discussing all the parables, Blomberg summarizes what they teach:

Jesus clearly has three main topics of interest: the graciousness of God, the demands of discipleship and the dangers of disobedience.... The central theme uniting all of the lessons of the parables is the kingdom of God. It is both present and future. It includes both a reign and a realm. It involves both personal transformation and social reform. (page 326)

Blomberg's book offers a reasonable approach that avoids fanciful allegory on the one hand and reductionistic summaries on the other. By focusing on main characters, it suggests where to look for each parable's significance, and a controlled way to develop the teachings of the parables for modern audiences.

WHAT THE GOSPELS TEACH US
ABOUT GOD

By Michael Morrison

The Gospels are books about Jesus Christ. But these four books also tell us much about God the Father. Even though he is often hidden behind the scenes, he is the most important person in the story. Everything depends on him. Even Jesus' importance is best understood when it is seen in relationship to God — Jesus is the Son of God, the the One sent by God, the Messiah anointed by God. Jesus' importance is received from God; his authority, power and teaching come from God the Father. His mission was to serve God, to bring glory to God, to further God's purpose and God's kingdom and God's plan for the salvation of his people.

The Gospels make no effort to prove that God exists — they seem to assume that the readers already believe in the God revealed in the Old Testament. They believe that he is eternal, almighty, personal, omnipotent, omniscient, holy, righteous and gracious.

A basic understanding of God is assumed in the Gospels, and important additional information about him is revealed. Let us survey the four Gospels to see how Jesus and the apostles understood God.

1. Did Jesus speak with authority? Matt. 7:29. Where did he get his authority? John 5:19;8:28; 12:49; 14:10. Where did he come from? John 8:42. Why was he sent? Luke 4:43; John 3:17; 4:34; 5:36; 6:38-39; 9:4.

Comment: These are just a few of the scriptures that tell us that God the Father sent Jesus the Son into the world to accomplish the Father's purpose. In John, more than 30 verses tell us that the Father sent the Son, and in 14 additional verses, Jesus refers to "the one who sent me." Jesus is telling us something about God — not only is Jesus identified as the one who was sent, the Father is identified and described in terms of his relationship to Jesus. The God we are interacting with is the one who sent Jesus.

2. During Jesus' ministry, it was revealed that he was the Son of God. What did he then reveal about the Father? John 1:18; 14:9; 17:26; 17:4. And what did the Father himself reveal about Jesus? Matt. 3:17; 17:5.

Comment: Jesus shows us what God the Father is like. He shows us the Father's love, his compassion and mercy, his righteousness, humility, authority, words, work and truth — even his glory. In Jesus Christ, the Father is made visible so that we can know him. We worship a Father who is very much like his Son.

Although the Father is greater than the Son, they are also one. They have a reciprocal relationship: the Son is in the Father, and the Father is in the Son. Jesus brings glory to the Father, and the Father gives glory to the Son. The Son testifies concerning the Father, and the Father testifies concerning the Son.

3. In the Sermon on the Mount, Jesus taught about the Father. What kind of love does the Father have? Matt. 5:45. Can he be trusted to take care of us? Matt. 6:8, 26-32;18:14. How should we respond to him? Matt. 5:44; 6:33.

4. Does God reward his children? Matt. 6:1-6. How do we speak to him? Luke 11:1-13;18:1-8. What are we to pray for? Matt. 5:44; 7:11; 9:38; 18:19. Whose will is to be done, in prayer as well as in other aspects of life? Matt. 6:10; 7:21; 12;50;26:39, 42.

5. What is the Father's role in the work of the Son? Matt. 11:25-27; 13:11; 16:17;19:26; 20:23. People can come to the Father only through Jesus Christ, but how do people get to Jesus? John 6:44, 65.

Comment: Jesus' ministry was all done under the direction of the Father. Throughout the Gospels we are reminded that Jesus worked according to a plan. It was predicted in Scripture, and it had to be done in a particular way to fulfill what God had already predicted.

The Father directed Jesus in what to do and what to say, and the Son was obedient. Jesus prayed often, and he knew his Father's will. His authority and power came from the Father, and the Father supported him and honored him for his work.

6. How did Jesus describe his relationship with God? John 3:35; 5:20; 10:17; 14:3;17:24. What special term did he call him? Mark 14:36. Where was he to go after his work on earth had been done? John 13:1; 14:28; 16:10; 20:17.

Comment: In the Old Testament, God is called Father less than 1 percent of the time, never in prayer. Yet Jesus always addressed God in this way (except when he quoted an Old Testament prayer). His disciples only rarely called God Father; almost all the occurrences of "Father" are spoken by Jesus.

Jesus had an unusually close relationship with God, as shown by the word Abba. This was an Aramaic word for father, used by children and adults to refer to their human fathers. Jesus used this familiar term when he prayed, and apparently he taught his disciples to use it, too. Paul used this Aramaic word when he wrote to the church at Rome, confident that they also knew the word because it had been taught to them (Rom. 8:15).

Abba shows a personal and close relationship — Jesus was aware that he had a unique relationship with God. He was loved by the Father, even before the world began, and he loved and trusted the Father. When his work was done, he returned to the Father to be with him in his glory.

7. May we also share in this relationship and look to God as our Father? Matt. 6:14-15, 32;7:11; John 1:12-13; 14:23. What does the Father send to us? John 14:26.

Comment: Jesus gave us the right to become children of God — yet we are not children in exactly the same way that Jesus is. He was a born Son of God; we are adopted children of God. We experience a Father-son relationship with God when we have faith in Jesus as the Son of God (John 8:42). We are to respond to him with worship, praise, honor, prayer, love, faith and obedience — to the Son as well as to the Father.

Parables of the Father

1. Some of Jesus' parables tell us what the Father is like. Jesus tells us that the Father will act like the king in the parable of the unmerciful servant (Matt. 18:23-35). Was the king willing to forgive the debt? Verse 27. Why was this forgiveness taken away? Verses 28-35. How did Jesus make the same point in the Sermon on the Mount? Matt. 6:15. How is it expressed in Luke 6:36?

2. In the parable of the workers (Matt. 20:1-15), the Father is like the landowner who paid each worker a day's wage, even if he worked only one hour. What does this tell us about God? Verse 15.

3. In the parable of the tenants (Matt. 21:33-43; Luke 20:9-16), the Father is like a landowner who eventually sent his son to collect rent. What happened to the son? Luke 20:15. And what happened to the tenants? Verse 16.

4. In the parable of the wedding banquet (Matt. 22:2-13), the Father is like a king who prepared a wedding banquet for his son. Who is invited to the wedding? Verse 9. What happens to those who don't respond properly? Verses 7, 11-13.

5. In the parable of the lost sheep and the parable of the lost coin (Luke 15:3-10), the Father is represented as a man or woman who seeks something that is lost. What is the point that Jesus made? Verses 7, 10. In the parable of the prodigal son, the Father eagerly desires the return of his son (verse 20). How does he greet him? Verses 22-24. What is the lesson we can learn? Verse

32.

Comment: These parables do not give a complete portrait of the Father, but they do sketch some important aspects. Here we see a Father who is generous, willing to forgive, eager to invite and eager for us to return. In fact, the Father is so eager for our salvation that he took the initiative to send his Son to seek for us, to invite us and to ensure that we can come.

In the parables, we also see another aspect of God: a Father who makes requirements, who is critical of people who do not rejoice when sinners turn to God. Moreover, the Father is willing to judge and punish those who disobey. "Be afraid," Jesus said, "of the One who can destroy both soul and body in hell" (Matt. 10:28). "Worship the Lord your God, and serve him only" (Matt. 4:10).

WHAT THE GOSPELS TEACH US ABOUT JESUS

By Michael Morrison

It is difficult to summarize in this short space what the Gospels say about Jesus Christ. These four books contain more than 100 pages of information about Jesus, and so much of it seems important. Perhaps we can summarize the Gospels by looking at three questions: 1) Who is this person? 2) What did he do? 3) What does he mean for us today?

Who is this person?

Jesus looked like an ordinary person. He was born in an ordinary way, in humble circumstances. Like other Jewish boys, he was circumcised. As a firstborn child, he was dedicated at the temple. Two pigeons were sacrificed, showing that the family was poor (Luke 2:24; Lev. 12:8).

Like other children, Jesus grew physically, intellectually and socially. Later, he was known as "the carpenter, the son of Mary" (Mark 6:3). He walked and worked like other people did. He ate, slept and became tired and hungry and thirsty. Later, he died, as all people do.

Jesus did have a special interest in religion. His family went to Jerusalem for the Passover every year, and when Jesus was 12, the temple teachers were surprised at how much he knew (Luke 2:46-47).

His cousin John was also religious — and quite out of the ordinary. John lived in the wilderness, eating strange food and wearing strange clothes. He preached repentance, and baptized people as a symbol of forgiveness. Crowds of people came to rededicate themselves to God. Jesus also came, and he was baptized.

Extraordinary behavior

At Jesus' baptism, something extraordinary happened — a voice from heaven, and something like a dove came upon him (Luke 3:22). This was a major turning point in his life. His behavior suddenly changed. He quit his job, moved to the desert and stopped eating for 40 days.

When Jesus came back to the synagogue at Nazareth, he practically claimed to be the Messiah when he said that God had anointed him to preach. He announced that he was the fulfillment of Scripture (Luke 4:16-29).

Jesus began to do some extraordinary things: turning water into wine, feeding thousands of people, healing all sorts of diseases, giving sight to the blind, even raising the dead. He commanded demons to leave, and they obeyed! Repent, he preached, for the kingdom of God is near.

Could this be the Messiah?

No way, said the experts. They liked Jesus when he was 12, not now. He disrupted temple-related businesses, turned over tables and drove out the animals (John 2:13-17). He publicly criticized the Jewish leaders, calling them blind leaders, snakes, children of the devil, sons of hell (Matt. 15:14; 23:15, 33; John 8:44).

And no one ever taught like Jesus did. What extraordinary things he said about himself! Such as, If you don't do what I say, you will not be in the kingdom of God. No one comes to God except through me. I am the judge of your eternity. I can forgive your sins (Matt. 7:26; 9:2-6;10:33; 16:27; John 5:22; 14:16).

Moses is not enough, Jesus said. Moses said one thing, but I teach something else (Matt. 5:21-39). He claimed to be greater than the temple, greater than Solomon and Jonah (Matt. 12:5-8, 41-42). He said that people should be more righteous than Pharisees, but he ignored their rules about ritual washings and Sabbath-keeping.

Who is this man? Where did he get these extraordinary ideas?

If Jesus didn't do any miracles, his teachings might have been ignored as ridiculous. But his miracles gave evidence that he really could forgive sin, he really could bring spiritual light to the blind and he really did have authority from God. This man could not be ignored.

The people saw Jesus' miracles, and they wondered, Could he really be the Messiah? (John 7:25-31, 40-44). Could this person who criticizes our traditions really be anointed by God?

Extraordinary shame

Jesus often called himself the Son of Man. Sometimes this phrase meant "an ordinary person." Sometimes it referred to an extraordinary person — someone "like a son of man" coming with the clouds of heaven, crowned and given great glory (Daniel 7:13-14). Jesus said that he would come in great glory, at the right hand of God (Matt. 24:30). This was such a bold claim that the high priest accused Jesus of blasphemy (Matt. 26:64).

Paradoxically, Jesus also used the phrase Son of Man to predict his own death on a cross (Matt. 20:18-19; 26:2) — but crucifixion was the most shameful way for any Jew to die. "Anyone who is hung on a tree is under God's curse" (Deut. 21:23).

How could anyone have both shame and glory? How could a blasphemer be honored by God? If Jesus were the Messiah, why did he say that the people would reject him and kill him? A dead Messiah made no sense.

That's why Peter said, Not so, Lord! We will never let this happen to you! But Peter could not stop the envy of the Jewish leaders, nor the injustice of the Roman rulers. Peter was powerless against sin and evil.

And so Jesus, once hailed by the people as a king, was soon rejected, betrayed, deserted, condemned, beaten and crucified. The disciples' hopes were crushed. Some left town; some planned to return to the fishing business.

The Gospels do not hide the shameful death of Jesus. Indeed, all four books spend a disproportionate amount of space on this tragic event. These books were designed to tell us what Jesus did (Acts 1:1), but they give a lot of space to Jesus' suffering and death. Could it be that his death is part of what he did? Could it be that his manner of death was part of his ministry? What made his death so newsworthy in the eyes of the Gospel writers?

Extraordinary revaluation

Even in death, Jesus was a controversial figure. One Jewish leader asked for permission to put him in a brand-new tomb. Other Jewish leaders posted a guard.

Early on a Sunday morning, some women came to put burial spices on his body, but they came back with a strange report. There was an earthquake, they said, and an angel rolled the stone away, the guards fainted and Jesus suddenly appeared to the women.

The disciples "did not believe the women, because their words seemed to them like nonsense" (Luke 24:11). Even after Peter examined the evidence, "he went away, wondering to himself what had happened" (verse 12).

It was not long before Peter became convinced about what had happened. But why? If God wanted Jesus to be alive, why did he allow him to die in the first place? Is this what Jesus was all about?

"Beginning with Moses and all the Prophets, Jesus explained to them what was said in all the Scriptures concerning himself" (verse 27). The disciples began to learn a new understanding of Jesus — not just his resurrection, but also the purpose of his death, the meaning of his life and most astonishing of all, who he was.

Who was this man from Nazareth? He called himself the Son of Man. Blind men and a Canaanite woman called him Son of David, another name for the Messiah. Demons called him Son of God — but could they be right?

Nathanael, Peter and Martha also called him the Son of God. He accepted that title in front of the high priest, and was condemned for it. The crowds ridiculed him for it, but the centurion said, "Surely he was the Son of God!" Mark, Luke and John begin their books by calling him the Son of God —

not a child of God in the same way that believers are, but Son in an unprecedented way.

Extraordinary person

Despite appearances, Jesus did not begin in the usual way, Matthew and Luke tell us — he was conceived by the Spirit of God. Even when he was a baby, the Magi worshiped him. His disciples fell on their knees and worshiped him (Matt. 2:11; 14:33; 28:9, 17).

John tells us something even more astounding: that Jesus was, from the beginning of time, the Word of God, who "was with God, and the Word was God." Through him all things had been created (John 1:1-3). John calls him "God the One and Only" (verse 18). Thomas called him "My Lord and my God" (John 20:28). Jesus said he had the glory of God "before the world began" (John 17:5).

Who was this person? He was God, worthy of worship and honor and absolute obedience.

How could Jews ever come to believe such an idea? Not easily! But the Gospel writers had seen the evidence, and they report to us the evidence that convinced them. They describe for us a Jesus who is both ordinary and extraordinary at the same time.

Well, if Jesus was God in human flesh, what was he doing on the cross? Why does it seem that the focal point of his ministry is an ignominious death? The Gospels do not give us many details why (other New Testament books give us much more). Jesus did say that he would draw people to himself through the cross (John 12:32). His death would be a means of acquiring disciples.

Jesus said that his death had been predicted in the Old Testament (Matt. 26:24; Mark 9:12; Luke 24:46). So we can look to the Old Testament to learn more. But where does the Old Testament predict someone sent by God to die for others?

In Luke 22:37, Jesus pointed the way by quoting a specific prophecy that "must be fulfilled in me." He quoted from Isaiah 53, which describes a servant who carries our sins, suffers and dies, brings forgiveness, and is honored by God. Jesus saw himself as that servant. He is the one who would "give his life as a ransom for many" (Matt. 20:28).

As a ransom for many, as a sin-bearing sacrifice, Jesus accomplished more in his death than he did in all his miracles. This is the reason he came (John 12:27). There was no other way to achieve his purpose (Matt. 26:42).

What then are we supposed to do with this person? How is he relevant to us today?

John tells us that he wrote his Gospel so that we would believe that Jesus is the Messiah, the Son of God, and by believing we may have eternal life through him (John 20:31). We can have eternal life only by being forgiven, and it is only through the death of Christ that we can be forgiven. It is to him we must respond. We should fall to our knees and confess, My Lord and my God.

WHAT THE GOSPELS TEACH US ABOUT THE HOLY SPIRIT

By Michael Morrison

The Holy Spirit was an essential part of Jesus' ministry. Not only was Jesus enlivened by the Spirit, Jesus also taught his disciples that the Holy Spirit would be an essential part of their ministry.

1. When and how did the Holy Spirit begin the life of Jesus? Matt. 1:18, 20; Luke 1:35. What did the Holy Spirit do to Jesus at the beginning of his ministry? Luke 3:22; John 1:32-33.

Christ "made himself nothing" (Phil. 2:7), and the Holy Spirit caused Jesus to begin growing in Mary's womb. Although the Spirit remained in Jesus from that moment on, a visible sign was given at his baptism that the Holy Spirit was empowering him.

However, Jesus was not the first person to be given God's Spirit. The Old Testament describes a variety of people who were given power, wisdom and understanding by the Spirit. Jesus said that David — and presumably all other writers of Scripture — spoke by the Holy Spirit in the Psalms (Matt. 22:43).

But in the first century, the Jews had gone a long time without a Spirit-filled prophet. They were waiting for someone to come in the spirit and power of Elijah.

2. Before Jesus was born, was John the Baptist filled with the Holy Spirit? Luke 1:15. Even while Jesus was in Mary's womb, who was filled with the Spirit? Verse 41. What was Elizabeth inspired to say? Verses 42-45. Several months later, what was her husband, Zechariah, inspired by the Spirit to prophesy? Verse 67. And shortly after Jesus was born, did the Holy Spirit move upon yet another person? Luke 2:25-27.

3. After Jesus was baptized and filled with the Holy Spirit, what did the Spirit lead him to do? Luke 4:1. After his victory over the satanic temptations, was he drained of power? Verse 14. What did he tell the people that the Spirit was leading him to do? Verse 18. What emotion filled him because of the Holy Spirit? Luke 10:21.

4. John tells us that God gave Jesus the Holy Spirit without limit (John 3:34). He was filled and led by the Spirit in all his work. One work in particular showed that he was empowered by the Spirit. What did that miracle prove? Matt. 12:28. In his ministry, how did Jesus fulfill a prophecy about God's Spirit? Verses 15-18.

Jesus' comment about "blasphemy against the Spirit" (v. 31) refers to people who become enemies of God (Isa. 63:10). The Pharisees became worse than unbelievers — they were actively resisting the power of God. By calling Jesus' power satanic, they were fighting against God, making themselves enemies of the only power able to lead them to salvation and forgiveness.

5. What did John the Baptist predict that Jesus would do with the Spirit? John 1:33. When was this done? John 7:39. Is it Jesus who sends the Spirit, or is it the Father? Luke 11:13;John 4:10; 7:37; 14:16, 26; 15:26; 16:7.

Jesus sent the disciples out to preach, heal and cast out demons, and they presumably did this with the same power Jesus had, the Holy Spirit. The Spirit was living with them, but was not yet in them (John 14:17). They would be filled with the Holy Spirit after Jesus had been glorified. Both the Father and the Son would send the Holy Spirit to live within the believers.

6. What does the Holy Spirit do in a person's life? John 3:5; 6:63. What does the Spirit bring to our minds? John 14:26; 15:26. What is the focus of this spiritual work? John 15:26; 16:13-14.

The Spirit of God does not teach us truths about math, but about the Truth, Jesus himself, the way of salvation (John 14:6). The Spirit enabled the disciples to understand what Jesus had taught, and to understand what was "yet to come" — his death and resurrection. By causing the disciples to understand, the Spirit enabled them to preach the good news of life through Jesus Christ.

Jesus sent his disciples with a message, told them to receive the Holy Spirit (John 15:27;20:21-23) and to wait until they received the "power from on high" they needed (Luke 24:49). The gospel work of the church is done in the power of the Holy Spirit.

Through the Spirit-led disciples, the world hears the message of truth, the message of Jesus — but many people do not accept that message (John 14:17). In this way, the Holy Spirit convicts the world of guilt in regard to unbelief and judgment (John 16:8-11). The world may be hostile, but even in times of persecution, the Holy Spirit speaks through the disciples (Luke 12:11-12).

Disciples are baptized into the name of the Father, Son, and Holy Spirit (Matt. 28:19). The Spirit is as much a part of our identity as the Father and the Son are.

Jesus said that he would go away, and yet live in his disciples (John 14:18; Matt. 28:20). He lives in us by means of the Holy Spirit, the Counselor who continues the teaching work of Jesus.

WHAT THE GOSPELS TEACH US
ABOUT THE SCRIPTURES

By Michael Morrison

The Scriptures were an important part of Jesus' work. He used the Old Testament as an authoritative basis for beliefs and behavior. He used the Hebrew Bible to prove his points, to explain his mission and ministry, and to communicate God's will for his people.

Jesus and the Pharisees agreed that God had inspired the Scriptures. Jesus disagreed with them about interpretations, but they all agreed on the basic belief that these writings were true and authoritative.

Since Jesus agreed with the Pharisees on this point, he did not have an occasion to list all his beliefs about Scripture, nor to explain the reasons he had for his beliefs. However, Jesus used the Scriptures so often that we are able to see what he believed about Scripture. The disciples who wrote the Gospels also used Scripture frequently, and we can tell by the way they used the Scriptures that they held the same beliefs.

1. According to Jesus, who wrote the Torah? Matt. 8:4; 19:8. Did he also say that God was the author of at least two of the commands? Matt. 15:4; 22:31-32. How was a human author able to write the words of God? Verse 43. Did the prophets accurately report words God said about himself? Matt. 9:13; 11:10; 12:18; 15:8-9.

2. Matthew mentions numerous Old Testament verses that were fulfilled by Jesus Christ. Who was the source of these verses? Matt. 1:22; 2:15. Matthew tells us that various scriptures were spoken "through" the prophets Isaiah, Jeremiah, Daniel (Matt. 2:17; 3:3; 13:35;24:15). Who was the source?

3. Did Jesus expect all the words of the prophets to be fulfilled? Matt. 5:17-18; 26:24,31, 54, 56. Did he chide the Pharisees for not understanding the prophets? Matt. 12:7;21:16, 42. Did he consider the Scriptures, even though they were written hundreds of years earlier, to apply to his own day? Matt. 15:7; 19:8.

4. How did Jesus use Scripture as a decisive answer to doctrinal questions? Matt. 12:3-5;19:4; 22:31-32. How did he quote Deuteronomy in response to Satan's temptations? Matt. 4:4, 7, 10. Does this suggest a greater-than-human authority in the Scriptures?

Our Lord clearly had a high view of Scripture. He always treated it as true, as conclusive proof, as correct teaching. It was God communicating through human authors. The message was true.

Jesus understood his own mission in terms of the Old Testament

Scriptures: "I have come to fulfill the Law and the Prophets. Everything in them must be fulfilled. I must do this because it has been inspired by the Holy Spirit, and what is written must come to pass. Doctrinal errors exist because you do not know what the Scriptures say. They are the standard of truth" (paraphrase of Matt. 5:17-18; 22:29; 26:54).

5. What was Jesus' attitude toward the Old Testament laws? Matt. 5:18-19. Did Jesus advise people to obey all the laws? Matt. 15:4; 19:17-19; 22:37-40. Did Jesus tell people to obey ritual laws? Matt. 8:4. To obey the Pharisees when they taught the law of Moses? Matt. 23:2-3. Should people obey in even the smallest details? Matt. 5:19; 23:23.

Jesus taught people to obey every law in Scripture, because all the laws had divine authority. The laws told God's old covenant people what he wanted them to do, and they were supposed to do it all.

The ritual laws are still part of Scripture. They describe what God told a specific people to do at a certain time in history. But those laws were not given to the Christian church, and the covenant that framed those laws has been surpassed. Just as we do not have to obey all the instructions God gave to Abraham, we do not have to obey all the instructions God gave to the Israelites.

Those laws were inspired by God for a temporary purpose: "All the Prophets and the Law prophesied until John" (Matt. 11:13).

6. Does the law of Moses give the perfect will of God? Matt. 19:8. Where did Jesus find authoritative guidance? Verses 4-5. Is it enough to keep the letter of the law? Matt. 5:21-22,27-28. Was the law of Moses too strict, or too lenient? Verses 31-32. By what authority did Jesus say this? Verses 22, 28, 32, 34. What is the higher standard that Jesus taught? Matt. 7:12; 22:37-40.

Although Jesus had a high respect for the Old Testament, he taught that it was not a complete guide for godly living. The law of Moses allowed divorce, but divorce is not good. Jesus taught a higher principle, the golden rule, the way of love and mercy. The law of Moses included love, but it did not identify love as the most important principle. Jesus did.

Jesus had high standards about the way humans should treat one another — he was stricter than the Pharisees. But when it came to ritual purity and Sabbath rules, Jesus was more permissive than the Pharisees. Jesus often touched unclean people, and he often healed on the Sabbath even though he could have waited until later.

"When it came to morals (e.g., divorce) Jesus' interpretation was stricter than most of his contemporaries. When it came to [worship] laws (e.g., the Sabbath) Jesus' interpretation was comparatively lenient. Jesus' emphasis seems to have fallen on compassion as over against holiness" (Craig Evans, "Old Testament in the Gospels," *Dictionary of Jesus and the Gospels,* InterVarsity, 1992, p. 581).

In the Sermon on the Mount, Jesus quoted several laws from the Torah, and then gave his own teaching as the complete word on the subject. In doing this, he put his own words on the level as Scripture, as authoritative instruction from God. His words will never pass away, and it is by his words that people will be judged (Matt. 24:35; 7:24-27; John 12:48). He is the only one who can help us know God (Matt. 11:27).

Jesus spoke with authority; his judgments are certain, and his predictions are guaranteed to come to pass. The Holy Spirit taught his words to the disciples (John 14:26), just as the Spirit inspired the Old Testament writers. These sayings of Jesus suggest that more Scripture was yet to be written, the Scriptures we now call the New Testament. These are the writings that give us the words by which we will be judged — words from and about Jesus Christ.

7. Did Jesus see his own ministry in terms of Old Testament prophecies? Luke 4:16-21. Did he believe that the prophets foretold his suffering, death and resurrection? Luke 18:31-33. Which prophecy of Isaiah applied specifically to him? Luke 22:37. Did he believe that the prophecies were certain to come true? Luke 24:44-47. Did he believe that other prophecies were certain to be fulfilled in the future? Luke 21:22.

Jesus, as a Galilean rabbi who taught in synagogues, would naturally root his ministry in the Old Testament Scriptures. The Bible was the foundation for many of his teachings, for explaining his mission as the Messiah, and for predicting the future judgment. Our Lord was confident that the Scriptures are trustworthy because he believed them to be inspired by God. He based his life and mission on this conviction.

Many of his teachings have Old Testament roots. The parable of the Good Samaritan, for example, reflects the story in 2 Chronicles 28:8-15—the men of Samaria gave food, clothes and medicine to Jews, and used donkeys to help transport them to Jericho. The parable of humility (Luke 14:7-14) develops the thought of Proverbs 25:6-7.

Jesus often referred to Old Testament characters: Abel, Noah, Abraham, Lot's wife, Isaac, Jacob, Moses, Solomon, the Queen of Sheba, Jonah and others. Although he corrected the Pharisees on other matters of biblical interpretation, their acceptance of the biblical story did not have to be corrected.

8. In the Gospel of John, how does Jesus describe the giver of the law?

John 7:19, 22. Did he quote part of the law to support the validity of his own teachings? John 8:17-18. Did he expect biblical prophecies to come true in his own ministry? John 13:18; 15:25; 19:24. Which Old Testament author wrote about Jesus? John 5:46.

9. In addition to the books of Moses, what else was included in "the law"? John 10:34. How likely was this word to be true? Verse 35.

Jesus quoted Psalm 82:6, which describes God criticizing leaders who fail to do their duty to help the oppressed. With some irony, he calls these leaders "gods" — mighty ones, elohim, and he gives judgment on them (Ps. 86:1). He calls them "gods" and children of the Most High, but notes that they die like all other human rulers (verses 6-7). The word of God — his judgment on them — came to these unjust leaders.

Jesus is not commenting on the now-dead leaders, nor on the psalm itself. He is using it as a "from the lesser to the greater" argument: "If he called these people gods, these unjust people to whom the judgment of God came, why do you accuse me of blasphemy when I say that I am the son of God? If he can call unjust people gods, why can't I call myself the son of God?"

In making this argument, Jesus mentions, almost as a parenthetical thought, that "Scripture cannot be broken." He was not trying to prove this idea. Rather, it was a point on which he and the Pharisees agreed, and all he needed to do was to mention it. Human words can be broken. They can fail, but Scripture cannot. Its words are trustworthy, because they are inspired by God. The Scriptures are the standard of truth, the accurate record of God's revelation, and the ultimate authority for all matters of doctrine, faith and practice.

WHAT THE GOSPELS TEACH US
ABOUT ANGELS AND DEMONS

By Michael Morrison

Angels

Angels are spirit beings, messengers and servants of God. They have a special role in four major events of Jesus' life, and Jesus referred to them on occasion as he taught about other subjects.

The Gospels are not designed to answer all our questions about angels. They give us only incidental information as angels enter the story.

Angels appear before Jesus does. Gabriel appeared to Zechariah to announce that he would have a son, John the Baptist (Luke 1:11-19). Gabriel also told Mary that she would have a son, Jesus (vv. 26-38). Joseph was told about it by an angel in a dream (Matthew 1:20-24).

An angel announced the birth of Jesus to shepherds, and a host of angels sang praises (Luke 2:9-15). An angel again appeared to Joseph in a dream to tell him to flee to Egypt, and when it was safe to return (Matthew 2:13, 19).

Angels are mentioned again in Jesus' temptation. Satan quoted a verse about angelic protection, and angels ministered to Jesus after the temptation (Matthew 4:6, 11). An angel helped Jesus in Gethsemane during a later temptation (Luke 22:43).

Angels had an important role in the resurrection, too, as mentioned in all four Gospels. An angel rolled back the stone and told the women that Jesus was risen (Matthew 28:2-5). The women saw one or two angels inside the tomb (Mark 16:5; Luke 24:4, 23; John 20:11). Divine messengers showed the importance of the resurrection.

Jesus said that angels will again play a major role when he returns. Angels will come with him and will gather the elect for salvation and evildoers for destruction (Matthew 13:39-49;24:31).

Jesus could have had legions of angels, but he did not ask for them (Matthew 26:53). He will have them when he returns. Angels will be involved in the judgment (Luke 12:8-9). Perhaps this is when people will see angels "ascending and descending upon the Son of Man" (John 1:51).

Angels may appear as a person, or with unusual glory (Luke 2:9; 24:4). They do not die and do not marry, which apparently means that they have no sexuality and do not reproduce (Luke 20:35-36).

Jesus said that "little ones who believe in me" have angels in heaven who care for them (Matthew 18:6, 10). Angels rejoice when people turn to God, and they bring the righteous to paradise (Luke 15:10; 16:22).

Demons

Jesus also said that the devil has "his angels" (Matt. 25:41). These are more commonly called demons, or evil or unclean spirits. The chief demon is Satan (which means "the adversary"), also called the devil (one who leads others astray), Beelzebul (lord of the house), the evil one, the enemy, the tempter, or the prince of this world.

More than any other section of Scripture, the Gospels often mention demons — but as with angels, the Gospels do not answer all our questions — they simply give us incidental information about demons as they touch on the story of Jesus. In almost all cases, the stress is that Jesus already has absolute power over all evil spirits.

Demons caused a wide variety of problems for people: illness, muteness, blindness, screaming, partial paralysis, unusual strength, convulsions, wounds and insanity. Some people were completely possessed by multiple demons; others were only partially influenced.

Jewish and pagan exorcists had elaborate rituals and words (Matt. 12:27; Mark 9:38), but Jesus simply told the demons to leave, and they did. He used his own authority over them. He gave that authority to his disciples (Matt. 10:1; Luke 10:17), but they were not always successful (Mark 9:18).

Satan is the chief enemy of the gospel (Matt. 13:19), but he cannot stop it. Jesus defeated him in several ways. Jesus resisted his temptations (Matt. 4:1-11), liberated his captives (Luke 13:16) and thwarted his desire through prayer (Luke 22:31-32).

In a parable, Jesus described himself as tying up Satan and taking his possessions (Matt. 12:29). He spoke of seeing Satan fall (Luke 10:18). Through his death on the cross, Jesus drove Satan out (John 12:31-32). Satan was condemned (John 16:11).

Just as our salvation and God's kingdom is already here, but not yet in its fullness, so also is Satan's defeat. He has been defeated, but he still works against the gospel. Jesus predicted that victory would be complete at the end of the age (Matt. 13:39-42; 25:41). There is a time appointed for the devil and his angels to be punished (Matt. 8:29).

THE GOSPELS AND THE GOSPEL

By Jim Herst

After a three-year study (1991-94), George Barna arrived at a sobering conclusion: "Spiritually speaking, many Christians try to run before they have learned to walk. Lacking the fundamentals, they eventually get snarled up in their faith, hindered by the absence of a strong foundation on which to build their faith."

Barna, founder and president of The Barna Research Group of Glendale, California, believes that most Christians do not live with a holistic biblical worldview. "Their decisions," he says, "are made 'off-the-cuff,' based on whatever seems right at the moment — without prayer, without a biblical checkpoint, without a true concern for how Jesus might have dealt with the same situation" (*The Barna Report,* vol. 2., 1994).

Many Christians do not know God's word well enough. Is it any wonder that the faith of so many is weak? "Faith comes by hearing and what is heard comes through the word of Christ," wrote Paul in his letter to the Romans (10:17). So why not read the words of Christ, beginning with the Gospel of Matthew?

You probably know many individual scriptures and parables from this Gospel. But have you ever read it right through, as a story? When you do, it will give you a different impression.

We suggest you use a modern version, such as the New International Version, or the New King James. We've given you some notes and background information. We also prepared an outline, which may help as a road map. But now we would like to get out of your way and let you begin to read Matthew's words for yourself. Matthew's Gospel has 28 chapters. If you read one a day, you can read through the book in four weeks.

The major purpose of the Gospel writers was to record Jesus' teachings on the kingdom of God and to proclaim the good news of salvation that God offers us through Jesus.

It is common for Christians today to speak about "the four Gospels" — referring to Matthew, Mark, Luke and John. And that's fine as far as popular usage goes. But we should always remember that these four books do not reflect four different gospels, or four different messages. One of the great foundational doctrines of the New Testament is that there is only one gospel, "the gospel of Jesus Christ" (Matthew 1:1).

The early church never spoke of "the Gospel of Matthew," "the Gospel of Mark" or "of Luke" or "of John." They distinguished these four accounts of the "one story" by using the Greek preposition *kata,* meaning "according to." The church used the terms "the Gospel according to Matthew" or "the Gospel according to Mark." For them, it was always the one and the same gospel, brought into being by four different authors. King's College professor Graham Stanton puts it well when he describes the writings of the evangelists as "One Gospel: Four Gospellers" (*Gospel Truth? New Light on Jesus and the Gospels,* p. 96).

In fact, the word gospel was not originally used in a literary sense of a Gospel writing; it always designated the Christian message of salvation through Jesus Christ. It was not until the year A.D. 150 that the word was first used in the sense of a Gospel writing.

The English word gospel comes from the Middle English word godspel, literally "good spell," with the idea of being a "good tale." The Greek word behind the concept is *euangelion,* meaning "good news." This good news is that we can have eternal life through Jesus Christ our Lord. It is nowhere better described than in Paul's letter to the church at Corinth: "Now I would remind you, brothers and sisters, of the good news that I proclaimed to you … that Christ died for our sins in accordance with all the scriptures, and that he was buried, and that he was raised on the third day in accordance with the scriptures, and that he appeared to Cephas and then to the twelve" (1 Corinthians 15:1, 3-5).

This gospel is "the power of God for salvation to everyone who has faith" (Romans 1:16). It was preached and received "not as a human word but as what it really is, God's word, which is also at work in you believers" (1 Thessalonians 2:13). It is "a message by which you and your entire household will be saved" (Acts 11:14).

EXPLORE THE GOSPELS: MATTHEW

Who was Matthew?

Early church tradition attributes this Gospel to Matthew, the tax collector chosen by Jesus to be an apostle (10:3). He was also known as Levi (compare 9:9-13 with Luke 5:27-31). None of the four Gospels actually names its author. It was the message, not who was writing that was considered important.

What this book means for us today

Matthew's Gospel is a call to take Jesus seriously and to follow him. It is not enough to mouth the name of Jesus; we must be his disciples, just as the people of his day had to. Just knowing about him is not enough. Jesus said, "Not everyone who says to me 'Lord, Lord' will enter the kingdom of heaven, but only he who does the will of my father in heaven" (7:21).

"Discipleship involves following Jesus. This notion of following Jesus suggests that the disciples are to be 'with' Jesus (e.g. 9:15; 12:20; 26:38-40) as those who accompany him (e.g. 9:19), align themselves with him over against his opponents (e.g. 9:10-17; 12:1-8) and therefore experience persecution (e.g. 5:10-12; 10:24-25), learn from him (e.g. 5:1 10:24; 13:26), model their lives after his example (e.g. 20:25-28), and come after him by assuming for themselves the journey of self-denial and cross-bearing (10:38-39; 16:24-28; compare 16:24-28)" ("The Major Characters of Matthew's Story: Their Function and Significance," David Bauer, *Interpretation,* October 1992, p. 362).

Jesus calls upon us to forsake everything and follow him. But he also promises that "everyone who has left houses or brothers or sisters or father or mother or children or fields for my sake will receive a hundred times as much and will inherit eternal life" (Matthew 19:29).

Matthew wrote a marvelous proclamation of hope in the Messiah. As you read, listen to his clear message: Jesus is the Christ, the King of kings, and Lord of lords. Jesus Christ has gained the victory over evil and death. Your death. Re-dedicate yourself

to him. Make him the Lord of your life, even as Matthew the tax collector did nearly two thousand years ago.

Road map of Matthew

The Gospel of Matthew has been divided into 28 chapters, and the chapters are divided into verses.

These chapters and verses are a later addition. They have the advantage of making it easy to locate specific verses, passages and quotations. But they have the disadvantage of interrupting the continuity and theme of the book. Most of the time we "access it" like a telephone directory rather than read it like a story.

Matthew wrote his gospel as a carefully organized continuous narrative. It has three major sections, each of which has sub-sections. You may find it helpful to follow this outline to help you navigate as you read through the story for yourself.

1. The preparation for Jesus' ministry (1:1- 4:11)
 a. The genealogy of Jesus (1:1-17).
 b. The announcement to Joseph of the birth of Jesus (1:18- 25).
 c. The visit of the Magi to worship Jesus (2:1-12).
 d. The flight of Joseph, Mary and Jesus into Egypt (2:11-23).
 e. The ministry of John the Baptist (3:1-12);
 f. The baptism of Jesus (3:13-17).
 g. The testing of Jesus by Satan in the wilderness (4:1-11).

2. The ministry of Jesus (4:12-25:46)

This section is organized into five blocks of narrative interspersed with five long discourses:

- In the Sermon on the Mount (5:1-7:29), Jesus discusses the law, worship and good deeds.
- In the commission to the disciples (9:35-10:42), Jesus expands the scope of his ministry.
- The third discourse (13:1-52) contains seven parables on the kingdom of heaven.
- The fourth discourse provides instructions concerning the community of faith (18:1-35).
- In the final discourse, Jesus pronounces seven woes on the Pharisees, laments over Jerusalem and preaches about the end times (23:1-25:46).

The five blocks of narrative (4:12-25; 8:1-9:34; 11:1-12:50; 13:53-17:27; and 19:1-22:46) discuss Jesus' miracles, his superiority over John the Baptist, his disputes with the religious leaders, and further teachings on the kingdom of heaven.

3. The crucifixion and resurrection (26:17-30)

a. First, Jesus predicts his betrayal (26:1-5), is anointed at Bethany (26:6-16) and eats the Last Supper with his disciples (26:17-30).

b. Then Jesus is betrayed by Judas Iscariot (26:6-16) is mocked before the high priest (26: 57-68) and is denied three times by Simon Peter (26:69-75).

c. Finally, Jesus is tried by Pilate and scourged (27:1-31), is subjected to an agonizing death on the cross (27:32-57) and is buried in a new tomb, which is then sealed and guarded (27:57-66).

d. But the story does not end there. The tomb is found empty because Jesus has risen (28:1-15), and the risen Christ commissions the disciples to preach the good news in all the world (28:16-20)!

Matthew and the Second Coming

Matthew emphasizes the future aspect of Jesus' work more than the other Gospel writers do. Matthew alone uses the word *parousia,* which has become the technical term for Jesus' second coming (Matthew 24:3, 27, 37, 39). Moreover,

> "Only Matthew has a series of parables which turn on judgment and which can be interpreted in terms of the second coming. Only he has the parable of the wise and foolish virgins and the shut door (25:1-13); the parable of the sheep and the goats and the final judgment (25:31-46); the parable of the talents and the casting out of the unsatisfactory servant (25:14-30)" (William Barclay, *Introduction to the First Three Gospels,* pp. 170-171).

61

FORTY-TWO MEN AND FIVE WOMEN: A STUDY OF MATTHEW 1:1-16

By Michael Morrison

Many modern readers feel that the New Testament begins in the most boring way possible: a list of unusual and hard-to-pronounce names. However, ancient readers would have found a number of interesting things in this list.

The ancestors of Jesus, the Messiah, the son of David, the son of Abraham:

- Abraham
- Isaac
- Jacob
- Judah
- Perez, whose mother was Tamar
- Hezron
- Ram
- Amminadab
- Nahshon
- Salmon
- Boaz, whose mother was Rahab
- Obed, whose mother was Ruth
- Jesse
- King David
- Solomon, whose mother had been Uriah's wife
- Rehoboam
- Abijah
- Asa
- Jehoshaphat
- Jehoram
- Uzziah
- Jotham
- Ahaz
- Hezekiah
- Manasseh
- Amon
- Josiah

- Jeconiah, at the time of the exile to Babylon
- Shealtiel
- Zerubbabel
- Abihud
- Eliakim
- Azor
- Zadok
- Akim
- Elihud
- Eleazar
- Matthan
- Jacob
- Joseph, the husband of Mary; Mary was the mother of Jesus the Messiah.

List adapted from Matthew 1:1-16. NIV 2011 used in this chapter.

Women in the list

Matthew wanted to present evidence that Jesus is the Messiah. Everyone expected the Messiah to be descended from David, so Matthew began by showing that Jesus meets that requirement.

Biblical genealogies usually list only men. Matthew's list is unusual because it includes five women. Even more surprising, Matthew did not mention women who were highly esteemed—Sarah, Rebekah, Rachel and Leah. Instead, he mentioned women who were somewhat embarrassing:

1) **Tamar**, who committed incest. Genesis 38 tells the seedy story. Judah and a Canaanite woman had three sons. The first one married Tamar, but he died before they had any children. Following ancient Middle Eastern custom, his brother was supposed to marry the widow and engender an heir for the dead brother. The second son did not want to do this, and he died. Time passed, and Tamar saw that Judah's third son was not going to marry her, so she pretended to be a prostitute and had sex with Judah, her father-in-law. Her twin sons became the ancestors of most of the Jewish people.

2) **Rahab** the prostitute. When the Israelites were about to conquer the land of Canaan, they sent spies into Jericho, who stayed at "the house of a prostitute named Rahab" (Joshua 2:1). The king of Jericho wanted to kill the spies, but Rahab helped them escape. When Jericho was destroyed, Rahab and her family were spared (Joshua 6:25). The Old Testament does not tell us what happened to Rahab, but Matthew tells us that she was an ancestor of

King David.

3) **Ruth** the Moabitess. The biblical book of Ruth says that a Jewish family moved to Moab, and the sons married Moabite women. The men died, and two of the widows moved to Bethlehem. Following ancient custom, a relative was supposed to marry the young widow so the dead man would have an heir. So Boaz married Ruth. Deuteronomy 23:3 says that Moabites could not "enter the assembly of the Lord, even down to the tenth generation." Nevertheless, in fewer than 10 generations, God anointed one of those descendants as Israel's king.

4) The wife of Uriah the Hittite. Curiously, Matthew does not mention her name. But his readers would know the story of **Bathsheba** from 2 Samuel 11. While Uriah was fighting battles for David, David was stealing his wife. Bathsheba became pregnant, and David arranged for Uriah's death. The child died, but David's second child with Bathsheba was Solomon, the next king.

5) **Mary**, mother of Jesus. Mary was accused of a scandal, but Matthew explains that there was no scandal: Mary became pregnant before marriage by a special act of God (Matthew 1:18).

Why these women?

Why did Matthew mention these women? One theory is that the women were immoral. Indeed, some were, but Ruth was not, and the way in which Rahab become an ancestor of David is not known; she may have been completely moral after coming to know God. Nor would Matthew want to imply that Mary was immoral.

Another theory is that the women were Gentiles. Some were, but we do not know about Tamar and Bathsheba. Matthew says that the gospel should be preached to all nations (28:19), and it would indirectly support his point to mention Gentiles in the ancestry of the Savior. Although genealogies were often designed to support ethnic authenticity, Matthew uses his genealogy to point out ethnic impurity.

Perhaps Matthew's purpose was simply that all of the women are irregularities in the royal lineage of Judah, and that people should therefore not be surprised that the birth of the Messiah involves some irregularity as well. Jesus was not born as a "pure" person, but as an ordinary person, with moral and ethnic impurity in his ancestry, just as we all have.

THE VIRGIN WILL GIVE BIRTH TO A SON:
A STUDY OF MATTHEW 1:18-23

By Michael Morrison

In his book about Jesus, Matthew frequently says that Jesus fulfilled verses from the Old Testament. One example comes in the story of Jesus' birth.

Miraculous beginnings (verses 18-21)

"This is how the birth of Jesus Christ came about," Matthew begins. "His mother Mary was pledged to be married to Joseph, but before they came together, she was found to be with child through the Holy Spirit" (NIV 2011 used throughout this chapter).

Joseph knew how most girls become pregnant, and he knew that he was not the father. But "because Joseph her husband was a righteous man and did not want to expose her to public disgrace, he had in mind to divorce her quietly."

Joseph and Mary were legally obligated to marry, and they were considered husband and wife. If Mary had sex with another man, it would be considered adultery, and Deuteronomy 22:23-24 required death for most such cases. Joseph did not want to humiliate Mary, but he wanted to call off the wedding.

"But after he had considered this, an angel of the Lord appeared to him in a dream and said, 'Joseph son of David, do not be afraid to take Mary home as your wife, because what is conceived in her is from the Holy Spirit.'"

The angel also announced that God had a special role for the child: "She will give birth to a son, and you are to give him the name Jesus, because he will save his people from their sins."

The name Jesus is the Greek form of Joshua, which means "God saves." Jesus was a common name in those days, because many Jewish parents gave their children names that expressed faith in God. Many first-century Jews wanted God to save them from the Romans. The angel announced a different kind of Messiah—one who would save the people from their own sins.

A fulfillment of Scripture (verses 22-23)

Matthew tells us that "all this took place to fulfill what the Lord had said through the prophet: 'The virgin will be with child and will give birth to a son, and they will call him Immanuel'—which means, 'God with us.'"

But no one called Mary's child "Immanuel." No one talks about "Immanuel of Nazareth." The angel said his name should be *Jesus*. Immanuel was someone else.

Matthew is quoting Isaiah 7:14. In context, that is *not* a prophecy about

the Messiah. Rather, it is the prediction of a child in the days of Ahaz, king of Judah, some 700 years before Jesus. Enemies were threatening to invade Judah, and Isaiah tells Ahaz not to worry. Isaiah gives him a time frame: a woman will conceive, and before her son is weaned, Assyria will take care of the enemies (Isaiah 7:1-17).

Ahaz presumably knew who the virgin was— perhaps his daughter—and she conceived in the normal way, after marriage. She had a boy and named him Immanuel, meaning "God with us." She did not expect the boy himself to be God; rather, she was expressing belief that God was helping his people.

Isaiah's prophecy was fulfilled in the days of Ahaz, and Matthew says it was fulfilled *again* by the birth of Jesus. Jesus gave the verse a significance far greater than anyone had imagined: It was indeed a virgin who conceived, and her son was indeed God, who had come to be with his people.

Jesus did not have to bear the *name* Immanuel—he fulfilled the scripture in an unexpected way. What the boy Immanuel could signify only in his name, Jesus fulfilled in reality.

The Greeks had a word for it: πληρόω

The Greek verb *plēroō* means "to make full." John uses this word to say that a house was "filled with the fragrance of the perfume" (John 12:3). *Plēroō* is often used in connection with Scripture, and the traditional translation is that a scripture was "fulfilled."

Many people assume that this means that a prediction has come true. But in some cases, the scripture is not even a prediction. Matthew 2:15 says that Jesus fulfilled a scripture when he returned from Egypt. Matthew quotes Hosea, who says: "When Israel was a child, I loved him, and out of Egypt I called my son." Hosea 11:1 is referring to the past, not the future.

Matthew says that this event in Israel's past was given a new significance in the life of Jesus. Hosea used the word "son" in a figurative way to refer to the nation of Israel; Matthew is saying that a similar thing happened to the child who was *literally* God's Son. He *filled* the scripture with new meaning; he gave it a new and deeper significance.

JESUS: TEMPTED ON OUR BEHALF

By Joseph Tkach

Scripture tells us that Jesus, our High Priest, was "tempted in every way, just as we are—yet he did not sin" (Hebrews 4:15). This powerful truth is represented in the historic Christian teaching that Jesus, in his humanity, is the "vicarious man."

Vicarious is a Latin word that means "in place of another," or "on another's behalf." Through the Incarnation, the eternal Son of God, while remaining God, became human. Calvin referred to this as the "wondrous exchange." T. F. Torrance used the word *substitution:* "In the incarnation, the Son of God abased himself, substituted himself in our place, interposed himself between us and God the Father, taking all our shame and curse upon himself, not as a third person, but as one who is God himself" (*Atonement*, p. 151). In one of his books, our friend Chris Kettler refers to "the deep interaction between Christ's humanity and our humanity at the level of our being, the ontological level."

In his vicarious humanity, Jesus represents all humanity. He is the second Adam who is far superior to the first. Representing us, Jesus was baptized for us—the sinless one baptized for sinful humanity. Our baptism then is a participation in his. Representing us, Jesus was crucified and died for us so that we may live (Romans 6:4). Then Jesus rose from the grave, making us alive with him (Ephesians 2:4-5). Then he ascended, seating us with him in the heavenly realms (Ephesians 2:6). Everything Jesus did, he did in our place, on our behalf. And that includes being tempted on our behalf.

I find it encouraging to know that Jesus went through the same temptations I face and overcame them in my place, on my behalf. To face our temptations and overcome them was one of the reasons Jesus went into the wilderness following his baptism. Even though the enemy was there to interfere, Jesus prevailed. He is the overcomer—on my behalf, in my place. Understanding this makes a world of difference!

Many people face a crisis concerning their identity. There are three unhelpful ways that people typically identify themselves: by what they do, by what others say about them and by what they possess. It's interesting to note that the three temptations faced by Jesus in the wilderness had to do with all three of these identity factors.

You will recall that in the Gospel accounts of Jesus' temptation in the wilderness (in Matthew and Luke), the Holy Spirit led Jesus into the wilderness to be tempted by the enemy. Jesus did not go through these trials alone. He was accompanied by the Holy Spirit. He was never alone—just as we are never alone.

After 40 days of prayer and fasting, the enemy came to Jesus and said, "If..." Now that's a big word, and I suggest that many of our own temptations start with the word "if." "If I could just..." "If you are..." "If you had your way..." etc. Satan taunted Jesus with the words, "If you are the Son of God..." In doing so, Satan was tempting Jesus to doubt his true identity in relationship to his heavenly Father—to lead him to think he needed to prove his identity and act in certain ways to secure it for himself.

Satan sends similar temptations our way—calling into question our relationship to God and leading us to think that we, by our own efforts, must achieve our identity as children of God. But Jesus exposes the lies of these temptations hidden behind all of the "ifs."

Jesus' first temptation involved the false assumption, *I am what I do*. Satan said, "If you are the Son of God, command these stones to become loaves of bread." In other words, prove to yourself that you really are the Son of God. See if you have miraculous powers to feed yourself and demonstrate your self-sufficiency!

The second temptation involved the false assumption, *I am what others say about me*. Satan said to Jesus, "If you are the Son of God, throw yourself down and let the angels rescue you." In other words, prove to yourself that you are the Son of God by seeing if the angels will obey your command and then if others witnessing this spectacle will confirm to who you are.

Jesus' third temptation involved the false assumption, *I am what I possess*. Satan said, "If you are the Son of God, fall down and worship me and I will give you all the kingdoms of the world." In other words, prove you are the Son of God by having all the rulers of the world under your authority as you ought to. Simply submit to my authority to take possession of them all.

Jesus saw through the false assumptions behind each temptation. With each one he replied, "It's a lie!" For Jesus, there was no "*If* I am the Son of God," but always "*Because* I AM the Son of God." Jesus knew there was nothing he needed to do or possess to be who he truly was. Jesus knew who he was and remained secure in his relationship with the Father, confident in the Father's faithfulness. Under the pressure of temptation, the Holy Spirit, who had sent him into the wilderness in the first place, was there to remind him. Knowing who he was, Jesus had no need to prove it to himself. He had no need to act independently from his Father, out of unbelief, as if he could not trust his Father's love and provision.

Torrance reminds us that Jesus, being the Son of God, did not need to go through and overcome temptation for himself. In his vicarious humanity, Jesus met and overcame these temptations on our behalf: "It was for our sakes and in our place that Jesus lived that vicarious life in utter reliance upon God and in laying hold upon his mercy and goodness" (*Incarnation,* p. 125). Jesus did this for us knowing clearly who he was—the Son of God and the Son of Man.

For us to be delivered from temptations in our lives, it's essential that we know who we truly are. As sinners saved by grace, we have a new identity—we are Jesus' beloved brothers and sisters, God's dearly loved children. This is not an identity we earn, and certainly not one others can give us. No, it's something God has given to us through the vicarious humanity of his Son. We simply trust him to be who he is for us and then receive from him this new identity with much thanksgiving.

We take strength knowing that Jesus overcame for us the deceit of Satan's subtle, yet powerful temptations concerning the nature and source of our true identity. As we live in Christ, secure in that identity, we will find that what used to tempt us and make us fall becomes less and less powerful. We grow in strength as we embrace and live into our true identity—secure in knowing it is ours in relationship with the triune God who is faithful and full of love for us his children.

If we are not secure in our true identity, temptations likely will set us back. We may doubt we are Christians, or that God loves us unconditionally. We might be tempted to think that being tempted means God has begun to withdraw from us. But knowing our true identity as God's dearly beloved children is a freely-given gift. We can rest secure knowing that Jesus, in his vicarious humanity, overcame all temptation for us—in our place and on our behalf. Knowing this enables us to stand back up when we fall (and we will), make whatever amends we need to make, and trust God to lead us forward. In fact, confessing that we have fallen and are in need of God's forgiveness are signs that God remains unconditionally faithful to us. Were he not, had he actually abandoned us, we never would turn back to him to receive again his freely-given grace and thus be renewed in his welcoming embrace.

Let us look to Jesus who was tempted in every way we are, yet without sin. Let us rely on his mercy, his love, his strength. And let us praise God because Jesus Christ, the vicarious human, has overcome for us.

MATTHEW 5:17-19 AND THE "LAW"

By Paul Kroll

Do Jesus' words in Matthew 5:17-19 tell Christians they must keep the seventh-day Sabbath? Some people believe these verses make Sabbath-keeping binding on Christians. Others conclude the Sabbath is not in view in this passage. To discover the answer, let us begin by quoting the verses in question:

> Do not think that I have come to abolish the Law or the Prophets; I have come not to abolish them but to fulfill them. I tell you the truth, until heaven and earth disappear, not the smallest letter, not the least stroke of a pen, will by any means disappear from the Law until everything is accomplished. Anyone who breaks one of the least of these commandments and teaches others to do the same will be called least in the kingdom of heaven, but whoever practices and teaches these commands will be called great in the kingdom of heaven.

We see right away that Jesus did not mention the Sabbath or the Ten Commandments in these verses. To read Jesus' statement as having these laws specifically in mind is to bring in ideas that were not stated by Jesus.

Nonetheless, there are certain phrases in this text that need further study: Jesus' assertion that he did not come to abolish the Law; that he came to fulfill it; that not the smallest part of the Law would disappear till everything was accomplished; that whoever broke the commandments he was speaking about or taught others to break them would be of little reputation in the kingdom. What do all these things mean in terms of the Sabbath? By looking closely at the key phrases in this Scripture, we will learn some surprising things.

"Abolish Law and Prophets"

First, we see that Jesus spoke of "the Law *and* the Prophets" as not being abolished. What did he mean by this phrase? The "Law and the Prophets" was a regular expression Jews of Jesus' day used to refer to the entire Old Testament. (See Matthew 7:12; 22:40; Acts 24:14;28:23; Romans 3:21.) The Old Testament comprises the Holy Scriptures or the sacred writings of the Jewish faith. It was through these writings that Jews thought they could understand the will of God and have eternal life (John 5:39, 45).

What Jesus said, then, was the Old Testament as a body of "God-breathed" literature would not be set aside or abolished. His concern was not specifically the Sabbath or the Ten Commandments. It was the entire Old Testament.

"To fulfill them"

Jesus also said he came not to abolish the Law or the Prophets, that is, the Holy Scriptures, but to "fulfill them" (Matthew 5:17). We should notice that Jesus did not tell Christians to "fulfill" these Scriptures down to the smallest letter and least stroke of a pen. He said *he* came to fulfill the Holy Scriptures.

What did he mean by this? The Greek word for "fulfill" is *plerosai*. According to Greek scholars, the nuance and meaning of this word is difficult to express in English, and several possibilities have been offered. These are summarized by four options:

1. Jesus came to accomplish or obey the Holy Scriptures,
2. to bring out the full meaning of the Holy Scriptures,
3. to bring those Scriptures to their intended completion,
4. to emphasize that the Scriptures point to him as Messiah and are fulfilled in his salvation work.

After reviewing several ways of looking at the word "fulfill," the *Expositor's Commentary* concluded by saying: "The best interpretation of these difficult verses says that Jesus fulfills the Law and the Prophets in that they point to him, and he is their fulfillment. The antithesis is not between 'abolish' and 'keep' but between 'abolish' and 'fulfill'" (page 143).

Let's see how this possibility works out. It is certainly a proper understanding of Jesus' intent to say that he came to fulfill the Law and the Prophets in *himself*—in his life and salvation work, and that the Scriptures pointed to him.

The book of Matthew was written to prove from the Jewish Scriptures that Jesus fulfilled the requirements of messiahship. Matthew often said Jesus acted "to fulfill" what was said through one prophet or another (Matthew 1:22; 2:5, 15,17, 23; 4:14; 8:17, etc.). One can read through the book of Matthew and note all the times that a reference is made to the Old Testament as being fulfilled in Jesus. It is surprising, indeed.

Jesus said in Matthew 3:15that "all righteousness" should be fulfilled in his actions. Luke 24:25-27, 44-45 and John 5:39-47 are also instructive on this point. These verses show that Jesus was interested in showing how the Hebrew Scriptures had himself as their object. He was the Messiah of whom all the Jewish holy writings had spoken of.

The *Tyndale New Testament Commentary* on Matthew offers another view of "fulfill." It emphasizes that Jesus was bringing the meaning of the Scriptures to their intended completion. It says: "Jesus is bringing that to which the Old Testament looked forward; his teaching will transcend the Old Testament revelation, but, far from abolishing it, is itself its intended culmination" (page 114).

But is the keeping of the "holy time" requirement of the Sabbath something Jesus meant to bring forward for Christians to follow? Since the context does not mention the Sabbath in Matthew 5:17-19, we would have no basis to insist that he did.

"Not the smallest letter"

Jesus also said that "not the smallest letter, not the least stroke of a pen" from the entire body of the Jewish Holy Scriptures would disappear until "everything is accomplished." Some believe that by saying this, Jesus was saying that Christians should keep the seventh-day Sabbath.

Let's ask again what the context tells us, and where such a conclusion would lead us. As we saw, Jesus did not mention the Sabbath or the Ten Commandments in Matthew 5:17-19. In order to say that Jesus had the Sabbath in mind, we would be forced to say that he was commanding Christians to follow *all* the laws of the Law and Prophets, or the Old Testament. At the least, we would have to conclude he was making the entire Law of Moses binding on Christians.

Based on the argument above, we would have to take Jesus' words as enjoining *every single commandment and regulation* in the Law of Moses on Christians! The reason is because Jesus said that "not the smallest letter, not the least stroke of a pen" from the entire body of the Jewish Holy Scriptures would disappear until "everything is accomplished."

To ask again: Did Jesus mean Christians had to keep *all* the regulations of the Law of Moses, including the "holy time" regulations of the Sabbath, or strict tithing, or the food laws? Consider what that line of reasoning would demand.

Christians would be obligated to keep all the sacrificial, ceremonial and civil laws described in the Law of Moses. They would have to keep every single law mentioned in Genesis through Deuteronomy — and the rest of the Old Testament. The Jews calculated that there were 613 laws in their Holy Scriptures. Christians, then, based on the idea that Jesus was telling his disciples to keep the regulations of the Law and the Prophets, would have to keep all 613 laws. No wonder the apostle Paul said that thinking in these terms was wrongheaded (Galatians 3:10).

To pick a few examples of this line of reasoning, Christian men would have to be physically circumcised. All Christians would have to offer sacrifices. Men, at least, would have to travel to Jerusalem to keep the annual festivals. Christians would have to keep the various purification rituals. One of these rituals specified that individuals who came in contact with dead bodies would be "unclean" for seven days. They would have to ceremonially wash themselves on the third and seventh day (Numbers 19:11-13). If any person failed to do this, he or she would be "cut off from Israel" (verse 13). There are many dozens of such laws in the Law of Moses that would have to be followed.

Obviously, when we see the implications, we have to conclude that Jesus could not having been telling Christians to keep all the old covenant Law. But if he was not saying this, then we have no justification for saying his words demand we keep the Sabbath as "holy time," because he did not specifically mention this command — or the Ten Commandments.

"Everything is accomplished"

Jesus said that until heaven and earth ceased to exist, nothing would disappear from the law "until everything is accomplished" (5:18). But heaven and earth will pass away, and by contrast, Jesus' own words will remain forever (Matthew 24:35). They have a greater validity than the Law because Jesus is greater than Moses.

The meaning of "until everything is accomplished" has several possibilities. It is suggested by the *Tyndale New Testament Commentary* that the translation: "Until what it [the Law] looks forward to arrives" gives the best sense of this phrase. This links the thought with the idea of "fulfillment" in verse 17. This also seems to be the thrust of Paul's comments regarding the relationship of the Law and Jesus' earthly ministry (Galatians 3:19, 23-25).

The *Tyndale New Testament Commentary* expresses the interpretation of "accomplished" in these words:

> The law remains valid until it reaches its intended culmination; this it is now doing in the ministry and teaching of Jesus. This verse does not state, therefore, as it is sometimes interpreted, that every regulation in the Old Testament law remains binding after the coming of Jesus. The law is unalterable, but that does not justify its application beyond the purpose for which it was intended. (page 115)

The *Tyndale* commentary also makes the same point in these words:

> This passage does not therefore state that every Old Testament regulation is eternally valid. This view is not found anywhere in the New Testament, which consistently sees Jesus as introducing a new situation, for which the law prepared (Galatians 3:24), but which now transcends it. The focus is now on Jesus and his teaching, and in this

light the validity of Old Testament rules must now be examined. Some will be found to have fulfilled their role, and be no longer applicable…others will be reinterpreted. (page 117)

This explanation must be the correct one, or else the early Christian church and the apostles violated Matthew 5:17-19 by telling gentile Christians that circumcision and keeping the Law of Moses was not necessary. The book of Galatians would also have been in error on this point. And the book of Hebrews would have been in extraordinary violation of Jesus' words, too, since it states that the entire sacrificial system, the temple worship and Levitical priesthood had been annulled.

However, these books are in agreement with the principle mentioned above. They explain that some old covenant religious regulations have fulfilled their role and others need reinterpretation. This is the situation that holds with the ceremonial weekly Sabbath "holy time" regulation. It fulfilled its role in old covenant times and can be interpreted spiritually for Christians as the spiritual Sabbath rest we now have in Christ.

"Least of these commandments"

In Matthew 5:19 Jesus also said that if anyone broke "one of the least of these commandments" and taught others to do so, that person would be called "least" in the kingdom. Those who practiced and taught these commands of which he spoke would be called "great" in that kingdom. How do these words fit into the discussion?

One explanation of this phrase is that "these commandments" refer to the teaching of Jesus in Matthew 5-7, and not to the Old Testament or its law. His reinterpretation of old covenant law was certainly the subject of much of the Sermon on the Mount.

After discussing the Law and the Prophets, Jesus went on to give six units of teaching, each introduced by the phrase, "You have heard that it was said… But I say to you" (Matthew 5:21-48). In those six units, Jesus gave varied examples of how the principles he was discussing should work out in practice among his disciples. He began each section with how Jews might have taught and applied a literal understanding of Old Testament law. Then Jesus gave his more discerning view — the real intent or aim of the law in general, and the six examples he chose in particular.

To summarize, he mentioned the following subjects: *murder and anger,* based on the sixth commandment (5:21-26); *adultery,* the seventh commandment (5:27-30); *divorce,* from Deuteronomy 24:1 (5:31-32); *swearing and oaths,* summarizing teaching from such scriptures as Leviticus 19:12 and

Numbers 30:2 (5:33-37); *legal rights,* quoted from Exodus 21:24-25, Leviticus 24:20, and Deuteronomy 19:21 (5:38-42); and the principle of *loving one's neighbor,* from Leviticus 19:18 (5:43-47).

What we notice is that the examples Jesus chose come from *all* five books of Moses. These six principles are then summarized as the greater righteousness of Jesus' disciples (5:48). The disciples of Jesus, in contrast to the scribes and Pharisees, must be "perfect," that is, have a life totally motivated by the will of God. Jesus contrasted this new and radical righteousness (5:20) with the scrupulous religious observance of old covenant demands practiced by Pharisees and other Jewish religious teachers (6:1-8. 16-18).

Jesus did not come to annul the Holy Scriptures *as a body of holy writings* since they were "God breathed" words of the Creator. But they were not an end in themselves, as many Jews thought. Jesus had come to bring the truth to which those Scriptures pointed (John 1:17).

The law of Christ

If we look carefully at the context of the verse in which Jesus spoke of fulfilling the Law, particularly at what follows Matthew 5:17-19, we will note that Jesus was redefining the teaching from the Law and the Prophets. He was pointing out which principles from the Holy Scriptures had an eternal validity and their intended purpose, and how both were to be understood.

In short, Jesus was creating a spiritual law, which we may call the "law of Christ" (John 13:33-35) — and this becomes the norm for Christian living, not the old covenant law. This is demonstrated by the fact that one cannot find in the teaching in Matthew 5-6 any discussion of ceremonial laws such as the Sabbath and annual festival "holy time" regulations — a hallmark of Jewish religious observance based on old covenant commands.

While Jews concerned themselves with what Moses and their traditions said, Jesus superseded that approach to God with his own instruction. He became the standard of truth (John 1:17). In referring to both the Law of Moses and the tradition of the elders, Jesus boldly proclaimed, "But I say to you" (Matthew 5:22, 28, 32, 34, 39, 44). At the end of the Sermon, Jesus told his hearers that the wise person is one "who hears *these words of mine* and puts them into practice" (Matthew 7:24).

The orientation of the new covenant is to Christ and the cross, not to Moses and the tables of stone. The great sermon of the new covenant is not the one given on Mt. Sinai, but by Jesus Christ (John 1:17). He explained the spiritual-moral principles of the new covenant that apply to Christians. These are amply discussed in several places in the New Testament (in Galatians 5:22-25, for example). We should note that these places do not contain any mention of such ceremonial regulations as keeping a specific day of the week.

Matthew concluded his gospel with the following words of Jesus: "Go and make disciples of all nations, baptizing them in the name of the Father and of the Son and of the Holy Spirit, and teaching them to obey everything I have commanded you" (Matthew 28:19-20). The disciples are to teach and do the commands Jesus gave, not legalistically follow the Law of Moses (John 15:12-13). Since Jesus did not command Sabbath-keeping in Matthew 5:17-19, we cannot use this Scripture to justify teaching it.

In the interest of fairness, we should point out that some scholars object to the view that Jesus was referring to his own commandments in Matthew 5:19. The word for "commandment," *entole,* elsewhere in Matthew always refers to the Old Testament law. These scholars insist the expression "least of these commandments" would be better understood in the context as referring to the law as expounded in the Old Testament. If so, how are we to understand Jesus' command to his disciples — to respect and teach the "least of these commandments"?

We have already seen that Jesus cannot be telling his disciples to keep each of the 613 regulations of the Law. That would lead to a logical absurdity, violate his own teaching in Matthew 5, and stand in conflict with other New Testament teachings and writings. (Since Jesus didn't mention the Sabbath in Matthew 5, we cannot use this Scripture to insist that one of "these commandments" was the Sabbath "holy time" regulation.)

It cannot be a literal observance of the Law of Moses that interests Jesus — this is seen by what he says in Matthew 5:21-48, where he radically *reinterprets* the commands of the Law. If it were a literal observance that Jesus wanted, the Gospel of Mark was in specific violation of Jesus' command, because it *interpreted* Jesus' view of the laws of "uncleanness" and said he had abrogated these Old Testament food regulations. See Mark 7:19 in any modern translation.)

What such Scriptures show is that Jesus left the question of interpretation and application of the Law of Moses open to changing circumstances. We can see this in his teaching in Matthew 5:21-48 and elsewhere. Of course, the Old Testament must be respected, and it has value as the word of God, but it is also time-bound to a certain extent. This practical view of the Law is demonstrated in the rest of the New Testament. It allows, for example, the apostles to understand that the ceremonial and sacrificial laws are no longer binding.

Nonetheless, Christians are to respect the Old Testament as the Holy Scriptures of God. They are profitable, when used wisely, for "teaching, rebuking, correcting and training in righteousness," and can make one "wise for salvation through faith in Christ Jesus" (2 Timothy 3:15-16). But no one should place faith in the Law itself, for while the Law came through Moses, grace and truth have come through Jesus. Under grace, Christians are not required to keep a specific "holy time," go to a "holy place" such as the temple, or be under the authority of the holy levitical priesthood (John 4:21-24). These were ceremonial regulations, and Christians do not need to keep them.

MATTHEW 5: SERMON ON THE MOUNT

Even non-Christians have heard of the Sermon on the Mount.
Christians have heard many sermons on it, but still find parts of it
hard to understand—and hard to apply in our lives.

By Michael Morrison

John Stott writes: "The Sermon on the Mount is probably the best-known part of the teaching of Jesus, though arguably it is the least understood, and certainly it is the least obeyed" (*The Message of the Sermon on the Mount,* InterVarsity Press, 1978, p. 15). Let's study it again. Perhaps we will find new treasures as well as old.

The beatitudes

"When [Jesus] saw the crowds, he went up on a mountainside and sat down. His disciples came to him, and he began to teach them" (Matt. 5:1-2). The crowds probably followed him, as they often did. The sermon was not designed for the disciples only. Jesus told them to spread his teachings throughout the world, and Matthew wrote it down for more than a billion people to read. These teachings are for everyone who is willing to listen.

First come the beatitudes (the word "beatitude" comes from the Latin word for blessed):

"Blessed are the poor in spirit, for theirs is the kingdom of heaven" (v. 3). What does it mean to be "poor in spirit"? Low self-esteem, low interest in spiritual things? Not necessarily. Many religious Jews called themselves "the poor," for they often *were* poor, and they looked to God to supply their daily needs. So Jesus may have been referring to the faithful.

But "poor in spirit" suggests something more. Poor people know that they have needs. The poor in spirit know that they need God; they feel a lack in their lives. They do not imagine that they are doing God any favors by serving him. But Jesus says that the kingdom is for people like them. It is the humble, the dependent, who are given the kingdom of heaven. They must trust in the mercy of God.

"Blessed are those who mourn, for they will be comforted" (v. 4). This statement includes an irony, since the word for "blessed" can also mean "happy." Happy are the sad, Jesus says for at least they have the comfort of knowing that their trials are temporary. Everything will be set right. But note that the beatitudes are not commands – Jesus is not saying it is spiritually superior to mourn. But in this world, many people are already mourning, and Jesus says that they will be comforted – presumably by the coming of the kingdom.

"Blessed are the meek, for they will inherit the earth" (v. 5). In ancient society, land was often taken away from the meek. But in God's way of doing things, that will also be set right.

"Blessed are those who hunger and thirst for righteousness, for they will be filled" (v. 6). Those who ache and yearn for justice (the Greek word for righteousness also means justice), will receive what they seek. Those who suffer from evil, who want things to be set right, will be rewarded. In this age, God's people suffer from injustice, and we long for justice. Jesus assures us that our hopes will not be thwarted.

"Blessed are the merciful, for they will be shown mercy" (v. 7). We need mercy in the day of judgment. Jesus is saying that we therefore should show mercy in this age. It is inconsistent for anyone to want justice, and yet cheat others, or to want mercy and yet be unmerciful. If we want the good life, we must live a good life.

"Blessed are the pure in heart, for they will see God" (v. 8). A pure heart has only one desire. Those who seek only God will be sure to find him. Our desire will be rewarded.

"Blessed are the peacemakers, for they will be called children of God" (v. 9). The poor will not achieve their rights through violence. God's children need to rely on him. We should show mercy and humility, not anger and strife. We cannot live in harmony with a kingdom of righteousness by acting unrighteously. Since we want the peace of God's kingdom, we should live in the way of peace.

"Blessed are those who are persecuted because of righteousness, for theirs is the kingdom of heaven" (v. 10). Good people sometimes suffer because they are good. People take advantage of the meek. They may even resent those who do good, because a good example makes the bad people look worse. And sometimes the righteous, by helping the oppressed, weaken the social customs and rules that have given power to the wicked. We do not *seek* to be persecuted, but nevertheless, wicked people often persecute the righteous. Be of good cheer, Jesus says. Hang in there. The kingdom of heaven belongs to people like this.

Jesus then addresses his disciples more directly, using the second-person "you": "**Blessed are you when people insult you,** persecute you and falsely say all kinds of evil against you because of me. Rejoice and be glad, because great is your reward in heaven, for in the same way they persecuted the prophets who were before you" (vs. 11-12).

There is an important phrase in this verse: "because of me." Jesus expects that his disciples will be persecuted not just for being good, but because of their association with Jesus. So, when you are persecuted, rejoice and be glad—at least you are doing enough to be noticed. You are making a difference in this world, and you are sure to be rewarded.

Making a difference

Jesus also gave some short parable-like sayings about the way that his followers should affect the world: "You are the salt of the earth. But if the salt loses its saltiness, how can it be made salty again? It is no longer good for anything, except to be thrown out and trampled by men" (v. 13).

If salt lost its flavor, it would be worthless, for its flavor is what makes it valued. Salt is good precisely because it tastes different than other things. In the same way, Jesus' disciples are scattered in the world—but if they are just like the world, they are not doing any good.

"You are the light of the world. A city on a hill cannot be hidden. Neither do people light a lamp and put it under a bowl. Instead they put it on its stand, and it gives light to everyone in the house" (vs. 14-15). The disciples are not to hide themselves—they are to be seen. Their example is part of their message.

"In the same way, let your light shine before men, that they may see your good deeds and praise your Father in heaven" (v. 16). Later, Jesus criticized the Pharisees for doing works in order to be seen (6:1). But good works should be seen—for God's praise, not our own.

Superior righteousness

How should the disciples live? Jesus will get to that in verses 21-48. But he begins with a caution: When you hear what I say, you might wonder if I am trying to eliminate the Scriptures. I'm not. I am doing and teaching exactly what the Scriptures say I should. What I say will be surprising, but don't get me wrong.

"Do not think that I have come to abolish the Law or the Prophets; I have not come to abolish them but to fulfill them" (v. 17). Many people focus here on the Law, and assume that the question is whether Jesus will do away with Old Testament laws. This makes the verse very difficult to interpret, since everyone agrees that Jesus Christ caused some laws to become obsolete, and that this was part of his purpose. Just how many laws are involved may be disputed, but everyone agrees that Jesus came to abolish at least some laws.

Jesus is not talking about laws (plural). He is talking about the Law (singular)—the Torah, the first five books of the Scriptures. He is also talking about the Prophets, another major section of the Bible. This verse is not about individual laws, but about the Scriptures as a whole. Jesus did not come to do away with the Scriptures, but to fulfill them.

This involved obedience, of course, but it went further. God wants his children to do more than follow rules. When Jesus fulfilled the Torah, it was not just a matter of obedience—he completed all that the Torah had ever pointed to. He did what Israel as a nation was not able to do.

Jesus then said, "I tell you the truth, until heaven and earth disappear, not the smallest letter, not the least stroke of a pen, will by any means disappear from the Law until everything is accomplished" (v. 18).

But Christians don't have to circumcise their children, build booths out of tree branches, and wear blue threads in tassels. Everyone agrees that we don't have to keep these laws. So what did Jesus mean when he said that none of the Law would disappear? For practical purposes, haven't those laws disappeared?

There are three basic approaches to this. First, we can recognize that these laws have not disappeared. They are still in the Torah—but being in Torah doesn't mean that we have to do them. This is true, but it does not seem to be what Jesus intended here.

A second approach is to say that Christians do keep these laws, but that we do so by having faith in Christ. We keep the law of circumcision in our hearts (Rom. 1:29) and we keep all ritual laws through faith. This is true, but it may not be what Jesus was saying right here.

A third approach is to observe that 1) none of the Law could become obsolete until everything was accomplished, and 2) everyone agrees that at least some of the Law has become obsolete. So we conclude 3) that everything was accomplished. Jesus fulfilled his mission, and the old covenant law is now obsolete.

However, why would Jesus say "until heaven and earth disappear"? Was it simply to emphasize the certainty of what he was saying? Why mention two "untils" if only one of them was relevant? I don't know. But I do know that there are many Old Testament laws that Christians do not have to keep, and verses 17-20 do not tell us which laws are which. If we quote these verses only for the laws we happen to like, we are misusing these verses. They do not teach the permanent validity of all laws, because not all laws are permanent.

These commandments

Jesus then goes on to say, "Anyone who breaks one of the least of these commandments and teaches others to do the same will be called least in the kingdom of heaven, but whoever practices and teaches these commands will be called great in the kingdom of heaven" (v. 19).

What are "these" commandments? Is Jesus referring to commandments in the Law of Moses, or to his own commands, which he will soon give? We must take into account the fact that verse 19 begins with the word "therefore" (which the NIV 1984 does not include; the NIV 2011 does).

There is a logical connection between verses 18 and 19. Is it, The Law will remain, so these commandments should be taught? That would imply that Jesus was talking about the Law. But there are commandments in the Torah that are obsolete and should not be taught as law. So Jesus cannot be saying that we should teach all the laws of the Old Testament. That would contradict the rest of the New Testament.

More likely, the logical connection between verses 18 and 19 is different, focusing more on "until all is accomplished," the closest phrase. The thought would be like this: All the Law will remain until everything is accomplished, and therefore (since Jesus did accomplish everything), we are to teach these laws (the laws of Jesus that we will soon read) instead of the old laws that he critiques. This makes better sense in the context of the sermon, and in the New Testament.

It is Jesus' commandments that should be taught (Matt. 7:24; 28:20). Jesus explains why: "For I tell you that unless your righteousness surpasses that of the Pharisees and the teachers of the law, you will certainly not enter the kingdom of heaven" (v. 20).

The Pharisees were known for detailed obedience, tithing even on their herbs. But true righteousness is a matter of the heart, of a person's character, not just conforming to certain rules. Jesus is not saying that we need better obedience to the same laws, but rather obedience to better laws, and he will soon illustrate what he means.

But we are not as righteous as we should be. We all need mercy, and we enter the kingdom not through our own righteousness, but in another way, as Jesus explained in verses 3-10. Paul explained it as the gift of righteousness, as justification by faith, as the perfect righteousness of Jesus being attributed to us as we become united to him through faith. But Jesus does not explain all that here.

Here is a summary of this section: Do not think that Jesus came to abolish the Scriptures. He came to do what they said. Every law remained in force until Jesus accomplished all that he was sent to do. Now he gives a new standard of righteousness, and we must conform to his standard and teach it.

But I say...

Jesus then gives six contrasts between the old teachings and the new. Six times he quotes a traditional teaching, most often from the Torah itself, and six times he explains that the old way is not enough. He offers a more exacting standard of righteousness.

Do not despise

"You have heard that it was said to the people long ago, 'Do not murder, and anyone who murders will be subject to judgment'" (v. 21). This is a quote from the Torah and a summary of its civil laws. People heard this when Scripture was read to them. In the days before printing, people more often heard Scripture than they read it.

Who said this "to the people long ago"? God himself, at Mt. Sinai. Jesus is not quoting a distorted tradition of the Jews—he is quoting the Torah. He then contrasts it with a more rigorous standard:

"But I tell you that anyone who is angry with his brother will be subject to judgment" (v. 22). Perhaps the Torah really meant this, but Jesus does not reason on that basis. He does not mention any authority for his teaching. It is true simply because he is the one who says it.

We will be judged on our anger. Someone who wants to kill, or wishes that someone else were dead, is a murderer in the heart, even if they are unable or unwilling to carry out the deed. However, not all anger is sin. Jesus himself was sometimes angry. But Jesus states it boldly: Anyone who is angry will be subject to divine judgment. The principle is stated in stark terms; the exceptions are not listed. Here and elsewhere in the sermon, we must realize that Jesus phrases his demands in an extreme form. We cannot lift sayings out of the sermon and act as if none of them have any exceptions.

Jesus then says, "Again, anyone who says to his brother, 'Raca,' is answerable to the Sanhedrin. But anyone who says, 'You fool!' will be in danger of the fire of hell" (v. 22). Jesus is not referring new cases to the Jewish leaders. More likely, in the saying about "raca," he is quoting something that the scribes were already teaching. Next, he says that the penalty for evil attitudes goes much further than a civil court—it goes all the way to the final judgment.

Jesus himself called people "fool" (Matt. 23:17, same Greek word). We cannot take these sayings as legalistic rules that must be enforced to the letter. No, they are startling statements designed to make a point. Here, the point is that we should not despise other people. This principle is beyond the intent of the Torah, but it is the true righteousness that characterizes the kingdom of God.

Jesus then gives two parables to illustrate: "Therefore, if you are offering your gift at the altar and there remember that your brother has something against you, leave your gift there in front of the altar. First go and be reconciled to your brother; then come and offer your gift" (vs. 23-24).

Jesus lived in an old covenant age, and his affirmation of old covenant laws does not mean that they are still in force today. His parable points out that interpersonal relationships have priority over sacrifices. If someone has something against you (whether justified or not), that person should have taken the first step, but if that person does not, do not wait. Take the initiative.

However, it is not always possible. Jesus is not giving a new law, but stating a principle in bold terms: we should try to reconcile.

"Settle matters quickly with your adversary who is taking you to court. Do it while you are still with him on the way, or he may hand you over to the judge, and the judge may hand you over to the officer, and you may be thrown into prison. I tell you the truth, you will not get out until you have paid the last penny" (vs. 25-26).

Again, it is not always possible to settle matters out of court. Nor should we let false accusers get away with extortion. Nor is Jesus making a prediction that the civil courts will never have mercy. Again we see that we cannot treat Jesus' words as precise laws. Nor is he simply giving us wise advice about how to stay out of debtors' prison. Rather, he is telling us to seek peace because that is the way of true righteousness.

Do not lust

"You have heard that it was said, 'Do not commit adultery'" (v. 27). God said it on Mt. Sinai. But Jesus tells us "that anyone who looks at a woman lustfully has already committed adultery with her in his heart."

The tenth commandment prohibited lust, but the seventh commandment did not. It prohibited "adultery"—a behavior that could be regulated by civil laws and penalties. Jesus makes no attempt to have Scriptural support behind his teaching. He does not need it. He is the living Word, and has more authority than the written Word.

Jesus' teaching falls into a pattern: The old law says one thing, but true righteousness requires much more. He then gives extreme statements to drive the point home. When it comes to adultery, he says, "If your right eye causes you to sin, gouge it out and throw it away. It is better for you to lose one part of your body than for your whole body to be thrown into hell. And if your right hand causes you to sin, cut it off and throw it away. It is better for you to lose one part of your body than for your whole body to go into hell" (vs. 29-30).

Yes, it is better to lose a body part than to lose eternal life. But that is not really our choice, because eyes and hands cannot cause us to sin, and if we remove them, we have committed another sin. Sin originates in the heart, and what we need is a changed heart. Jesus' point is that we need surgery on our thoughts. We need extreme measures to eliminate sin.

Do not divorce

"It has been said, 'Anyone who divorces his wife must give her a certificate of divorce'" (v. 31). This refers to Deuteronomy 24:1-4, which accepts the certificate of divorce as an already established custom among the Israelites. This law did not allow a remarried woman to remarry her first husband, but other than this rare situation, it did not make any restrictions. The Law of Moses permitted divorce, but Jesus did not.

"But I tell you that anyone who divorces his wife, except for marital unfaithfulness, causes her to become an adulteress, and anyone who marries the divorced woman commits adultery" (v. 32). This is a hard saying, both to understand and to apply. Suppose an evil man puts away his wife for no reason at all. Is she automatically a sinner? And is it a sin for anyone to marry this victim of divorce?

It would be a mistake for us to treat Jesus' statement as an unalterable law. Paul was inspired to realize that there is another legitimate exception for divorce (1 Cor. 7:15). Although this is a study of the Sermon on the Mount, we must remember that Matthew 5 is not the last word on the subject of divorce. What we learn here is only part of the picture.

Jesus' saying here is a shocking statement designed to make a point—in this case the point that divorce always involves sin. God intended for marriages to be life-long, and we must strive to keep them the way he intended. Jesus did not attempt to discuss what we should do when things go wrong.

Do not swear

"Again, you have heard that it was said to the people long ago, 'Do not break your oath, but keep the oaths you have made to the Lord'" (v. 33). These principles are taught in Scripture (Num. 30:2; Deut. 23:31). But what the Torah clearly allowed, Jesus did not:

"But I tell you, Do not swear at all: either by heaven, for it is God's throne;

or by the earth, for it is his footstool; or by Jerusalem, for it is the city of the Great King" (Matt. 5:34-35). Apparently the Jewish leaders allowed people to take oaths in these names, perhaps to avoid pronouncing the holy name of God.

"And do not swear by your head, for you cannot make even one hair white or black. Simply let your 'Yes' be 'Yes,' and your 'No,' 'No'; anything beyond this comes from the evil one" (vs. 36-37). The principle is simple: honesty—but the point is made in a startling way. Exceptions are allowed.

Jesus himself said more than Yes and No. He often said Amen, Amen. He said that heaven and earth would pass away, but his words would not. He called God as witness that what he was saying was true. Paul also wrote some oath-like affirmations, rather than simply saying Yes (Rom. 7:1, 2 Cor. 1:23).

So we see again that we should not take the bold statements of the Sermon on the Mount as prohibitions that must be enforced exactly as written. We should have simple honesty, but we can on occasion emphasize the truth of what we are saying.

In a court of law, to use a modern example, we are allowed to "swear" to tell the truth, and ask God to help us tell the truth. It is nitpicking to say that "affirm" is acceptable but "swear" is not. In a court of law, these words mean the same thing—and both are more than a simple Yes.

Do not seek revenge

Jesus again quotes the Torah: "You have heard that it was said, 'Eye for eye, and tooth for tooth'" (v. 38). It is sometimes said that this was merely a maximum limit for vengeance in the Old Testament. It was indeed a maximum, but it was sometimes a minimum, too (Lev. 24:19; Deut. 19:21).

But what the Torah required, Jesus prohibited: "But I tell you, Do not resist an evil person" (v. 39). But Jesus himself resisted evil persons. He drove moneychangers out of the temple. The apostles resisted false teachers. Paul objected when soldiers started to flog him. Jesus' statement is again an exaggeration: It *is* permissible to resist evil persons. Jesus would allow us, for example, to resist evil persons by reporting crime to the police.

Jesus' next statements must be seen as exaggerations, too. That does not mean we can dismiss them as irrelevant. Rather, we must receive the principle, and we must allow it to challenge our behavior, without turning these rules into a new law-code as if exceptions were never allowed.

"If someone strikes you on the right cheek, turn to him the other also." In some circumstances, of course, it would be better to walk away, as Peter did (Acts 12:9). Nor is it wrong to voice an objection, as Paul did (Acts 23:3).

Jesus is teaching a principle, not a rule that must be kept in a rigid way.

"And if someone wants to sue you and take your tunic, let him have your cloak as well. If someone forces you to go one mile, go with him two miles. Give to the one who asks you, and do not turn away from the one who wants to borrow from you" (vs. 40-42). If people sue you for ten thousand dollars, you do not have to give them twenty thousand. If someone steals your car, you do not have to give your truck as well. If a drunk asks for ten dollars, you do not have to give anything.

The point in Jesus' extreme sayings is not that we have to let people take advantage of us, nor that we should reward them for doing so. Rather, it is that we should not take revenge. Try to make peace; do not try to hurt others.

Do not hate

"You have heard that it was said, 'Love your neighbor and hate your enemy'" (v. 43). The Torah commands love, and it commanded Israel to kill all the Canaanites and to punish all evil-doers.

"But I tell you: Love your enemies and pray for those who persecute you" (v. 44). Jesus teaches a different way, a way less like the world. Why? What is the model for all this radical righteousness?

"That you may be sons of your Father in heaven" (v. 45). We are to be like he is, and he loved his enemies so much that he sent his Son to die for them. We cannot send our children to die for our enemies, but we are to love them just as much and pray for them to be blessed. We fall short of the standard that Jesus says is right. But our frequent failures do not mean that we should quit trying.

Jesus reminds us that God "causes his sun to rise on the evil and the good, and sends rain on the righteous and the unrighteous" (v. 45). He is merciful to all.

"If you love those who love you, what reward will you get? Are not even the tax collectors doing that? And if you greet only your brothers, what are you doing more than others? Do not even pagans do that?" (vs. 46-47). We are called to do more than what is natural, more than unconverted people do. Our inability to be perfect does not change our calling to seek to improve.

Our love for others is to be complete, to extend to all peoples, and that is what Jesus means when he says, "Be perfect, therefore, as your heavenly Father is perfect" (v. 48).

Old teaching	Source	New teaching	Evidence of exaggeration
Do not murder, and anyone who murders will be subject to judgment	Quote from Ex. 20:13, and summary of OT civil laws about murder	Anyone who is angry with a brother will be subject to judgment	Jesus was sometimes angry; not all anger is sin
		Anyone who says, 'fool!' will be in danger of hell	Jesus called people "fool"
		First be reconciled to your brother	It is not always possible
		Settle matters out of court	It is not always possible
		You will not get out until you have paid the last penny	Sometimes debts are forgiven
Do not commit adultery	Quote from Ex. 20:14	anyone who lusts has already committed adultery	Eyes and hands cannot cause sin; and removing them is a sin
		If your eye or hand causes you to sin, remove it	
Anyone who divorces his wife must give her a certificate of divorce	Reference to Deut. 24:1-4	Anyone who divorces his wife, except for marital unfaithfulness, causes her to become an adulteress, and anyone who marries the divorced woman commits adultery	Paul allowed another exception
			The man commits adultery, too.
			If she does not remarry, she is not an adulteress.
Keep the oaths you have made to the Lord	Accurate paraphrase of Num. 30:2 and Deut. 23:31	Do not swear at all	No need to say "affirm" instead of "swear"

		Let your 'Yes' be 'Yes'	Jesus and Paul said more than "Yes" to affirm their words
Eye for eye, and tooth for tooth	Quote from Lev. 24:19; Deut. 19:21	Do not resist an evil person

Turn the other cheek

Give double what they ask | Nonviolent resistance is permissible; Jesus even used some force

We can object or walk away

Not always required – do not reward evildoers |
| Love your neighbor

hate your enemy | Quote from Lev. 19:18

Exaggeration of Torah | Love your enemies and pray for them

Be perfect | humanly impossible |
| **Summary** | Usually a quote or paraphrase of Torah | Even more is required — who can obey these startling demands? | Exceptions often exist |

MATTHEW 6:
SERMON ON THE MOUNT, PART 2

By Michael Morrison

Jesus teaches a high standard of righteousness, requiring sincerity in the heart. In startling words, he warns us against anger, adultery, oaths and vengeance. He says that we must love even our enemies (Matthew 5).

The Pharisees were known for strict standards, but our righteousness should be better than theirs (which could be rather dismaying, if we forget about the mercy promised earlier in the Sermon). True righteousness is internal. In chapter six, Jesus illustrates this point by denouncing religion done for show.

Secret charity

"Be careful not to do your 'acts of righteousness' before men, to be seen by them. If you do, you will have no reward from your Father in heaven. So when you give to the needy, do not announce it with trumpets, as the hypocrites do in the synagogues and on the streets, to be honored by men. I tell you the truth, they have received their reward in full" (vs. 1-2).

In Jesus' day, some people made a show of religion. They made sure that people could see them doing good. They received the admiration of many, but that is all they will receive, says Jesus, because they are only play-acting. Their good works were done not to serve God, but to serve public opinion and to serve self. It is the wrong attitude, and God will not reward it.

Religious show-offs can be seen today in pulpits, or setting up chairs, or leading Bible study groups, or writing for church newspapers. They may be feeding the poor and preaching the gospel. On the outside, it looks like sincere service; but the attitude may be quite different.

"When you give to the needy, do not let your left hand know what your right hand is doing, so that your giving may be in secret. Then your Father, who sees what is done in secret, will reward you" (vs. 3-4).

Our "hand," of course, doesn't know anything. Jesus is using a figure of speech to say that alms-giving shouldn't be done for show, either for others or for self-congratulation. We do it for God, not to make ourselves look good.

But it is not literally true that charity must be secret. Jesus has already said that we should let our good deeds be seen so that people will praise God (5:16). The focus is on attitude, not appearance. Our motive should be to do good for God's glory, not for our own glory.

Secret prayer

Jesus said something similar about prayer: "When you pray, do not be like the hypocrites, for they love to pray standing in the synagogues and on the street corners to be seen by men. I tell you the truth, they have received their reward in full. But when you pray, go into your room, close the door and pray to your Father, who is unseen. Then your Father, who sees what is done in secret, will reward you" (vs. 5-6).

Jesus is not creating a rule against public prayer. Jesus himself sometimes prayed in public. His point is that we should pray not just to be seen—or for that matter, neither should we avoid prayer out of fear of public opinion. Prayer is done for God, not for appearance.

"And when you pray, do not keep on babbling like pagans, for they think they will be heard because of their many words. Do not be like them, for your Father knows what you need before you ask him" (vs. 7-8). God knows our needs, but we should still ask (Phil. 4:6), and we should be persistent (Luke 18:1-8). But the effectiveness of prayer depends on God, not us. We do not have to achieve a certain number of words, a set length of time, a particular posture or a special eloquence.

Jesus then gave a sample prayer—a model of simplicity. It may be used as an outline, but other outlines are also acceptable.

"This, then, is how you should pray: 'Our Father in heaven, hallowed be your name, your kingdom come, your will be done on earth as it is in heaven'" (Matt. 6:9-10). This prayer begins with simple praise—nothing elaborate, just an expression of desire that God would be honored and that earth would be responsive to his will.

"Give us today our daily bread" (v. 11). This acknowledges that our lives depend on our powerful Father. Although we may go to the store to buy that bread, we should remember that God is the one who makes it possible. We depend on him day by day.

"Forgive us our debts, as we also have forgiven our debtors. And lead us not into temptation, but deliver us from the evil one" (vs. 12-13). We need not only food, but also a relationship with God, a relationship that we often betray and are therefore often in need of forgiveness. And this prayer reminds us that we should be merciful to others if we ask God to be merciful to us. We know we are not spiritual giants—we need divine help so we can resist temptations.

That ends the prayer; Jesus then emphasizes again our responsibility to forgive one another. The better we understand how good God is and how far short we fall, the better we will understand our need for mercy, and so we should be willing to forgive others (vs. 14-15).

Is God's forgiveness conditional on our forgiveness?

However, this sounds conditional: I won't do this unless you do that. But there is a big problem with that: humans aren't very good about forgiving. None of us are perfect, and none of us forgive perfectly. And is Jesus telling us to do something that God himself won't do? Are we supposed to forgive others unconditionally, while he himself puts forgiveness on a conditional basis? If God's forgiveness is conditional, and we forgive in the way that he has forgiven us, then we should not forgive anyone unless *they* have forgiven everyone – and they shouldn't forgive unless everyone else forgives everyone else. That would place us in a chain that never moves.

If our forgiveness is based on whether we forgive, then our salvation is dependent on what we do – on our works. So theologically and practically, the face-value reading of Matt. 6:14-15 has problems. Now we can add to the discussion the point that Jesus died for our sins, before we were even born, and scriptures say that he has nailed our sins to the cross, and has reconciled the whole world to himself.

On one side, we have this teaching in Matthew 6 that makes it sound like forgiveness is conditional. And on the other side, we have verses that make it sound like all our sins are already forgiven – and this would include the sin of not forgiving. So how do we combine these two ideas? Either we have misunderstood the verses on one side, or we have misunderstood verses on the other side.

Now we can bring another point into the discussion: that Jesus often taught in an exaggerated way. If you eye offends you, gouge it out. When you pray, go into your room (and yet Jesus did not always pray inside). When you give to the needy, don't let your left hand know what your right hand is doing. Do not resist an evil person (and yet Paul did). Don't say anything more than yes or no (but yet Paul did). Do not call anyone your Father – and yet we all do.

Now we can see that Matthew 6:14-15 is another example of exaggeration. This does not mean that we can ignore it – Jesus had an important point to make, the serious importance of forgiving other people. If we want God to forgive us, then we should forgive others. If we want to live in a kingdom in which forgiveness is given to us, then we need to be living in that way ourselves.

In the same way, if we want to be loved by God, we should love others. If we fail to love others, we cannot change the nature of God to love. But it is still true that if we want to be loved, then we should also love. Although this may be expressed in a conditional way, the function of the saying is to encourage us to love, to forgive. Paul expresses it as a command: "Bear with each other and forgive one another if any of you has a grievance against someone. Forgive as the Lord forgave you" (Col. 3:13). Here is is expressed as an example, but not a condition.

In the Lord's prayer, we ask for daily bread, even though we (in most cases) already have it. In the same way, we ask for forgiveness even though we already have it. It is an acknowledgement that we have done something wrong, that it does affect our relationship with God, and that he is willing to forgive. It is part of what it means to look to him for salvation as a gift rather than as something we earn through our performance.

Secret fasting

Jesus then addresses another religious behavior: "When you fast, do not look somber as the hypocrites do, for they disfigure their faces to show men they are fasting. I tell you the truth, they have received their reward in full. But when you fast, put oil on your head and wash your face, so that it will not be obvious to men that you are fasting, but only to your Father, who is unseen; and your Father, who sees what is done in secret, will reward you" (vs. 16-18).

When we fast, we groom ourselves as normal, for we are fasting to God, not to impress people. Again, the focus is on the attitude, not on whether somebody happens to find out that we are fasting. If someone asks us if we are fasting, we can answer truthfully—but neither should we hope that they ask. Our goal is not to show off, but to seek God.

In all three areas, Jesus made the same point. Whether we give alms, pray or fast, we do it "in secret"—without regard to whether people see. We do not make a show of it, but neither do we need to hide it. We just do it to God, for God, and he will reward us. The reward, like our activity, may be hidden, but it is real, and it is growing.

Heavenly treasures

Our focus should be on pleasing God, on doing his will, on valuing his rewards rather than the temporary rewards of this world. Public praise is one form of short-lived reward. Jesus now turns to the shallowness of physical things. "Do not store up for yourselves treasures on earth, where moth and rust destroy, and where thieves break in and steal. But store up for yourselves treasures in heaven, where moth and rust do not destroy, and where thieves do not break in and steal" (vs. 19-20).

Earthly riches are temporary, and Jesus is advising us to make a better investment—to seek the permanent values of God through quiet charity, unshowy prayer and secret fasting.

If we take Jesus too literally, we might think that he is making a rule against retirement savings. But his point is really about our heart—what it is that we treasure. We should value the heavenly rewards even more than we do the earthly savings. "For where your treasure is, there your heart will be also" (v. 21). If we value the things that God values, then our heart will be right and our behavior will be right, too.

"The eye is the lamp of the body. If your eyes are good, your whole body will be full of light. But if your eyes are bad, your whole body will be full of darkness. If then the light within you is darkness, how great is that darkness!" (vs. 22-23).

Here Jesus seems to be using a proverb of his day, applying it to the desire for money. If we look at things in a good way, we will see opportunities to do good, to be generous. But if we look selfishly, enviously, we will be in moral darkness, corrupted by our desires.

What are we looking for in life—to get or to give? Are our bank accounts designed to serve ourselves, or to enable us to serve others? We are improved or corrupted by our goals. And if the inside is corrupt, if we are seeking only the rewards of this world, we are corrupt indeed.

What motivates us? Is it money, or is it God? "No one can serve two masters. Either he will hate the one and love the other, or he will be devoted to the one and despise the other. You cannot serve both God and Money" (v. 24). Neither can we serve God and public opinion. We must serve God alone, without any competition.

How might a person "serve" money? By thinking that it can bring us happiness, by considering it all powerful, by valuing it highly. Those attitudes are more properly given to God. He is the one who can give us happiness; he is the true source of security and life; he is the power that can help us most. We are to value him more than anything else, to treasure him, to put him first.

True security

"Therefore I tell you, do not worry … saying, 'What shall we eat?' or 'What shall we drink?' or 'What shall we wear?' For the pagans run after all these things, and your heavenly Father knows that you need them" (vs. 25-32). God, a good Father, will take care of us if we put him first. We need not worry about human opinion, and we do not need to worry about money and things.

"But seek first his kingdom and his righteousness, and all these things will be given to you as well" (v. 33). We will live long enough, we will eat enough, we will have enough, if we have God.

MATTHEW 7:
SERMON ON THE MOUNT, PART 3

By Michael Morrison

In Matthew 5, Jesus explains that true righteousness is internal, a matter of the heart, not just of behavior. In chapter 6, he explains that our religious activities must be sincere, not performances designed to make us look good. In those chapters, Jesus addresses two problems that occur when people focus on external behavior as the main definition of righteousness: external behavior is not all that God wants, and people are tempted to pretend instead of being changed in the heart.

In chapter 7, Jesus addresses a third problem of having a focus on behavior: People who equate righteousness with behavior tend to judge or criticize others.

The speck in someone's eye

"Do not judge," Jesus said, "or you too will be judged. For in the same way you judge others, you will be judged, and with the measure you use, it will be measured to you" (Matt. 7:1-2). Jesus' audience knew the kind of judging Jesus was talking about: the condemning attitude held by the people Jesus had already criticized—the hypocrites who focused on external behaviors (see John 7:49 for an example).

But those who are quick to condemn, those who feel superior to others, will be condemned by God. All have sinned, and everyone needs mercy. But some people find it hard to admit that they need mercy, and find it hard to extend any mercy. So Jesus is warning that the way we treat other people may be the way that God treats us. The more we feel our own need for mercy, the less judgmental we will be toward others.

Jesus then gives a humorous, exaggerated illustration of what he means: "Why do you look at the speck of sawdust in your brother's eye and pay no attention to the plank in your own eye?" (Matt. 7:3). In other words, how can you complain about someone's sin when you have a bigger one?

"How can you say to your brother, 'Let me take the speck out of your eye,' when all the time there is a plank in your own eye? You hypocrite, first take the plank out of your own eye, and then you will see clearly to remove the speck from your brother's eye" (vs. 4-5). Jesus' audience must have laughed at this cartoonish depiction of hypocrites.

The hypocrite was claiming to help someone else identify sin. He was claiming to be wise, claiming to be zealous for the law. But Jesus is saying that the man is unqualified to help. He is a hypocrite, a play-actor, a pretender. He needs to get sin out of his own life first, to realize that his own sin is large.

How can the plank be removed? Jesus did not explain that here, but we know from elsewhere that sin can be removed only through God's grace. Only after experiencing mercy can a person really help others.

"Do not give dogs what is sacred; do not throw your pearls to pigs" (v. 6) is usually interpreted to mean that we should be wise in the way we preach the gospel. That may be true, but the context here has nothing to do with the gospel. If we keep this proverb in context, it could have an ironic sense: "Hypocrite, keep your pearls of wisdom to yourself. If you think the other person is a sinner, don't waste your words on him, for he won't appreciate what you say, and will just get mad at you." This would be a humorous way to cap off Jesus' main point: Do not judge.

Good gifts from God

Jesus has already talked about prayer and our need for faith (chapter 6). Now he mentions them again: "Ask and it will be given to you; seek and you will find; knock and the door will be opened to you. For everyone who asks receives; he who seeks finds; and to him who knocks, the door will be opened" (vs. 7-8). Jesus is describing an attitude of trust, of reliance on God. Why can we have such faith? Because God is trustworthy.

Jesus then makes a simple comparison: "Which of you, if his son asks for bread, will give him a stone? Or if he asks for a fish, will give him a snake? If you, then, though you are evil, know how to give good gifts to your children, how much more will your Father in heaven give good gifts to those who ask him!" (vs. 9-11). If even sinners take care of their children, then we can certainly rely on God, who is perfect, to take care of his children. He will supply our needs.

But we don't always get what we want, and sometimes our greatest need is discipline. Jesus is not commenting on those things—his point here is simply that we can trust God.

Jesus' next comment is the golden rule. The thought is similar to verse 2. God will treat us the way we treat others, so we should "do to others what you would have them do to you" (v. 12). Since God gives good things to us, we should do good to others. If we want to be treated kindly, to be given the benefit of the doubt, to be forgiven, then we need to be gracious toward others. If we would like someone to help us when we need help, then we need to be willing to help them when they need it.

The golden rule, said Jesus, "sums up the Law and the Prophets" (v. 12).

This common-sense rule is what the Torah is really about. All those sacrifices should have told us that we need mercy. All those civil laws should have told us to treat others fairly. The golden rule gives us a focus to clarify God's way of life. It can be easily stated, but it is not easily done. So Jesus ends his sermon with some warnings.

The narrow gate

"Enter through the narrow gate," Jesus advises. "For wide is the gate and broad is the road that leads to destruction, and many enter through it. But small is the gate and narrow the road that leads to life, and only a few find it" (vs. 13-14).

The path of least resistance leads to ruin. Christianity is not the most popular path. It involves self-denial, it involves thinking for oneself, it requires a willingness to step out in faith even if no one else is. We cannot just go along with the majority. Nor can we prefer a little bandwagon just because it is little. Truth cannot be measured by popularity or rarity.

"Watch out for false prophets," Jesus warned. "They come to you in sheep's clothing, but inwardly they are ferocious wolves" (v. 15). False preachers look good on the outside, but their motives are selfish. How can we tell whether they are false?

"By their fruit you will recognize them." It may take some time, but we will eventually see whether the preacher is trying to benefit himself, or whether he is truly serving others. But appearances can be misleading for a time. The agents of sin try to look like angels of God. Even the false prophets look good for a while.

Is there a faster way to tell? Yes, there is—Jesus will get to it in a moment. But first, Jesus warns the false prophets: "Every tree that does not bear good fruit is cut down and thrown into the fire" (v. 19).

Building on a rock

The Sermon on the Mount ends with a challenge. Now that people have heard Jesus, they must choose whether to obey. "Not everyone who says to me, 'Lord, Lord,' will enter the kingdom of heaven, but only he who does the will of my Father who is in heaven" (v. 21). Jesus is implying that everyone must call him Lord. But words alone are not enough.

Not even miracles in Jesus' name are enough: "Many will say to me on that day, 'Lord, Lord, did we not prophesy in your name, and in your name drive out demons and perform many miracles?' Then I will tell them plainly, 'I never knew you. Away from me, you evildoers!'" (vs. 22-23). Here Jesus implies that he will be the judge of all humanity. People will plead their case before him, and their eternity is described as being with or being excluded from Jesus.

How can anyone be saved? Hear the parable of the wise and foolish builders: "Therefore everyone who hears these words of mine and puts them into practice..." Jesus equates his words with the will of the Father. Everyone must obey Jesus in the same way that they obey God. People will be judged by the way they respond to Jesus. We all fall short, and we all need mercy, and that mercy is found in Jesus.

A person who builds on Jesus "is like a wise man who built his house on the rock. The rain came down, the streams rose, and the winds blew and beat against that house; yet it did not fall, because it had its foundation on the rock" (vs. 24-25). But we do not have to wait for the storm to come in order to know what the end result will be. A person who builds on a faulty foundation will come to ruin. Anyone who tries to have a spiritual life on any basis other than Jesus is building on sand.

"When Jesus had finished saying these things, the crowds were amazed at his teaching, because he taught as one who had authority, and not as their teachers of the law" (vs. 28-29). Moses spoke in the name of the Lord, and the scribes spoke in the name of Moses. But Jesus is the Lord, and he spoke with his own authority. He claimed to teach absolute truth, to be the judge of all humanity, to be the key to eternity.

Jesus is not like the teachers of the law. What the law said was not enough, and behavior is not enough. We need the words of Jesus, and he sets a standard that no one can attain. We need mercy, but with Jesus, we can be confident. Our eternity depends on how we respond to Jesus.

MATTHEW 9:
THE PURPOSE OF HEALINGS

By Michael Morrison

Matthew 9, like most other chapters in Matthew, tells of several events in the life of Christ. But these are not random reports—Matthew sometimes puts stories next to each other because they shed light on each other. They give physical examples of spiritual truths. In chapter 9, Matthew tells several stories that are also found in Mark and Luke—but Matthew's version is much shorter, more to the point.

Authority to forgive

When Jesus returned to Capernaum, "some men brought to him a paralyzed man, lying on a mat. When Jesus saw their faith, he said to the man, 'Take heart, son; your sins are forgiven.'" (verses 1-2; NIV 2011 used in this chapter). In faith, they brought this man to Jesus to be healed, and instead of healing him, Jesus simply said that his sins were forgiven. The man's most serious problem was not his paralysis—it was his sins—and Jesus took care of that first.

But some of the teachers of the law were thinking, "This fellow is blaspheming!" (v. 3). Only God can forgive sin, they thought, so Jesus is claiming too much for himself.

Jesus knew what they were thinking, scolded them for their evil thoughts, and challenged them: "Which is easier: to say, 'Your sins are forgiven,' or to say, 'Get up and walk'? But I want you to know that the Son of Man has authority on earth to forgive sins. So he said to the paralyzed man, 'Get up, take your mat and go home.' Then the man got up and went home" (vv. 5-7).

It is easy to talk about divine forgiveness, but it is hard to prove that it has really happened. So Jesus performed a miracle of healing in order to show that he had authority to forgive sins. His mission on earth was not to heal everyone's physical diseases, and he didn't even heal everyone in Judea. Rather, his mission was to announce forgiveness—and that he was the source of forgiveness. This miracle was designed not to announce physical healings, but to announce something more important: spiritual healing.

"When the crowd saw this…they praised God" (v. 8)—but not everyone was happy.

Eating with sinners

After this incident, Jesus "saw a man named Matthew sitting at the tax collector's booth. 'Follow me,' he told him, and Matthew got up and followed him" (v. 9). The fact that Matthew had a "booth" suggests that he collected taxes from people transporting goods through the area—perhaps even from fishermen taking their catch into town to sell. He was a customs agent, a toll-road cashier, and a Roman-appointed highway robber. But he left his lucrative job to follow Jesus, and the first thing he did was invite Jesus to a banquet with his friends.

"While Jesus was having dinner at Matthew's house, many tax collectors and 'sinners' came and ate with him and his disciples" (v. 10). It would be like a pastor going to a party at a Mafia mansion.

The Pharisees noticed the kind of company that Jesus kept, but they did not challenge him directly. Instead, they asked his disciples, "Why does your teacher eat with tax collectors and 'sinners'?" (v. 11). The disciples may have been a little puzzled themselves, and eventually Jesus gave the answer: "It is not the healthy who need a doctor, but the sick. But go and learn what this means: 'I desire mercy, not sacrifice' [Hosea 6:6]. For I have not come to call the righteous, but sinners" (v. 12). He had authority to forgive – this was a spiritual healing, too.

Just as a doctor associates with the sick, Jesus associated with sinners because those are the sort of people he came to help. (Everyone is a sinner, but that isn't the point that Jesus is making here.) He called people to be holy, but he didn't require them to be perfect before he called them.

Just as we need mercy more than judgment, God wants us to extend mercy more than judgment. If we do everything that God tells us to do (i.e., sacrifice) but fail to have mercy for others, we have failed.

The new and the old

The Pharisees were not the only ones who were puzzled by the ministry of Jesus. The disciples of John the Baptist asked this question: "How is it that we and the Pharisees fast, but your disciples do not fast?" (v. 14). They fasted because they were sorry that the nation had strayed so far from God.

Jesus replied: "How can the guests of the bridegroom mourn while he is with them? The time will come when the bridegroom will be taken from them; then they will fast" (v. 15). There is no need to mourn while I am here, he said—but he hinted that he would eventually be "taken"—removed by force—and then his disciples would mourn and fast.

Jesus then gave a puzzling proverb: "No one sews a patch of unshrunk cloth on an old garment, for the patch will pull away from the garment, making the tear worse. Neither do people pour new wine into old wineskins.

If they do, the skins will burst, the wine will run out and the wineskins will be ruined. No, they pour new wine into new wineskins, and both are preserved" (vv. 16-17).

Jesus did not come to "patch" the Pharisee approach to pleasing God. He was not trying to add mercy to the sacrifices that the Pharisees taught, nor was he trying to pour new ideas into an old framework. Rather, he was starting all over, bringing something new. We call it the new covenant.

Raising the dead, healing the unclean

Matthew then connects another story to this one by telling us: "While he was saying this, a synagogue leader came and knelt before him and said, 'My daughter has just died. But come and put your hand on her, and she will live'" (v. 18). Here is an unusual religious leader—one who had faith in Jesus. Jesus went and raised the girl from the dead (v. 25), but while he was on the way, someone else came to him for healing:

"Just then a woman who had been subject to bleeding for twelve years came up behind him and touched the edge of his cloak. She said to herself, 'If I only touch his cloak, I will be healed.' Jesus turned and saw her. 'Take heart, daughter,' he said, 'your faith has healed you.' And the woman was healed at that moment" (vv. 20-22).

The woman was unclean because of the bleeding. The Law of Moses said that people should not touch her. Jesus had a new approach. Instead of avoiding her, he healed her when she touched him. Matthew highlights the reason: faith.

Faith is what prompted men to bring a paralyzed friend. Faith is what motivated Matthew to leave his job. Faith brought a religious leader to seek life for a dead daughter, a woman to seek healing for continual bleeding, and blind men to seek for sight (v. 29). All sorts of ailments, but one source of healing: Jesus.

The spiritual significance is clear: Jesus forgives sin, gives new life and new direction in life. He makes us clean and helps us see. This new wine is not poured into the old framework of Moses—it creates its own framework. The ministry of Jesus is built around the mission of mercy.

Things to think about

- If I were paralyzed, would I rather hear a word of forgiveness, or a command to rise? (vv. 2, 6)
- Under what circumstances would a pastor go to a party with the Mafia? (v. 10)

- Are there ways in which I try to use the gospel to patch an old garment? (v. 16)
- Is there anything unclean in my life, any longstanding sin, for which I need to go to Jesus for healing? (v. 20)
- Does the example of Jesus encourage me to change the way that I look at other people?

MATTHEW 13:
PARABLES OF THE KINGDOM

By Michael Morrison

We need to make sure that our description of the kingdom is compatible with the description Jesus gave. Jesus often preached about the kingdom of God—but what did he say about it? Did he describe peace and prosperity, health and wealth, law and order? Did he get into details of governmental organization?

No, we do not need to know those things. The most important thing we need to know about the kingdom is how we get there in the first place—and when Jesus described the kingdom, that is what he talked about.

Let's begin with Matthew 13, the largest collection of kingdom parables. Several times Jesus said, "The kingdom of God is like..." and then he would tell a story. We know many of these parables, but a few details may surprise us.

Parable of the sower

A farmer went out to sow his seed. As he was scattering the seed, some fell along the path, and the birds came and ate it up. Some fell on rocky places, where it did not have much soil. It sprang up quickly, because the soil was shallow. But when the sun came up, the plants were scorched, and they withered because they had no root. Other seed fell among thorns, which grew up and choked the plants. Still other seed fell on good soil, where it produced a crop—a hundred, sixty or thirty times what was sown. (Matthew 13:3-9; NIV 2011 used in this chapter)

The story is easy to understand. We can picture a man scattering wheat seeds, and we understand about birds, thorns and sunshine. But Jesus had a spiritual purpose in this story, and the disciples found it puzzling. So they asked Jesus, "Why do you speak to the people in parables?" (v. 10).

Jesus told them that it was not yet time for people to understand the "secrets of the kingdom of heaven" (v. 11). He is saying that this parable is actually about the kingdom of God—something we see again in verse 19. Most of the people in the crowd were not spiritually responsive (vs. 13-15), and so Jesus was not giving them more than they could handle. But Jesus taught his disciples the spiritual significance of the story—and they have published it for us.

When anyone hears the message about the kingdom and does not understand it, the evil one comes and snatches away what was sown in their heart. This is the seed sown along the path. (v. 19)

When we preach the gospel, Jesus says, some people do not understand it. That's just the way it is in this world. Don't get upset if people think you are talking nonsense.

The seed falling on rocky ground refers to someone who hears the word and at once receives it with joy. But since they have no root, they last only a short time. When trouble or persecution comes because of the word, they quickly fall away. (vs. 20-21)

Some people like the gospel as a novelty. But then they get bored with it, and when it doesn't solve their problems, they quit. So when we share the gospel, some of the people who respond will eventually fall away. Don't be surprised; that's just the way some people are.

The seed falling among the thorns refers to someone who hears the word, but the worries of this life and the deceitfulness of wealth choke the word, making it unfruitful. (v. 22)

People do not have to be rich to be deceived by riches. All sorts of people can be distracted by the worries of this world, and some drop out for that reason. They are more worried about this world than they are about eternity.

But the seed falling on good soil refers to someone who hears the word and understands it. This is the one who produces a crop, yielding a hundred, sixty or thirty times what was sown. (v. 23)

Jesus wants us to be this kind of person. Seeds don't have a choice as to what kind of soil they fall on, but we have a choice as to what kind of soil we will be for the seed. We can choose to respond to the gospel. When trials come, we can choose to stick with the gospel, or to fall away. When life gets boring or worrisome, we can choose whether to bear fruit for the kingdom. That's the kind of message Jesus gives us.

Parable of the weeds

Jesus told them another parable:

> The kingdom of heaven is like a man who sowed good seed in his field. But while everyone was sleeping, his enemy came and sowed weeds among the wheat, and went away. When the wheat sprouted and formed heads, then the weeds also appeared.
>
> The owner's servants came to him and said, "Sir, didn't you sow good seed in your field? Where then did the weeds come from?"
>
> "An enemy did this," he replied.
>
> The servants asked him, "Do you want us to go and pull them up?"
>
> "No," he answered, "because while you are pulling the weeds, you may uproot the wheat with them. Let both grow together until the

harvest. At that time I will tell the harvesters: First collect the weeds and tie them in bundles to be burned; then gather the wheat and bring it into my barn." (Matthew 13:24-30)

Jesus explains the parable for us in verses 37-43. The good seeds are the disciples, spread by Jesus throughout the world. The weeds are bad people, spread by the devil. The bad people are mixed in with the good, and this is what the kingdom of God is like. God allows this; it is part of his plan. Jesus is describing a world in which Satan is active—the age we live in today. The kingdom of God starts small, like seeds, and it is growing now, and God is waiting to see which plants will bear fruit. Don't be too hasty, he tells his servants. Wait and see. There will be a harvest.

In farming, weeds can never produce grain. But when it comes to the gospel, fruitless folks can be changed. What looks like a weed one day may begin bearing fruit another day. It depends on each person's choice, and the kingdom of God gives people time to choose. But this will not go on forever. There will come a judgment, and the weeds will be removed from the kingdom (v. 41). God lets good and bad grow together, but he doesn't want the bad to stay bad. He wants them to change, and he will keep only the good. (How we become "good" is covered in other places.)

This parable, and the previous one, describes an age in which we have spiritual enemies. It does not describe the world after Jesus returns. Rather, it's a time when enemies snatch away the message that was sown in people's hearts, and cause weeds to grow among God's people. The kingdom of God, as described in these parables, is not a utopia in which everything is perfect. It is a time of struggle, trials, worries and deceit—but it is also a time of growth that leads toward God's harvest.

In these parables, the harvest is at "the end of the age." The harvest is the time when God's people will be resurrected to be with the Lord forever. These descriptions of the kingdom *end* with the return of Christ, rather than beginning with it. These parables describe a kingdom that exists in this age, a kingdom that will also include a future judgment.

When Jesus preached the gospel of the kingdom of God, this is the way he described it. He was not preaching about a golden age of peace and prosperity, but a long period of growth in which his disciples are to produce fruit for the kingdom.

Parables of growth

The next story is about growth:

He told them another parable: "The kingdom of heaven is like a mustard seed, which a man took and planted in his field. Though it is the smallest of all seeds, yet when it grows, it is the largest of garden plants and becomes a tree, so that the birds come and perch in its branches." (vs. 31-32)

Here Jesus described the kingdom not just as a seed, but as the *smallest* seed. Jesus is not describing a kingdom that arrives in a blaze of glory—he is describing a kingdom that begins very small. This is not what the Jews expected, but this is the kingdom that Jesus said was near. The kingdom is a story about gradual growth.

In the next parable, perhaps the shortest parable of all, Jesus compares the kingdom to a small amount of yeast.

> Again he asked, "What shall I compare the kingdom of God to? It is like yeast that a woman took and mixed into about sixty pounds of flour until it worked all through the dough. (Matthew 13:33)

When yeast is first mixed into bread dough, it is not very noticeable, but a small amount eventually produces a large result. The kingdom begins small and inconspicuous, but it grows large. In the parable of the wheat, it also produces a crop for harvest.

The small beginning of the kingdom would have surprised Jesus' listeners. They were hoping that a Messiah would lead the Jewish people to a great victory over the Romans. They were hoping to become an independent nation, with the power of David's kingdom and the wealth of Solomon's. But Jesus was announcing that the kingdom must begin in a very small way.

These parables do not describe a future golden age. They do not fit well with a kingdom that begins in a blaze of glory at Jesus' return. Rather, these parables describe the kingdom of God that exists for many years before the return of Christ. These parables describe a long, slow growth process for the kingdom.

The kingdom of God is not just a seed, and it is not just a fully grown plant. It is the entire story—something small that grows into something large.

Hidden treasures

> The kingdom of heaven is like treasure hidden in a field. When a man found it, he hid it again, and then in his joy went and sold all he had and bought that field.
>
> Again, the kingdom of heaven is like a merchant looking for fine pearls. When he found one of great value, he went away and sold everything he had and bought it. (vs. 44-46)

Again, the story begins with the kingdom small and hidden—but it does not remain hidden. The traditional interpretation of these parables is that when we hear the message of the kingdom, we should be so full of joy that we are willing to give up everything else. That is true.

But we can never "buy" the kingdom or earn our salvation. Rather, in these parables (like other parables in this chapter), it may be that *Jesus* is the main character. He is the one who sees hidden treasure in his people (the field), and gives everything he has to purchase the prize. The value may not be evident right now, but it is there.

Good fish, bad fish

Once again, the kingdom of heaven is like a net that was let down into the lake and caught all kinds of fish. When it was full, the fishermen pulled it up on the shore. Then they sat down and collected the good fish in baskets, but threw the bad away. This is how it will be at the end of the age. The angels will come and separate the wicked from the righteous and throw them into the blazing furnace, where there will be weeping and gnashing of teeth. (vs. 47-50)

The kingdom of God captures both good and bad people. The message is given to both. They live together and are given a chance to change and grow. Eventually the time comes when judgment is made, and God keeps the good. He loves the bad, he seeks the bad, he wants the bad, but he does not want them to stay bad. But some people choose to stay bad. God gives each person time, but eventually there is a judgment. That is what the kingdom of God is like.

Again, these parables *end* with the day of judgment. When Jesus described the kingdom, he did not describe the world after his return. Rather, he described the world in this age, the age in which we hear the gospel, choose to respond, and choose to be faithful.

When we hear the gospel, we should respond. Though trials come our way, we need to keep our eyes on the goal. Though this life has its worries, we should not let them distract us. Through faith, we enter the kingdom of God, and through faithfulness, we stay in the kingdom of God, and through faith, we bear fruit for the kingdom.

JESUS WALKS ON THE WATER

Editor's note: This is an edited transcript of a small group discussion led by Dan Rogers.

Dan Rogers: Good morning, everyone. We've had a nice service so far, and it's now time for the section where we talk about God's word – take a look at it, and see not only what it said, but what it's saying to us today.

Our selection for today is from Matthew chapter 14 verses 22-32. This is the well-known story of Jesus walking on the water, and Peter's attempt to walk on the water. Before we talk about the actual text itself, the action takes place on the Sea of Galilee. I wonder if any of you know anything about the Sea of Galilee? Have you ever been there? Have you ever seen it? Is there anything you could share what's about?

Person5: I knew we're going to be studying this. It brought to mind the time when I did go to see the Sea of Galilee and I didn't realize how big it was. It's really huge and we saw a boat that they've pulled up from the bottom of the sea. It looks so tiny... That's what really stuck with me.

Dan: That small of a boat on that huge body of water. Right. I think we have a picture here on our TV screen of the Sea of Galilee and the type of boat that was common among the fishermen of that day. The boat is kind of interesting. You can't see the sail, because the sail is down, but that center mast was for a sail. Then they had four positions for rowers. The boat could accommodate as many as 15 people, which, looking at the boat seem that would be pretty crowded out there on the Sea of Galilee.

From behind you can get kind of the imagery of this how big that sea is. They call it a sea, but it's actually fresh water, and it's the lowest freshwater lake on earth. I have some dimensions of it here, which are kind of interesting. As Pat said, it's quite big, 33 miles in circumference, 13 miles long, approximately 8 miles wide at its widest point, 64 square miles are covered by Sea of Galilee. It's 200 feet deep and 682 feet below sea level. It's fed primarily by the Jordan River. It's located 27 miles east of the Mediterranean and 60 miles northeast of Jerusalem. That's a good day's walk.

Storms come up on that lake. Does anybody know anything about the storms that frequent the Sea of Galilee? Has anybody read anything, or have you ever seen it in a movie? What did it look like?

Person6: It seemed like it's very violent. It's very strong.

Dan: Living here in Southern California, we're familiar with the phenomenon known as the "Santa Ana winds," and you know how they come. They come down through the canyons. That's what happens there.

There are canyons on east and west sides of the sea and the wind gets funneled through them, and at times particularly when ... It really catches speed going through those canyons, you can have some pretty serious weather out there of the sea. They've seen waves as high as at least 10 feet [Wow.] out on the Sea of Galilee. No. You usually think of a lake as pretty calm, but this one at times betrays its calmness and can turn violent very quickly and almost without warning. That gives us a little bit of maybe background of what we're dealing with. A pretty big size lake or sea, and a pretty small boat in comparison, is what we're going to be dealing here in the story.

Let's take a look then in Matthew chapter 14, and we begin reading in verse 22, which says, "Immediately, Jesus made the disciples get into the boat and go on ahead of him to the other side, while he dismissed the crowd. After he dismissed them he went up on a mountainside by himself to pray."

Now, this is interesting. Why do you think that Jesus wanted to get rid of the disciples, which immediately he made them? He didn't ask them – he *made* them get into the boat. What do you think is going on here?

Person5: I think after what we've read about the hugeness of everything that went on before, I think he needed a time just to be alone and also the time to be recharged by the prayer.

Dan: What's the context that we find in the story in, in the book of Matthew? What things have just happened and Jesus' life and the life of the disciples?

Person1: He just fed the 5000.

Dan: Right. He just fed the 5000. That was probably a day's work, feeding over 5000 people. Charles, you had a comment?

Person7: I was going to echo what Julie said, and it was the fact that there's a period here of several parables that Jesus is teaching. This is in a period of a lot of teaching right now as well…so he probably needed some time alone after all this teaching.

Person3: John the Baptist.

Dan: John the Baptist. What happened to him?

Person1: Was beheaded.

Dan: Yes. John the Baptist had just been killed. What relationship did he have to Jesus?

Person3: He was his cousin.

Dan: His cousin. Yeah. This is a pretty hefty blow, the death of your cousin. What about Jesus' disciples? Did they have any relationship with John the Baptist?

Person3: Yes. They were followers.

Dan: Yes, they had been followers of John the Baptist, at least several of them, before Jesus. Here we have some people who knew John quite well, were very close to him, and now he's dead. They feed the 5000. I think Jesus says, "I need some alone time."

Jesus was the Son of God. Why did he need alone time? What's with that? Here he is praying. Since he's the Son of God, why is he praying and why is he seeking time to be alone?

Person6: I think he's modeling for us, for one thing. I think he truly had a need to be alone with his Father, and on top of that, he's modeling how we ought to respond during a time of stress. That the right to do is to go to God and seek his face and seek that solitude and quiet stillness.

Dan: There was something he couldn't do with his disciples, the group around him all the time, because they were always arguing, bickering, doing something, and he just needed some alone time, but here again I bring up the point: He's the Son of God. Was he praying to himself? How does he pray to God when he's the Son of God? Why is he praying? Why does he need to pray?

Person3: He's totally human, totally in his emotions.

Dan: He's, as well as being fully God, fully human and living out his humanity as a human, and so humans need to have alone times. They need to pray, particularly in situations like this.

We find that he went up on a mountainside by himself to pray. Now, I'm struck by the fact that he liked to go up on a mountain. Have you ever found it interesting to go up on a mountain to pray?

Person1: Mm-hmm (Affirmative)

Dan: Why? What is it about going up on a mountain to pray that makes it special?

Person1: Being in God's nature. Just seeing his majesty just lay before you and it just makes you feel closer to God.

Dan: When you get up higher you feel closer to him. [Laughter] I think there is truth to that and seeing his creation.

Person7: It helps you to find your place. As you go up, you can look back from where you're coming, you're looking back over your city or your town, and because you realize how vast that is and how small you are in comparison to the greater creation.

Dan: Right. It gives you some perspective, doesn't it? Isn't it interesting that how many times in the Bible significant events take place on mountains?

We call it a "mountain-top experience." Going up to the mountain and coming back down, like Moses did. He had a rather miraculous thing happen to him after he came down from the mountain, didn't he?

Kind of interesting. Miraculous things happen to people when they come down back off the mountain, so let's see if something miraculous happens. Of course, we know the story, it did. Let's read on: "When evening came, he was there alone, but the boat was already a considerable distance from land buffeted by waves because the wind was against it."

What strikes me there is, how was Jesus supposed to catch up with his disciples? What do you think they thought?

Person5: He hadn't told them…. They didn't know.

Person7: All we know is he dismissed them.

Someone: He told them to go.

Person1: They probably didn't know he was going to rejoin them.

Dan: Or when. That's kind of an unusual situation. How do you think they felt?

Person3: I think they were worried.

Dan: They may have been worried. Yeah, worried about Jesus. Worried about what was happening, what was going to happen to their ministry that he said they have, and this is unusual. He disappears. We don't know when we'll see him. We'll go, "This is a big lake. We're going to cross the lake. When will we see Jesus again? Maybe he'll get a boat tomorrow and get across."

Person6: I wonder if the disciples even wondered if Jesus knew that they were in trouble, that they were in the midst of a big storm. He's off somewhere and they're in the boat, and they probably didn't even know that Jesus already had an overview, but they were just … He doesn't know we're out here drowning…

Person5: But they did go in faith that he told them to go, and they did it.

Dan: Yeah, and they are a considerable distance, as the New International Version translates that, considerable distance out in the water this time. They're being buffeted by the waves, and I love this phrase, "Because the wind was against it." What do you think they mean by the wind was against it?

Person3: It is pushing it.

Dan: Pushing the boat?

Person3: Yes.

Dan: Do you think it was pushing them the way they wanted to go?

Person6: No. I think pushing them out further into danger.

Dan: Right. They would like to have maybe rowed to shore. Remember they have four oars in there. The sails are of no use right now, but they were probably manning those oars and rowing for all they were worth, but the wind just wouldn't let go of them. Now, if you know anything about Jewish cosmology, and you probably do, there are two places that you expect to encounter demons. You know what two places in Jewish cosmology they were?

Person7: Water is one of them.

Dan: Right, on the water, out on the sea. Remember in the book of Revelation where all these evil looking critters come from?

Person5: Out of the sea.

Dan: It's dangerous going out in the sea. Because you might encounter something out there. And the other place would be the wilderness, out in the desert. They're a little worried about something going on here that maybe more than meets the eye, and I think there's a hint when Matthew says, "The wind was against it." I think maybe he means more than physically, that things are not going the way they should. We're experienced fishermen. This doesn't look right, what's happening here tonight.

Person3: They were no longer in control.

Dan: Yeah. That's another good point. They had lost control. I think that's an excellent point. Because we know someone is going to come who takes control, who has control. Kind of a lesson for them that they don't have control of their lives or their situation. In verse 25 we read, "During the fourth watch of the night..." Does anybody have a translation that tells you what time that is?

Person6: Three o'clock in the morning, that's why it's early.

Dan: Three, and that's early. Three o'clock in the morning. "During the fourth watch of the night, Jesus went out to them walking on the lake." Walking on the lake – why was Jesus walking on the lake? Why didn't he fly? I mean, good grief, if you're going to do a miracle, why not do a big one? Why not fly? Why not suddenly appear in the boat with them? Why do you think Jesus might have been walking on the water?

Person3: Amongst the waves that were terrifying them.

Dan: He was there at ease.

Person3: Yeah. At ease walking right to them.

Dan: Yeah. I think we forget that these waves are great, and yet Jesus comes out just walking like I think we've seen in the movies, on a peaceful little lake. He's walking through these waves and the sea is bouncing up and down around him and he's walking across it.

Person5: Perhaps it's to reassure them, too, that as (because being very versed in the Old Testament), they knew they had the story of Exodus in the turmoil and everything that went on there, and the big waves that God stilled.

Dan: Very good. There's a little imagery there, walking between the waters and not being harmed by the waters if you're the chosen of God. There's a testimony as to who he was. He's walking like the Israelites walked through the Red Sea, and he's come down from the mountain like Moses. There's a lot going on here that the imagery... Do you think the disciples got all this imagery at that time? [Laughter]

Someone: They're hanging on to the boat.

Person7: Earlier you were saying that this issue of evil spirits or demons in the water is a potential... He's walked on top of the water, or is anything there that we may have missed, that Jesus is on *top* of the water, on top of any evil spirits that might be there? I don't know...

Dan: Yeah. It could be. Go back to Barbara's point that he is in control of all things. It's amazing, but yeah, this demonstrates his control, his peace, his promise, his faith, a lot of things. Again, the disciples had no thoughts about these things right now. Twenty years later, they reflect back, maybe, and to figure this out, but now, they're just scared. We find that "Jesus went after them walking on the lake. When the disciples saw him walking on the lake, they were terrified." Evidently, they didn't recognize him? Why do you think they didn't recognize him?

Person5: There's too much turbulence?

Dan: Too much turbulence. Okay.

Someone: Waves throwing up.

Person2: They're expecting demons.

Person3: It's a ghost.

Dan: You tend to see what you expect to see, not what is always really there.

Person6: Plus it seems so unbelievable. I mean, it's not something you would expect. That would not be something that I would immediate come to the conclusion that oh, it's Jesus. When you're already scared of demons and all those things out in the water, like you just explained, that your first assumption would probably be it's a ghost, or a demon, or something evil.

Dan: Fear hinders your vision. When you're afraid, it's harder to see Jesus, because you're worried. Your mind is where?

Person1: Your own personal storm.

Dan: Right. Where is Jesus?

Person2: He's there.

Person5: But he doesn't come to them until, or at least they don't see him, until after a lot has really happened.

Dan: Yeah. He is there, but they don't see him. Even when they see him, they don't recognize him. Isn't that a question that people tend to ask when they're in a crisis: Where is God? He's there, but we don't see him because we're not expecting him, and we're not looking for him, and really knowing that he is there.

Person6: What strikes me on this is it doesn't say that Jesus came and just calmed the storm and then walked across. Maybe I'm missing something here, but the way I read it, he's walking through the storm.

Dan: Right. That's the way it appears to me, too. That's how I read it. He's walking right through the midst of the storm, which really is amazing. He's walking on the lake and they were terrified. They said, "It's a ghost." They cried out in fear like a little girl. Oh no. That's not in there... [Laughter]

Dan: Had these fellows ever been out on the sea before? Yeah. They were fishermen. Most of them. Had they ever been out on that lake? Yeah. It was probably, maybe, one of their boats, unless they rented or borrowed it from someone, and yet these brave, experienced seamen are terrified. Something out of the ordinary is definitely happening here. Now they thought they saw a ghost. Did the disciples believe in ghosts?

Someone: Probably not.

Person3: They had them in their background.

Person6: Maybe it's still in there somewhere.

Dan: Yeah. You fall back on what you've grown up with, what you've heard. Did the Jewish people believe in disembodied spirits roaming the earth? Yeah, they did. Is Jesus a disembodied spirit?

Person5: They think he is. [Laughter] He's walking on the water.

Dan: There might be an interesting message here from Matthew (and other New Testament writers as well) of the reality of Jesus' humanity, that he is not some disembodied spirit who they perceive as a man. He *is* a man. He's not a ghost. He's not a disembodied spirit. He's a man, but he's a man who is walking on the water. How do you think he did that? What technique did he use to walk on the water?

Person3: He's God.

Dan: He is God, but he's operating, he's fully human. How could he do this?

Person3: By the Spirit.

Dan: I would say by the Spirit. That's the way he seems to have done everything in his ministry, is by the Spirit. He might say that same happened to Moses coming down from the mountain and glowing. He was a man, but he glowed by the Spirit. Let's say Jesus was a man, but walking down off the mountain and parting the sea, he walked like a man, but through the power of the Holy Spirit. It also shows Jesus is in control, like what Barbara's raised there. He's in control. He's in control of what?

Everything. You mean even storms?

Dan: He's in control. The forces of nature. Who in the world could be in charge of all creation?

Someone: God.

Dan: Yeah. The Creator. Who else would be in charge of all the creation, but the Creator.

"They say, 'It's a ghost,' and they cried out in fear, but Jesus immediately said to them, 'Take courage. It is I. Don't be afraid.'" Have you ever noticed how many times Jesus had to say to his disciples, Don't be afraid? Take courage, don't fear, and don't be afraid. Why do you think he had to continually encourage them not to be afraid?

Person5: There was a lot against them.

Dan: We're fearful. When things get against us, we get fearful. What have we seen that fear does to you, though, when you have that kind of fear?

Person2: Blind you.

Dan: It blinds you. Yeah.

Person3: Makes you crazy.

Person1: You start questioning everything.

Dan: Questioning, doubting ...

Person3: Can't see the truth.

Dan: Fearing. Can't see.

Person5: You can't do anything.

Person2: It paralyzes.

Dan: It kind of reminds me of the fellow who buried a talent because he was afraid. Everybody else did well. His problem was not that he only had the one. His problem was he was afraid, and when you're afraid, as Barbara said, you do crazy stuff, stuff that's not right, and you lack faith. You don't trust God, and you just make things worse. Isn't it challenging as a human not to be afraid?

We're going to find out, as we read on in the story, what a challenge it is. Verse 8, "Lord, if it's you ...," [Don't you love Peter's cry?] "If it's you [he's still having a little trouble], Peter replied, tell me to come to you on the water."

Now, notice that Peter didn't say, "Let me come to you on the water," or

"Can I come to you on the water?" He said, "*Command* me to come to you on the water." Why do you think he put it that way? Why did he ask Jesus to command him to come to him on the water?

Person3: He wanted Jesus to make it possible that he could come, because he was afraid.

Dan: He was afraid, but he felt what? If Jesus commands ...

Person3: ... it would happen, because he's seen it.

Dan: All right.

Someone: He just thought, he's been seeing it.

Person6: He wanted to make sure it was going to work. [Laughter]

Dan: If it didn't work, whose fault was it going to be?

Several: Jesus'.

Dan: Can we ever do that?

Person7: Yes.

Dan: Oh, God, you have left me down. I asked you for this and I prayed about it. I prayed about it, and it didn't happen. It didn't turn out the way you wanted it. I don't know what's going on with you, God, but you're not listening or something out there. Yeah, I think there was a little human tendency there to "let's put this on God. I have nothing to do with it. If I fail, it's God's fault."

"So Jesus eventually said, 'Come.' Then Peter got down out of the boat." Would you have gotten down out of the boat?

Person5: Probably not.

Person3: I would hope so.

Dan: You notice that the 11 did not get down out of the boat? There was only one out of the 12 who did, but that's what? Peter's personality? Peter's nature? The others were saying, "Let's see how this thing works out. If Peter makes it, maybe we'll walk, too, but first, let Peter go." Peter got down out of the boat and walked on the water. How cool is that? Peter is walking on the water.

"He came towards Jesus, but when he saw the wind, he was afraid." What happened here? He saw the wind and was afraid. He walking on water.

Person3: He took his eyes off Jesus.

Dan: Very good. Fear blinded him, and now he couldn't see Jesus, because he's afraid. He saw what? The wind?

Person5: He saw what was going on immediately around him and said, "This is impossible."

Dan: Thankfully, we never do that. [Laughter] I think we can understand it. God, I know you're there, but look's going on around me? Oh, my goodness. What's going to happen next? I am impressed that Peter walked on the water. "He saw the wind and he was afraid and beginning to sink, cried out, 'Lord, save me.'" What do you think of his actions there? He starts to sink.

Person5: He knew who to turn to.

Dan: He knew who to turn to. Let's give Peter a lot of credit. He realized "I'm not in control, but I have a feeling Jesus, you are. [Barb: And you love me.] I need you to save me." Isn't it the cry of all humanity, or should be, "Lord Jesus, save me"?

Person6: I like it that he didn't yell to his friends. Throw him the oar over here.

Someone: Throw me a line.

Dan: You get the feeling that he was past the point of no return? There's a gospel account of Peter swimming. We know Peter could swim. Being a fisherman, we would assume he was a pretty good fisherman having grown up on the lakes, spent his life out there fishing, but at this point, he realizes he can't swim back to the boat. There is no alternative if Jesus doesn't save him. He's a goner.

"Immediately [verse 31], Jesus reached out his hand and caught him. 'You of little faith,' he said. 'Why did you doubt?' When they climbed into the boat, the wind died down. Then those who were in the boat worshiped him, saying, 'Truly, you are the Son of God.'" What do you make of Jesus' words to Peter, "You of little faith, why did you doubt?"

Person3: He was teaching him.

Dan: What do you think the message was?

Person3: He had to believe.

Dan: He needed to believe. He should have had more belief.

Person3: In Jesus.

Dan: Right.

Person5: I think it also probably looks ahead to the time at the crucifixion when Peter said, "I'll never give up on you," and he did, and Jesus is saying, "Don't doubt."

Person6: I think I take these words as very tender words, I guess. Because his first reaction was to save Peter, and to grab him and pull him out, and then he told them, oh, come on. It wasn't that he let him struggle or sink, or he could have dived after him really, but he took it easy on him. He saved him first, and I see these as very tender words even though they're strong. He saved him first and then he taught him.

Dan: Yeah. Some of us might say, "Well, let him learn his lesson. Let's have him drown almost and... I think you're right – Jesus was kind in his admonition. I don't even know if it's a rebuke. Peter, he says, had little faith.

Person5: But he had some.

Dan: He had some. How much faith do I have?

Person3: And how much do the disciples have? They didn't go.

Dan: They didn't even go out on the water.

Person3: But he was working with him. [Dan: Yeah.] individually...

Dan: I think the point it is, can you be saved with little faith?

Person3: Yes.

Person5: Yes.

Person3: Or with no faith.

Dan: Virtually no faith, because Jesus has faith for you. We have to trust not in our own faith, but on the faith that Jesus has.

Person6: He supplies for us.

Dan: Yeah, he had a little faith, but he was still saved. What condition was Peter in, do you think, when he got back in the boat?

Person3: Wet. [Laughter.]

Person1: Ghostly looking, looking very wet as a sheet.

Dan: Probably. Do you imagine the water was hot or cold?

Several: Cold.

Dan: And the wind was blowing. I think he might have even turned blue. How do you think he feels all wet and frozen lying there on the boat and all the other 11 looking at him?

Person3: Humble, embarrassed.

Person5: But yet he did walk on water for a little bit. "Did that really happen?" He had to be thinking about that, too.

Person7: Jesus was so full of love that in this ... I have to see that Peter's gained some additional love for Jesus, and he recognizes that "I desperately need you" and I have to see his heart growing even more there.

Dan: Then Jesus tells the storm to stop, and Peter's thinking, "yeah, now, after I'm back in the boat. Why didn't you do that before, when I was walking out there?" Anything we can learn from that?

Person3: He would have learned.

Dan: The storm actually helped Peter, didn't it?

Person3: Yes.

Dan: Did storms in our lives ever help us? They're not very pleasant ... We don't like them.... God seems to saves us out of most of them. He will save us for all eternity, but sometimes you get wet.

Person3: Cold.

Dan: He lets you get wet.

Someone: Hungry.

Dan: Then in saving you, you don't come out unscathed. Why do you think Jesus didn't stop the storm until it was over, though?

Person6: It would have had far less impact, I think, than if he would have calmed the storm. With this scenario, he didn't just calm the storm. They also walked on the water. They almost drowned. He was there in the midst...

Dan: ...of the storm.

Person5: In the midst – I just thought of that, too – in the midst of the trial and the crisis. Jesus was there when he was walking on the water, and he was still in the midst of the storm, and he was still cold and shivering, and all of that, but he was still there. He did perform the miracles, too, in the midst of the trial, in the midst of the crisis.

Dan: Right. That's amazing. And you know, has God promised us no problems in life? Do you read that? ...persecution... Jesus has never promised us no storms, but what has he promised us?

Person3: Storms.

Someone: That he will be with us.

Dan: He promised that he will be with us in those storms.

Person3: To the end.

Dan: Right, to the very end, and he will save us.

Person6: Even with little faith.

Dan: Even with a little faith that we have, he will still save us. Any lessons that you take away from this story today from this biblical account, anything that really just particularly stands out in your mind?

Person6: I think for me, there are several, but the one of them that just keeps popping in my mind is as a mother of two small children, the approach of that graceful loving way of dealing, the way Jesus dealt with their tantrums sometimes, or their doubts, or their fears, and how Jesus approached almost as a parent to them, how tender and full of mercy and love it was, even when they were in the midst of a crisis, tantrum, or doubt or a fear. As a mom, I think I just really want to take that same approach in life to deal with my children in a tender way, a loving way, even when there's only very little faith, and even when there's a lot of doubt whether I'm doing the right thing for them. They doubt me, I can still be there in a loving way, on that level. Of course, there's a deeper level as well as far as my personal relationship with Jesus, and the storms that I do go through and knowing that he will pull me out. He might not calm the storm, but he will be there and he won't let me drown.

Dan: Okay. Very good. What else?

Person3: There's lessons on many levels. There's the blessing of training, that Jesus was training his disciples through this whole experience about the storms and in saving them, like Suzie said about them.

Dan: Even when he is not visibly present.

Person3: Right.

Dan: You still have faith and he will save you.

Person7: The modeling at the start of the story, we have Jesus going up to the mountainside to be with his Father to recharge his batteries, to get some peace after having fed the 5000, knowing what is yet to come in his ministry, just spending a time alone with God, just a reminder that even in the midst of struggles, we need to cling to our Father.

Person5: I think that was one that I got, too, is that he was there getting close to his Father, getting recharged, but he knew about the disciples. He knew the problem they were having and he did go rescue them.

Dan: Right. How do you think maybe this speaks to people who ask that question, "When bad things happen, where is God?" How does this speak to that?

Person7: He's there. You may not see him. The storm may blind us, but he's there. We have to look for him.

Dan: He's not only there in spirit. How else is he there, do you think?

Person2: He's physically present.

Dan: Physically present, and not only in his being, but in whatever humans may be there as well. God is present, and there is no good but of God, so whatever happens to us in storms, if it's not Jesus who pulled us up ... What if it's a rowboat that came out and pulled Peter out of the water? Was Jesus still there?

Person3: Yes.

Person2: Absolutely.

Dan: Yeah. Peter's present in the people in the rowboat. You know the old joke about you know guy was waiting on his housetop in the flood for the Lord to save him, and the rowboat came up and he said, "No thanks. The Lord is going to save me." The helicopter came, "He said, No thanks. The Lord's going to save me." He drowned and went to heaven. When he's in heaven he said, "Lord what happened? You didn't save me." He said, "Well I sent a rowboat and a helicopter for you." [Laughter]

Sometimes we don't see the ways. Again, we're blind to the ways that God comes to us. We look for God to come to us in the way we *want* him to come, and the way we expect him to come, and when it's not that way, sometimes we're blind to it and don't see it.

Person1: I think also how much has our faith grown through each storm we face. Does our faith grow each time? Or do we allow more doubt?

Dan: I think you make a good point. One of the things about Peter was he had some faith, he thought, and he walked on the water, but even at our highest points, when we have faith to walk on water, as humans, we still revert, and then the next time, didn't learn the lesson at all. Now we doubt. Now we're sinking, and you'd think, Well, Peter, if you walked on water a while..."

Person1: Why didn't you keep going?

Dan: Why didn't he keep going? We humans, we're up and down. Thank God, it's not our faith that saves us.

Person6: What I love about this Jesus who's so fully human, he must have felt the storm and the boat rocking, and he must have been getting wet and cold. He was in the storm with them. He was not the one who was miraculously all dry and probably didn't feel the cold. He must have felt all the elements in the midst of the storm. He put himself there. To me, it's what makes Jesus so approachable knowing that I'm in a storm. "You might not calm the storm, but I know you know what it feels like."

Dan: Yeah. There's a lot to learn from this story, isn't it?

All right. Well, that concludes our message portion of the service today. We'll sing the final hymn, and have a closing prayer, and dismiss for the day.

MORE PARABLES OF THE KINGDOM

Matthew 13 is the largest collection of parables that are specifically said to be about the kingdom of God. But Matthew has five additional parables describing the kingdom of God, and Mark has another. A brief analysis of these parables will show that Jesus did not describe the kingdom as an ideal age after his return. Rather, he described the kingdom as an age leading up to the final judgment.

The growing seed

> This is what the kingdom of God is like. A man scatters seed on the ground. Night and day, whether he sleeps or gets up, the seed sprouts and grows, though he does not know how. All by itself the soil produces grain—first the stalk, then the head, then the full kernel in the head. As soon as the grain is ripe, he puts the sickle to it, because the harvest has come. (Mark 4:26-29; NIV 2011 throughout this chapter)

This parable, like the parable of the mustard seed and the parable of yeast in the dough, is a story of growth. The kingdom of God is not just a seed, not just a harvest—it involves the whole story of growth—a growth that occurs whether or not humans notice it or understand the way it works. The gospel produces its fruit in people's lives, and then comes the harvest—the judgment.

The unmerciful servant

> The kingdom of heaven is like a king who wanted to settle accounts with his servants. As he began the settlement, a man who owed him ten thousand bags of gold was brought to him. Since he was not able to pay, the master ordered that he and his wife and his children and all that he had be sold to repay the debt.
>
> At this the servant fell on his knees before him. "Be patient with me," he begged, "and I will pay back everything." The servant's master took pity on him, canceled the debt and let him go.
>
> But when that servant went out, he found one of his fellow servants who owed him a hundred silver coins. He grabbed him and began to choke him. "Pay back what you owe me!" he demanded.
>
> His fellow servant fell to his knees and begged him, "Be patient with me, and I will pay it back."
>
> But he refused. Instead, he went off and had the man thrown into prison until he could pay the debt. When the other servants saw what

had happened, they were outraged and went and told their master everything that had happened.

Then the master called the servant in. "You wicked servant," he said, "I canceled all that debt of yours because you begged me to. Shouldn't you have had mercy on your fellow servant just as I had on you?" In anger his master handed him over to the jailers to be tortured, until he should pay back all he owed.

This is how my heavenly Father will treat each of you unless you forgive your brother or sister from your heart. (Matthew 18:23-35)

This entire story is what the kingdom is like, Jesus said. It's about judgment, and about the King forgiving our debts, and about our need to forgive one another. And it is also about severe consequences for those who don't.

The kingdom of God involves a time in which people are forgiven, and are likewise expected to be forgiving toward one another. The amount we owe God, so to speak, is thousands of times greater than whatever anyone might owe to us. Since he has been merciful toward us, we are to be merciful to others.

Some of the detail is exaggeration. God does not torture people in an effort to make them repay what they owe. No amount of suffering could possibly pay off our transgressions against God. This detail is a rhetorical device, used to emphasize the importance of responding to God's grace; it is not a commentary on the purpose of hell.

We do not forgive others as well as God forgives us. We always fall short in that—but this is not the unforgiveable sin. God forgives us of this failure, too. However, whenever we fail to forgive others, it shows that we have failed to appreciate how much God has forgiven us, and that we are still striving, at least in part, to earn something that has already been given to us. We live in a self-imposed torture of feeling that God is angry at us, when he really is not. We will not *experience* the forgiveness of God unless we are forgiving toward others.

The main point for us right now is that this parable describes life in this age, not our situation after Christ's return.

The vineyard workers

The kingdom of heaven is like a landowner who went out early in the morning to hire workers for his vineyard. He agreed to pay them a denarius for the day and sent them into his vineyard.

About nine in the morning he went out and saw others standing in the marketplace doing nothing. He told them, "You also go and work in my vineyard, and I will pay you whatever is right." So they went.

He went out again about noon and about three in the afternoon and did the same thing. About five in the afternoon he went out and found still others standing around. He asked them, "Why have you been standing here all day long doing nothing?"

"Because no one has hired us," they answered.

He said to them, "You also go and work in my vineyard."

When evening came, the owner of the vineyard said to his foreman, "Call the workers and pay them their wages, beginning with the last ones hired and going on to the first."

The workers who were hired about five in the afternoon came and each received a denarius. So when those came who were hired first, they expected to receive more. But each one of them also received a denarius. When they received it, they began to grumble against the landowner. "These who were hired last worked only one hour," they said, "and you have made them equal to us who have borne the burden of the work and the heat of the day."

But he answered one of them, "I am not being unfair to you, friend. Didn't you agree to work for a denarius? Take your pay and go. I want to give the one who was hired last the same as I gave you. Don't I have the right to do what I want with my own money? Or are you envious because I am generous?"

So the last will be first, and the first will be last. (Matt. 20:1-16)

The kingdom of heaven is an age in which we work before we are rewarded. Some work much, and others work only a little, but all are paid. This does not mean that we earn our salvation, of course; work simply provides the setting of the parable. The point is that God is generous, and he is so generous that it troubles some people.

If Jesus were describing the world after his return, the parable would not be very relevant to his audience, nor to us. The work he describes as part of the kingdom is the work we are doing now, in this age, and the grace that some people complain about is grace that can be seen in this age. Some people work long and hard to do God's will, and others work less, but in one respect the Master treats them all the same: He forgives them, whether their debt is large or small.

This parable presents us with two questions: 1) Do we think that God is too liberal? 2) Are we willing to do our best, even if it's difficult, even if others get the same reward for doing less?

The wedding clothes

The kingdom of heaven is like a king who prepared a wedding banquet for his son. He sent his servants to those who had been invited to the banquet to tell them to come, but they refused to come.

Then he sent some more servants and said, "Tell those who have been invited that I have prepared my dinner: My oxen and fattened cattle have been butchered, and everything is ready. Come to the wedding banquet."

But they paid no attention and went off—one to his field, another to his business. The rest seized his servants, mistreated them and killed them. The king was enraged. He sent his army and destroyed those murderers and burned their city.

Then he said to his servants, "The wedding banquet is ready, but those I invited did not deserve to come. So go to the street corners and invite to the banquet anyone you find." So the servants went out into the streets and gathered all the people they could find, the bad as well as the good, and the wedding hall was filled with guests.

But when the king came in to see the guests, he noticed a man there who was not wearing wedding clothes. He asked, "How did you get in here without wedding clothes, friend ?" The man was speechless.

Then the king told the attendants, "Tie him hand and foot, and throw him outside, into the darkness, where there will be weeping and gnashing of teeth."

For many are invited, but few are chosen. (Matthew 22:2-14)

Here, Jesus compared the kingdom to a wedding feast—not the banquet itself, but to the invitations. Jesus is not talking about what it will be like after we get there, but rather how we get there in the first place. The original invitees are the unbelieving Jews, but they ignored the message and persecuted the messengers.

God then invites everyone else, both good and bad, and that includes us. But God does not want bad people to stay bad. Eventually a day of judgment will come, when we will need to be clothed in the righteousness of Christ. The main point of the parable—what people need to know about the kingdom of God—is that the invitations are going out now, and we need to respond to them.

The wise and foolish virgins

At that time the kingdom of heaven will be like ten virgins who took their lamps and went out to meet the bridegroom. Five of them were foolish and five were wise. The foolish ones took their lamps but did not take any oil with them. The wise ones, however, took oil in jars along with their lamps. The bridegroom was a long time in coming, and they all became drowsy and fell asleep.

At midnight the cry rang out: "Here's the bridegroom! Come out to meet him!"

Then all the virgins woke up and trimmed their lamps. The foolish ones said to the wise, "Give us some of your oil; our lamps are going out."

"No," they replied, "there may not be enough for both us and you. Instead, go to those who sell oil and buy some for yourselves."

But while they were on their way to buy the oil, the bridegroom arrived. The virgins who were ready went in with him to the wedding banquet. And the door was shut.

Later the others also came. "Lord, Lord," they said, "open the door for us!"

But he replied, "Truly I tell you, I don't know you."

Therefore keep watch, because you do not know the day or the hour. (Matthew 25:1-13)

Jesus is talking about the day that the master will return (Matthew 24:50), and he is saying that the kingdom will then be like a wedding for which some people will be unprepared. Not everyone who wants to attend will be permitted to.

Jesus' point is not to make a prediction, but to encourage his disciples to be wise, to be prepared, to be always ready. The parable about the future is really an exhortation for today. Jesus does not say here what the oil represents, or how we "buy" more, or how we can be prepared. The point is simply that we need to be prepared.

The bags of gold

The traditional name of this next story is the parable of talents, from the Greek word *talanton*. Anciently, this was a large amount of money; the NIV 2011 has attempted to give the approximate value by translating it as "bags of gold." The precise dollar figure is not important; it represents everything that God has given to us. Some people get more than others, but God wants us to use whatever amount we have.

Again, it [the kingdom of God, v. 1] will be like a man going on a journey, who called his servants and entrusted his wealth to them. To one he gave five bags of gold, to another two bags, and to another one bag, each according to his ability. Then he went on his journey. The man who had received five bags of gold went at once and put his money to work and gained five bags more. So also, the one with two bags of gold gained two more. But the man who had received one bag went off, dug a hole in the ground and hid his master's money.

After a long time the master of those servants returned and settled accounts with them. The man who had received five bags of gold brought the other five. "Master," he said, "you entrusted me with five bags of gold. See, I have gained five more."

His master replied, "Well done, good and faithful servant! You have been faithful with a few things; I will put you in charge of many things. Come and share your master's happiness!"

The man with two bags of gold also came. "Master," he said, "you entrusted me with two bags of gold; see, I have gained two more."

His master replied, "Well done, good and faithful servant! You have been faithful with a few things; I will put you in charge of many things. Come and share your master's happiness!"

Then the man who had received one bag of gold came. "Master," he said, "I knew that you are a hard man, harvesting where you have not sown and gathering where you have not scattered seed. So I was afraid and went out and hid your gold in the ground. See, here is what belongs to you."

His master replied, "You wicked, lazy servant! So you knew that I harvest where I have not sown and gather where I have not scattered seed? Well then, you should have put my money on deposit with the bankers, so that when I returned I would have received it back with interest.

"So take the bag of gold from him and give it to the one who has ten bags. For whoever has will be given more, and they will have an abundance. Whoever does not have, even what they have will be taken from them. And throw that worthless servant outside, into the darkness, where there will be weeping and gnashing of teeth." (Matthew 25:14-30)

Just as the good seeds produce grain for the harvest, here the good servants work for their master. There is a long time period, and the people are expected to do something, and to have some results. Those who fail to respond to the King will not be rewarded, and will miss out on the blessings of the kingdom.

The King determines how much to reward each person. He is the one who determines when to call each worker, and he determines when he will return for judgment. When Christ returns, the kingdom of God will be like the return of a wealthy landowner. Faithful servants will be rewarded; fearful and lazy servants will be excluded from the blessings.

The focus is more on the present than it is on the future. Jesus told the parable because it is relevant to the way we live now. Some will work hard and bear much fruit; others will bear less fruit, but both will be rewarded generously, and both will share in the master's happiness.

Jesus wants the gospel to have results in our lives. He does not want us to think that he is hard, or that he makes unreasonable demands. We do not need to be afraid, or to use that as an excuse for doing nothing. Rather, we are to grow—at least a little, hopefully more. Jesus wants us to be about our Father's business. He doesn't always spell out exactly what we are to do, but he wants us to at least make an effort, to try while we can.

Conclusion

We have now looked at all the parables that Jesus specifically said described the kingdom. Let's try to summarize what he said.

First, the kingdom of God begins in a small way. It is not conspicuous. Many people will not notice it. Others will hear about it and want to be part of it, but will fall away for one reason or another. The kingdom has too much work, too many trials. It is not the utopia that some people want it to be, and some people prefer the things of this world. But others treasure it so much that they are willing to give up everything for it.

The kingdom begins with God. He is the one who sows the seed; he is the one who hires the workers and gives the talents. He is the one who seeks a harvest, who sets the standards, who makes the judgments, who gives both grace and duties. He tells us to forgive others and to work for the kingdom.

When Jesus used parables to describe the kingdom, he did not describe a wonderful world that comes only after the King returns. Rather, he described a time of trials, choices and growth, and then a judgment when the King returns. Jesus does not describe what the kingdom looks like after that. God's kingdom includes both positive consequences and negative consequences. Jesus described our own age as a time of invitation, testing and growth.

The kingdom of God is now in a stage of growth, in which we are given grace, and given opportunity to bear fruit. We are expected to be forgiving, to be working, and to be ready. For the time will come when the kingdom will be like a harvest, when accounts will be paid, and decisions will be made as to who enjoys the celebration.

MATTHEW 16:
WHAT KIND OF MESSIAH?

By Michael Morrison

Jesus praised Peter for accurately identifying him as the Messiah, and he promised him great authority. But in almost the next breath, Jesus gave Peter one of the strongest rebukes in all of Scripture. The incident, and the teaching of Jesus that surrounds it, tells us much about the purpose of the Messiah.

Seeking a sign

First, some "Pharisees and Sadducees came to Jesus and tested him by asking him to show them a sign from heaven" (Matt. 16:1). Jesus had already done many miracles, but the Jewish leaders wanted special proof. Jesus refused to take their test, because they were asking the wrong questions.

He responded by quoting proverbs about the weather: "When evening comes, you say, 'It will be fair weather, for the sky is red,' and in the morning, 'Today it will be stormy, for the sky is red and overcast.' You know how to interpret the appearance of the sky, but you cannot interpret the signs of the times" (vv. 2-3). They could not interpret the signs because they were looking for the wrong kind of signs.

Beware of wrong ideas

Matthew changes the scene, but still has the same subject in mind. "When they went across the lake, the disciples forgot to take bread. 'Be careful,' Jesus said to them. 'Be on your guard against the yeast of the Pharisees and Sadducees'" (vv. 5-6). Jesus meant this as a metaphor, but the disciples thought he was warning them about real yeast. Instead of asking Jesus what he meant, "they discussed this among themselves and said, 'It is because we didn't bring any bread'" (v. 7).

But Jesus knew what they were discussing, and asked them: "You of little faith, why are you talking among yourselves about having no bread? Do you still not understand? Don't you remember the five loaves for the five thousand, and how many basketfuls you gathered?... How is it you don't understand that I was not talking to you about bread? But be on your guard against the yeast of the Pharisees and Sadducees" (vv. 8-11).

I am not worried about bread, he seemed to say. If we need to, we can make some more. The disciples then understood that Jesus was using a figure of speech: "He was not telling them to guard against the yeast used in bread, but against the teaching of the Pharisees and Sadducees" (v. 12).

Although Jesus could have had various teachings in mind, Matthew puts it in the context of ideas about a Messiah. The Jewish leaders had just asked for proof that Jesus was the Messiah. They had ideas about what a Messiah would do, but they were wrong, so Jesus tells his disciples not to listen to them.

'You are the Messiah'

The next scene that Matthew describes occurs north of Galilee, in a gentile area ruled by Herod's son Philip. It was a safe place to discuss the word *Messiah* without any bystanders getting the wrong idea. "When Jesus came to the region of Caesarea Philippi, he asked his disciples, 'Who do people say the Son of Man is?' (v. 13).

"They replied, 'Some say John the Baptist; others say Elijah; and still others, Jeremiah or one of the prophets'" (v. 14). It is doubtful that they thought Jesus was really John or Jeremiah come back from the dead. Rather, they were guessing what sort of prophet he was: a miracle-worker like Elijah, or doomsayer like Jeremiah, or some other messenger from God.

"'But what about you?' he asked. 'Who do you say I am?' Simon Peter answered, 'You are the Messiah, the Son of the living God.' Jesus replied, 'Blessed are you, Simon son of Jonah, for this was not revealed to you by flesh and blood, but by my Father in heaven'" (v. 15-17). Peter probably thought the idea was his own, but Jesus tells him that the thought actually came from God. Jesus accepts the titles that Peter has given him, and reinforces them by revealing a special role for Peter:

"And I tell you that you are Peter [Greek *Petros*], and on this rock [*petra*] I will build my church, and the gates of Hades will not overcome it" (v. 18). Some interpreters conclude that the "rock" on which Jesus built his church is Peter; others say it is his confession. Even if Jesus means Peter, however, he is not predicting apostolic succession or hierarchy. Jesus used Peter to build the church, but he also used the other apostles (Eph. 2:20). And he promised that death would never conquer the church.

Jesus promised Peter authority: "I will give you the keys of the kingdom of heaven; whatever you bind on earth will be bound in heaven, and whatever you loose on earth will be loosed in heaven" (v. 19). The meaning of this verse is widely debated, but the safest interpretation seems to be that Peter would open the gates of heaven to more people by preaching the gospel. When rabbis spoke of "binding" and "loosing," they were talking about which commandments were required for the kingdom. Jesus apparently meant that through the gospel, Peter would tell people that by God's grace, Jesus was the Way into the kingdom of God. In Matthew 18:18, Jesus expanded this role to all the apostles. Their teachings are authoritative guides for us.

Then Jesus "warned his disciples not to tell anyone that he was the Messiah" (v. 20). Since people had the wrong concept of the Messiah, they would only misunderstand if the disciples used that word for Jesus.

A Messiah who dies

Jesus then taught his disciples what his role as Messiah really was. It was not to raise an army or bring prosperity. "Jesus began to explain to his disciples that he must go to Jerusalem and suffer many things at the hands of the elders, the chief priests and the teachers of the law, and that he must be killed and on the third day be raised to life" (v. 21). The Son of God had to die and be raised.

This was so far out of Peter's concept that "Peter took him aside and began to rebuke him." Just a few minutes before, Peter had proclaimed Jesus to be a representative of God; now he tries to correct him. "'Never, Lord!' he said. 'This shall never happen to you!'" (v. 22). We can prevent that, he seemed to say.

But Jesus told him that he was completely wrong: "Get behind me, Satan! You are a stumbling block to me; you do not have in mind the concerns of God, but merely human concerns" (v. 23). Through his ignorance and preconceptions, Peter was tempting Jesus to use power for his own benefit, just as Satan had tempted Jesus earlier. But the Son of God did not come to serve himself—he came to give himself.

Jesus had a different approach: "Those who want to be my disciples must deny themselves and take up their cross and follow me. For those who want to save their life will lose it, but those who lose their life for me will find it" (vv. 24-25). Jesus is not talking just about martyrs—he is also talking about people who lose their lives metaphorically, giving up self-centeredness, egoism and self-seeking. The selfish life will fail, but if we give our lives to the service of Jesus, we enter new life, eternal life.

"What good will it be for someone to gain the whole world, yet forfeit their soul? Or what can anyone give in exchange for their soul?" (v. 26). Even if you conquer the entire Roman Empire, what good would it do you, if you use military methods to do it? You would then be no better than the Romans. The bigger battle, and the real reason that we need a Messiah, is spiritual transformation, transformation from the stress, fear and anxious care of selfish living to the inner rest and peace of life in Jesus Christ.

Things to think about

- What kind of "messiah" do people look for today?
- How do modern hopes and desires affect my expectations of what I want Jesus to do for me?
- Is special revelation still required for people to say that Jesus is the Messiah?
- Does the church today have the power to bind and loose?
- In what way do Christians lose their lives for Jesus?

MATTHEW 18: PARABLE OF THE UNFORGIVING SERVANT

By Joseph Tkach

It's hard to forgive

Jesus often said that God is merciful. But he also said, in a statement that can send chills up the spine, "If you do not forgive others, neither will your Father forgive your trespasses" (Matt. 6:15, NRSV in this chapter). Do we have to forgive everyone? Apparently so—yet no one does it perfectly. We don't do anything perfectly. So how can we ever hope for the Father to forgive us?

Examples

After a brief romance, George and Judy married. After an equally brief marriage, Judy walked out on him, crushing his ego like an eggshell on a railroad track. Even 10 years later, George has deep scars from his wound. Is Judy's "sorry, but I want to move on" an apology? Is there ever an acceptable apology for that sort of betrayal?

Bob was the youngest child in a family of seven. He "borrowed" all of his parents' money and lost it in gambling. He's broke now, and the older siblings have to take care of the elderly parents. How can they forgive Bob, when they are still suffering from what he did?

Or perhaps you know someone like Susan, Chris or Karl. Susan was abused by her stepfather, and 30 years later she still struggles with a distorted self-image. Chris was paralyzed in an accident caused by a drunk driver. Karl was left an orphan when his father committed suicide. The sinners are dead, and can't repent or apologize. Can these victims forgive the people who caused them such pain, or would that trivialize the sin?

What other choice do we have, though? If we hang on to anger, it will eventually eat us from the inside out, like acid in an iron pot. We will become bitter, ulcerated, depressed and unpleasant—we add to our own damage and pain. Anger raises our blood pressure and hurts our heart. For our own health, we need to forgive—but it's hard to forgive.

Forgiving another believer

"Peter came to Jesus and asked, 'Lord, how many times shall I forgive my brother when he sins against me? Up to seven times?' Jesus answered, 'I tell you, not seven times, but seventy-seven times'" (Matt. 18:21-22, NIV).

Imagine that someone in the church has hurt your feelings, and the person says "sorry." And he or she does it again, and says "sorry." And it happens again, and again you hear "sorry." And again, and again, and again. At what point are you going to say, "I don't think you're really sorry?" Maybe the person *isn't* sorry, but Jesus says to forgive them anyway, even 77 times. Try saying "I forgive you" that many times! It might be good therapy.

Jesus said "forgive," not "forget," and there is an important difference. Jesus has not forgotten who betrayed him, or deserted him, or ordered his execution, but Jesus does not harbor grudges about it. He wants those people to accept the forgiveness that he offers—he died for them as well as for everyone else. (When the Bible says that God does not remember our sins any more, it is not talking about forgetfulness—it is using the word *remember* in the sense of taking action on something. Ex. 2:24 is an example of this meaning of "remember.")

Jesus then told a parable that explains why we should forgive:

> Therefore, the kingdom of heaven is like a king who wanted to settle accounts with his servants. As he began the settlement, a man who owed him ten thousand talents [an enormous amount] was brought to him. Since he was not able to pay, the master ordered that he and his wife and his children and all that he had be sold to repay the debt. (Matthew 18:23-25).

The king represents God, and the debt corresponds to our sins. We are totally unable to pay for our sins. Even selling ourselves into slavery would pay only a small fraction of the debt. We can't work our way out of this one.

> The servant fell on his knees before him. "Be patient with me," he begged, "and I will pay back everything." The servant's master took pity on him, canceled the debt and let him go. (verses 26-27)

We can't pay our debt, but if we ask for mercy, God will give us more than we ask. That's what the kingdom of God is like. (As an aside here, we can see that the servant didn't have a totally accurate understanding of God's grace. He asked for mercy, but it seems that he still thought he could do something to repay his debt. That's like a lot of Christians today, who don't really believe they are forgiven unless they have done some kind of penance. Yet God forgives them anyway, even if they don't understand how sweeping his forgiveness really is.)

So far, so good. It would be a great parable if Jesus just stopped right here. But Jesus did not stop here, and the second part of the parable makes me squirm a little. But I have to remember that Peter's question is not whether *he* is forgiven, but whether he has to forgive others—and this is the task that we frequently face.

The unmerciful servant

> But when that servant went out, he found one of his fellow servants who owed him a hundred denarii. He grabbed him and began to choke him. "Pay back what you owe me!" he demanded. (verse 28)

The first servant was determined to pay off his own debt by collecting every cent he could. A hundred denarii was a significant amount, but it was only a tiny fraction of the 10,000 talents. But every penny counts, the servant must have thought, and he even used a little violence to underscore his determination to collect. Christians today do this as well. When they think they have to earn God's respect through obedience and good works, they look down on people who aren't trying as hard as they are.

> His fellow servant fell to his knees and begged him, 'Be patient with me, and I will pay you back' [which is what the first servant had said to his master]. But he refused. Instead, he went off and had the man thrown into prison until he could pay the debt. (vs. 29-30)

He wanted the man's relatives to cough up the money to get the guy out of jail. He was playing hardball in a desperate attempt to gather enough cash to impress the king with his sincerity.

When the other servants saw what had happened, they were greatly distressed and went and told their master everything that had happened. Then the master called the servant in. "You wicked servant," he said, "I canceled all that debt of yours because you begged me to. Shouldn't you have had mercy on your fellow servant just as I had on you?" (vs. 31-33)

This chapter is about life in a community, not just between one person and God. This is a small reminder in this parable that our actions affect other people, and that we should encourage one another to give mercy, just as we have been given mercy.

Here is where the parable turns into a warning:

In anger his master turned him over to the jailers to be tortured, until he should pay back all he owed. This is how my heavenly Father will treat each of you unless you forgive your brother from your heart. (vs. 34-35)

Shocking!—Jesus represents God as taking away the forgiveness he once gave, and inflicting punishment, knowing quite well that the man will never be able to "pay back all he owed."

But Jesus is not attempting to tell us about the nature of eternal punishment—he is simply presenting this as a warning, with terms appropriate to the parable, that we must forgive others not grudgingly, but from the heart.

Faulty forgiveness

But is Jesus laying on us an impossible burden? It is easy to say "you are forgiven," but it is difficult to mean it in our heart. Aren't we still angry at the injustice that was done to us? Don't we still hurt when we think about it? Don't we still want the person to be punished for what was done? What are we to do with the vial of bitterness we have accumulated in our thoughts?

If this parable had been longer, maybe it would have gone something like this:

"And the wicked servant said, 'O my king, you are right. You have been patient with me; I should be just as patient with my fellow servants. Please do not throw me in jail. Have mercy on me again. I will forgive the people who ask me for mercy.' And the king said, 'You are forgiven.'

"And the wicked servant went out and found a woman who owed him 50 denarii, and he demanded to be repaid within a week. The woman was exceedingly sorrowful, and sold herself into slavery to pay the debt. And since she did not ask for mercy, none was given.

"The other servants found out about this and reported it to the king, and the king was angry and called the wicked servant in again, saying: 'You wicked servant! I forgave your huge debt because you asked me to. Can you not see that the poor woman wanted mercy even though she was afraid to ask?' Therefore I will throw you into outer darkness, where there will be weeping and gnashing of teeth.'

"The wicked servant then said: 'O my king, you are right again. If you forgive me this time, I will sell some of my possessions to redeem the woman from slavery.' 'Well done,' said the king, 'you may go.' And the wicked servant went out and straightway forgot what he had promised.

"And he was reported to the king again, was threatened with punishment again, asked for mercy again, and was forgiven again. And I ask you, how many times will the king forgive—seven times? Nay, he will do it seventy-seven times. That is what the kingdom of heaven is like. God is even more merciful than what he tells us to be."

In other words, God even forgives our imperfect attempts at forgiveness, as long as we look to him for mercy.

The key to forgiving

The better we understand that we are forgiven, the better we can forgive others. That does not mean thinking (as the wicked servant may have), "Thanks for your patience; I will still try to repay all that I owe." If we have that attitude, then we still overestimate our abilities, and we will still expect people to pay all that they owe us—groveling for everything they've done to us.

But the truth (which the wicked servant could have known, if he had listened carefully) is that when God forgives us, we are forgiven. There is no debt to repay. There's nothing to work off, no penance to perform, no need to prove how sincere we were this time. It's forgiven—it's gone.

Another point from the parable that will help us forgive others: We have been forgiven an enormous debt; the sins that people commit against us are much smaller. Even if someone beats you to a bloody mess and nails you to die on a cross, God has forgiven *you* more than that. Perhaps you find that hard to believe, as I do, but this is the point of what Jesus is saying, and he has earned the right to say it.

Forgiveness does not mean that we pretend like nothing ever happened. It does not mean trusting a swindler with money, trusting a wife-beater to not get abusive again, or appointing a child-molester to be a youth pastor. However, forgiving means that we do not harbor grudges, we do not seek vengeance. It means letting go of our need to get even. It means praying for our enemies. It means seeing ourselves in their shoes, knowing that God has, for the sake of Christ, forgiven us all our sins too. No groveling required. God does not want us to sin again, but his mercy lasts forever.

God wants us to forgive, and he knows that it's hard. He wants us to obey him in everything, and he knows that we don't. That's why our salvation does not depend on our performance, but on the righteousness of Christ. Our salvation does not depend on our performance in keeping the law, or in having enough faith, or in forgiving as well as we ought. In all these areas, we are sinners who fall short of the glory of God.

Our salvation depends not on us, but on Christ, and on our connection to him. He is the one who forgives with the sincerity and frequency that is required, and when our lives are hidden in Christ (Col. 3:3), God attributes Christ's perfect obedience, including his perfect forgiveness, to us.

God wants us to forgive others because he forgives us. He forgives us far more generously than 77 times. The point is that we are to realize our need for mercy, look to him for mercy, depend on his mercy, and instead of harboring our hurts and nursing our grievances, we need to ask him to help us begin to forgive others.

In this world of sin and ignorance, offenses are inevitable. We've all been hurt. So, what's the worst thing that has happened to *you?* What resentment do you carry? For our own good, we need to let our resentments go. Jesus will help us—that's something worth praying about.

PARABLE OF WORKERS
IN THE VINEYARD

By Joseph Tkach

A parable of unfairness

The parable of the workers in the vineyard is in Matthew 20. Some men worked all day long in the heat of the day. Some worked only half a day, and some worked only one hour, but they all got paid the same amount, a day's wage. Some got exactly what they agreed to, but others got more. However, the men who worked all day long said, "That's not fair. We worked all day long, and it's not fair to pay us the same as those who worked less" (my paraphrase; see verse 12).

But the men who worked all day got exactly what they had agreed to before they began work (verse 4). The only reason they got upset was because other people got more than they deserved.

What did the paymaster say? He said: "Don't I have the right to do what I want with my own money? Or are you envious because I am generous?" (verse 15).

The boss said he would give them a fair day's wage for a fair day's work, and that's what he did—and yet the workers complained. Why? Because they compared themselves with others and they got the shorter end of the stick. They got their hopes up, and then they were disappointed.

But the landowner said: "I am doing you no wrong. If you think it's not fair, the problem is in what you expected, not in what you actually got. If it hadn't been for the amount I paid the newcomers, you would be quite happy with what I gave you. The problem is in your expectations, not in what I did. You accuse me of being bad, simply because I was good to someone else (see verse 15).

How would you react to this? What would you think if your boss gave a bonus to the newest employees, but not to the old faithful workers? It would not be very good for morale, would it? But Jesus was not giving us payroll advice here—he was telling a parable about the kingdom of God (verse 1).

The parable reflected something that was happening in Jesus' ministry. God was giving salvation to people who hadn't worked very hard, and the religious leaders said: "That's not fair. You can't be generous to them. We've been working hard, and they have hardly been working." And Jesus replied, "I am bringing good news to sinners, not to the righteous." His teaching threatened to undermine the normal motive for doing good.

Where do we fit in?

We might like to think that we have worked all day long, bearing the burdens and the heat of the day, deserving a good reward. But we have not.

It doesn't matter how long you've been in the church or how many sacrifices you have made; those are nothing in comparison to what God is giving us. Paul worked harder than any of us; he made more sacrifices for the gospel than we realize, but he counted it all as a loss for Christ. It was nothing.

The time we've spent in the church is nothing to God. The work we've done is nothing compared to what he can do. Even at our best, as another parable says, we are unprofitable servants (Luke 17:10). Jesus has bought our entire lives; he has fair claim on every thought and every action. We cannot possibly give him anything on top of that—even if we do everything he commands.

We are really like the workers who worked only one hour and got a whole day's wage. We just barely got started, and we were paid like we actually did something useful. Is that fair? Maybe we shouldn't even ask the question. If the judgment is in our favor, we shouldn't ask for another opinion!

Do we think of ourselves as people who have worked long and hard? Do we think we deserve more than we are getting? Or do we see ourselves as people who are getting an undeserved gift, regardless of how long we've worked?

THE HERO WHO WOULDN'T

At several times in Jesus' ministry, he attracted crowds of people who wanted to make him king, but he refused. He sent them away, or he slipped away, because if thousands of people started to proclaim him king, there would be a confrontation with the Romans and the Jewish leaders, and it was not yet time for that. But eventually the time came.

It was less than one week before his crucifixion, on what is now called Palm Sunday. Jesus told two of his disciples where they would find a donkey, and what they were to do with it.

> As they approached Jerusalem and came to Bethphage on the Mount of Olives, Jesus sent two disciples, saying to them, 'Go to the village ahead of you, and at once you will find a donkey tied there, with her colt by her. Untie them and bring them to me. If anyone says anything to you, tell him that the Lord needs them, and he will send them right away. (Matthew 21:1-3)

The Lord needs them — this is what a king might say when conscripting supplies from the people. We are taking this because we need it. In this case, Jesus needed the donkey. What did he need it for? It was just for show — a very special show — a symbolism that would tell the people that Jesus was the Messiah, the king.

A king of peace

Verses 4-5: "This took place to fulfill what was spoken through the prophet: 'Say to the Daughter of Zion, "See, your king comes to you, gentle and riding on a donkey, on a colt, the foal of a donkey."'" Jesus was doing this to fulfill a prophecy of Zechariah 9:9. Zion's king was predicted to come on a donkey.

At first glance, this does not seem like a very kingly way to come into the city. In the Roman world, kings rode horses, sitting up high, leading their armies. The military parade showed how powerful a king they were.

But this was not the sort of king that Jesus was, and it was not the sort of king that Zechariah had predicted. Zechariah did not predict a military hero coming back from battle. He was predicting a king of peace, a king who did not need to show off his army.

The context of Zechariah makes it clear. The very next verse in Zechariah says: "I will take away the chariots from Ephraim and the war-horses from Jerusalem, and the battle bow will be broken. He will proclaim peace to the nations. His rule will extend from sea to sea and from the Euphrates to the ends of the earth."

This king will have peace. Weapons will not be needed. War horses will not be needed. The king rides on a donkey as a symbol of peace.

The problem is that many people in Jesus' day didn't keep this part of the prophecy in mind. They knew from Zechariah that the Messiah would ride into town on a donkey, but they also expected the Messiah to wage war, to bring peace through military victory.

Jesus had another plan in mind, and that is part of the story. Let's pick it up again in Matthew 21:6-7: "The disciples went and did as Jesus had instructed them. They brought the donkey and the colt, placed their cloaks on them, and Jesus sat on them." Jesus sat on the cloaks.

Verse 8: "A very large crowd spread their cloaks on the road, while others cut branches from the trees and spread them on the road."

This parade must have gone at a slow pace. The donkey wasn't galloping. It was a leisurely procession that gave people enough time to cut tree branches and line the road with branches and cloaks. This was a sign of great honor in that society. People don't throw their clothes into the street just for fun. It meant a great deal. It showed great honor and deference. The people knew that the Messiah would come into town on a donkey, and Jesus was practically blowing a trumpet and saying, I am the Messiah.

This event is commonly called "the triumphal entry" into Jerusalem. But there is little indication of triumph here. There are no spoils of war, no military parade. Jesus is using ordinary things — little things. He uses a donkey and a colt. He uses the clothes that people take off on the spur of the moment. Jesus uses little things.

"The crowds that went ahead of him and those that followed shouted, 'Hosanna to the Son of David!' 'Blessed is he who comes in the name of the Lord!' 'Hosanna in the highest!'" (verse 9).

The people were singing Psalm 118, a messianic psalm, and they sang it for Jesus. Hosanna means "save us." It was a prayer that said, "We need to be saved." It was praise because it said, "You are capable of saving us." They called Jesus the Son of David —the Messiah. They said he was coming in the name of the Lord. This is the King God had sent them.

"Save us now, O King of Israel! We welcome you. We honor you with our palm branches. We pave the streets for you with the clothes off our backs. We praise you and look to you for the salvation we need." It must have been an air of tremendous excitement. People had this sense that the most exciting moment in their life was just around the corner.

But not everyone liked the party. The Pharisees complained. "Jesus," they said, "tell your people to stop this. They are getting too excited. Tell them to be quiet."

And Jesus said, "If these people didn't do it, then God would raise up stones to sing praises for me. This is something that has to be done in God's plan. I have to be hailed as a king."

Verses 10-11: "When Jesus entered Jerusalem, the whole city was stirred and asked, 'Who is this?' The crowds answered, 'This is Jesus, the prophet from Nazareth in Galilee.'"

Who is this man who rides into town on a donkey, who claims to be the Messiah fulfilling Zechariah's prophecy? It is Jesus.

A great disappointment

If we fast forward a few days and a few chapters, to chapter 27, we will find that the crowds were yelling something quite different. They were yelling "Crucify him, crucify him!" They were jeering: "If you are the king of Israel, then save yourself."

One day, the crowds were praising Jesus as a hero. Not long after that, they were so angry at him that they wanted him to be killed. What happened to turn the tide of public opinion? The Gospel writers don't tell us right here, but we see the picture in other parts of the Gospels. The people were looking for a king who would drive the Romans out of Judea. They were looking for a king who would give them food, safety, and prosperity – material things.

But Jesus just wasn't that sort of king. The people had wanted to make him king before, and he had refused,

143

because they had the wrong idea about what a king is. Even his own disciples had the wrong idea. Jesus was the Messiah, but not the sort of Messiah they were looking for.

The people hailed him as a hero, but he wouldn't perform the way a hero was supposed to. He wouldn't do what they wanted. They called him a Savior, but he didn't bring the kind of salvation they wanted. Instead of kicking the Romans out of Judea, he kicked the Jewish moneychangers out of the temple — and that's all. This was not a hero — this was a disappointment.

Then, in chapter 21, Jesus told the parable of the tenants, and his conclusion was definitely not a way to win a popularity contest: "The kingdom of God will be taken away from you and given to a people who will produce its fruit" (verse 43).

Jesus is saying that the main problem around here is not the Romans — it is you. You are not producing the fruit you should be for the kingdom of God. The kingdom of God comes by conquering sin, not by conquering foreign armies. Sin is not conquered through physical power, but through righteousness, meekness, and submission. Death, the ultimate enemy, can be conquered only through death.

So Jesus did not do what the people expected. The people were disappointed, and many were angry. That kind of emotional roller coaster can happen sometimes after an intense emotional high. This guy won't be a hero, so get rid of him. Crucify the imposter.

All according to plan

Ironically, this is the very reason that Jesus had come to Jerusalem, because this is the kind of hero he was. He was a hero who would be crucified. He wouldn't do what the people wanted — he was heroic enough to do what the people *needed*. The people's biggest enemy was not the Romans — it was sin. The Romans were a temporary problem; sin was a problem with eternal consequences.

The people were concerned about the quality of life; Jesus was concerned about life itself – eternal life. He came that the people might have life, and the only way they could have it was through his death as a sacrifice for their sins.

The people were singing psalms. They were involved in religious activity. They were preparing for Passover, in worship of God, and yet they were completely unaware of what God was doing in their midst. They were missing the spiritual reason God had come. Even as Jesus rode on a lowly donkey, the people were thinking of power and pageantry. They wanted their king to be like Gentile kings.

Jesus knew all this as he was riding the donkey. He knew that the praises of the people would soon pass away. He knew that he would soon be thrust into public ridicule and shame, pain and death. He knew the people needed exactly that, and he was hero enough to ignore their desires and instead, do what they needed.

What kind of king were the crowds looking for? Someone someone who would give them what they wanted? They were willing to follow Jesus only if he was going in the direction they liked, only if he was going to save them in the way they wanted to be saved — a physical salvation, a peace achieved through violence, and a material prosperity.

They were not willing to follow Jesus, because he was not going the way they wanted him to go. They called him king only as long as he was traveling in the direction they thought was right, but they were not willing to let him re-direct their expectations.

It still happens today

The people had a different priority, a different god. They wanted a god in their own image, instead of God the way he reveals himself to be. Instead of serving God, they wanted God to serve them. That happens today, too. People hail Jesus as their Savior. They sing hosanna. They praise Jesus. They participate in the parade — and yet in time they disappear. Their enthusiasm fades, and they fade away. Jesus is not what they wanted him to be.

When Jesus came into Jerusalem riding on a donkey, people thought he was a king riding into his capital city, where he would sit on a throne. But Jesus was riding into Jerusalem where he knew he would be crucified.

It is the same today. When we follow Jesus, we take up our cross to follow him. If our life is pleasant sometimes, then thank the Lord, but we should never forget that we are following in the footsteps of a crucified hero who disappointed his own people.

We did not become Christian because it was the popular thing to do, or it's what our parents or friends expected us to do. We joined this parade because we believed in Jesus. We believed in a man who saves us through his death. We did not join this parade to get power. We did not join in order to tell Jesus what we want him to do for us. We joined it because we were willing for Jesus to tell us what to do, even if it cost the clothes off of our backs, even if it cost us our lives. We have to be willing to follow Jesus to shame and death, because we know that by doing so, we will also follow him to glory and life forever.

The whole world will someday praise Jesus Christ. Revelation 7:9-10 says,

After this I looked, and there before me was a great multitude that no one could count, from every nation, tribe, people and language, standing before the throne and in front of the Lamb. They were wearing white robes and were holding palm branches in their hands. And they cried out in a loud voice: "Salvation belongs to our God, who sits on the throne, and to the Lamb."

That is a victory song. Salvation belongs to the Lamb who was slain. This will really be a triumphal celebration. Who are these people? The book of Revelation tells us: The people who gave their lives in service to Jesus Christ. The victory celebration is reserved for people who gave their lives. This is the victory of Jesus Christ. This is glory and power and life forever.

But not everyone can see this. In Matthew 21, we see what some people do with Jesus. They praise him, and soon fall away. The disciples were not much different than the crowds, were they? They all fell away. They all lacked faith. They all refused to follow where Jesus was going.

Supernatural help needed

How can we be sure that we are not one of them? We are no better than the crowds, no better than the disciples who fell away. Human strength and power cannot overcome sin and unfaithfulness. That is why Jesus came on a donkey instead of a war-horse. Human strength cannot overcome sin. Spiritual victory comes through meekness, through reliance on God.

It is only through the Holy Spirit that we can have the spiritual strength to be faithful. It is only through the help of the Spirit that we can have faith in a resurrection, so that we can see beyond the things of this world. We have to see beyond the fame that the world can give, and we have to see beyond the shame that the world can give. One is just as fleeting as the other.

And it is only through the Holy Spirit that we can see beyond the wealth of this world, or the good things of this life. Only through the Spirit can we believe in promises of a new heavens and new earth, promises that are so real to us that we are willing to give up the promises that humans make. When we see the beauty of God, the things of this world seem like cheap plastic. When we see the glory of God, the trials of this world seem like momentary troubles.

When we see the joy set before us, only then will we be willing to follow Jesus to his cross. Only then will we let him crucify our sinful desires, to put to death the deeds of the flesh. We have to ask the Holy Spirit to help us see more clearly the things he wants us to see.

It is only through the Holy Spirit that we can understand that we need a hero like Jesus. It is only the Holy Spirit who convicts us of sin, who convinces us that we are sinners in desperate need of spiritual salvation. It is the Holy Spirit who enables us to believe the gospel that we can live only because Jesus died for us, that our sins are forgiven only because he died for us.

It is only the Holy Spirit who convinces us that a crucified hero is exactly the sort of hero we need. It is only then, only when we recognize him for the kind of Savior that he is — and that we need that kind of Savior — that we will be willing to follow him wherever he goes.

People like a Savior full of love and forgiveness. People like a Savior who answers prayers as soon as we ask. But when we find out that our Savior also allows pain in our lives, we are disappointed — even though that pain can help us mature in the faith.

When we find out that our Savior sometimes disciplines us, we don't like it as much, even though his discipline is always motivated by love. When we find out that the Savior also punishes, when we find out that the one who forgives is also one who condemns, we have a Savior that not everybody likes.

But we cannot pick and choose what sort of Savior we are going to welcome. We have to welcome the only Savior that exists, the Savior who is revealed to us in the Bible. We cannot demand a Savior who serves our desires — we have to accept a Savior who takes care of our *needs,* and he lays his life on the line to take care of those needs. We have to trust him in everything else, and we have to follow him wherever he goes, even if he goes into pain and shame.

It is good to sing hosanna. If we didn't do it, God would raise up others to do it. Hosanna must be sung. But we need to remember what it means: "Save us!" We need a Savior, and we need to sing about him. But Jesus wants us to do more than sing — he wants us to follow him, even to the cross, even to where it hurts. We have to give up our expectations of what a Savior should do for us, and be willing to accept what Jesus actually gives us. We can't do this on our own. It must be done by the Holy Spirit working in us, living in us, changing us to be more like Christ.

Join the parade

In the first century, people in Jerusalem had the privilege of participating in a historic parade, now known as the triumphal entry of Jesus Christ. They didn't know it at the time, but they got a chance to see God, and to welcome him. Some of them never knew what had passed them by.

This happens today, too. People hear something about Jesus, and don't realize what an opportunity is passing them by. But others have the chance to praise God, and to welcome him. Can you join the parade? Can you sing Hosanna to the king? Can you follow him even when he goes into the valley of the shadow of death? Can you welcome this king into your life? Can you let him take your life and shape it the way he wants to?

Jesus can use little things. That is his method of triumphal entry. He can say, The Lord needs this. The Lord needs this person. He has a job for this person to do. The Lord needs praise, and he invites us to join this parade — not just for a moment, but for life…eternal. The Lord needs this person. The Lord needs you, and he needs what you have. It may not be much, but it is what he needs.

Are you willing to praise him? Are you willing to follow him? Is he the sort of hero you are willing to follow? Is he the sort of hero you need to follow? If you can accept it, the answer is yes. This is our hero. This is our Savior. This is our King, gentle, riding on a donkey, hearing the people cheer as he rides toward his death.

WHAT MATTHEW 24 TELLS US
ABOUT "THE END"

By Paul Kroll

D.A. Carson, a New Testament scholar, begins his commentary on Matthew 24 with the following words: "Few chapters of the Bible have called forth more disagreement among interpreters than Matthew 24 and its parallels in Mark 13 and Luke 21. The history of the interpretation of this chapter is immensely complex" (*The Expositor's Bible Commentary*, volume 8, page 488).

Carson's statement underlines the difficulties people have encountered when trying to interpret Matthew 24. As we try to understand what Jesus was saying in this chapter, we would do well to approach it with caution and avoid simplistic views and dogmatism.

Seeing things in context

Studying Matthew 24 in the larger context of preceding chapters will help us avoid interpretation pitfalls. We may be surprised to learn that the background to Matthew 24 actually begins at least as far back as chapter 16:21. There, we are given the following summary statement: "From that time Jesus began to explain to his disciples that he must go to Jerusalem and suffer many things at the hands of the elders, chief priests and teachers of the law, and that he must be killed and on the third day be raised to life."

By his comments, Jesus set the stage for what appeared to be to the disciples a showdown in Jerusalem between himself and the religious authorities. He continued telling his disciples about this imminent conflict as they made their way to Jerusalem (20:17-19).

During the time Jesus was explaining that he was to suffer at Jerusalem, he took Peter, James and John up a high mountain. There, they experienced the transfiguration (17:1-13). This of itself must have made the disciples wonder whether the establishment of the kingdom of God was close at hand (17:10-12).

Jesus also told the disciples they would sit on 12 thrones judging Israel "when the Son of Man sits on his glorious throne" (19:28). No doubt, this sparked additional questions about the time and manner of the coming of the kingdom of God. Jesus' talking about the kingdom even prompted the mother of James and John to ask him to give special positions in the kingdom to her two sons (20:20-21).

Then came the triumphal entry into Jerusalem, in which Jesus rode into the city on a donkey (21:1-11). This, said Matthew, fulfilled what the prophet

Zechariah had spoken, and which was thought to refer to the Messiah. The entire city was stirred, wondering what would happen as Jesus arrived. In Jerusalem, he overturned the moneylender's tables and took other actions to demonstrate his messianic authority (21:12-27). "Who is this?" people asked in response (21:10).

Next, in 21:43 Jesus told the chief priests and elders of the people: "I tell you that the kingdom of God will be taken away from you and given to a people who will produce its fruit." His audience knew he was talking about them. Jesus' statement could have been taken as an implication that he was ready to establish his messianic kingdom, but the religious leaders would not be a part of it.

Is the kingdom to be established?

The disciples who heard this must have wondered what was going to happen. Was Jesus ready to announce his messiahship? Was he ready to put down the Roman authority? Was he on the verge of bringing in the kingdom of God? Would there be a war, and what would happen to Jerusalem and the temple?

We now come to Matthew 22 and verse 15. Here the scene begins with the Pharisees laying plans to trap Jesus by asking him a question regarding the paying of taxes. They hoped to use his answer as the basis for accusing Jesus of rebelling against the Roman authority. But Jesus answered rather cleverly, and their plan was foiled.

That same day the Sadducees also had an encounter with Jesus (22:23-32). Not believing in the resurrection, they asked him a trick question about seven brothers marrying one woman. Whose wife would she be in the resurrection?, they asked. Jesus answered them indirectly by telling them they didn't understand their own Scriptures. He confounded them by pointing out that there is no marriage in the kingdom.

Next, the Pharisees and Sadducees together tested Jesus on the meaning of the greatest commandment in the law (22:36). He answered wisely by quoting Leviticus 19:18 and Deuteronomy 6:5. Then Jesus asked them a trick question about whose son the Messiah was to be (22:42). They did not know how to answer him: "No one could say a word in reply, and from that day on no one dared to ask him any more questions" (22:46).

Chapter 23 shows Jesus criticizing the teachers of the law and the Pharisees. Toward the end of the chapter, Jesus talked about sending them prophets, wise men and teachers whom they would flog, pursue, kill and crucify. He placed the responsibility of all the slain prophets on their shoulders. The tension was obviously mounting, and the disciples must have been wondering about the meaning of these hostile encounters. Was Jesus about to take control as Messiah?

Then, in a prayer to Jerusalem, Jesus spoke of its house as becoming desolate. This is connected to his cryptic comment: "For I tell you, you will not see me again until you say, 'Blessed is he who comes in the name of the Lord'" (23:39). The disciples must have become increasingly puzzled, curious and anxious about the things Jesus was saying. Was he about to proclaim himself?

Temple to be destroyed

After these things, Jesus left the temple. As he was walking away, his breathless disciples pointed to its buildings. In Mark's words, they said, "Look, Teacher! What massive stones! What magnificent buildings!" (13:1). Luke says the disciples remarked how the temple was "adorned with beautiful stones and with gifts dedicated to God" (21:5).

Think of what must have been going through the disciples' minds. Jesus' comments about Jerusalem's desolation and his confrontation with the religious leaders both frightened and excited the disciples. They must have wondered why he was speaking of impending doom on Judaism and its institutions. Wasn't the Messiah coming to glorify both? By their comments about the temple, it seems as if the concerned and confused disciples were thinking, Surely, nothing can happen to this beautiful temple in which God dwells!?

Jesus then made the disciples more curious and frightened. He brushed aside their lavish praise of the temple. "Do you see all these things?" he asked. "I tell you the truth, not one stone here will be left on another; every one will be thrown down" (24:2).

This must have been shocking to the disciples. They thought the Messiah was going to save Jerusalem and the temple, not allow both to be destroyed. As Jesus spoke of these things, the disciples must have thought about the end of gentile rulership and the glory of Israel, both which are prophesied so many times in the Hebrew Scriptures. They knew these events would occur at "the time of the end" (Daniel 8:17; 11:35, 40; 12:4, 9). It was at this time that the Messiah would appear or "come" to usher in the kingdom of God. This meant Israel would arise to national greatness as the spearhead of that kingdom.

When will this happen?

The disciples, who believed Jesus was that Messiah, were naturally anxious to know if the "time of the end" had come. There was great expectation that

Jesus was about to announce that he was the messiah (John 12:12-18). It's not surprising, then, that the disciples pressed Jesus about the nature and timing of his "coming."

As Jesus was sitting on the Mount of Olives, the excited disciples came to him privately to get some inside information. "'Tell us,' they said, 'when will this happen, and what will be the sign of your coming and of the end of the age?'" (24:3). They wanted to know when the things Jesus said about Jerusalem would take place, for they undoubtedly associated these with the end of the age and his "coming."

When the disciples asked about his "coming," they didn't have a "second" coming in mind. In their thinking, the Messiah would come and immediately establish his government in Jerusalem, and it would last "forever." There would be no "first" and "second" coming.

There is another vital point to notice about Matthew 24:3, for it is a kind of summary statement of the content of chapter 24. Let us repeat the disciples' question, italicizing some important words: "Tell us," they said, "when will *this* happen, and what will be the *sign* of your coming and of the *end* of the age?" (24:3). They wanted to know when the things Jesus said about Jerusalem would take place, for they associated these with the end of the age and his "coming."

Disciples' three questions

The disciples were really asking three questions. First, they wanted to know when "this" would happen. The "this" could be a reference to the destruction of Jerusalem and the temple, which Jesus had just finished describing as being threatened with destruction. Second, they wanted to know what the "sign" of his coming was, which as we shall see, Jesus finally gave them in 24:30. Third, the disciples also wanted to know when the "end of the age" would occur. This is something Jesus told the disciples they could not know (24:36).

If we separate out the three questions, and see how Jesus answered each of them, we can clear up a number of problems or misinterpretations associated with Matthew 24. Jesus was telling his disciples that Jerusalem and the temple (the "this") would, indeed, be destroyed i n *their* day. But the "sign" they asked about, Jesus said, would be associated with his coming, not with the destruction of the city. Finally, as to the disciples' third question, Jesus said, no one could know the answer to the question of when he would return and "the end" of the age would occur.

In Matthew 24 are three questions, and each is answered individually in Jesus' reply. We can still have Jesus' return and the "end of the age" occur in the future, and Jerusalem be destroyed in the past, in A.D. 70, just as Jesus prophesied.

That is not to say the disciples separated out the destruction of Jerusalem from "the end," because they almost certainly didn't. And they most likely thought that the events would occur almost immediately.

Let us see how these questions play out in Matthew 24. First, we note that Jesus didn't seem particularly interested in talking about the circumstances of "the end." It was his disciples who provoked the questions, and Jesus obliged them by providing some comments.

We also realize that almost certainly the disciples' questions about "the end" were based on a wrong conclusion—that all the events would occur almost immediately, and all at the same time. Hence, it's not surprising that they thought Jesus' "coming" as Messiah was extremely close, in the sense that it might happen within days or weeks. Still, they wanted a physical "sign" of his coming as a confirmation. With this private and secret knowledge they would be able to place themselves at the most advantageous position when Jesus made his move.

We should see Jesus' comments in Matthew 24 in that context. In short, the disciples provoke the discussion. They think Jesus is about to assume power, and they want to know exactly when this will happen. They want a preparatory sign. But the disciples totally misunderstood Jesus' mission.

"The end" is not yet

Rather than answering the disciples' questions on their terms, Jesus used the occasion to teach them three important things. One, he taught them that the scenario they were asking about was much more complicated than their simplistic notions. Two, they could not know when Jesus would "come," or as we would say, "return." Three, they should worry about or "watch" their relationship with God and not worry about "watching" world or local events.

Let's now notice how Jesus' conversation with his disciples unfolded, keeping these principles and the prior discussion in mind. The first thing he did was warn the disciples not to be deceived by traumatic events that might make it appear as though "the end" was near (Matthew 24:4-8). Tumultuous things would happen in the world, but "the end is still to come" (verse 6).

Next, Jesus told his disciples that they would be persecuted and put to death (24:9-13). How shocking that must have seemed! They must have wondered, "What is all this talk about persecution and death?" The Messiah's people would be triumphant and victorious, not butchered and destroyed, they thought.

Jesus then began talking about a gospel to be preached to the whole world. After this, "the end" would come (24:14). This must have also been confusing to the disciples. They probably thought the Messiah would "come" first, then establish his kingdom. Only after that would the word of the Lord go forth to all the earth (Isaiah 2:1-4).

Next, Jesus seemed to backtrack and forecast a dire warning for the temple. The abomination of desolation would be seen in the holy place, and those in Judea would have to flee to the mountains (24:15-16). These would be dreadful times indeed for the Jews. "For then there will be great distress, unequaled from the beginning of the world until now—and never to be equaled again," said Jesus (24:21). Things would get so bad that no one would survive if those days weren't cut short.

Though Jesus mentioned what would happen in the world at large, Jesus was talking primarily about what would happen in Judea and Jerusalem. Luke uses the phrase "there will be great distress in the *land*" to describe the context of Jesus' comments (Luke 21:23). The temple, Jerusalem and Judea were the focus of Jesus' warning, not the entire world. The warning Jesus gave about impending doom was primarily for Jews in Jerusalem and Judea. The events of A.D. 66-70 confirmed this.

Flight on the Sabbath?

It's not surprising, then, that Jesus said, "Pray that your flight will not take place in winter or on the Sabbath" (24:20). Some have wondered why he would make this statement if the church was not required to observe the Sabbath? Since the Sabbath is no longer a concern for Christians, why would it be mentioned as a significant problem?

The Jews believed it was wrong to take long journeys on the Sabbath. They apparently even had a measurement for the maximum distance that could be traveled on this day, which was called a "Sabbath day's walk" or journey (Acts 1:12). In Luke's example it was the distance between the Mount of Olives, on the perimeter of Jerusalem, and the city itself. But Jesus said that people who were in Judea would need to flee far away into the hills. A Sabbath's day walk would not get them out of harm's way. Jesus knew that those listening to him believed you should not do the kind of traveling that his warning required.

This explains why Jesus told his disciples to pray that their flight would not have to occur on the Sabbath. He gave this admonition in the context of their current understanding of the Law of Moses. We can paraphrase Jesus' thought in this way: I know you don't believe in traveling long distances on the Sabbath, and you won't do it because of what you think the law demands. So if the things to befall Jerusalem fall on the Sabbath, you will be caught and killed. I can then only offer you this advice: You better pray that the need to flee doesn't occur on the Sabbath. Even if they did choose to flee on the Sabbath, the restrictions imposed by other Jews would make escape difficult.

As stated earlier, we can understand this part of Jesus' explanation to refer to the destruction of Jerusalem, which occurred in A.D. 70. Jewish Christians in Jerusalem, who still kept the Law of Moses (Acts 21:17-26), would be caught up in these events and have to flee. They would have to deal with their belief about the Sabbath regulations, if circumstances demanded a flight on that day.

Still not the "sign"

Meanwhile, Jesus continued with his discourse, which had the purpose of answering the disciples' three questions about when he would come. But we note that so far all he has done is tell them when he will *not* come. Jesus has separated out the calamity to occur at Jerusalem from the "sign" and the coming of "the end."

At this point, the disciples must have thought that the destruction in Jerusalem and Judea was the "sign" of the end they were looking for. But they were mistaken, and Jesus pointed out their error. Jesus said, "If anyone says to you, 'Look, here is the Christ!' or, 'There he is!' do not believe it" (24:23). Do not believe it? What were the disciples to make of this? They must have wondered, We asked when Jesus would establish the kingdom and we asked him to give us a sign of this event, and he keeps talking about when the end is *not* and everything that *looks* like a sign he says *isn't* a sign.

Nevertheless, Jesus continued to tell the disciples when he would not come or appear. "If anyone tells you, 'There he is, out in the desert,' do not go out; or, 'Here he is, in the inner rooms,' do not believe it" (24:26). Jesus was driving home the point that his disciples should not be deceived either by world events or by people claiming to know when the "sign" of "the end" had occurred. Perhaps he was even meaning to tell them that the fall of Jerusalem and the temple were not the harbinger of "the end."

Now we come to verse 29, where Jesus began telling the disciples about the "sign" of his coming, which was the answer to their second question. The sun and moon would be darkened and "stars" (perhaps comets or meteorites) would fall from the sky (24:29). The solar system itself would be shaken.

Finally, Jesus gave the disciples the "sign" they were waiting for. He said: "At that time the *sign* of the Son of Man will appear in the sky, and all the nations of the earth will mourn. They will see the Son of Man coming on the clouds of the sky, with power and great glory" (24:30).

Basically, the "sign" of Jesus' coming, as he gave it, was his coming! There is a lesson here for us. Quite simply, there is *no* advance sign of Jesus' coming for us to be able to predict. He comes when he comes, and the people who are then alive will know it when it happens.

Next, Jesus asked the disciples to learn a lesson from the fig tree (24:32-34). As soon as the tree's twigs got tender and its leaves came out, they knew summer was near. "Even so," said Jesus, "when you see all these things, you know that it is near, right at the door" (24:33).

"All these things"

What are "all these things"? Are they only wars, famines and earthquakes in various places? No. These are only the beginning of sorrows. There are many other sorrows as well before "the end." Does "all these things" end at the appearance of false preachers and the preaching of the gospel? No, again. Is "all these things" fulfilled with the distress in Jerusalem and the destruction of the temple? No, it is not. What, then, must "all things" include?

Before we answer, let us digress a moment to describe what may have been an after-the-fact lesson that the church of the apostles' day had to learn, and which the synoptic Gospels talk about. The fall of Jerusalem in A.D. 70, the destruction of the temple, and the death of many Jewish religious leaders (and at least some of the apostles) must have been a surprise to the church. It's almost certain the church believed that Jesus would return right after these events. But he didn't return, and some Christians must have been disturbed by this fact.

However, the Gospels show that much more had to happen than just the destruction of the city and temple before Jesus would return. The church should not assume that because Jerusalem fell and Jesus did not return that it had been misled. The Gospels repeated Jesus' thought for the benefit of the church: Until you see the "sign" of the Son of Man appear in the sky, do not listen to those who say he has already come, or is about to come.

"No one knows"

We now come to the real lesson that Jesus wanted to get across in the dialogue of Matthew 24. That is, Jesus' discourse in Matthew 24 is not so much to be taken as a prophecy, but as a Christian living lesson. Matthew 24 is Jesus' warning that his disciples always need to be spiritually ready precisely because they *cannot* know when he will return. The parables in Matthew 25 continue that same theme.

In Matthew 24:36, Jesus said, "No one knows about that day or hour, not even the angels in heaven, nor the Son, but only the Father." This is Jesus' plain statement that he did not know when the end of the age would come.

That may seem shocking, since he was the Son of God, but nonetheless it is clear.

Accepting this point clears up a lot of confusion about chapter 24. It tells us that Jesus was not meaning to prophesy about the specific time of "the end" or of his return, since he himself did not know when it would be. Matthew 24 was to be a lesson in spiritual awareness, not awareness of world events nor a "when" prophecy. To repeat, Jesus could not have been prophesying about when "the end" would happen. How could he have, if he said he didn't know when his return would occur?

What we see in subsequent history is that Jerusalem has been the focal point of many turbulent events and times. For example, in A.D. 1099, the Christian Crusaders surrounded Jerusalem and massacred all the inhabitants. And during World War I, in 1917, British General Allenby took the city from the Turkish empire. And we are all quite aware of the central role Jerusalem and Judea continue to play in the strife between Jews and Arabs.

To summarize, Jesus told his disciples that the answer to their question about when the end would come was: "You can't know it, and not even I know it." That seems to be a difficult lesson to learn. After his resurrection, the disciples still pressed Jesus on the matter. They asked: "Lord, are you at this time going to restore the kingdom to Israel?" (Acts 1:6). Again, Jesus told them: "It is not for you to know the times or dates the Father has set by his own authority" (verse 7).

Despite Jesus' clear teaching, many Christians throughout the centuries have repeated the mistake of the apostles. Many have tried to prognosticate when "the end" would come, and have almost always said it would be "very soon." But history has proven Jesus right and every prognosticator wrong. Quite simply, we cannot know when "the end" will come.

What are we to "watch"?

So what are we to do in the meantime, while we await Jesus' return? Jesus gave the answer to his disciples, and it is our answer as well. He said: "Keep watch, because you do not know on what day your Lord will come.... So you also must be ready, because the Son of Man will come at an hour when you do not expect him" (24:42, 44).

Watching world events is not what Jesus was speaking about here. What all Christians must "watch" is their relationship with God. They are always to be ready to meet their Maker.

Jesus then went on to describe in the rest of chapter 24 and throughout chapter 25 what is really important to "watch." In the parable of the faithful servant, Jesus told his disciples to avoid worldly sins and the threat of being overcome by the attractiveness of sin (24:45-51). The lesson? Jesus said, "The master of that servant will come on a day when he does not expect him and at an hour he is not aware of" (24:50).

In the parable of the ten virgins, Jesus repeated his theme (25:1-25). Some of the virgins are not ready when the day of reckoning comes. They are shut out of the kingdom. The lesson? Jesus said: "Keep watch, because you do not know the day or the hour" (25:13).

In the parable of the talents, Jesus spoke of himself as going on a journey (25:14-30). He was probably referring to his stay in heaven before his return. In the meantime, the servants are to be faithful with the things they have been entrusted.

In the parable of the sheep and goats Jesus spoke of the shepherding responsibility the disciples would be given during his absence. Here he switched their thinking from the "when" of his return to the consequences of that return on their eternal life. His coming and the resurrection would be judgment day for them. That is the time when Jesus will separate his sheep (his true followers) from the goats (the evil shepherds).

Jesus presented the parable in terms of the disciples' relationship to his physical needs. They fed him when he was hungry, gave water to him when he was thirsty, invited him in when he was a stranger, and clothed him when he was naked. The disciples were surprised, and they said they never saw him in any of these needy states.

But Jesus had a lesson in shepherding in mind. He said: "I tell you the truth, whatever you did for one of the least of these brothers of mine, you did for me" (25:40). Who is a brother of Jesus? One of his true followers. Jesus, then, was telling his disciples to be good stewards and shepherds of the flock — the church.

Thus ends the long discourse in which Jesus answered the disciples' three questions: When will Jerusalem and the temple be destroyed? What would be the "sign" of his coming? When would "the end" of the age occur?

Jesus' point in brief

Let us summarize the entire discussion. The disciples are concerned by Jesus' teaching that the temple buildings will be destroyed. They ask when this will happen, and when "the end" and his "coming" will occur. As stated earlier, they probably thought that Jesus would then and there take the mantle of messiahship and inaugurate the kingdom of God in all its power.

Jesus warns them against such thinking. There will be a delay before "the end." Jerusalem and the temple will be destroyed, but the life of the church will continue. Future times will be characterized by violent persecution of his followers and terrible tribulation in Judea. The disciples are shocked. They think Messiah's disciples will be immediately and eminently victorious, the Promised Land easily conquered and the worship of God restored. What is this talk about the destruction of the temple and the persecution of his followers?

But there is more shocking teaching. The only "sign" that the disciples will have of Jesus coming will be his actual coming. This "sign" will have no predictive value because it comes too late. Jesus' point leads to his discussion that no one can prophesy when "the end" will occur or when he will come. In fact, not even Jesus knew the time. Only the Father did.

Jesus has taken the disciples' wrong-headed concern and turned it into a spiritual lesson. In the words of D.A. Carson: "The disciples' questions are answered, and the reader is exhorted to look forward to the Lord's return and meanwhile to live responsibly, faithfully, compassionately, and courageously while the Master is away (24:45-25:46)" (*ibid,* page 495).

"Amen, Come, Lord Jesus" (Revelation 22:20).

MATTHEW 24:20 – WHY PRAY NOT TO FLEE ON THE SABBATH?

What did Jesus mean: "Pray that your flight will not take place in winter or on the Sabbath" (Matthew 24:20)?

By Paul Kroll

If Sabbath observance was not a concern for Christians when Matthew wrote his Gospel, why did he mention Jesus' words about fleeing on the Sabbath? Some people claim this is a command from Jesus for Christians to keep the Sabbath rest. Is this true?

We begin our explanation by noting an important point about Jesus' statement. If we carefully read his words in Matthew 24:20, we find no command from his lips for Christians to observe a Sabbath rest. He simply advises Christians that for circumstantial reasons, they should pray that the need to flee will not arise on the Sabbath or in winter. Why it would not be prudent to flee in winter is obvious. Adverse weather conditions would hamper flight and put those fleeing at risk from the elements. But why would fleeing on the Sabbath day be a problem?

Here is where we have to be aware of Jewish customs and practices regarding the Sabbath. Jesus gave his warning to the disciples because of the possibility that Jewish people in Jerusalem and Judea would have prevented Christians from fleeing on the Sabbath. Please note that the warning was given "to those who are in Judea" (verse 16), not to disciples in other parts of the world. It is preserved only in Matthew's Gospel, which was probably written to Jewish Christians.

Thus, the passage tells us more about the religious practices and social regulations regarding the Sabbath of non-Christian Jews in Jerusalem and Judea, than what the church would be doing about it. The context in which the warning about fleeing is given leads us to conclude that it has nothing to do with any supposed command for Christians to keep the Sabbath rest. Jesus gave his warning not because the church would be keeping the Sabbath but because Christians in Judea and Jerusalem might find it difficult or impossible to flee on this day,

Since the Jews honored Moses' laws, they believed it was wrong to take long journeys on the Sabbath. They apparently even had a measurement for the distance to be traveled on this day, which was called a "Sabbath day's walk" or journey (Acts 1:12). This was a short distance. In Luke's example it was the distance between the Mount of Olives, on the perimeter of Jerusalem, and the city itself. But Jesus' warning was given in the context of a catastrophe on the city and Judea, which would have required getting much further out of the area than a limited "Sabbath day's walk" might allow.

Further, the gates of Jerusalem were locked on the Sabbath day, which would have prevented people from fleeing the city. The Jews also had authority to police their own people regarding certain religious matters. The zealots especially, no doubt, would have tried to prevent fellow Jews from taking long journeys on the Sabbath. And they would have tried to prevent anyone from fleeing Jerusalem and Judea while the war with the Romans was in progress (A.D. 66-70). Such fleeing would have been considered a traitorous action by the Jews battling the Romans.

But Jesus said that people who were in all of Judea at the time of the crisis at Jerusalem would need to *immediately* flee far away into the hills. Jesus gave the warning in Matthew 24:20because he knew that the Jews would not allow the kind of escape in troubling times on the Sabbath that his warning required. His warning was not a command to rest on the Sabbath any more than it was a command to rest in winter. These were simply inconvenient times to flee.

Warning for the future?

Those who interpret Matthew 24 as applying only to a future time claim the warning in verse 20 has nothing to do with the practices of Jews in the first century. Thus, Jewish customs with regard to the Sabbath would not have any relevance for explaining this verse. They note that Jewish authorities today – an example for the future, they believe – would not prevent people from fleeing the city or the area of ancient Judea. Matthew 24, they claim, is a warning for the future "time of the end" of the world. In this context, they teach that verse 20 is, indeed, a command for the Sabbath to be kept.

Does this theory have any validity? In fact, this idea of a future context to the warning in verse 20 is fraught with difficulties. Let's briefly look at some of the problems.

First, we have no idea what Jewish authorities might or might not allow during an unknown future time when it is claimed that all of the Holy Land will be in the throes of military, social and natural destruction and upheaval. Today's modern military power is overwhelming in its ability to pinpoint, corner and destroy. When Israel invaded Palestinian territory in April 2002 to prevent suicide bombers from killing Israelis, there was no escape for groups of people from any town, and certainly not from the area. The fact is, we have no way of knowing what might or might not be possible in terms of fleeing an area to safety – and any escape seems doubtful at best.

Second, leaving this hypothetical argument aside, we need to once again repeat that there is no command in Matthew 24:20 for Christians to keep the Sabbath. Jesus doesn't say, "Keep the Sabbath holy." He says that those who are in Judea should hope they don't need to flee in winter or on the Sabbath day. That is not a command to keep a rest day; it is advice about adverse conditions for fleeing.

Third, if the warnings given throughout Matthew 24, including those about fleeing on the Sabbath, were meant only for some future "end times," then they would have had no meaning for the Christians to whom they were originally spoken, and then written. The hearers would have been confused by the meaning of such assertions. The existence of these warnings – in a future scenario – would require an explanation to the effect that Jesus was talking only to people living in some distant "end time." But no such explanation is evident in Matthew 24:20. The disciples who first heard these warnings are addressed throughout the chapter. In fact, Jesus says the following after giving such warnings as the one about fleeing on the Sabbath: "I tell you the truth, this generation will certainly not pass away until all these things have happened" (verse 34).

Fourth, the idea that Matthew 24 refers to specific events in some future "end time" is speculation. Christians have been trying to understand how to interpret this chapter without great success or agreement for 1900 years. For example, some Christians believe that *all* the events mentioned in Matthew 24 were fulfilled before A.D. 70 and have no application for the subsequent history of the church, or for the future. The interpretation that these events are yet future is by no means proven.

Conclusion

The point is that we cannot use one speculative assertion (that Matthew 24 refers to a future time) as the basis for a dogmatic assertion about another unproved claim (that the Sabbath should be kept). Even here, before we lose our mooring, let us repeat a third time that verse 20 contains no command to keep the Sabbath. In fact, one can read the New Testament from Matthew through Revelation and he or she will not find a single instance in which the church is commanded to keep the Sabbath as "holy time."

Given all the above considerations, we can only conclude that Matthew 24:20 as written was a warning to Christians living at the time the book was written, and not specifically to Christians living in a supposed future time of "the end" of the world. The warning was given to Christians of that day living in Judea and Jerusalem because they would find it difficult or impossible to flee on a Sabbath day if circumstances demanded it. There is no command in this verse to keep the Sabbath as "holy time."

GOOD NEWS IN AN ALABASTER JAR

By Michael Morrison

Matthew 26 records an interesting episode in the life of Jesus, just two days before he was killed. This was an action-packed week, filled with highly significant events — and this event is no exception. In Matthew 26, we find a description of Jesus being anointed with perfume. The story begins in verses 1-2:

> When Jesus had finished saying all these things, he said to his disciples, "As you know, the Passover is two days away — and the Son of Man will be handed over to be crucified."

Jesus knows that his time is short – he has only two days to live – but his disciples seem to be unaware of it. Jesus will soon be given another opportunity to tell his disciples about his impending death.

Then there is an abrupt change of scene, in which Matthew tells us what is happening in another place at about the same time:

> The chief priests and the elders of the people assembled in the palace of the high priest, whose name was Caiaphas, and they plotted to arrest Jesus in some sly way and kill him. "But not during the Feast," they said, "or there may be a riot among the people." (verses 3-5)

Jesus anointed with perfume

Matthew then takes us back to Jesus:

> While Jesus was in Bethany [two miles east of Jerusalem] in the home of a man known as Simon the Leper, a woman came to him with an alabaster jar of very expensive perfume, which she poured on his head as he was reclining at the table. (verses 6-7).

A whole jar of perfume! The smell would have filled the entire room.

> When the disciples saw this, they were indignant. "Why this waste?" they asked. "This perfume could have been sold at a high price and the money given to the poor."

> Aware of this, Jesus said to them, "Why are you bothering this woman? She has done a beautiful thing to me. The poor you will always have with you, but you will not always have me. When she poured this perfume on my body, she did it to prepare me for burial."

Then Jesus, with special emphasis, said,

> I tell you the truth, wherever this gospel is preached throughout

the world, what she has done will also be told, in memory of her. (verses 8-13)

Why is this so important?

I would like to ask a follow-up question: Why is this story so important that it will be told wherever the gospel message goes?

The woman had done a nice favor for Jesus, and it was appropriate for Jesus to thank her in a nice way. But surely this does not mean that the disciples, no matter where they went in the world, would have to tell this story everywhere they told the gospel? If the disciples were running short of time, couldn't they just preach the gospel and skip this particular story? No, said Jesus. Wherever the gospel is preached, this story must be told, too. It is practically as important as the gospel itself!

When the disciples were inspired to write the stories of what Jesus did, they also wrote the story of what this woman did. In the Gospel accounts, it is on an equal level with the teachings and miracles of Jesus. What this woman did is an essential part of the story of Jesus.

That is not just long ago and far away. It also applies right now, and right here. Wherever the gospel goes, this story must be told, too. Why is that?

The context: Jesus' death

This section of Matthew is about Jesus' death. It begins in verse 2 with Jesus mentioning his death. It moves in verse 3 to the conspiracy to kill Jesus. And in verse 12, Jesus connects the anointing with his burial.

Right after Jesus says that this story will be told around the world, Matthew tells us in verse 14 that Judas went out and conspired with the chief priests to betray Jesus. This anointing with perfume was the last straw for Judas. He was so upset about this waste of money that he went out to betray his master for 30 pieces of silver – ironically, money that he himself would waste. He eventually saw that there was something more important than money – but that is a different story. Our focus today is on the story of what the woman did. That is the story that must be told everywhere the gospel goes.

The story is set in the context of Jesus' death. It is part of the introduction to what is called "the passion" – Jesus' suffering and death. That helps make the story significant. There are several points of resemblance between what this woman did and what Jesus did on the cross. Her action was in some ways a parable, a drama that portrayed spiritual truth about Jesus.

Many of Jesus' own actions were object lessons for spiritual truths. He did many more miracles than could be recorded in the Bible, but some are reported to us because they have special significance.

The miracle of feeding 5,000 people, for example, helps show that Jesus is the bread of life. Just as he gives food for physical life, so also he gives what we need for eternal life. The fact that he could do something we can see, gives us assurance that he can do something we cannot see. Just as he heals diseases, so also he forgives sins. The physical action pictures a spiritual truth.

This is also true of what this woman did for Jesus. What she did illustrates for us some lessons about the sacrifice of Jesus Christ. It also pictures the way that we should respond to Jesus. What this woman did is a miniature picture of the gospel itself. That is why this story is so important that it has become part of the gospel message. It can help us explain the nature of the gospel.

A powerful devotion

Let's look at three ways in which this anointing resembles the sacrifice of Jesus himself.

Let's give this woman a name. John 12 tells us that she was Mary, sister of Lazarus, and that this was shortly after Jesus had raised Lazarus from the dead. The story can be told without that particular fact — the action is more important than who did it — but it does help us understand a little more of what went on behind the scenes. (It is not exactly certain that the story in John 12 is the same incident as we read about in Matthew 26, but that question does not affect the point we wish to make here.)

First, we can see that Mary was motivated to do this out of love. Nobody told her to do it. It was not commanded. It was just something Mary took upon herself to do, and she did it out of love.

Jesus also made his sacrifice out of love. He had no obligation to die for us, but he chose to do it, willingly, motivated by love. Even while we were sinners, he loved us with incredible intensity.

Mary may have known that Jesus was soon to die, but perhaps not. The disciples didn't understand that Jesus was going to die, and Mary probably didn't, either. Otherwise, she would have saved the perfume for the actual burial. She seems to have poured the perfume on Jesus simply because she had an incredibly intense devotion to Jesus. She was overwhelmed with love. Maybe it was a response to the resurrection of Lazarus.

Mary may have bought that perfume to anoint the dead body of her brother. Now that Lazarus was alive, Mary did not need the perfume for him — thanks to what Jesus had done. How could Mary thank Jesus for his wonderful gift of life? Why, she could use that same perfume to lavish it on Jesus, as a token of her thanks and love. Mary was praising Jesus, honoring Jesus—in effect, worshipping Jesus, sacrificing to Jesus.

Many people today are concerned with right beliefs. Right beliefs are good. We need them. Many people today are concerned with right behavior. Right behavior is good. We need it — but we need something else, too, and that is something that Mary demonstrates for us. Mary shows us right *emotion,* right feeling. The heart we need for God is an intensely personal devotion, a powerful dedication of ourselves to his service.

This intensity of emotion is unusual, and like most unusual things, this was criticized. This kind of devotion was not within the ordinary range of acceptable behavior. People would call Mary eccentric, maybe even out of her right mind. Society says, Don't get carried away with your emotions. Mary did. Her society criticized her, but Jesus praised her. Society says, Moderation in all things. Mary was not moderate. Her society criticized her, but Jesus praised her. The jury of 12 men said this is wrong, but Jesus said, she is better than you all.

Mary had an intense affection and devotion for Jesus. We can see it when she sat at Jesus' feet listening to him teach. She was a contemplative person who liked to think. Here, she is an expressive person — expressive not in words but in actions. Her quiet nature did not prevent her from making a powerful statement — more powerful than words could have possibly done.

An enormous sacrifice

The second way in which Mary's action was like the sacrifice of Jesus is that it was a sacrifice. This was some incredibly expensive perfume. Mary could have sold it for a large amount. Mark tells us it was worth about one year's wages — the amount of money that a working person would earn in an entire year. In today's economy, it might be worth several thousand dollars.

Can you imagine one jar of perfume that costs several thousand dollars? Now, can you imagine taking that and just pouring it out? Thousands of dollars evaporating into thin air — gone forever. A year's worth of work, gone, just like that.

This shows us something of the intensity of Mary's love for Jesus. She must have known what she was doing, and how much it had cost her. But she did not care. Her love for Jesus was so great that she was not concerned about the cost. She was probably happy about it — she was getting a chance to demonstrate her devotion to Jesus. If she had sorrow, it was not about how much she was giving up, but that she had so little to give. Love often expresses itself in self-sacrifice, with little thought for self.

If an offering is to be meaningful, it should cost us something, and it should be done out of our own free will. We should give up something that is of value to us. Worship always involves sacrifice — sacrifice of money, time or pride, or all three. Maybe it requires everything we have, and everything we are.

The disciples were concerned with self. They wanted to be great in the kingdom of God. But Mary was achieving greatness already, through her devotion to Jesus. She was not concerned for self and what she would get out of it. She was concerned for nothing but Jesus, and in that, she was already great.

Concern about the money

The disciples suggested that the money could be given to the poor. It wasn't just Judas who objected to this "waste" of money. All the disciples were indignant.

It is good to give money to the poor. The traditional Jewish understanding of righteousness included giving money to the poor, and apparently the disciples sometimes did it. (When Judas went out from the last supper, the disciples thought that he might be going to give something to the poor. If Jesus had never given any money to the poor in the previous three years, the disciples probably would not guess that he would start right then. Charity seems to have been part of what they normally did.)

When someone has lots of money, it is appropriate to share some of it with those who need it. That is a good use of money. But in this case, Mary had picked an even better use of the money. She used it in an act of tremendous devotion, an act of worship. That is a legitimate use of money, too.

Some Christians make a religion out of social work, and they do it very well. Social work can be part of the Christian faith. But some unfortunately see that as the only form of religion, and they have forgotten about devotion to Jesus. Social work is good, but it is not supreme. Jesus is supreme — and our devotion to *him* will cause us to help the people who need help. It's a question of priorities, and Jesus must always be first. For Christian service to really count, it must be done for Christ. We are serving him. Even when we are helping other people, we are serving Christ.

What Mary did, from an observer's perspective, was a big sacrifice. But because she was willing, it was for her a small price to pay, a token of her love. Jesus' crucifixion, from all perspectives, was a tremendous sacrifice, but he was willing to make it. For the joy set before him he endured the cross. He knew that glory was waiting not just for him, but for all who would be saved by what he did. He was willing to pay the price—and he was happy that he was able to pay the price, because he knew how valuable the result would be.

As *we* grasp the enormity of his sacrifice, we cannot help but respond in love and devotion — and there is no sacrifice too great. Nothing we do could ever compare to what he has done for us. Our love for him causes us to *live* for him, to give all that we are.

Extravagant sacrifice

The third way in which Mary's action was similar to Jesus' crucifixion is that it was extravagant. It was far more than what was necessary. It was outrageous! Mary was not a calculating person who thought, what is the least I can do? How much do I have to spend to be enough? What is my duty?

Nor was she tied down to tradition. Mary did not think, How do other women show respect for a rabbi? She was not afraid of public opinion. Her love freed her from that fear. She was not afraid to do something out of the ordinary. Mary did not ask the disciples if it was OK. No, Mary broke traditions. She broke the limits of what is public propriety. Mary didn't even ask Jesus if it was OK. She just seized the opportunity, and did it. She did what she could, because only that expressed her devotion to Jesus. Her love was so great that it called for an exceptional act of creative devotion.

The disciples didn't object to the anointing in itself. They didn't object to perfume. What they objected to was the extravagance. This was just *too much* of a good thing — way too much. This was ridiculous, wasteful, even sinful.

No so, said Jesus. What she has done is a beautiful thing, Jesus said. It had an aesthetic value, like a beautiful work of art, a beautiful piece of music. It was a beautiful *action* — a beauty that defies cost analysis. It is impossible to put a price on such personal devotion.

Sometimes we are too concerned about the usefulness of something. I often think that way. But that may mean that I do only the ordinary things, never the unusual, never the beautiful, never anything heroic, never anything requiring faith.

The disciples wanted the money to be put to good use, for something practical, like food for the hungry. That *is* a very good use for money. It was the ordinary thing to do, the normal thing to do, even a respectable thing to do. But *usefulness* is not the most important thing in the universe. Usefulness is not our god. Efficiency is not our god. Public opinion is not our god. Traditional boundaries of politeness are not our god. *Jesus* is our God, and it is useful to use up our material resources to honor and glorify him.

Maybe there aren't any tangible results, but a sacrifice of love and devotion *has a usefulness of its own.* An act of great beauty has a usefulness of its own when it is done for Jesus Christ. Mary's act of extravagant waste was actually a picture of spiritual beauty — a heavenly fragrance. It pictured the sacrifice of Jesus Christ in a way that words could not. It was extravagant, and that is part of its beauty. God himself is extravagant.

Now, when something is done out of the ordinary, *someone* is going to complain about it. Someone is not going to understand the motive, or understand the beauty, or they are going to say, "That's not right. We don't do things that way." To them, it seems that mediocrity is better than intense emotion. But Jesus praises extravagance, not mediocrity.

God gave us an extravagant gift in the person of Jesus Christ. It was an outrageous gift, worth far more than what we deserve. Grace is extravagant. Jesus gave everything he had for us. He gave his very life. He gave more than necessary — he died for the whole world, and yet the whole world does not accept him. He died even for the people who reject him.

What a waste!, some people might think, but it was really an act of love, of sacrifice, of extravagance. Some people said, "That can't be right. That's not the way God normally acts with us." But God does things out of the ordinary. Jesus shows us total commitment, total sacrifice, so that we might respond to him with all that we have.

An extravagant response

We need to respond to Jesus the same way that Mary did — with a supreme focus on him, a single-minded love that counts everything else loss for Jesus Christ, a love that does not ask how *little* we can do to get by, a love that is not worried about public opinion, a love that is no longer concerned about what is within the boundaries of normal devotion — a love that is willing to be extravagant.

When Mary poured perfume on Jesus, she was not only picturing some aspects of what Jesus did on the cross, she also pictured the way that we should respond to Jesus, with such complete devotion, such willingness to sacrifice, such willingness to go beyond the boundaries of normal and to have an extraordinary love for Jesus.

Have you ever done anything extravagant for Jesus Christ? Have you ever done anything so outrageous for him that other people thought you were foolish? Have you ever been so bold with love that other people have criticized what you did? Some of us have. Maybe it was a long time ago. Whenever it was, it was sweet-smelling aroma offered to God.

The example of Mary tells me that I am too reserved. I am too often concerned with what others think. I am not loving Jesus as much as I ought. I am too concerned with myself. I need to think more about actions of extraordinary beauty. God has been extravagant with me. He has lavished on me the riches of his grace. He has repeatedly given me things I did not deserve and things I did not appreciate the way I ought. His grace toward me abounds and abounds and abounds. How do I respond to him who gave his life for me?

SOLD...FOR THIRTY PIECES OF SILVER

By Joyce Catherwood

Skimming the pages of a book about Jesus recently, my eye fell on a caption: "The Messiah sold for thirty pieces of silver."

I was struck by the enormity of the meaning of that caption and even the absurdity of it. The Messiah, the Savior, the One by whom all things were created, sold for 30 pieces of silver! I am always disarmed by the humility of our Lord who, time and time again, suffered indignities and insults at the hands of his own creatures. In this instance, that it was done by one of his own disciples must have been a source of great sadness for him. The procession to the cross, ugly and violent as it was, had to be triggered by someone, and so it was Judas who set it off. It was to be expected, of course, but that didn't make it any easier for Jesus.

When Judas left the upper room to betray Jesus, he had already made arrangements with the chief priests, who wanted the charismatic teacher and his ministry destroyed. Jesus had been with his disciples in the home of Mary of Bethany six days before the last supper.

At great expense and with a heart brimming with devotion, Mary had poured perfume on Jesus' feet and reverently wiped them with her hair. The disciples, and in particular Judas, objected vehemently to her anointing, claiming it was a waste of money that could have been used for the poor. This was hypocritical criticism by Judas, who had already stolen funds from the money bag.

Jesus defended Mary and held her up as a shining and beautiful example. The fact that Jesus took Mary's side, telling the disciples to leave her alone, must have ignited rage in Judas. He left Mary's home and went directly to the chief priests and elders inquiring what they would give him if he delivered Jesus over to them. Delighted, they counted out 30 silver coins, a sum equal to compensation for a dead slave. Thus the series of events that would be the most tragic in all of human history, and yet the most important and meaningful, began to unfold.

Though Judas' conduct was especially hurtful and destructive, the reaction of the rest of the disciples was also disheartening for Jesus. In the end, with the exception of John, Jesus was deserted by his disciples, who fled into hiding behind closed doors.

Their lack of support added even more misery to the crushing weight of the cross that he bore. Starting with Mary's anointing, only the women in his close circle of companions somehow understood that he needed the reassurance of his beloved friends.

What would my reaction have been had I been there? I like to think it would have been the same as Mary's. On the other hand, to paraphrase a line from a praise song, would I have been ashamed, hearing my own mocking voice call out among the scoffers?

Even though it all started with 30 pieces of silver and betrayal, Jesus' lonely path to Golgotha ended gloriously by ushering in the salvation of all humanity.

PILATE'S WIFE

Matthew 27:11-66

By Joyce Catherwood

I woke up suddenly, startled and shaken. I stared at the ceiling, momentarily relieved, thinking my nightmare about Jesus was only a dream. But angry voices coming through the windows of our residence brought me back to reality. My heart sank. I had been deeply disturbed by the news of Jesus' arrest as I retired for the evening. I didn't know why he had been taken and accused of crimes that could cost his life. He had helped so many in need.

From my window, I could see the judgment seat where my husband Pilate, the Roman governor, conducted public hearings. I heard him shout: "Which one do you want me to release to you: Barabbas, or Jesus, who is called Christ?" I knew this could only mean that events throughout the night had not gone well for Jesus. Pilate may have naively thought the hostile crowd would free him. But the mob had been enraged by wild accusations from the jealous chief priests and elders, so they screamed for Jesus to be crucified. Some of these were the same people who only weeks before had followed him everywhere receiving healing and hope.

Jesus stood there so alone, despised and rejected. He was not a criminal. I knew that, and my husband knew that, but things were out of control. Someone had to intervene. So I grabbed a servant by the arm and told him to go tell Pilate not to have anything to do with those proceedings, and that I had suffered greatly because of a dream about Jesus. But it was too late. My husband gave into their demands. In a cowardly attempt to rid himself of any responsibility, he washed his hands in front of the crowd, declaring he was innocent of Jesus' blood. I moved from the window and slumped to the floor, weeping. My soul ached for this compassionate, humble man who traveled everywhere healing and delivering the oppressed.

As Jesus hung on the cross, the brilliant afternoon sun gave way to an ominous darkness. Then as Jesus gasped his last breath, the earth shook, splitting rocks and leveling structures. Tombs broke open, releasing dead people who came back to life. All of Jerusalem had been brought to its knees. But not for long. These terrifying events weren't enough to stop the Jewish leaders. They scrambled to Pilate and conspired with him to secure Jesus' grave so his disciples could not steal his body and claim he rose from the dead.

Three days have now passed, and Jesus' followers are indeed proclaiming he is alive! They insist they have seen him! Those who came back from their graves now walk the streets of Jerusalem. I am overjoyed! I dare not tell my husband, but I will not rest until I learn more about this amazing man who defied death and promises eternal life.

EXPLORE THE GOSPELS: MARK

By Jim Herst

A Bible, especially if it is an older version, can look about as inviting to read as a telephone directory. But don't let that first impression put you off. Behind the intimidating facade is a fascinating story.

Mark's Gospel has only 16 chapters. Taking a chapter a day, you could read the book in just over two weeks. Any Bible will do, but we suggest you use a version in modern English, such as The New International Version or The New Revised Standard Version.

Who was Mark?

This gospel is traditionally attributed to John Mark, the man who accompanied Barnabas and Paul on their first missionary journey (Acts 13). John Mark abandoned that mission early, which greatly disappointed Paul, who refused to take him on a later journey (Acts 15:36-38).

Barnabas was willing to give the young man another chance, and took him on a mission to Cyprus. Mark made good and was later reconciled with Paul, who subsequently wrote that he was a useful helper (2 Timothy 4:11).

We do not know for certain when Mark wrote, or to whom. However, there is evidence that he wrote in Rome to encourage Gentile Christians, and to prove that Jesus was the promised Messiah.

Outline of the book

Forget it! You don't need an outline. Mark didn't organize his Gospel neatly in topics, as Matthew did. Mark is less interested in composing literature than in telling his readers who Jesus is and what he did.

If Mark had lived today, he could have worked for CNN. He brings you the action as Jesus' ministry unfolds. His Gospel reads like an eye-witness report of key events in Jesus' life. You are there as he is baptized, performs miracles, chooses his disciples, heals, upsets the establishment, is arrested, tried and crucified. Verbs like "run," "shout," and "amaze" abound in this book. Mark's favorite adverb is *euthys,* meaning "immediately" or 'at once,' which occurs 10 times in chapter 1 alone.

Mark "presents a rapid succession of vivid pictures of Jesus in action — his true identity revealed by what he does, not by what he says (18 miracles are described, and only four parables). It is Jesus on the move" (*Life Application Bible,* p. 1676). The evangelist often interrupts one story to begin another, going back to the first later. Chronology is reckoned in days and, in the account of Jesus' trial and crucifixion, hours.

Mark concentrates on miracles and the revolutionary nature of Jesus' teaching (1:22) to emphasize his authority. Dramatic signs at crucial events also reveal Jesus to be the supreme Servant of God, performing the Father's will with authority and power.

At Jesus' baptism, heaven is "torn open" (1:10); at his death, the temple curtain is torn in two from top to bottom (15:38). Mark shows how, in Jesus, God has broken into human history. Jesus urgently proclaims: "The kingdom of God is near. Repent and believe the good news!" (1:15).

Mark may have been an eyewitness to some of this. It is also possible that he got many of the details from Peter, the flamboyant disciple who was one of Jesus' intimate friends. Mark's Gospel is therefore an excellent introduction to Jesus Christ, who he was and what he stands for.

Hidden identity

Mark's Gospel shows that Jesus tried to keep his identity hidden until the end of his ministry. He knew he would be misunderstood. The Jews were expecting a Messiah who would deliver them from the Romans by force of power. But Jesus had come to deliver them from sin by his atoning death.

He silenced the demons who acknowledged him as God's Servant and Son (1:23-25, 34; 3:11-12). When he healed people, he asked them to keep quiet about it (1:43-45; 5:43; 7:36; 8:26). Jesus even forbade his disciples from making public his Messiahship (8:30; 9:9) until the time was right.

Jesus was the Son of God

But after Jesus had accomplished his mission, there was no need for caution. Everyone needed to know the good news. So Mark wastes no time in getting down to business. He opens with "The beginning of the Gospel about Jesus Christ, the Son of God" (1:1). He tells us that when Jesus was baptized, a heavenly voice proclaimed: "You are my Son, the Beloved; with you I am well pleased" (1:11).

Mark tells us that Jesus had the authority to forgive sin, a prerogative of God (2:5-12). Evil spirits recognized Jesus as the Holy One of God (1:24), the Son of God (3:11) and Son of the Most High God (5:7-8). The supernatural world acknowledged Jesus' true identity as the Son of God.

However, Mark also shows that no one in the human realm fully understood this. Even Peter, who professed Jesus to be the Christ, failed to realize Jesus' purpose: to die, and after three days to rise again (8:31). In Mark's Gospel, the first human acknowledgement that Jesus is the Son of God comes, astonishingly, from a Roman centurion who sees Jesus on the cross (15:39).

Today, enthusiastic believers still try to make Jesus a cult super-hero. Such well-meaning devotion can distort and dilute the true nature of his life and work. The Gospel of Mark warns its readers not to proclaim Jesus other than what he really is — the Son of God, who came to die on our behalf.

Down to earth

Mark shows us that Jesus was a servant. He helped people, and he commands us to do likewise: "Whoever wants to become great among you must be your servant, and whoever wants to be first must be slave of all. For even the Son of Man did not come to be served, but to serve, and to give his life as a ransom for many" (10:43-45).

Mark does not portray the disciples as spiritual giants. Rather, he emphasizes their lack of understanding. Even though they forsook everything to follow Jesus, they needed to be reminded about the importance of unselfish service: "If anyone wants to be first, he must be the very last, and the servant of all" (9:35).

The original disciples had serious failings. But Jesus loved them, and persisted with them. That should be encouraging to us as we struggle to follow our Lord and Savior.

> Ironically, it is the "minor" characters in Mark who display the trait of unselfish service, giving us a rich legacy to learn from: "The poor widow gives out of her need, her whole living" (12:41-44). An unnamed woman uses expensive ointment to anoint Jesus ahead of time for his burial (14:3-9). Joseph of Arimathea takes courage and approaches Pilate for the right to bury Jesus (15:43). Women go to anoint Jesus' body at the grave (16:1-3). ("Losing Life for Others in the Face of Death: Mark's Standards of Judgment," *Interpretation,* October 1993, pp. 361-362)

Jesus tells us to deny ourselves in order to serve him and to further the gospel: "Whoever loses his life for me and for the gospel will save it" (8:35). Jesus is the ultimate example of service, and he died on our behalf. This, indeed, is the great paradox of the gospel: By giving up our lives in service to our Lord and Master, we gain eternal life through him.

Downward mobility

The Gospel of Mark is an antidote for a secular society bent on "upward mobility" – being first at all costs. On the contrary, Mark teaches us that our lives must truly reflect the "downward mobility" of the cross.

As you read Mark, ask God to show you how you can model your life on his Son who "came not to be served, but to serve, and to give his life a ransom for many" (10:44-45).

A LESSON IN HUMILITY (MARK 1:1-8)

By J. Michael Feazell

The beginning of the good news about Jesus the Messiah, the Son of God, as it is written in Isaiah the prophet: "I will send my messenger ahead of you, who will prepare your way"— "a voice of one calling in the wilderness, 'Prepare the way for the Lord, make straight paths for him.'" (NIV 2011)

And so John the Baptist appeared in the wilderness, preaching a baptism of repentance for the forgiveness of sins. The whole Judean countryside and all the people of Jerusalem went out to him. Confessing their sins, they were baptized by him in the Jordan River. John wore clothing made of camel's hair, with a leather belt around his waist, and he ate locusts and wild honey. And this was his message: "After me comes the one more powerful than I, the straps of whose sandals I am not worthy to stoop down and untie. I baptize you with water, but he will baptize you with the Holy Spirit."

Who would you say was the greatest man ever born? If you are a Christian, you might say, "Why, Jesus Christ, of course!" Suppose Jesus himself were asked the question. What do you suppose he would say?

You might be surprised to know that Jesus did once attribute that distinction of greatness to a certain man. He told his disciples, "I tell you, among those born of women there is no one greater than John; yet the one who is least in the kingdom of God is greater than he" (Luke 7:28).

Major celebrity

John the Baptizer was an amazingly popular figure. Everybody in Jerusalem and people from all over the Judean countryside went out to listen to him preach. But they didn't just listen--they responded; they confessed their sins and were baptized! Not only was John popular, he was also successful.

For all his popularity and success, though, John was strikingly different from the average man. Many people respond to great popularity and success with a certain degree of pride and swagger. But from the beginning, John the Baptizer was different.

'Not about me'

Perhaps you have seen the slogan, "It's not about me."

That was the root of John's message. He preached about someone else, someone who would come after him whose sandal thongs John did not consider himself even worthy to tie.

John wasn't interested in the limelight. He wasn't interested in the praise or admiration of others. He was interested in preparing the way for someone else, and he didn't let personal ambition get in the way of doing his job well.

Baptism

John was a baptizer. Among the preparations he made for the coming of Christ was the task of preaching a baptism of repentance for the forgiveness of sins. It was into this kind of baptism that the people listening to him entered.

Baptism was not an invention of John, nor was it unique to the Israelites. From ancient times, baptism was a well-known symbol, an outward sign, of a new spiritual birth, of entering into a new form of life.

For those whom John baptized, it marked their confession that they were sinners. When we admit we are sinners, we are laying aside our human pride and confessing the truth of what we really are. But we are not making that confession blindly. We are making it in the light of the revealed knowledge that God loves us immeasurably, and that he has made atonement for us in Jesus Christ.

In other words, because God has revealed to us that he is *for* us, we are *free* in Christ both to fearlessly acknowledge our sinfulness before God, and *free* to accept God's gift of atonement and his new creation of us in Jesus Christ.

Because we have met with the grace of God in Jesus Christ, we can entrust ourselves to him fully and without reservation. Safe in his love, we can give over to him even the crushing burdens of our darkest sins and fears.

New creation

Within that confession of our sinfulness is our recognition that we need God's forgiveness. We admit that we are rebels who have betrayed God's love, and we place ourselves at his mercy, having now renounced our rebellion and pledged faithful obedience.

But actually becoming that new person, entering that new life, turning over that new leaf, is another question entirely. When we try to do that, we find ourselves failing--fighting our old ways, but losing so often we can easily fall into despair.

That is, *unless we trust God to be who he really is for us in Jesus Christ!*

In Christ, we are a new creation (see 2 Corinthians 5:17 and Galatians 6:15). And we are set free (Galatians 5:1)! God has freed us to be the new, redeemed, healed and complete persons he has made us to be in Christ. We can use that gift of freedom to hear and obey our heavenly Father, or we can reject it and continue to live as though God had not made us his covenant partner, as though he had not made us the beloved recipients of his overflowing grace in Christ (verse 13).

No longer must we live in spiritual bondage, struggling in vain to grasp here and there a little respect, dignity, security and love in this heartless world. No longer must everything in life be about us and our anxieties about not getting all the things we think we want. No longer must we live in opposition to God, ourselves and our neighbor.

The Holy Spirit both gives us ears to hear God's command and provides us our new life in Christ. In that new life provided by the Holy Spirit, we are free to choose to be the person in Christ God has already chosen us to be. To do otherwise is not freedom, but a return to bondage.

In Christ

All this repenting, believing and passing through the waters of baptism have meaning *only because God gives them meaning*. Only because the Son of God took the indescribable action of becoming one of us--living sinlessly as one of us, dying on the cross as one of us, being resurrected as one of us, ascending to and being received by the Father as one of us, does any of it make any sense at all.

It makes sense because God, *in his divine freedom to be who he wants to be for our sakes,* makes it make sense. We are saved by God's grace--his love, his utter faithfulness to his redemptive purpose for the humanity he loves so much that in Christ he took humanity itself into himself.

A lesson in humility

God was pleased to have all his fullness dwell in Jesus Christ, and through Christ to reconcile to himself all things in heaven and earth through Christ's death (see Colossians 1:19-20).

That is the way God chose to make us into a new creation. The Son of God took humanity into himself, and in his perfect obedient sacrifice of love, he reconciled humanity to God. It is to this God, the God who in immeasurable love humbled himself to take all our burdens upon himself, including our ugliest sins, and turn us into a new and beautiful creation in his Son, that we owe complete allegiance and obedience.

John's ministry was a ministry of humility. Baptism is an expression of humility. The Son of God humbled himself to become one of us for our sakes. And the new life in Christ that is given to us by our Creator and Redeemer is a life of humility.

It's not about me. If it were about me, what would I do? How can I heal my own past, my present and future? How can I redeem my own faults, sins, betrayals and rebellion? How can I secure my future or the future of those I care about?

No, thank God, it's not about me. It's all about Jesus Christ, the Son of God incarnate (in the flesh) for our sakes. He is the one who heals our personal history, redeems our every dark sin, secures our future and gives us deep peace and rest.

Praise be to God that we can drop all our airs of superiority and pride, and humble ourselves before the mighty hand of God, because he is truly our all in all.

For reflection:
- How did Mark describe the gospel (v. 1)?
- What prophecy did John fulfill (vs. 2-3)?
- How are repentance and humility related?
- Why can we confess our sins without fear?

A LESSON IN TRANSITION (MARK 1:1-8)

By J. Michael Feazell

The beginning of the good news about Jesus the Messiah, the Son of God, as it is written in Isaiah the prophet: "I will send my messenger ahead of you, who will prepare your way"— "a voice of one calling in the wilderness, 'Prepare the way for the Lord, make straight paths for him.'" (NIV 2011)

And so John the Baptist appeared in the wilderness, preaching a baptism of repentance for the forgiveness of sins. The whole Judean countryside and all the people of Jerusalem went out to him. Confessing their sins, they were baptized by him in the Jordan River. John wore clothing made of camel's hair, with a leather belt around his waist, and he ate locusts and wild honey. And this was his message: "After me comes the one more powerful than I, the straps of whose sandals I am not worthy to stoop down and untie. I baptize you with water, but he will baptize you with the Holy Spirit."

How would you describe the message of John the Baptist? Mark said that John preached "a baptism of repentance for the forgiveness of sins," but that his *message* was, "After me will come one more powerful than I, the thongs of whose sandals I am not worthy to stoop down and untie. I baptize you with water, but he will baptize you with the Holy Spirit."

To set the context, Mark cites the words of Isaiah, combining them with a well-known prophecy from Malachi 3:1, about the messenger whom God would send to "prepare the way for the Lord."

What is the connection between preparing the way for the Lord and repentance for the forgiveness of sins? And what does that have to do with John's message that one more powerful than he would come, one who would baptize with the Holy Spirit? Let's begin in Malachi.

Time to repent

The prophecy Mark quoted from Malachi warned about a coming day of judgment against unfaithful Israel and Judah. In Malachi 2:17, the prophet declared, "You have wearied the Lord with your words ... By saying, "All who do evil are good in the eyes of the LORD, and he is pleased with them" or "Where is the God of justice?"

The next verse, Malachi 3:1, is the one Mark used in describing the role of John the Baptist. It is the answer to the rhetorical question just posed by Israel. Here is what the God of justice is going to do.

"'I will send my messenger, who will prepare the way before me. Then suddenly the Lord you are seeking will come to his temple; the messenger of the covenant, whom you desire, will come," says the LORD Almighty."

But, says verses 2-5, the Lord's coming will entail a powerful cleansing and purifying of his people. He will set things right and deliver the weak and disadvantaged from their cruel oppressors. "But who can endure the day of his coming? Who can stand when he appears? For he will be like a refiner's fire or a launderer's soap."

What can this mean, considering God's unchanging faithfulness, but a call to repentance — a call to turn back to God? God will never turn from his covenant faithfulness despite Israel's unfaithfulness, and for this reason Israel will not be destroyed (v. 6). Therefore God will, in his grace and love, save all who will turn to him (v. 7). It may have appeared for a time that there was nothing to gain by serving God and that only evildoers prosper (vs. 14-15), but that was never really the case (v. 16). God never leaves nor forsakes those who put their trust in him (vs. 16-18).

Therefore, God says, before this great and dreadful day of judgment comes, he would send them the prophet Elijah, who would bring together as one the hearts of the fathers and the children, that is, the hearts of Abraham, Isaac and Jacob united with the hearts of the generation upon which this judgment would fall.

Transitions

In this righteous way (see Romans 3:21-22 and Matthew 3:15), through the sudden coming of the Lord to his temple in cleansing judgment and forgiving grace, preceded by the voice of preparation crying in the wilderness, God would bring together the old with the new.

The Genesis creation would find its redemption in its transition into the new creation in Jesus Christ. The old covenant would find its fulfillment in its transition into the new covenant in Jesus Christ (see Jeremiah 31:31; 2 Corinthians 3:14).

The prophets of Israel would find their climax in John the Baptist (see Matthew 11:11 and Luke 16:16) and their fulfillment in the transition to the One whose sandals John knew he was "not worthy to stoop down and untie" (Mark 1:7). And wretched sinners like you and me would find love, forgiveness and redemption in the welcoming arms of the Father as he transitions us into his new creation in Jesus Christ (see 2 Corinthians 5:17 and Romans 8:38-39).

The "beginning of the good news about Jesus Christ" (Mark 1:1), rooted in creation itself and expressing itself unceasingly throughout history in God's faithfulness to his covenant promises, finds its grand consummation in the One who "will baptize you with Holy Spirit" (v. 8).

In Christ, God has brought together all things in heaven and earth and reconciled them to himself in his new creation (see Colossians 1:19-20 and Ephesians 1:9-10).

That is why Paul instructed the church at Galatia, "Neither circumcision nor uncircumcision means anything; what counts is the new creation" (Galatians 6:15).

New creation

Let's be honest. It might be encouraging or even inspiring to hear that we are a new creation, but the truth is, we don't often *feel* very much like a new creation. We usually feel more like a struggling creation, a tired, worried, barely-hanging-on-by-our-fingernails creation.

Don't let that get you down. That is how things are right now, but it will not always be so. The day will come when the new creation God has already made you to be in Christ will be fully unveiled (Colossians 3:1-4). And when that happens, there will be no more crying, no more pain and no more death (Revelation 21:4).

Even now, our hope lies in this: God has proven in Christ his love for us and his faithfulness to us (consider Romans 5:6-8). He has made our cause his own. He has taken responsibility for us, sins and all. He has taken us under his wing, and he will never let us go. That is why we trust him.

God, who proved himself faithful to faithless Israel, is exactly the same God who is faithful to faithless you and me. He is the same from the beginning, which means he has and always will be *for you,* working to help and to heal, and not to condemn (consider John 3:17).

If you have turned your back on God, don't ever think he has turned his back on you. Quite the contrary. He's got the porch light on and dinner on the table, waiting for you to come home.

For reflection:

- How was John the Baptist related to the beginning of the gospel of Jesus Christ (v. 1)?
- How did John fulfill the prophecies about preparing the way for the Lord (vs. 2-4)?
- What is the connection between forgiveness and judgment?
- What does John's message about a greater one to come mean for you?

For further reading:

The Mediation of Christ, by Thomas F. Torrance

A LESSON ABOUT POWER (MARK 1:1-8)

By J. Michael Feazell

The beginning of the good news about Jesus the Messiah, the Son of God, as it is written in Isaiah the prophet: "I will send my messenger ahead of you, who will prepare your way"— "a voice of one calling in the wilderness, 'Prepare the way for the Lord, make straight paths for him.'" (NIV 2011)

And so John the Baptist appeared in the wilderness, preaching a baptism of repentance for the forgiveness of sins. The whole Judean countryside and all the people of Jerusalem went out to him. Confessing their sins, they were baptized by him in the Jordan River. John wore clothing made of camel's hair, with a leather belt around his waist, and he ate locusts and wild honey. And this was his message: "After me comes the one more powerful than I, the straps of whose sandals I am not worthy to stoop down and untie. I baptize you with water, but he will baptize you with the Holy Spirit."

Baptism is not unique to Christianity. The use of water in purification and cleansing rites is as old as recorded history, and for a devoted first-century Jew, ritual washings were a regular part of life.

Unlike ritual washings, however, baptism involved the complete bathing of the entire body, and for first-century Jews it was reserved for proselytes, or gentile converts to the Jewish faith. If a gentile became a proselyte, besides keeping the Sabbath and avoiding defiled meat, he had to undergo certain rituals. He had to be circumcised, because circumcision was the mark of the Abrahamic covenant. A sacrifice had to be made for him to make a blood atonement for his sins. And he had to be baptized as a sign of his cleansing from past pollutions and the beginning of his new, purified life as a member of the household of God.

But John was calling for Jews—already members of the covenant people — to be baptized as though they were in no better standing with God than gentiles. Indeed, John's message was a declaration that God's prophesied judgment on faithless Israel was near, and that only those who humbled themselves and turned back to God would be spared.

But for those who would turn to God, who would make their confession and undergo this watery sign of commitment to a new life before God, something even greater was in store. There lay ahead a baptism that was not merely a sign or a ritual, but the real thing — the actual cleansing of the heart and mind that would result not merely in new behavior but in an entirely new person!

This baptism would be one that only the Son of God could provide, and he would provide it by sending the Holy Spirit to dwell both with and in the people of God.

Power

"I am going to send you what my Father has promised; but stay in the city until you have been clothed with power from on high" (Luke 24:49). Jesus was referring to the Holy Spirit, described in Acts 2:2 as a powerful wind and flames of fire.

It might be tempting to think about this "power" that the Holy Spirit provides as something we can use to make us stronger than others, wiser than others, braver than others, or more talented, healthier or wealthier than others. But the Holy Spirit is God, not a genie in a bottle to grant our every wish.

Indeed, God loves us dearly, cares for us tenderly and moves mountains to help us in our need. But God's priority is to make us like Jesus Christ, and Jesus left us an example of suffering for righteousness' sake (see 1 Peter 3:17-18), not of amassing fortune and fame.

Triune God

There is only one God — Father, Son and Holy Spirit. There is no Holy Spirit, therefore, except the one sent by the Father and the Son to minister their presence with you and in you for your redemption. The Holy Spirit does not draw attention to himself, but leads us to the Son who presents us to the Father (compare John 14:26; 16:13-14).

The Spirit does not have his own agenda, but only the agenda of the Father and the Son, who sent him. That agenda is human redemption and salvation — the *gospel* agenda. The Spirit is not a prima donna, a showboat, an entertainer, a circus or a side show. The Spirit is God, and he is God with the Father and the Son and no other way.

Our heavenly Father is the Father of Jesus Christ, the Father who loved the world so much that he sent his Son to save the world (see John 3:16-17) and who, with the Son, sent the Holy Spirit so that he and the Son would always be with us and in us (see John 14:16-19).

That means that any other idea you have about God — about him being mad at you, for example, about him being unsure about what he is finally going to do with you, about him not listening to you or not caring about you or not loving you — is pure fiction.

The God who has revealed himself fully in Jesus Christ is the only God there is. He is the God who loves you, who sent his Son to save you and his Spirit to make you what you are in Christ. He is the God who *will not be without you* and there is no other God but this one — Father, Son and Holy Spirit.

That means that the Holy Spirit empowers you, not for human means and ends, but for God's means and ends, which have to do with conforming you to the image of Christ, not with granting you the life — style of the rich and famous.

Baptism of the Spirit

To be baptized with the Holy Spirit (Mark 1:8) is to be baptized into the baptism of Jesus Christ. It is to enter into new life in Christ — the life of the kingdom of God. When Jesus was baptized in water, the Holy Spirit came upon him, and when we enter into Jesus' baptism, we enter the fellowship of the Holy Spirit who ministers to all the saints the things of Christ. Our baptism in water is a sign of the baptism we receive in Jesus, which is ministered to us from the Father by the Holy Spirit.

The gifts of the Spirit, then (see 1 Corinthians 12:7-11; 27-31), whether tongues or healing or administration or teaching or whatever they might be, are for the benefit of the body of Christ, and not for personal acclaim or gain (2 Peter 4:10). They are not to enable us to stand out among people or appear to be closer to God than others. They are not to make us feel more spiritual or more saved or more righteous than others. Rather, they are to enable us to share in Christ's work of love and redemption.

The Holy Spirit lives in us, unites us with the Father and the Son and transforms us into the image of Christ. If you are looking for riches, talk to an investment counselor. But if you are looking for hope, courage, endurance, love, mercy and help in time of need, talk to God. He'll send you the Holy Spirit.

For reflection:

- What is the meaning of baptism?
- What is baptism with the Holy Spirit?
- Who is the Holy Spirit?
- What is the Holy Spirit doing in the world? In the church? In your life?

For further reading:

The Outpouring of the Holy Spirit by Karl Barth (*Church Dogmatics,* vol. I, part 2, sections 16-18)
Understanding the Trinity, by Alister McGrath

A LESSON ABOUT BAPTISM (MARK 1:9-11)

By J. Michael Feazell

> At that time Jesus came from Nazareth in Galilee and was baptized by John in the Jordan. Just as Jesus was coming up out of the water, he saw heaven being torn open and the Spirit descending on him like a dove. And a voice came from heaven: "You are my Son, whom I love; with you I am well pleased." (NIV 2011)

Have you ever wondered why Jesus, who was sinless, would need to be baptized? After all, baptism is a sign of our sins being washed away, and Jesus didn't have any sins to wash away. Or did he?

Bore our sins

Jesus was sinless, and yet he, the sinless one, bore the sins of the whole world. Paul tells us in 2 Corinthians 5:21 that God made Jesus to be sin for our sakes, even though Jesus himself was sinless, "so that in him we might become the righteousness of God."

In keeping with God's purpose, Jesus was baptized for our sakes, not for his own. His baptism, like his death and resurrection, was a dramatic expression of God's grace toward sinful humanity.

When we are baptized, we are baptized into the baptism of Jesus Christ — a baptism that is directly linked to Jesus' sinless life and his death and resurrection on our behalf.

As us and for us

The Son of God became one of us in order to represent all of us before God. This is what Christians mean by "representative atonement." Because Jesus is human, one of us, he is able to represent all of us before God. But Jesus is more than our representative. He also took all of our sins upon himself, bearing our sins and their penalty in our place. That is what Christians mean by "substitutionary atonement." Jesus represents us before God, and he also substitutes for us before God. In substituting for us, he carries away our sins; in representing us, his righteousness is attributed to us. He is our "alpha and omega." Our salvation is in Jesus Christ, and him only, from beginning to end.

God's beloved

The voice from heaven said to Jesus, "You are my Son, whom I love; with you I am well pleased." But remember, Jesus is God's Son, beloved of God, for our sakes and as our representative. In saying this to Jesus, God says it to every person for whom Jesus died and rose again. In Christ, God says this to you and he says it to me.

In his baptism for us, Jesus embodies from both sides the promised relationship of love between God and his people. As God, he represents God to us. As human, he represents humanity to God. And this relationship that God has created between himself and humanity in the person Jesus Christ is the fulfillment of everything God promised to Israel, to the House of David, and through Israel to all of the world. In Christ, God has demonstrated in person his utter faithfulness to his covenant of love and redemption. God saves us because he loves us and wants us saved, and he did it in Jesus Christ.

Religion teaches us to think of salvation in terms of laws, i.e., God saves the lawkeepers and destroys the lawbreakers. But the gospel tells us that salvation is God's gift to sinners, i.e., God makes sinners righteous in Christ, their perfect representative before God. That's why we need to trust him for our salvation — it comes only through him, and not through our deeds. It is his commitment to us and his faithfulness to us that saves us, not our commitment and faithfulness to him. When we trust in Christ, we participate in Christ's perfect commitment and faithfulness on our behalf.

It is only because we are God's chosen ones, holy and beloved, that we can clothe ourselves "with compassion, kindness, humility, gentleness and patience" (Colossians 3:12). Because God identifies us with Jesus, and this even while we were still sinners (Romans 5:8), we are freed to walk with him in the paths of his love. God acted in Christ to make us righteous. We receive his righteousness; we do not generate our own, and in receiving his righteousness, we begin to walk in his ways.

Remember, Jesus did not come to vindicate the law, but to vindicate people — sinners, to be precise. Christians ought not fall for the religious (as opposed to gospel) idea that God is more concerned about the law than he is about people. Paul wrote: "But when the fullness of time [the "Today" of Hebrews 3:13 and 4:7] had come, God sent his Son, born of a woman, born under the law, in order to redeem those who were under the law, so that we might receive adoption as children" (Galatians 4:4-5, New Revised Standard Version).

When God says to Jesus, "You are my Son, the Beloved; with you I am well pleased," he is saying it also to all who are in Christ, because Christ has identified himself with humanity as one of us (Hebrews 2:16-17), both substituting for us and representing us in the presence of God.

A certain future

Because of sin, the only future for humanity is disaster — unless, that is, God is faithful to his covenant love. All the biblical descriptions of hell, whether pictured as outer darkness or a furnace of fire, with all its torment and anguish, are exactly what we would have to look forward to were it not for God's absolute faithfulness to his promises of forgiveness and redemption.

It is precisely the horror of hell that Jesus took on himself in our place; but hell could not defeat him or hold him; he broke its power and disarmed it and led it captive in his parade of victory over all powers and authorities (Ephesians 3:8-9; Colossians 2:13-15; 1 Peter 3:18-22). Captivity of every sort, whether the captivity of hell, of addiction, of human tyranny or of sin, has all been led captive by Jesus, our victorious Savior.

Struggle and failure

Yet even though we know all this, and even though we are fully committed to living godly lives in the light of Jesus Christ, we still fall short and do things that are contrary to the love of God.

But don't let that get you down. That is how things are right now, but it will not always be so. The day will come when the new creation that God has already made you to be in Christ (2 Corinthians 5:17; Galatians 6:15) will be fully unveiled (Colossians 3:1-4). And when that happens, there will be no more crying, no more pain and no more death (Revelation 21:4).

Trust him

Even now, our hope lies in this: God has proven in Christ his love for us and his faithfulness to us (consider Romans 5:6-8). He has made our cause his own. He has taken responsibility for us — sins and all. He has taken us under his wing, and he will never let us go. That is why we trust him.

God, who proves himself faithful to faithless Israel, is exactly the same God who is faithful to faithless you and me. He is the same from the beginning, which means he has and always will be for you, working to help and to heal, and not to condemn (consider John 3:17).

If you have turned your back on God, don't ever think he has turned his back on you. Quite the contrary. He's got the porch light on and dinner on the table, waiting for you to come home.

For reflection:

- How is Jesus' baptism related to our baptism?
- Why did the voice from heaven say, "With you I am well pleased" (Mark 1:11)?
- Is it hard for you to accept the fact that in Christ you are beloved by God (v. 11)?

A LESSON ABOUT TEMPTATION
(MARK 1:12-13)

By J. Michael Feazell

> At once the Spirit sent him out into the wilderness, and he was in the wilderness forty days, being tempted by Satan. He was with the wild animals, and angels attended him. (NIV 2011)

"I can resist anything but temptation!" says the bumper sticker. It's funny, but as with so many things, one of the reasons it is funny is because sometimes it is all too true. As Christians, we know that temptation toward sinful, illegal or destructive things needs to be resisted, and yet we often find ourselves losing the battle. That is not only frustrating, it can get downright depressing. It can even make us start to question whether God still loves and cares about us.

More than a role model

The fact that Jesus was tempted in all points like as we are (Hebrews 4:15), teaches us at least two things. One thing it teaches us is that just as Jesus overcame every temptation, so we need to follow his example and make every effort not to fall to temptation either. But there is so much more here, and it makes all the difference. If Jesus were merely a great role model that we should follow, there would be no hope for us. Following Jesus would then just be another of the world's many religions — humanly devised systems of coping with bad behavior and plagued consciences.

The other thing these temptation passages teach us is that Jesus overcame every temptation in our place, as one of us, both representing us and substituting for us before God. Notice where Hebrews 4 places the emphasis: First, Jesus is presented as an incomparable High Priest (v. 14). The job of a high priest is to mediate on behalf of the people toward God. He offers the sacrifices and acts as the go-between to get everything straightened out between sinning people and God. In religion, this concept keeps people mindful of the need to behave better and establishes a hierarchy of humans that can exercise control over the masses.

Gospel not another religion

But the gospel is not another religion. The gospel tells us that the real and true High Priest is God himself, the Second Person of the triune God — the one who became Jesus Christ. He died and rose from the dead in glory, and now is in heaven as a glorified man and the Son of God at once, making actual peace between sinning humans and God.

Jesus did not sin; he took all the sin of humanity onto his own head. But all the sin in the world was no match for the Son of God. In him, sin, all sin, found its demise. In Christ, God destroyed the work of the devil and defeated sin — our sin — once and for all. This is not religion; it is the gospel.

That is why Hebrews 4 emphasizes the truth that Jesus sympathizes with us in our weaknesses, and the truth that because of Jesus doing what he did regarding sin, we can come with boldness to the throne of grace to receive mercy and find grace to help in time of need.

We find the same emphasis in Hebrews 2:17-18. He became like us humans in every respect for the express purpose of being a merciful and faithful high priest in the service of God. He can help those who are being tested because he was tested like they are. How does he help them? By his sacrifice of atonement (restoration to fellowship with God) and by being merciful (he forgives you) and faithful (he'll do it every time).

Trust him

How do you get in on all this grace and mercy? Hebrews 3 says, "Take care, brothers and sisters, that none of you may have an evil, unbelieving heart that turns away from the living God" (v. 12, New Revised Standard Version). It goes on to say, "But encourage one another daily, as long as it is called Today, so that none of you may be hardened by sin's deceitfulness" (v. 13). How does sin deceive us? One way is by telling us, in effect: "Ha! God won't forgive you this time. You've crossed the line, pal, and the jig's up. His mercy only goes so far, you know, and frankly, it's reserved for those who clean up their act and stay in shape — not for the likes of you, sinbag."

Look how verse 14 puts it: "For we have become partners of Christ, if only we hold our first confidence firm to the end" (NRSV). In other words, trust him. Trust him to do what he says he does for you — forgives you. Trust him to be what he says he is for you — faithful. Trust him to know what he's doing. Trust him to love you the way he says he loves you. Trust him to be the Creator and the Redeemer of his Creation that he claims to be.

How can you lose out on such a great salvation? The same way you would lose out on a million dollars if you got a letter from the bank telling you someone had put it in your account, but you didn't believe the bank and never went to take it out — *by* not believing. By not trusting the giver of the gift. By not trusting God to love you and forgive you and transform you and make you his own child like he tells you he has already done (Ephesians 2:4-6; Colossians 1:13-14, 22; 2:13; 1 John 3:2).

Good news

The gospel really is good news! Trouble is, for many of us, it seems too good to be true. We want to have at least a short list of "do's and don'ts" to separate the wheat from the chaff. But God gave us no list. He gave us himself. In Christ, we have everything we need for salvation. He saves us; not Hail Marys or holy days or verbose prayers or even great worship music and perfect doctrinal understanding. We're not worth saving because we convince him we are; we're worth saving because he decided we are and did it.

We devote ourselves to love and good works and righteous living because Christ has given us a new mind and heart, not because we figured out by intensive study that "we'd better or else." And even so, we fall to temptation far more often than we wish we would. But in spite of our failures, it is Christ who saves, so who will bring a charge against us? Paul figured nobody could — and make it stick, that is — because nothing "in all creation, will be able to separate us from the love of God that is in Christ Jesus our Lord" (Romans 8:39).

So, why bring a charge against yourself? The only thing charging yourself can do is erode your trust in Christ to be the Forgiver and Grace-giver that he says he is for you.

For the love of us

Consider Jesus' temptation. First, the Spirit drove him into the desert. That reminds us that Father, Son and Holy Spirit are one God with one purpose for us, and that purpose is the redemption of the entire creation. Why the wilderness? Because the wilderness is the barren habitation of lizards, snakes, scorpions, barbed plants, buzzards and such like. It is representative of the world of sin, the world of the devil, the world of lies, deception and death.

It was there, on the devil's own turf, so to speak, that Jesus encountered the devil and defanged his power to overpower humanity. Jesus was at his weakest, physically speaking, after 40 days without food, but even at his weakest, he made short work of the devil's best stuff—satisfaction of physical appetites ("turn these stones into bread"), power, wealth and influence ("rule all the kingdoms of the world"), and self-indulgent arrogance ("show how important you are by jumping off the temple wall and making the angels catch you").

When it was over, the angels waited on him. He ate a legitimate meal, provided from the Father by the angels, not a meal the devil offered. And all this was only the starting point of his long journey to Jerusalem to be murdered, buried and resurrected to glory — as one of us for all of us.

What more could we ask? The very God we are afraid doesn't like us, is fed up with us and won't forgive us again, is the God who loved us so much that he sent his Son, not to condemn the world, but to save the world (John 3:16-17).

Take heart

In Christ, God has done for us what we could never do for ourselves. He has taken our sins on himself, forgiven us, reconciled us with himself and made us a new creation in Christ—redeemed, healed in mind, spirit and body and perfectly unified with him. Though we do not yet see what he has made us to be in Christ, we can trust his word that at his appearing, we will be like him (1 John 3:2).

In our own temptations, then, we can take heart. Christ is with us, drawing us to him and away from sin, but when we do sin, we have an advocate with the Father, Jesus Christ, the Righteous One, who not only set the example for us, but also made atonement for the sins of the whole world, including ours (1 John 2:1-2).

Trust him. He did it for you!

A LESSON ABOUT FULFILLMENT
(MARK 1:14-15)

By J. Michael Feazell

> After John was put in prison, Jesus went into Galilee, proclaiming the good news of God. "The time has come," he said. "The kingdom of God has come near. Repent and believe the good news!" (NIV 2011)

John's message of repentance was over; the time had come for Jesus' message to begin. Jesus' message is not identical to John's. John was preaching about a time to come; Jesus preached that the time had come. John preached a baptism of repentance for the remission of sins; Jesus preached that the kingdom itself was at hand, so believe the gospel. John did not preach the gospel; he preached that the gospel bearer was coming (for more on this, see Introduction to Mark).

Repentance and faith

Jesus preached the gospel, the good news that God had fulfilled his promises to Israel by sending the Messiah, or the Anointed One, to save the people. As a whole, however, the nation rejected Jesus as Messiah, because he did not fit the commonly accepted profile of what the Messiah should do. The Messiah was expected to lead the Jews to victory over the Roman occupation forces and restore the nation to a place of dominance in the world. Jesus showed no signs of becoming such a Messiah. Even John the Baptist finally began to wonder whether Jesus was really the one sent by God (Matthew 11:3).

The Messiah God sent was different from the one the people expected, because God's purpose in the world was different from what the people expected. The people expected God to vanquish their enemies and make their nation great. But God's purpose was to make a new covenant with the people, to write his laws in their hearts.

In the very midst of Israel's rejection of God's Messiah, a rejection in which every human shares, God chose to bring all sin to a head and destroy it once and for all. In that act of turning the pinnacle of human rebellion and opposition to himself into the means of human salvation, God not only fulfilled all his promises to Israel for their redemption (Acts 13:32-33), but also his word of promise for all the world (Genesis 22:18).

In other words, we are saved by God's act of salvation on our behalf, not by our repentance and faith. Were it not for the righteousness and the faith of the Son of God, we would not have repentance and faith. Our repentance and faith have meaning only because they are taken up into Jesus' righteousness and faith on our behalf and given meaning in him, for they neither have meaning nor substance on their own.

Not a transaction

It is a popular notion that repentance and faith are two different things. The idea is that a person has to repent of all his sins and then ask Jesus to come into his life, and then, on the basis of this repentance and commitment to Jesus, God will forgive the person's sins and grant him salvation.

That is not the gospel. The gospel is not a transaction. It is not a deal. It is not a tit for tat, nor an I'll-do-this-if-you-do-that arrangement. When we believe the gospel we are not causing God to save us. We are not satisfying some prerequisite. What we are doing when we believe the gospel is trusting God's word that he has already saved us through what he has already done for us in Jesus Christ. Our faith enables us to enjoy the gift we already have; it doesn't cause God to give it to us.

The gospel is good news. It is the good news that God loved everybody so much that he did something to save them from the destruction and alienation of sin. What God did — send his Son — he did purely and simply because he wanted to, not because we did something, or said something, or thought something in our hearts to bring it about.

We are saved because God already, in Christ, did everything necessary to make our salvation the reality that it is. Jesus said, "God so loved the world," not "God so loved several carefully picked ones." For us to repent and believe the gospel is to turn from our empty lives, ignorant of God's love and grace, and turn to belief in God's word about who he is for us and what he has done for us in Christ. It is a matter of believing a thing that is already true. And it is a matter of believing it because God tells us that it is true.

That is not a transaction. It is not a matter of the gospel not applying to us unless or until we do the right thing. Salvation is not remuneration for repentance. It is not remuneration for faith. It is not remuneration for anything. It is a gift, and a gift given to the world is ours, whether we like it or not.

Role of faith

To believe that God has given you a gift is not a pathway to receive the gift. It's a gift, and it is given by grace, not by saying the magic words. But believing is the path to taking up, using and enjoying the gift. If you don't believe you have a gift, you'll never take it up and use it, and you'll never enjoy its benefits.

So it is with the gospel. The gospel is true for us because God made it true for us. It doesn't suddenly become true when we repent and believe. It does, however, suddenly become plain to us what God has given us when we repent and believe. And in belief, or faith, or trust, we can walk in the light of Christ, where we once walked in darkness because of unbelief. Our unbelief did not mean that the gospel was not so for us; it only meant that we could not sense it. We were in the dark about it. We didn't know that God had redeemed us in Christ long before we were ever born.

Redemption

The gospel was fulfilled when the Son of God became one of us for our sakes. He was the fulfillment of all the prophecies to Israel (Acts13:32-33), and the means by which Israel became a blessing to all nations (Genesis 22:18; Galatians 3:8). He transformed the meaning of human life, human history and human time. All times, from the creation to the end of the world, are redeemed in him. All of human history — past, present and future — including your personal history, are redeemed in him. Human life itself, including your human life, is redeemed in him, made new, saved (see Colossians 1:19-20; Ephesians 1:9-10).

This is not something we are waiting for — it is fulfilled already, though we do not yet experience its fullness. We still wait for the redemption of our bodies, as Paul said, when "this mortal shall put on immortality." We still wait for the revealing of the new, clean and righteous us, which is hidden with Christ in God and will be revealed with him in glory when he is revealed (Colossians 3:3-4). But we already walk by faith in the light of the knowledge of the Son of God, tasting and drawing on today the fulfillment of the reality that awaits us with Christ in the age to come. Christ has wrought a new creation (see 2 Corinthians 5:17; Galatians 6:15), which we do not yet see in full, but we are part of it. In believers, the age to come has already begun to manifest itself.

Approach

It is this light, the light of the gospel, that we seek to share with all those who still walk in the darkness of unbelief. When we share the gospel, we are not saying, "You are hanging by a thread over the fires of hell; say these words and God will change his mind about you." Instead we are saying, as Thomas F. Torrance put it,

> Jesus Christ died for you precisely because you are sinful and

utterly unworthy of him, and has thereby already made you his own before and apart from your ever believing in him…. He has believed for you, fulfilled your human response to God, even made your personal decision for you, so that he acknowledges you before God as one who has already responded to God in him, who has already believed in God through him…in all of which he has been fully and completely accepted by the Father, so that in Jesus Christ you are already accepted by him. Therefore, renounce yourself, take up your cross and follow Jesus as your Lord and Saviour. (*The Mediation of Christ,* page 94)

When we understand the gospel of the unconditional grace of God, we no longer rely upon our faith or our commitment, but upon what Jesus Christ has done for us. Indeed, the time is fulfilled, and the kingdom of God is at hand. Repent, and believe the gospel.

For further reading
The Mediation of Christ by Thomas F. Torrance.

For reflection
What is the scope of the reconciliation that God has worked in Jesus Christ? (Colossians 1:19-20; Ephesians 1:9-10).

A LESSON ABOUT FISHING (MARK 1:16-20)

By J. Michael Feazell

As Jesus walked beside the Sea of Galilee, he saw Simon and his brother Andrew casting a net into the lake, for they were fishermen. "Come, follow me," Jesus said, "and I will send you out to fish for people." At once they left their nets and followed him.

When he had gone a little farther, he saw James son of Zebedee and his brother John in a boat, preparing their nets. Without delay he called them, and they left their father Zebedee in the boat with the hired men and followed him. (NIV 2011)

When I was a small boy growing up in northern Louisiana, I went fishing every chance I got. By age six, though, we had moved to Southern California, and between the rigors of big city life and my family not having a lot of money, chances for fishing were dramatically fewer. Still, there were the occasional trips to the Malibu pier with a friend, and a couple of times a year my uncle took me out on one of the off-shore barges that local fishing enthusiasts flocked to. Between sessions of untangling lines with the elbow-to-elbow crowd on board, we usually managed to hook a couple of bonita, several mackerel and if we were really lucky, a small halibut.

We fished the Kern River a couple of times, as well as Lake Isabella and Lake Piru. As a boy, I had a clear definition of the difference between freshwater and saltwater fishing: Freshwater fishing is usually more relaxing, but the fish are smaller and you're less likely to catch one.

The kind of fishing the Zebedee boys were doing in Jesus' day was nothing like the hook, line and sinker kind I enjoy. What they did was work, hard work. They would have thought I was crazy if I had suggested: "Hey guys, let's take a break and go fishing. We all need some rest."

They had huge, heavy nets to cast out, draw in, unload, clean, dry and mend. They had hundreds of fish to process and sell. They had the boat to clean and repair. Fishing was not a sport or a break. It was their livelihood, and in many ways it was their life.

We are not told whether James and John liked their part in their dad's fishing business. All we know is that when Jesus called them, they left it and followed him. Presumably, Jesus said the same thing to them that he said to Simon and Andrew, "Come, follow me, and I will send you out to fish for people."

What did Jesus have in mind when he said, "fish for people"?

Most of us Bible types are quick to run analogies into the ground. Jesus, being a good bit smarter than we are and knowing a little something about analogies, probably was thinking more about the obvious parallels than the picky details that sometimes fill sermon time and Bible study sessions. Instead of casting nets to draw in fish for breakfast tables, these disciples would now be casting the gospel to draw in people for the kingdom of God.

In Mark's previous paragraph, he described Jesus as preaching, "Repent and believe the good news" (v. 15). It's a rather indiscriminate message. Like a net, it falls wherever it falls and, like fish, some people get caught in it while others swim obliviously by.

We count the fish who, by time and chance, escape the net, as lucky fellows who will grow a little bigger for the next time the net comes their way. We count the people who run from or dismiss the gospel as missing out on the best thing that could ever happen to them, and we pray that they might get caught next time the gospel splashes down around them.

However, as Jesus mentioned once in a parable, the fishing net gathers up a whole lot of stuff besides good-eatin' fish (Matthew 13:47-48). The net does not discriminate; it picks up every kind of fish out there, good and bad alike. At the end of the day the worthless ones have to be separated out and discarded.

Likewise, the gospel does not discriminate; it applies to the whole world (John 3:16; 1 John 2:1-2). But the only ones who can join the great celebration of the kingdom of God are the ones who believe that they really are in God's gracious net. If they won't trust God's word of love and grace for them, then the gospel of their salvation is meaningless to them, and they cannot even understand the kingdom of God, much less desire to be part of it. They prefer their own kingdom, the shriveled, selfish one they think is so grand. So they have to be tossed out of God's banquet room, where he had places set for everybody.

The kingdom of God is not a matter of choice; it's a matter of trust. Peter, Andrew, James and John trusted Jesus, which is why they followed him. It wasn't that they sized things up and chose, like choosing ice cream over spoiled milk. It was that they trusted this person who called them. He wasn't calling them to a finer and grander life; he was calling them to persecution and deprivation — and eventually to getting murdered.

If it was a choice issue, then only a foolish son would run off after an itinerant preacher instead of maintaining the family business and ensuring the care and security of his parents and siblings. But it was a trust issue — they trusted Jesus. Only in the light of trust can we see clearly that there really is no choice at all but to follow him.

Doubt

But let's face it, sometimes we doubt. We sin, and we doubt our standing with God. Our plans and hopes are frustrated, and we might doubt whether God cares. Bad things happen to us, and we might even doubt there is a God. Doubt is always just a downturn away, ready to move in on our often fragile faith.

But those ups and downs in the strength of our faith are all part of learning to trust Jesus Christ. God accepted his faith in our place and on our behalf, so it isn't a matter of how strong or weak our faith is — Jesus' faith before God on our behalf is what matters. Again, we rely on him, not on our faith.

Likewise, our success in overcoming is not what we should use as a measure of our standing with God. God accepted Jesus' righteousness in our place and on our behalf, so it isn't a matter of how much progress we make in overcoming — Jesus' righteousness on our behalf is what matters. That's why we rely on him, not on the level or steadiness of our success in overcoming. Indeed, the Spirit leads us into right behavior, but right behavior is no measure of our standing with God. We stand right with God for one reason only — God loved us so much that his Son took humanity into himself and through his life, death and resurrection made humanity righteous in his righteousness. That is the substance, the reality, of our righteous standing before God.

In spite of our sins

A friend who grew up as a foster child who was shuffled from home to home expressed how he had trouble trusting new foster parents. In the back of his mind, he believed that once the new parents discovered the extent of his faults and problems, they would reject him and send him on. He would try very hard to please the new family, desperately trying to measure up, but eventually he would have to pack up and move again.

Sometimes, we can feel a bit like that in our relationship with God. We want to believe his good word for us, but in the back of our mind, there is the nagging doubt that God won't really accept us in spite of our sins. So we make up all kinds of ways to keep ourselves on the straight and narrow, desperately trying to measure up to some semblance of a person decent enough for God to accept. And all the while, deep inside, we believe we are sunk, because in our most honest moments we know our sins are dark and many.

If we could only believe the gospel, we would believe that Christ died for us because we are sinners, and that in spite of our sins, he has determined not to be without us. He wants us to trust him to love us in spite of all we are, all the mess we've made of life, all the problems we've caused, people we've hurt, things we've said and places we've been. He wants us to trust him to be our righteousness, trust him to clean up our lives, and above all, to trust him to love us unconditionally and to never leave us nor forsake us.

The gospel is good news for bad people, and unlike fishing nets, it doesn't need washing and mending. It's perfect just the way it is.

Further reading
The Mediation of Christ by Thomas F. Torrance

For reflection
When have you felt as though God couldn't really love a person like you? Have you talked to him about it?

A LESSON ABOUT AUTHORITY
(MARK 1:21-28)

By J. Michael Feazell

They went to Capernaum, and when the Sabbath came, Jesus went into the synagogue and began to teach. The people were amazed at his teaching, because he taught them as one who had authority, not as the teachers of the law. Just then a man in their synagogue who was possessed by an impure spirit cried out, "What do you want with us, Jesus of Nazareth? Have you come to destroy us? I know who you are—the Holy One of God!"

"Be quiet!" said Jesus sternly. "Come out of him!" The impure spirit shook the man violently and came out of him with a shriek.

The people were all so amazed that they asked each other, "What is this? A new teaching—and with authority! He even gives orders to impure spirits and they obey him." News about him spread quickly over the whole region of Galilee. (NIV 2011)

The teachers of the law didn't speak with their own authority. They necessarily prefaced their comments with something like "There is a saying that..." or "Rabbi Such-and-Such said..." Even the prophets rightly attributed their pronouncements to "Thus says the Lord..." But Jesus said simply, "I say to you..."

Here was a man who spoke with his own authority, not in the name of another. That alone was amazing. But if that were not amazing enough, Jesus demonstrated his authority when he told an evil spirit what to do, and the evil spirit obeyed.

In Jesus' day, evil spirits were considered, even by many Jewish teachers, to be numerous and powerful, hanging around everywhere and doing whatever they could to inflict trouble and suffering. When someone seemed to be possessed of a demon, the exorcists, whether Jewish or pagan, used complicated magical rites and spells to compel the demon to leave. The power was in the magic, it was believed, so whoever knew the right incantations and ingredients and methods could use them to bring about the unseen conditions that would manipulate the spirit world.

But Jesus was astonishingly different. When the demon-possessed man disrupted the meeting, Jesus simply ordered the demon to leave, and it left. The people in the synagogue had never seen anything like it. Who could have such authority that even the evil spirits have to obey his straightforward word?

Not authoritarian

Jesus, the Son of God, had all the authority in the world—in the universe. God created all things through him and put all things under him. So even these spirits that turned evil, though he allowed them to exist, were completely subject to him (see Colossians 1:16; Ephesians 1:20-21).

Yet Jesus did not use his incomparable authority the way we humans tend to use our little sprigs of authority. "Man, proud man, drest in a little brief authority," wrote Shakespeare. For many humans, authority becomes merely a means of enriching oneself, of getting one's own way, of suppressing the truth, and of getting and holding the power to keep doing those things. Witness the parade of totalitarian regimes, corporate executive, government and ecclesiastical scandals, tyrannical parents, bosses, teachers, government officials and the like.

Not so with Jesus. He has all the authority there is, yet he uses it entirely differently from the way many people would. Let's look at a few examples:

He took action when necessary. Jesus did not stifle normal living by trying to prevent all possibility of something going wrong. He didn't post sentries at the doors to keep all potential demon-possessed-looking people from coming in. He simply dealt with the problem decisively when it arose.

He didn't overreact. Jesus didn't make a Broadway production out of making the demon leave. He didn't knock the demon around for a while, tell it off for 10 minutes, scream at it, kill it or declare war on all demons. He just made it go.

He didn't crow about it. Jesus didn't use the incident to further his image. He didn't print up flyers and bill himself as the one who tossed out the demon.

Servant authority

Jesus uses authority to serve, not to be served. And that is how he wants us to use whatever authority we might have. Whether our authority is at home, at work, or somewhere else, he wants us to use it to help others, not to make ourselves into big shots.

Later in Mark's Gospel, Jesus explained it to his disciples like this, "You know that those who are regarded as rulers of the Gentiles lord it over them, and their high officials exercise authority over them. Not so with you. Instead, whoever wants to become great among you must be your servant, and whoever wants to be first must be slave of all. For even the Son of Man did not come to be served, but to serve, and to give his life as a ransom for many" (Mark 10:42-45).

What a difference it makes when the authority we're subject to is a blessing instead of a curse. "When the wicked rule, the people groan," says

Proverbs 29:2. It is when authority is used to help, not to overpower, that those under it can rejoice.

Jesus doesn't overpower us to make us knuckle under. He serves us with patience and mercy, helping us grow to see how much we need him. Sin is a cruel, harsh, manipulative, unforgiving taskmaster. Jesus is compassionate, gracious, patient, loving and merciful. The authority of sin is fraudulent, but the authority of Jesus is absolute.

Walk with Jesus

Why not take your needs to Jesus? Give your problems to him and trust him to see you through them.

When it comes to Jesus' authority in our lives, how do you think he uses it? To help us, or to lord it over us? Many of us live as though we think Jesus uses his authority to lord it over us. We assume his love for us is conditioned on how well we behave. We feel discouraged and fearful that God no longer loves us when we fail to measure up in our obedience.

But Jesus uses his authority to help us, not to destroy us. He drives out the demons, not us. And literal evil spirits are not the only kind of demons Jesus has authority over and drives out for us. Sin itself is an enemy that does us damage and lords it over us. So are our fears and our doubts.

When our sins and fears start a commotion, it's time for us to take them to the one who knows how to handle them. We can take them to Jesus in prayer and trust him to know what to do.

What's your enemy? What habit, what sin, what fear plagues you, saps your courage and energy? What has you beaten down, enslaved? Whatever it is, it cannot withstand the authority of Jesus. When you give these battles to him, the complexion of the war changes — the enemy is on the run. When you stand close to Jesus, these enemies can't have the last word and can't push you around. When your attention is on Jesus, they don't seem so fearsome, so strong, because Jesus puts them into perspective as the puny weaklings they really are. In Jesus, you are bold and strong, and these bullying, fast-talking fears and sinful habits are weak and insignificant.

Why not take your needs to Jesus? Give your problems to him and trust him to see you through them. He's there for you, now and always.

For reflection:

Why were those at the synagogue amazed at Jesus' teaching?
Why did the evil spirits have to obey Jesus?
How did Jesus use authority?
How can Jesus help you?

A LESSON ABOUT ASKING (MARK 1:29-34)

By J. Michael Feazell

> As soon as they left the synagogue, they went with James and John to the home of Simon and Andrew. Simon's mother-in-law was in bed with a fever, and they immediately told Jesus about her. So he went to her, took her hand and helped her up. The fever left her and she began to wait on them.
>
> That evening after sunset the people brought to Jesus all the sick and demon-possessed. The whole town gathered at the door, and Jesus healed many who had various diseases. He also drove out many demons, but he would not let the demons speak because they knew who he was. (NIV 2011)

Even Jesus needed a rest. The synagogue let out in time for the Sabbath meal at noon, and Jesus went to the home of Simon and Andrew to eat. But even in a private setting, he was ready to help those who asked him. This wasn't a "big" miracle in terms of crowds and renown. It was a private, personal, family need. The household had come to know Jesus as one who cares and helps, so they made it a point to tell him about Simon's mother-in-law having a fever.

Take it to the Lord

We don't know whether Jesus knew about Simon's mother-in-law being sick before they told him. But we do know this: as soon as they told Jesus about her, he went to her and healed her.

That sounds like a good case for telling Jesus about things. Yes, there is no question that Jesus already knows what our needs are, but he wants us to learn to ask him to help us with them. The same goes for the needs of others. Jesus already knows what their needs are. But he wants us, his people who have his Spirit in us, to ask him to help. Simon's mother didn't ask Jesus to come to her; others did.

Why should we go through the traumas and crises of life alone? In the Psalms, God gives us examples of his people taking personal fears and concerns to him. When we lay out our problems before God, we know we have been listened to, and we know we are in the hands of someone who will do for us what is right and good.

"Even though I walk through the darkest valley, I will fear no evil, for you are with me; your rod and your staff, they comfort me" (Psalm 23:4).

Asking for help

When we ask Jesus to help, it shows certain things about us:

It shows that we know Jesus is the right one to ask.

It shows that we trust Jesus.

It shows that we care about the problems that Jesus cares about.

It shows that our hope is in Jesus.

It shows that our lives revolve around Jesus.

It shows that we belong to Jesus.

When we ask Jesus to help, it does certain things to us:

It reminds us of Jesus' power.

It reminds us of Jesus' love.

It reminds us that Jesus is in charge of everything.

It reminds us that Jesus knows our needs.

It reminds us that Jesus wants to help us.

It reminds us that Jesus listens to us.

It reminds us that Jesus does what is right and good for us.

When answers come

As soon as Jesus healed her, Simon's mother-in-law got up and started serving others. If we were to draw a principle from this, it would be that just as Peter's mother-in-law used the strength Jesus gave her to do good things for others, so we should devote what Jesus gives us to doing good for others. She did what she could do, and we should do what we can do. It all amounts to the same thing — taking care of each other.

Anyone can ask

After sunset the crowds arrived. The news had spread about how Jesus had cast out the demon, so the town brought their sick and demon-possessed to Simon's door, and Jesus healed them.

Jesus is good regardless of who asks. It's hard to imagine that everyone in town that night was a holy, righteous haloed saint.

Capernaum was like other towns, full of regular people who were regular sinners from every walk of life. But they came anyway, sins and all, and bathed in the glory of the Son of God. Jesus didn't ask them forty questions before he healed them. He didn't get out the sacred scales and weigh their sins against their good deeds. He just healed them. That's how he is.

Redeemer of his creation. He created in love and he redeems in love. He wants everyone to come to him, because in him is the only place healing and life truly exist. That evening in Galilee, the people of Capernaum had a taste in the here-and-now of the kingdom age to come.

Authority to help

When the Jewish exorcists and healers tried to cast out demons or heal fevers, they followed prescribed magic-like rituals, some of which are laid down in the Talmud. For example, according to William Barclay: "The Talmud actually lays down the method of dealing with it [a burning fever like that of Simon's mother-in-law]. A knife wholly made of iron was tied by a braid of hair to a thorn bush. On successive days there was repeated, first, Exodus 3:2-3; second, Exodus 3:4; and finally Exodus 3:5. Then a certain magical formula was pronounced, and thus the cure was supposed to be achieved."

Jesus amazed everyone because he didn't use any kind of ritual or incantation at all. He simply ordered demons to leave on his own authority, and they left. He simply told people to rise and walk, or touched their leprous skin, or took their hand and lifted them up and they were healed. His authority was and is the authority of the Maker and Ruler of all things.

That's why you can bring your problems to him. That's why you can trust him to do for you what is right and good. What's eating away at you right now? Why not take it to Jesus and ask him to help you?

Reflection:

1. Does Jesus perform only large miracles, or will he help you in small things?

2. What do you need to tell Jesus about?

For further reading:

Prayer: Finding the Heart's True Home, by Richard Foster

A LESSON ABOUT PRIORITIES
(MARK 1:35-39)

By J. Michael Feazell

> Very early in the morning, while it was still dark, Jesus got up, left the house and went off to a solitary place, where he prayed. Simon and his companions went to look for him, and when they found him, they exclaimed: "Everyone is looking for you!"
>
> Jesus replied, "Let us go somewhere else—to the nearby villages—so I can preach there also. That is why I have come." So he traveled throughout Galilee, preaching in their synagogues and driving out demons. (NIV 2011)

What's important? We usually consider whatever is the most urgent to be the most important. When we need to use the bathroom, for example, that need becomes both urgent and important, something that must for the moment take priority over everything else. Many things take a priority spot in our lives. Sometimes it might be a movie or television show we've been waiting to see. It might be a trip we want to take, or a special event we want to arrange or attend. Sometimes it might be something we want to buy, maybe a new CD, a pair of jeans, a computer, a car or a house. The priority might be a relationship, a job, a project. It might be an illness, a tragedy or a difficult ordeal.

Prayer a priority

Prayer is the kind of priority that lies at the root of all the others — at the root of life itself. It's a lot like eating; if we rarely eat, our physical health will suffer. We'll be weak and sick. It will affect our ability to carry on the activities of life. In a similar way, if we rarely pray, our spiritual life will lack vitality. We'll approach the challenges and successes of life on our own, as though we're not totally dependent on God even for life itself.

Without prayer, we fall into fear, anxious worry and even despair.

Without prayer, we begin to take credit for the good things in our lives, chalking them up to our skill, knowledge, wisdom and hard work. We begin to forget that all our skill, knowledge, wisdom and hard work are gifts of God—he gave us the mind, body and circumstances of life that enabled us to have and develop those attributes.

On the other hand, without prayer, we fall into fear, anxious worry and even despair at the failures, frustrations and bad events in our lives. We become unsure of God's love for us, unsure that he stands with us in our problems. We feel alone and afraid, doubtful about our ability to cope with what life is heaping onto us.

Prayer is the grease, we might say, that keeps the gears and wheels of life in good working order. Without prayer, we see ourselves as alone against the world, left to fend off the storms of life on our own wits and brawn. It is in the course of prayer that we learn to see the true state of things — that we are creatures within a creation, creatures dependent on our Maker and on all the other parts of the creation, and as such, never alone.

Hard to find time

It's a crowded, hectic world for most people. Opportunities for time alone, much less for prayer, are limited. Life has its immediate demands, its already scheduled priorities lined up to overwhelm us and keep us forever playing catch-up—jobs, classes, homework, housework, yard work, kids, church, health problems, car problems, home repairs, accidents, ants, traffic, crowds, lines, appointments and, oh yes, sleep.

Of course, there might well be a considerable amount of time that we could devote to prayer that we use on other things — things that don't really have the kind of priority that prayer should. For example, most of us have our favorite television show, and that's fine. But how often do we find ourselves sitting in front of the television — watching shows we don't really care about — just because nobody got up and turned the infernal thing off?

We make priorities out of things we care about. It isn't that we don't care about prayer, it's just that it often seems like just one more chore on top of all the other chores, and since God doesn't cry when he doesn't get his dinner or send collection agents out to repossess the washing machine, we tend to put prayer farther down the priority list.

It might be helpful to see prayer in a different light from that of one more chore to get done before (or after) turning off the light at night. Time with God is different from other time. It refreshes and rejuvenates. It relaxes the mind and body to release to God our worries, our anger, fear and anxiety. It's a better antidote to frustration than nibbling on donuts or chocolate bars. It fills our need for intimacy better than affairs or pornography. It's a far more productive way to handle anger than exploding at our spouses and children. It lasts; those alternatives don't.

Therapy, not duty

It's easy to view prayer as a duty, an obligation. When we do that, prayer becomes hard, something to put off, a burden and pressure all by itself. What a tragedy. We'd hardly consider talking to our best friends a duty. We talk to them because we like them. It's a lift to talk to them. It helps us feel better, reminds us we're not alone in this world, gives us strength to carry on.

It's harder with God. God's invisible. And he doesn't say much. Sometimes we wonder if he's even there at all. We have the Bible, but a book isn't the same as an oral conversation.

Talking to God takes place, you could say, in our heads, by faith, not by sight, touch or sound. We can't look God in the eye, smell him, shake his hand or pat his back. Instead, we "sense" his presence in some spiritual, unseen way. We believe. We trust. The Holy Spirit, also invisible, tasteless and odorless, communicates God's reality to us on a level other than our five physical senses. We don't understand it; we can only experience it.

Spending this time with God is great therapy. Therapy is remedial treatment of a bodily disorder, whether physical, emotional or psychological. When we think of prayer as much needed therapy, rather than as "our Christian duty," it puts prayer into a clearer perspective, I think. When we go through our daily, weekly, monthly routines without acknowledging God as the root and core of our lives (which he is), our attitudes, emotions, psyche, even our bodies, suffer the ill effects of trying to live as though we are self-existent — not dependent on God and his creation for our life and being.

To hand over our concerns to God, whether for ourselves or for others, reminds us that our lives and future are in God's hands. Even our past, with all its baggage of sin, selfishness and ignorance, is in God's redemptive hands. The act of acknowledging God as the loving, wise and powerful Being that he is, is remedial treatment for fear, worry and frustration. It's like an expert massage, removing tension and stress from our muscles, only better. Who wouldn't like a great massage every day?

Prayer is the perfect therapy for our tense, knotted and stressed spirits, and it's free! We can take a moment for a quick spiritual "rubdown" in the form of silent prayer just about any time we want during the day. And we can set aside time for a good, long session at times that work with our schedules. Think about it: if you had a certificate for a free full-body massage every day, you'd likely find a way to work it into your schedule as often as possible — even if you had to get up before everybody else and hightail it down to the gym at 5:30 a.m. You'd do that because you know what good therapy it is and how good it makes you feel. (If you are one who doesn't like or can't tolerate massages, please forgive the analogy.)

Not a substitute for action

There is another thing we can learn from Jesus' early morning hike to a solitary place for prayer. When it's time for action, it's time for action. When your child or your spouse needs your attention, it is not the time to go off and pray. When you need to repair a faucet, or make a call, or prepare a meal, it's not the time to disappear for an hour in a closet. We can and should be able to pray any time, any place, while we go about our business. The time to go to a solitary place for extended prayer is a time when we don't have other duties, responsibilities and obligations.

How did Jesus do it? In the instance cited in this passage, he got up early, before the regular day's activities began. You might find that other times work better for you. The point is, see prayer as a priority that will make all your other priorities more manageable and less stressful. Let your prayer time be a time to relax, to let God's love bathe and salve your frayed nerves, your taut emotions, your exhausted and frightened heart. Let prayer time be your time to rest in God, to let him renew your strength, brighten your hope, sharpen your faith.

Has prayer slipped to the bottom of your "to do" list? Why not set aside some time today for an overdue therapy session with the Master Therapist?

For reflection:

Does prayer seem like a chore to you? Why or why not?

Do you have trouble thinking of things to pray about? Have you thought of sitting quietly with God as a valuable part of your prayer time?

What are some of the ways prayer has helped you?

How would you describe "answered prayer"?

What is your favorite place for prayer?

Suggested Reading

Prayer: Finding the Heart's True Home, by Richard Foster

A LESSON ABOUT MISPERCEPTION
(MARK 1:40-45)

By J. Michael Feazell

A man with leprosy came to him and begged him on his knees, "If you are willing, you can make me clean."

Jesus was indignant. He reached out his hand and touched the man. "I am willing," he said. "Be clean!" Immediately the leprosy left him and he was cleansed.

Jesus sent him away at once with a strong warning: "See that you don't tell this to anyone. But go, show yourself to the priest and offer the sacrifices that Moses commanded for your cleansing, as a testimony to them." Instead he went out and began to talk freely, spreading the news. As a result, Jesus could no longer enter a town openly but stayed outside in lonely places. Yet the people still came to him from everywhere. (NIV 2011)

We are not going to talk about begging Jesus on our knees for healing. I suppose many people have taken this passage as an example of what to do when we sincerely desire to be healed of an affliction. But just about as many people have been disappointed to find that Jesus did not respond to them in the same way as he responded to this leper. So there is no sense in our pretending that if we go to Jesus on our knees and beg for healing that we will assuredly receive it. We believe that Jesus has given us the greatest healing of all — healing from our sins — but he does not always heal our physical ailments. We trust him to do what is right and good for us and to stand with us in our suffering.

Nor are we going to talk about offering the sacrifices that Moses commanded for cleansing. Much has been said and written about the differences between the old and the new biblical covenants; there is no need to cover that again here.

To obey or not to obey

The lesson we are going to consider in this article has to do with why Jesus did not want the healed leper to tell anyone about his healing. Jesus gave the healed leper the strong warning, "See that you don't tell this to anyone." But the former leper did not obey Jesus. He went straight out and freely spread the news. As a result of this man's disobedience, "Jesus could no longer enter a town openly but stayed outside in lonely places." Even in the lonely places, people came to him "from everywhere."

Should we applaud the former leper, or should we lament his disobedience to Jesus' strong warning? I am reluctant to try to answer that question, except to say that I have found that it is smarter to obey Jesus than not to obey Jesus.

In today's world we have the view that telling people about Jesus by whatever means we can muster is the most important activity in which we can be involved. So when we read that the healed leper went out and "began to talk freely, spreading the news," we tend to get excited and wish we could have that same overwhelming joy and evangelistic fervor. For this reason, many of us like to magnify healings and other miracles into advertisements and publicity opportunities for the gospel.

But Jesus did not want that man to go out and spread the news. Jesus wanted his identity as healer of the sick to remain secret. In verse 34, we read that Jesus would not let the demons speak because they knew who he was. Similarly, in chapter 8, Jesus asks the disciples, "Who do people say I am?" Peter replied, "You are the Christ." Jesus responded by warning the disciples not to tell anyone about him. That is the very opposite of what we might have expected. We want everyone to know about Jesus. But Jesus did not want everyone to know about him. What's going on?

Messianic secret

Why would Jesus want his disciples not to tell anyone about him? Here was the visible, flesh and blood, miracle-working Jesus walking and preaching all over the country. What better time for his followers to lead people to him and tell them who he was? Unlike today, when we must tell people to trust an invisible Jesus in faith, here Jesus was in the flesh. But Jesus was clear, strong, and even stern in saying, "Don't tell anyone who I am."

Perhaps one of the reasons Jesus gave this order lay in the expectations of the crowds who followed him. What did they want? What were they looking for?

In chapter 11, we find a clue. When Jesus entered Jerusalem the week before he was crucified, "Many people spread their cloaks on the road, while others spread branches they had cut in the fields. Those who went ahead and those who followed shouted, 'Hosanna!' 'Blessed is he who comes in the name of the Lord!' 'Blessed is the coming kingdom of our father David!' 'Hosanna in the highest heaven!'" (Mark 11:8-10).

When people heard that Jesus was the Messiah, they were happy to receive the news. The problem lay in definitions and expectations. What the people expected Messiah to be and to do was quite different from what Jesus the

Messiah came to be and to do. The people expected a king who would rally the people, and with the blessing of God, lead them to victory over their Roman conquerors and restore the kingdom of David in all its glory. They did not understand what Messiahship was all about. Their idea of Messiah was different from God's idea of Messiah. When they heard the term, they misunderstood it, because they had been conditioned to expect something else.

With this in mind, it becomes clearer why Jesus did not want his disciples or those he healed to spread the news about him. It was not the right time for the people to hear. The right time for the news to spread was after Jesus had been executed and raised from the dead. Only then could the real purpose of God in sending Messiah be understood for what it was.

Lesson

In our world today, there are many concepts about God. If you talk to 10 people on the street, you will likely find 10 different opinions about who God is, what God is like, how God deals with humans and what God expects of us. Surveys by George Barna have shown that even among Christians, ideas about who Jesus is, what grace is and how it works, sin, forgiveness, faith, repentance, obedience, etc., vary widely. How much more do ideas about Jesus vary among non-Christians?

Suppose I approach a stranger sitting on a park bench and ask him if he knows Jesus. Suppose the stranger's idea of Jesus is that of a long-haired, wispy-looking weakling. Suppose his mother used to tell him that Jesus didn't like it when he played cards. Suppose his most frequent exposure to the word Jesus was on a dirty cardboard "Do you know Jesus" placard glued in the parking garage of his apartment building.

People listen to friends. People listen to those who have proven they care.

What would likely be the first impression this man would have of me and my question? Would that promote the gospel?

Suppose, on the other hand, I met the man, and over a period of time developed a relationship with him. Suppose we became friends. Suppose I was not a flagrant hypocrite and that my life and the way I treated this friend usually reflected the love of God. Suppose he found out, as friends usually do, that I was a Christian. Would that tend to change his flawed perspective on Jesus and Christianity to a more accurate one?

A time to plant...

Ecclesiastes 3:1-8 points out that there is "a time for everything, a season for every activity under heaven" (New Living Translation). Among these are "a time to plant and a time to harvest" and "a time to be quiet and a time to speak up." The time to spread the news about Jesus came after his resurrection, not during his ministry; until his resurrection, there could not be sufficient understanding of who he really was. Even the disciples were consistently ignorant about Jesus' full identity and mission until after the resurrection (Mark 6:52; 8:17).

The same principle applies today — people are often not ready to hear and comprehend who Jesus is until they experience his resurrection life in his people, the church.

"Be careful how you live among your unbelieving neighbors. Even if they accuse you of doing wrong, they will see your honorable behavior, and they will believe and give honor to God when he comes to judge the world" (1 Peter 2:12, NLT). Peter does not say, "Press your unbelieving neighbors for a decision." His focus is on believers' "honorable behavior." Why? Because through our honorable behavior, our unbelieving neighbors see the living Christ in action. Peter says this will result in their belief at a time when God chooses ("when he comes to judge the world" implies God's timing, not ours).

"Most important of all," Peter says, is that we "continue to show deep love for each other" (1 Peter 4:8, NLT). In a similar vein, Paul wrote, "As we have opportunity, let us do good to all people, especially to those who belong to the family of believers" (Galatians 6:10).

Their instruction on evangelism centered on the witness of a godly life in Christ, not a well rehearsed speech. It is our lives in him that show people who Jesus really is.

Accurate perception

"Instead," Peter wrote, "you must worship Christ as Lord of your life. And if you are asked about your Christian hope, always be ready to explain it" (1 Peter 3:15, NLT). When a person asks about our Christian hope *because we live as though Christ is the Lord of our life,* then that person has a more accurate perspective of Jesus because he or she has seen Jesus in us. They ask because the Spirit prompts them, and the catalyst the Spirit uses is our godly behavior in Christ, the Lord of our life.

And our conversation, Paul said, should be "gracious and attractive so that you will have the right response for everyone" (Colossians 4:6, NLT). People listen to friends. People listen to those who have proven they care. People listen when the relationship is real, not artificial.

Peter wrote: "God has given each of you a gift from his great variety of spiritual gifts. Use them well to serve one another" (1 Peter 4:10). God has richly blessed us with active parts in his work of building up the body of Christ, the church, and reaching out with the gospel to nonbelievers. The greatest tool he has given us is his own life, ministered to us by the Holy Spirit and reflected in the way we live.

For reflection:

- What gifts has God given you? How do you manage them?
- Does God's generosity flow through you?
- Who is God nudging you to get to know better?
- When we pray for people, we tend to show them more active care. Which nonbelieving friends or neighbors are you actively praying for?

A LESSON ABOUT HEALING (MARK 2:1-12)

By J. Michael Feazell

A few days later, when Jesus again entered Capernaum, the people heard that he had come home. They gathered in such large numbers that there was no room left, not even outside the door, and he preached the word to them. Some men came, bringing to him a paralyzed man, carried by four of them. Since they could not get him to Jesus because of the crowd, they made an opening in the roof above Jesus by digging through it and then lowered the mat the man was lying on. When Jesus saw their faith, he said to the paralyzed man, "Son, your sins are forgiven."

Now some teachers of the law were sitting there, thinking to themselves, "Why does this fellow talk like that? He's blaspheming! Who can forgive sins but God alone?"

Immediately Jesus knew in his spirit that this was what they were thinking in their hearts, and he said to them, "Why are you thinking these things? Which is easier: to say to this paralyzed man, 'Your sins are forgiven,' or to say, 'Get up, take your mat and walk'? But I want you to know that the Son of Man has authority on earth to forgive sins." So he said to the man, "I tell you, get up, take your mat and go home." He got up, took his mat and walked out in full view of them all. This amazed everyone and they praised God, saying, "We have never seen anything like this!" (NIV 2011)

This is a story about a lame man whose friends believed that Jesus could heal him. At last they found a way to get their friend before Jesus by opening the roof and letting him down by ropes attached to his bed. But Jesus didn't heal the man's lameness — he forgave his sins.

The teachers of the law didn't like that, and with good cause. How could a mere man forgive sins, something that only God had authority to do? Jesus knew their thoughts, and he asked them a question, "Which is easier: to say to this paralyzed man, 'Your sins are forgiven,' or to say, 'Get up, take your mat and walk'?"

It's a rhetorical question. Both statements would be impossible for anyone but God. If Jesus had authority to make the lame walk by merely uttering the word, then he also had authority to forgive sins, because the power to do either was in God's domain, not man's.

Today, a team of doctors might be able to restore the ability to walk to people with certain kinds of problems. Even after the operation, however, the person would still need a long period of therapy and rehabilitation. But no one, not even the finest doctor, can simply say, "Rise up and walk," and cause it to happen.

Which is easier?

Which is easier to say to a paralyzed man, "Your sins are forgiven," or "Rise up and walk"? It seems to me that "Your sins are forgiven" is easier.

Why? Sins are between people and God, and their forgiveness is therefore invisible, like God is invisible. You can't see or taste the forgiveness of sins. You can see a leg fixed. It's physical. You can see the withered leg; you can see the whole leg; you can see the difference.

Anyone can say, "Your sins are forgiven," and there is no immediate evidence that the person is a fraud. If someone says to a paralytic, "Get up and walk," the evidence for or against the person's authority over sin is immediate and visible to all.

Evidence

The forgiveness of sins is something that becomes real to you as you believe it, not as you see it. The lame man in this story could not see his forgiveness; he could only decide whether to believe that what Jesus said was true. To believe it would lift a great burden of guilt and fear from his shoulders. It would bring joy, peace and comfort. To not believe it would leave him feeling the same old estrangement, alienation from God and fearful expectation of judgment.

The man's joy in being forgiven was experienced through faith, not through sight. The healing of his legs, on the other hand, was experienced through sight — he didn't need faith to walk; he simply had to get up.

Either way, it takes God, for no human could heal the legs or forgive the sins. That was Jesus' point. Sure, it's easy to say, "Your sins are forgiven," but how can anyone know for sure that the sins really are forgiven? So Jesus healed the man to show that when he says, "Your sins are forgiven," they really are forgiven.

By grace through faith

Salvation is by grace through faith. We receive it by grace — we don't do anything to get it; it's God's gift to us, free and clear. We don't get any document, title or deed as proof that it is done. We just have to believe it or not believe it.

If we don't believe the gospel — this amazing good news that in Christ's life, death and resurrection we are saved — how can we experience that salvation? How can we enjoy and benefit from the knowledge of something if we don't even believe it is so?

Unless we believe the gospel is true, we will go on living as though Christ had not died and been raised for us. But when we believe the gospel, we are overwhelmed by the joy of what Christ has done for us. We begin to live abundantly in his love — resting in his love for us as well as showing his love to those around us.

Can God heal your physical ailments? Yes. Does he heal the physical ailments of everyone who asks? No. What does he say to everyone who asks? He says what he said to the paralyzed man, "Your sins are forgiven." Which is more important?

A sign

Jesus told the Pharisees, "But I want you to know that the Son of Man has authority on earth to forgive sins." So he said to the man, 'I tell you, get up, take your mat and go home.'" To believers, this is unnecessary. We already believe that the Son of man has power to forgive sins. We don't need a sign of Jesus' power to demonstrate the fact that he has authority to forgive sins. We feel it and know it as the Holy Spirit bears witness with our spirit (Romans 8:16).

Believers didn't need visible signs that their sins are forgiven. Signs are usually for unbelievers. Paul was an unbeliever and an enemy of the gospel, in that he persecuted believers. When Jesus appeared to him in person on the road to Damascus, he became a believer. Many others became believers when they witnessed the signs given by Jesus and the apostles.

Sometimes, though, we wish we did have a sign, because we fall into doubt about the things God has told us. We sometimes doubt whether God really loves us. We often doubt whether God really has forgiven us. Sometimes we even doubt, though we hate to admit it, whether God is really there at all. And our doubt makes us worry all the more that if God is there, he must not love and forgive sinners and doubters like us.

Our Savior is Jesus. Faith doesn't save us, Jesus does. In our moments of strong faith, we trust him completely and all fear is gone. In our moments of doubt, we fear condemnation. May we learn to trust Jesus to have faith for us when we are in doubt, for it is his righteousness and his faith on our behalf that God accepts. Jesus represents us before God. He stands in for us. And it is for his sake that we are clean and saved. Let our faith be in Jesus, not in our faith.

Myth about physical healing

A rumor goes around that if people really trusted God for healing, they would be healed. So when people aren't healed, they feel guilty. They look for the supposed "secret sin" that is keeping them from being healed.

Christian friends and family may tell them they need to pray that God will show them their sins so that he can heal them. They might tell the sick person that he or she needs more faith, and prescribe more prayer and Bible study and fasting as the way to get God to heal them.

That's not gospel; it's religion. It's superstition. It reduces God to the level of the ancient pagan gods, tyrants, who cared little for the plight of humans and acted only when they had something to gain, or when a stronger god forced them to. The Father of Jesus Christ is not like those gods.

Religion, as a formula for getting right with God, has no place in the gospel. Our relationship with God is not a business transaction: you, human, bring me six chickens and say the magic words and then I will be good to you. Our relationship with God does not and did not start with us. It started with God, God sees it through, and its foundation is his love, not his convenience.

The reason we pray, as Jesus did, "Your will, not mine, be done," is that God's will for us is unwaveringly good, never bad. God is not vindictive; he is love. In this, in his commitment to love us and see us through all things, he does not change (Malachi 3:6). In this, Jesus Christ is the same, yesterday, today and forever (Hebrews 13:8). That's what all this covenant business is about — it's about God's faithfulness to be our God and for us to be his people. It's not about our faithfulness, because if it were, it would be over. God is faithful to his word of promise to love us regardless of what we do.

If we live as his enemies, in constant ungodliness, giving little or no regard to our Maker and Redeemer and his good plans for us, then our lives can never be anything more than the miserable, selfish stabs at happiness that we can conjure up for ourselves. But God is no less faithful to us, regardless of what we do. He continues to leave his door open and the porch light on, even when we are holed up in our shack with our door barred shut. He stands out there and knocks, even when we put in our earplugs and crawl under the bed.

The point is: God is faithful. That's how he is, and that's how he will always be. When you look at Jesus Christ, you see how God is. He sacrifices himself for sinners, and calls on the Father to forgive even those whose greed, pride, selfish ambition and jealousy led them to torture and murder him. In that, we all have a stake; we all have greed, pride, selfish ambition and jealousy. But for Christ's sake, God forgives us. Because he is faithful, because he is true to who he is: Lover and Redeemer of his creation.

We pray for healing, but we trust ourselves to the One who cares for us. We believe he will do what is right and good for us. We live by faith, resting in his hands, because he is good.

The main thing

Like the paralytic, we know our sins are forgiven, and that's what really matters. If we are healed physically too, that's an added blessing. But we should remember that the paralytic died. Lazarus, who was raised from the dead, died. Every person who was ever healed, eventually died, and unless Jesus comes back before we die, we'll die too, whether we were ever healed of a disease or not.

Physical healing is great, and we praise God for the wonderful healings he has given and continues to give, but we look ultimately to something that lasts forever. Like those cited as examples of faith in the book of Hebrews, we look for a better country, a permanent one, a heavenly one, promised to us by the One who is faithful (Hebrews 11:13-16). Praise God, our sins are forgiven!

For reflection

- Have you doubted God's love for you? What do you think caused your doubt?
- Why do you believe God has forgiven your sins?
- How would you describe God to a small child?
- What is the most memorable time in your life when God gave you help?

A LESSON ABOUT ASSUMPTIONS
(MARK 2:13-17)

By J. Michael Feazell

Once again Jesus went out beside the lake. A large crowd came to him, and he began to teach them. As he walked along, he saw Levi son of Alphaeus sitting at the tax collector's booth. "Follow me," Jesus told him, and Levi got up and followed him.

While Jesus was having dinner at Levi's house, many tax collectors and sinners were eating with him and his disciples, for there were many who followed him. When the teachers of the law who were Pharisees saw him eating with the sinners and tax collectors, they asked his disciples: "Why does he eat with tax collectors and sinners?"

On hearing this, Jesus said to them, "It is not the healthy who need a doctor, but the sick. I have not come to call the righteous, but sinners." (NIV 2011)

The Pharisees assumed that if a person ate with sinners, that person was a sinner, too. Levi was a Jew who worked for the Roman government. He was a tax collector. Tax collectors were renowned for their dishonesty. If that were not bad enough, they were also ritually unclean. They rubbed shoulders with gentiles. Their clothing touched the unclean garments of gentiles. Their dishes and eating utensils weren't purified.

Naturally, since Jesus and his disciples ate with such people, Jesus and his disciples were unclean, too. He ate not only with tax collectors, he ate with sinners in general.

Reversal

The Pharisees, of course, were right. According to the Law, an Israelite who placed himself in contact with ritually unclean people became unclean as well (Leviticus 15:7; Numbers 19:22).

But the Pharisees knew Jesus was no ordinary Israelite. They had seen his healing miracles. They had heard him forgive sins, and they had witnessed his power to cast out evil spirits. With such demonstrations, Jesus disturbed the Pharisees. Their authority was thrown into question. The applecart of their prestige and influence among the people was upset. Their agendas for preparing Israel for its Messiah conflicted with Jesus and his kingdom. Their interpretation of Israel's law was threatened.

When they caught Jesus blatantly flaunting the Law by consorting with sinners and eating with impure hands from impure dishes with impure people, they knew such a man could not be from God.

Their assumptions prevented them from seeing what was really going on. God was not interested in cleansed appearances; he was interested in cleansed hearts. Jesus was coming into contact with sinners. But instead of the sinners making him unclean, he was making them clean.

From this passage, we learn that the grace of God ministered through Jesus Christ isn't limited to righteous people. It extends to sinners, even to the kind of sinners that disturb righteous people.

Foolish assumption

The Pharisees were not happy. Jesus was eating with people a good man would have no business eating with. Such conduct proved to them that Jesus was not a good man.

Who could deny it? They saw it with their own eyes. They knew the facts. They knew the implications. And they were not the type to sit by and do nothing. They confronted Jesus' disciples.

Mark does not tell us what Jesus' disciples said. He only tells us that Jesus found out what the Pharisees were asking and answered the question himself. He told them that healthy people have no need of a physician, but rather those who have illness. It is interesting that the word Mark used here, which is translated "illness" in the NIV, and "sick" in most other translations, is *kakos,* which means "bad" or "evil."

Jesus continued, "I have not come to call the righteous, but sinners."

It may be that the conversation between the Pharisees and the disciples, and the one between the Pharisees and Jesus, took place well after the meal was over. That would make sense, considering the fact that if the conversations had taken place during the meal, then the Pharisees themselves would have been present at a meal with tax collectors and sinners.

Regardless of when the conversations took place, the Pharisees made a foolish assumption. Of course, they did not know it was foolish. They assumed that they were "healthy people," and that they had no need of a physician. They assumed that they were righteous, and that Jesus' call to sinners did not apply to them. They had found righteousness in their diligent faithfulness to do everything they believed God had required of his people in the law.

Trust and follow

Jesus said to Levi, "Follow me," and Levi got up and followed him. Levi found righteousness in the Son of God. He saw with his own eyes what the accusing Pharisees also saw but could not recognize. He saw what Paul described in his letter to the Romans: "In the gospel the righteousness of God is revealed—a righteousness that is by faith from first to last, just as it is written: 'The righteous will live by faith.'" (Romans 1:17).

Levi made no assumptions. He saw, he listened, and he believed. He trusted the One sent from God because he trusted God. May we, too, live by faith, not by assumptions.

For reflection

- Can a person be righteous apart from Jesus? (Mark 2:17)
- Are you too sinful for God to forgive?
- Why did Jesus spend so much time with sinners?

A LESSON ABOUT OLD AND NEW
(MARK 2:18-22)

By J. Michael Feazell

John's disciples and the Pharisees were fasting. Some people came and asked Jesus, "How is it that John's disciples and the disciples of the Pharisees are fasting, but yours are not?"

Jesus answered, "How can the guests of the bridegroom fast while he is with them? They cannot, so long as they have him with them. But the time will come when the bridegroom will be taken from them, and on that day they will fast.

"No one sews a patch of unshrunk cloth on an old garment. Otherwise, the new piece will pull away from the old, making the tear worse. And no one pours new wine into old wineskins. Otherwise, the wine will burst the skins, and both the wine and the wineskins will be ruined. No, they pour new wine into new wineskins" (Mark 2:18-22, NIV 2011).

The primary fast of the Jews was the Day of Atonement, one of the seven annual solemn assemblies of the Law of Moses. The Pharisees also fasted on the second and fourth days of every week. Apparently, the disciples of John were doing something similar. (The Pharisees didn't have disciples in the same sense as John or Jesus. The term "disciples of the Pharisees" might refer to anyone who followed the example of the Pharisees.)

Although such fasting was not part of the Law of Moses, by Jesus' day it had become an important expression of the Pharisees' meticulous devotion to the ceremonial law. To the Pharisees, if Jesus' disciples were not fasting, then it called into question their piety, sincerity and devotion toward the ceremonial law. Further, it called into question Jesus' attitude toward the ceremonial law. Jesus had already healed on the Sabbath, and his disciples had already been noticed picking grain on the Sabbath and eating without the prescribed ceremonial washing. Add to that the lack of fasting, and the Pharisees must have found this upstart rabbi increasingly troubling.

Incompatible

After Jesus was gone, fasting would have a place in the Christian community. It would remind believers of their dependence on God, of their need for God's mercy, and of the power of God for the salvation of those who believe the gospel. Until then, Jesus' disciples had no reason to fast. In the Bible, fasting is a sign of disaster, or a voluntary abasement during times of great stress or trial. But the presence of the Son of God on earth with his disciples was a time of joy, not of sorrow. The time for sorrow would come later, when Jesus was murdered and taken away.

In any case, fasting in the manner of the Pharisees, as a sign of their devotion to the ceremonial law, was incompatible with the new covenant Jesus was inaugurating. For Jesus' disciples, fasting while Jesus was with them would have been like sewing a new piece of cloth on an old garment — it would have been incompatible. Jesus' point was that the old has gone, the new has come. The two are not compatible. To put new wine in old skins ruins both the skins and the wine. New wine requires new skins.

Today, it's still easy to try to pour the new wine of the gospel into the old wineskins of the Law. Grace doesn't come easily to us. We like to have a way of measuring where we stand with God. The gospel tells us simply to trust God that he loves us and has forgiven all our sins for the sake of Christ. But we often want something more tangible than that. We want something we can sink our teeth into.

So we run back to the Law. The Law provides a way of measuring where we stand with God. If we avoid sexual sin, for example, and lying, and stealing, and murder, then we can have a firmer basis for feeling that God isn't mad at us. If we don't use crude language, if we don't watch entertainment that has sex and violence in it, if we help others, if we don't miss church, and so on, then we can rest easier about our relationship with God. Of course, these are good behavior patterns, part of the way we naturally desire to live when we have fellowship with God.

But even when we're successful in behaving well on the outside, a deeper problem remains. Doing good things doesn't solve the problem of our alienation from God. Our pride, our selfishness, the sin in our heart of hearts, is still there. And every once in a while, when our guard is down, what we really are inside squirts out to remind us that we're still sinners. Then we can either pretend we're not really that bad, or we can admit to ourselves what we're really like.

Not based on the Law

Fellowship with God is not based on the Law. It is based on God's faithfulness to his word of grace. God told Israel: "I the LORD do not change. So you, the descendants of Jacob, are not destroyed" (Malachi 3:6; compare Deuteronomy 4:31). God's free determination to do as he pleases is what gives us a positive relationship with him. He tells us through the words of Jesus in John 3:17: "God did not send his Son into the world to condemn the world, but to save the world through him."

John wrote, "God is love" (1 John 4:8). He did not write, "God is justice." If God were after justice, none of us would survive. But God has determined to dispense grace rather than condemnation. We are told, "Mercy triumphs over judgment" (James 2:13). How grateful we can be that God is the way he has chosen to be! God's devotion to us is the basis of our fellowship with him, devotion that God has demonstrated through Jesus Christ.

Rest

When we're really honest with ourselves, we know that despite constant trying, we still sin. Where does that leave us? We can either work harder and harder to keep up the whitewashed façade of personal righteousness, or we can turn it over to God and trust him to forgive us and make us righteous. If we take God at his word, then we can rely on him to do in us and for us what he says he has.

Faith gives us rest. It transforms godly living from a duty, from a way of proving ourselves, to a joy, to a way of taking part in the good life we can have with God in Christ (referring not to physical abundance, but to spiritual contentment, to the inner peace only God can provide, which is worth more than physical riches).

Most of us can use a good rest.

A LESSON ABOUT GOD'S LOVE
(MARK 2:23-28)

By J. Michael Feazell

One Sabbath Jesus was going through the grainfields, and as his disciples walked along, they began to pick some heads of grain. The Pharisees said to him, "Look, why are they doing what is unlawful on the Sabbath?"

He answered, "Have you never read what David did when he and his companions were hungry and in need? In the days of Abiathar the high priest, he entered the house of God and ate the consecrated bread, which is lawful only for priests to eat. And he also gave some to his companions."

Then he said to them, "The Sabbath was made for man, not man for the Sabbath. So the Son of Man is Lord even of the Sabbath." (NIV 2011)

The consecrated bread consisted of 12 loaves placed on the golden table outside the most holy place in the tent of meeting. It was a special offering to God, and was set out fresh every Sabbath. It was to be eaten only by the high priest and his sons (Leviticus 24:5-9).

Nevertheless, in the absence of any other food, David and his men ate it (1 Samuel 21:1-6). Jesus cited this incident as an example of how rules, even God-given ones, are not intended to take precedence over human need. In this way, Jesus tells us something important about divine rules: God made them, and he made them to serve humans, not to rule humans.

Love

In Jesus, God shows us that the core of authentic human life is love. The person who loves, Paul wrote, fulfills the law. We could say that the only reason the law of God exists is to point us toward the life of love. To love is to enter into the divine fellowship of the Holy Spirit, to dwell in the eternal love of the Father for the Son and of the Son for the Father.

People are more important than systems and programs. People are more important than rituals and religion. John wrote that if a person loves God, then that person will love his brother (1 John 4:20). William Barclay wrote: "The best way to worship God is to help men" (*Gospel of Mark*, Revised Edition, Saint Andrew Press, 1991, p. 64). It might be easy to think that loving God and loving one's neighbor are two different things. They are not. Our love for God is expressed precisely in how we treat others. If we are mean, hateful, cruel and inconsiderate of others, that is a demonstration of how devoted (or not devoted) we are to God.

God loves all people, even the ones we have no use for, the ones we treat as though they don't matter. When we behave poorly toward the people God loves, then we are behaving the same way toward God. God is interested in people, not in rituals for rituals' sake.

Sabbath

When it comes to the Sabbath, an idea has gotten around that the Sabbath is greater than God. Let me explain. It is as though God is the guardian or protector of the Sabbath, making sure that people keep the Sabbath holy, and finally awarding salvation only to those who are faithful Sabbathkeepers. In other words, in this kind of thinking, the main thing is the Sabbath; God is the enforcer of the Sabbath. God made the Sabbath, then made himself subject to it, then made people subject to it.

Jesus cleared all such convoluted recipes off the dinner table. He made things plain: people were not made to be servants of the Sabbath; the Sabbath was made to be a servant of people. Furthermore, Jesus was not talking to or about all people. He was talking to first-century Jewish teachers of the law. And he was talking about Israel, the specific humans to whom God gave the Sabbath.

For Christians to assume that the Sabbath commandment is for Christians is to misunderstand the covenant between God and Israel. And for Christians to hold out the Sabbath as a criterion of the truly faithful believers is to misunderstand the new covenant written on the hearts of all God's people, Jew and gentile alike.

Evangelism

The gospel declares God's love. It's interesting how carefully calculated step-by-step programs for evangelism seem to come and go, much like the latest fads in business and management.

The main reason most people come to church and keep coming to church and become believers is the same today as it was 2,000 years ago — they meet people who like them and accept them and become their friends.

Maybe one reason is that programs, by nature, are contrivances. They might work well for business endeavors, where advertising and manipulation of emotions is crucial to selling a product. But the gospel is not a product; it is a declaration of God's love.

Love doesn't come by programs. It comes in its own way in its own time. It is strengthened and proven in the crucible of self-sacrifice, patience and forbearance. It cannot be explained; it can only be lived. It's something you live out, not something you evaluate on a scale of measurable outcomes. It's messy, not predictable. Sometimes it hurts, sometimes it thrills. It's never static. It doesn't play by the rules; the rules can't keep up.

The main reason most people come to church and keep coming to church and become believers is the same today as it was 2,000 years ago — they meet people who like them and accept them and become their friends. Programs don't do it — love does it.

New command

Jesus gave a new command to his disciples: "A new command I give you: Love one another. As I have loved you, so you must love one another. By this everyone will know that you are my disciples, if you love one another" (John 13:34-35).

That's a novel thought in our highly organized, programmatic society. Suppose Christians were well known for being the kind of people anybody would enjoy having for a friend. Suppose they weren't known for being pushy and judgmental. Suppose they weren't known for well-rehearsed emotional spiels designed to press people into a so-called "decision for Christ."

Suppose they were genuine, caring and harmless people, who in the love of Christ loved others for who they are. Suppose they didn't make friends with people as part of some new evangelism program, but simply because faithful friendship is what Jesus Christ is all about.

Peter said we should always be ready to give an answer for the hope that lies within us (see 1 Peter 1:15). Paul said we should let our conversation always be full of grace, seasoned with salt, so that we may know how to answer everyone (see Colossians 4:6). Neither Peter nor Paul said we should press people to ask. Instead, we are told to live the life of love. We are to make no secret of our faith. But neither are we asked to push it on others.

The Holy Spirit moves people to ask. And the Holy Spirit works in us to give an answer that is "seasoned with salt" and full of "grace."

Some people call this kind of living "whole-life evangelism" or "relational evangelism" or "life-style evangelism," etc. But by giving it a name, we run the risk of turning it into a just another program.

Imagine a young man walking up to a young woman outside Lakeside Ice Cream Parlour and saying: "Excuse me. Do you know me? Well, I know you and I know you're miserable and pathetic and need a great husband. I can fix all that. If you'll just repeat after me these words, "I will marry you, and we'll live happily ever after." She'd slap his face, of course, or call 911, or jab him someplace with her keys.

That's not how good relationships start. Yet, something akin to that is how some Christians have been taught that a good relationship with Jesus Christ should begin. Thank God, he can and does clean up our messes and turn lemons into lemonade, but what makes us think that is how Jesus wants us to help people learn who he is for them?

Trust

Another word for what Jesus was confronting in this story is legalism. Legalism is incompatible with the gospel. Jesus Christ is who he is for us before we ever do anything. The gospel is the truth about the reconciliation God has already brought about in Jesus Christ (Colossians 1:19-20). Jesus' work of reconciliation doesn't depend on us. If it did, we'd never be reconciled, for our faith and our behavior are always substandard at best. God did what he did in Christ because he loved us, not because we loved him first (1 John 4:19).

That's why we can trust him for our salvation fully, from beginning to end. That is why we do not have to carry a burden of fear that our ever-present weakness in faith or behavior is the crack in the hull that will sink our salvation.

Jesus Christ is Lord of the Sabbath. We rest in him, not in our own works. His love binds us to himself, and he loves us for no other reason than that he wants to! He makes us new in himself, only because he loves us and has chosen freely not to be without us. Paul wrote, "Therefore, if anyone is in Christ, the new creation has come: The old has gone, the new is here!" (2 Cor. 5:17).

That's good news. God has made people — including you and me — his priority. He loves us, and we can't make him stop loving us. In that place of refuge, in the security of God's endless love for us, we are free to make him our priority. Therein lie the unshakable peace, joy, and fullness of life we so crave. Therein lies our true rest.

DOES MARK 2:27-28 COMMAND CHRISTIANS TO OBSERVE THE WEEKLY SABBATH?

By Paul Kroll

To find the answer to this question, let us begin by quoting Mark 2:27-28, which has Jesus saying the following to the Pharisees: "The Sabbath was made for man, not man for the Sabbath. So the Son of Man is Lord even of the Sabbath."

Sabbatarians generally make the following assumptions about this verse. They believe Jesus was commanding all people in all ages to observe the weekly Sabbath as "holy time." They reason that the Sabbath law could be changed or eliminated only if Jesus had specifically stated here that it was abrogated. But, Sabbatarians claim, Jesus by his word and actions in Mark 2:27-28 was implying that the Sabbath must be observed by all human beings. Therefore, they conclude that this passage in Mark is, in effect, a command to observe the Sabbath.

Is that what Mark 2:27-28 tells us? Let's look at the context of Mark 2 to see what Jesus' purpose was in saying what he did in verses 27 and 28. One Sabbath, Jesus and the disciples were picking heads of grain. Jesus' action and that of his disciples was immediately challenged by the Pharisees. "Why are they doing what is unlawful on the Sabbath?" they demanded to know (verse 24). The Pharisees had set themselves up as religious authorities, defining what could or could not be done on the Sabbath.

What the Pharisees objected to was Jesus and his disciples picking the heads of grain on the Sabbath. They regarded this as reaping. It was one of the many acts the teachers of the law had decided should be forbidden on the Sabbath. The people challenging Jesus in Mark 2:27-28 would all have rightly assumed that the Law of Moses commanded *them* to keep the Sabbath. As the old covenant people of God, they were obligated to observe it. The question for these people – not us – was *how* to keep it under certain circumstances.

To answer this question, Jesus countered their challenge with a question and an example of his own about David and his companions. He pointed out that on one occasion, because they were hungry, they ate the consecrated bread, which was unlawful for anyone to eat but the priests (verses 25-26). By his reference to this example, Jesus was pointing out that while David technically broke the Law of Moses, he was not condemned because such violations under certain conditions of need might be warranted. Jesus had applied this principle to what he and the disciples were doing when picking the heads of grain on the Sabbath.

Jesus' point was that although the action of David was contrary to the Law of Moses, he was not condemned for it. The issue in this passage, then, is how to interpret the Mosaic Law, and who has the ultimate authority to do so. Nothing is said about which group of people, or whether everyone, is commanded to keep the Sabbath as "holy time."

To drive home this explanation regarding the purpose of the weekly rest day, Jesus said to the Pharisees: "The Sabbath was made for man, not man for the Sabbath." What was his point? It was *not* whether or not Christians – or everyone – or a limited group – must observe the old covenant Sabbath. That doesn't come up at all in the conversation.

To repeat the point made earlier, Jesus was talking as a Jew to Jews under the old covenant. Jesus himself was a Jew, born under the Law (Galatians 4:4). In his person, Jesus basically kept the old covenant worship regulations.

The issue was how should the Sabbath law be interpreted and observed by those people, the Jews, to whom it applied. The Jewish teachers of the law, at least many of them, had made the Sabbath a burden for the people. Jesus was pointing out that human needs sometimes supersede legal requirements. His statement has no application to the question of whether Christians should or should not keep the Sabbath. The question was how should those who are *required* to keep the Sabbath (the Jews under the old covenant) do so in a particular circumstance.

Jesus was saying that the Sabbath, under the old covenant, was meant to serve human needs, not the other way around, thus the use of the expression that the "Sabbath was made for man." It was made for human need in a certain context, under the old covenant worship system as defined by the Law of Moses, until the Seed, Christ, should come.

Israelites were to rest from their work because they needed a rest from their agricultural toil. Through that rest they could worship God as the provider of all their needs, and as the God who had saved them from slave-like toil in Egypt. The Sabbath regulation was not given to Israel simply because God wanted people to keep religious rituals. It had a purpose for all those human beings to whom it was given. But it was given *only* to Israel under the old covenant.

Even Jews recognized that the Law of Moses, particularly its cultic observances such as weekly and annual Sabbath observance, applied only to national Israel. Jewish rabbis understood that non-Jews did not need to keep the Law of Moses, including the Sabbath rest. This law was given to Israel alone, and only for as long as the old covenant was in force.

In his conversation with the Pharisees in Mark 2, Jesus added another thought: "The Son of Man is Lord even of the Sabbath." Why did Jesus say this? Again, the issue was not about who should keep the Sabbath, but about who had authority or lordship in terms of deciding *how* it should be kept, when it was required. In the context in which the conversation occurs between Jesus and the Pharisees, the question of "who" should keep the Sabbath would never have come up. Everyone understood that the Jews under the old covenant Law were the ones who should keep it. The question was, to repeat, *how* should those who were required to keep the Sabbath, keep it – and who had the *authority* to determine how it should be kept.

What had happened is that the Pharisees, the religious leaders, had questioned Jesus' authority on the matter of his picking grain on the Sabbath. They had set themselves up above him on the issue of Sabbath interpretation. Yet, Jesus was the Word of God made flesh. Therefore, Jesus, who was God incarnate, had more authority than the human Pharisees to decide how the Sabbath should be observed – again, under the circumstances where it was required. He was, after all, the Lord of the law that had commanded Sabbath observance for old covenant Israel.

Jesus' statement says nothing about who should or should not keep the Sabbath. Of course Jesus is Lord of the Sabbath. He is Lord of every command ever given by God – including all the 613 commands (by rabbinical count) of the Law of Moses. Jesus is also Lord of all time and all days of the week, including Sunday, Monday, Tuesday, Wednesday, Thursday and Friday. Jesus is, after all, *Lord*. But his being Lord of the Sabbath does not mean to say it is commanded for all people. The Lord of Israel was Lord of the law of circumcision, given as a sign to the children of Israel. But the fact that God was Lord of the circumcision law does not of itself imply that all human beings must keep it. In all cases, we have to know which of all the laws God ever gave apply to new covenant Christians.

In summary, let us ask what has been and has not been said about the Sabbath in Mark 2:27. Jesus was addressing the Sabbath issue in the context of speaking to the religious leaders of old covenant Israel and the interpreters of the Law of Moses in his day. He was telling them as old covenant people how they should apply the law of the Sabbath, that is, with mercy and thought to human need. And he was telling them he had the authority to define how they should observe the Sabbath.

What isn't said here? The issue of whether Gentiles or Christians need to keep the Sabbath is not mentioned. Please note that. Jesus is not commanding Christians to observe the Sabbath as "holy time." Read the passage carefully: Jesus does not issue a command to keep the Sabbath. That is not the question under debate in this verse. Therefore, we should not import this idea into this passage of Scripture. That is, we shouldn't first assume that Christians must observe the Sabbath, and then claim that this idea is found in Mark 2:27-28, because it isn't there.

To conclude, Jesus' comments about the Sabbath being made for humanity reflect the idea that the Pharisees (as representatives of old covenant Israel) should have taught an enlightened Sabbath observance, not missing the reason why God gave the nation this holy time. Jesus' statement about being the Lord of the Sabbath challenged the Pharisees' attempt to subvert his authority in the matter and claim it for themselves.

A LESSON ABOUT APPEARANCES
(MARK 3:7-12)

By J. Michael Feazell

Jesus withdrew with his disciples to the lake, and a large crowd from Galilee followed. When they heard about all he was doing, many people came to him from Judea, Jerusalem, Idumea, and the regions across the Jordan and around Tyre and Sidon. Because of the crowd he told his disciples to have a small boat ready for him, to keep the people from crowding him. For he had healed many, so that those with diseases were pushing forward to touch him. Whenever the impure spirits saw him, they fell down before him and cried out, "You are the Son of God." But he gave them strict orders not to tell others about him. (NIV 2011)

Things are not always as they appear. That was certainly the case with Jesus. The crowd saw a miracle-worker, a remarkable man of God who could heal their diseases. They had come from all over the region, and the crowd was so thick that Jesus had a boat ready in case the crowd pressed him into the Sea of Galilee.

Crowds

Crowds are funny. Crowds don't have brains like people do. Crowds can't reason — they can only react, somewhat like an animal reacts. There may be voices of reason in a crowd, of course, but those voices are ordinarily as effective as shouting during a thunderclap.

Ecstatic crowds have been known to stampede and trample people at soccer matches. Such crowds have even, at times, crushed their own players in a mindless rush of bodies. Angry crowds have destroyed property and murdered people. People in crowds often suspend good judgment and do things they would never do if they were alone and thinking.

Crowds can be thrilled one moment and furious the next. Crowds are unpredictable, and for that reason, potentially dangerous. Evil people can stir up crowds to do evil things. Likewise, good people can calm crowds and set the people in the crowd back to straight thinking. A town clerk once did that in Ephesus, which saved Paul's life (see Acts 19:24-41).

Jesus knew about crowds. He took precautions, but he also knew that his time had not yet come. He knew he would be killed, but that evening at the shore of Galilee was not the time or the place. The time would be the season of Passover, and the place would be Jerusalem.

'Son of God'

The crowd saw Jesus as a healer of diseases. The demons saw something else. "You are the Son of God," they called out. Jesus ordered them to be silent.

It might appear that the term "Son of God" would have meant the same thing to that first-century crowd as it means to us today. It didn't. "Son of God" had several meanings in the ancient world. In gentile nations, it was not uncommon for kings to bear the title "son of god." Kings of Egypt were "sons of Ra," an Egyptian god. Many Roman emperors held the title, "son of god."

In the Old Testament, however, the term "son of God" referred to someone especially near to God. For example, angels were referred to as "sons of God" (Job 1:6). Israel itself was called the "son of God" (Exodus 4:22; Hosea 11:1). God referred to the king of Israel as "my son" (2 Samuel 7:14). The king is referred to as the "son of God" in the second Psalm — "You are my son; today I have begotten you."

Messiah

The demons knew that Jesus was especially dear to God. Maybe they even knew he was Emmanuel — God with us, or as John put it, "the one and only Son, who came from the Father, full of grace and truth" (John 1:14), or as in Hebrews, the Son by whom God made all things (Hebrews 1:2), the express image of God's person (verse 3). In any case, Jesus told them to be silent.

Why didn't Jesus want people to know who he was Jesus was indeed the Messiah, the anointed one, the king, the Son of David, the Son of God. But God's idea of Messiahship was radically different from the crowd's idea of Messiahship. Grace and truth, sacrifice and love were the marks of authentic Messiahship. But a conquering king with mighty armies overthrowing the Romans and leading Israel to national greatness was the Messiah the crowd wanted.

A crowd praised Jesus on Palm Sunday. A week later, a crowd, stirred up by evil men, demanded his execution. Jesus wasn't what the Messiah watchers were looking for. He had the popularity. He had the people's imagination and loyalty. He had the charisma. He had the devotion and support of God, as witnessed by his miracles.

But to the most zealous of the Messiah watchers, to men like Judas, it became more and more evident that Jesus was a fraud, a stubborn fool who for whatever reason would not declare himself and take the reins of leadership. To them, Jesus was a supreme disappointment — a man who could have restored the fortunes of Israel but wouldn't — a man who only appeared to be the chosen of God, a charlatan who was merely giving the people a cruel, false hope.

Savior

Jesus was not the Messiah they had been waiting for. Instead, he was far more than they could have ever dared dream or hope. He was more than they were yet capable of comprehending. He was YHWH himself, Immanuel, God With Us, come to his people as one of them, come to humanity as one of us all, come to deliver us all from the greatest oppression of all, come to restore us all to the household of God.

Mel Gibson's movie about the crucifixion of Jesus has sparked debate over whether the Jews killed Jesus. The debate itself belies ignorance of who Jesus was and why he came.

Jesus was a Jew, sent to his own people to be rejected by his own people (John 1:11). Yet others of his own received him (verse 12). Jesus was sent for the sake not only of Israel, but for the sake of the whole world (1 John 2:2). Does it make sense to blame Israel for being God's chosen people? To do so is to blame God for choosing Israel—for choosing Israel as his precious instrument for their vital part in the ultimate salvation of the world. Jesus was the representative of all Israel, the true and faithful Israelite for the sake of all Israel, and it is as the perfect Israelite that Jesus represents before God all people in the world.

Every human is to "blame" for the crucifixion of Jesus, because every human has sinned and fallen short of the glory of God (Romans 3:23). But Jesus gave himself freely, not because anyone "made" him, or because he "had" to. He did it because he loves humanity. It was God's free grace toward undeserving sinners that led to Jesus' crucifixion—undeserving sinners like you and me. The crowd that shouted, "Crucify him!" were no bigger sinners than those of us who sing "That Old Rugged Cross" on Easter morning. "Father, forgive them…" Jesus said. And the Father did.

Blame game

Would Christians who "blame" Jews for the crucifixion of Jesus prefer that Jesus not have been crucified? Would they prefer that he not have shed his blood for the sins of humanity and been raised from the dead? Jesus said of his life: "No one takes it from me, but I lay it down of my own accord. I have authority to lay it down and authority to take it up again. This command I received from my Father" (John 10:18).

Jesus' crucifixion was God's will, Jesus' will. God loved the world — Jews and gentiles alike — so much, that he sent his "only begotten" (King James Version), or "one and only" (NIV) Son to save the world by dying and rising from the dead (John 3:16).

There is no sense, no logic, no Christian love, in the historical epithet "Christ-killers" that some "Christians" have leveled at Jews. Every human bears responsibility, Jew and gentile alike, for the death of Jesus, and thank God for it; it is through this self-sacrificial means, this supreme expression of divine love and intimacy with humanity, that God has saved us all and restored us to fellowship with him and with each other.

He is risen! The Jesus who in his rejection by us all cried out, "Father, forgive them; they don't know what they are doing," is the same Jesus who rose in glory and is our Advocate with the Father. He is the same Jesus whose Spirit moves us to love one another as he commanded.

Blame the Jews for killing Jesus? Blame anyone for killing Jesus? Nothing could be farther from the heart of Jesus than setting blame, for all humanity is to blame, and in Jesus, all humanity is forever forgiven for all sin. For this purpose he came, and for this purpose he lives that we all might live in him, blameless before God.

Appearances

It was an otherwise ordinary day by the sea. Except for the crowd, the healings and the shouting demons. When it was over, the people went home. They went back to work. They weren't part of a crowd any more. They were people again; they could think and reason again.

They wondered about that day at the sea. They wondered who that amazing man was who healed the sick. They talked about him in their towns. He had inspired a sense of hope in them, whoever he was. Some said he was John the Baptist, come back to life. Others said the great prophet Elijah had returned. But things are not always as they appear. The day would come when they would hear of this man again. And what they would hear would change everything.

Maybe you need to see beyond appearances too. It might appear to you that your sins have the better of you. It might appear to you that God is fed up with you, sick and tired of your falling short, ready to spew you out of his mouth and wash his hands of you.

Things are not what they appear. God loves you and always will. Christ died for us, Paul says, while we were still sinners (Romans 5:10). Jesus didn't wait until you were behaving better before he loved you and saved you. Sin doesn't stand between God and you—God already took that barrier away.

That means you can stop worrying and trust him. He loves you, he saved you and he'll never let you go.

Don't believe the lies your sins tell you — despite what your sins say, God does still love you, and he won't ever turn his back on you. So why not take your struggles with sin to him — in faith that he's already forgiven you — and trust him to help you become more like him? He's right beside you.

ANOTHER LESSON
ABOUT AUTHORITY (MARK 3:13-19)

By J. Michael Feazell

Jesus went up on a mountainside and called to him those he wanted, and they came to him. He appointed twelve that they might be with him and that he might send them out to preach and to have authority to drive out demons. These are the twelve he appointed: Simon (to whom he gave the name Peter), James son of Zebedee and his brother John (to them he gave the name Boanerges, which means "sons of thunder"), Andrew, Philip, Bartholomew, Matthew, Thomas, James son of Alphaeus, Thaddaeus, Simon the Zealot and Judas Iscariot, who betrayed him. (NIV 2011)

"When the righteous are in authority, the people rejoice," says Proverbs 29:2 (KJV).

Who has authority over you? Do you see that person as a blessing? Or as a demon?

Jesus' idea of authority was not the same as that of the typical human. Once, when a dispute broke out among the disciples about which one of them was the greatest, Jesus told them, "The kings of the Gentiles lord it over them; and those who have authority over them are called 'Benefactors.' But not so with you, but let him who is the greatest among you become as the youngest, and the leader as the servant" (Luke 22:25-26, NASB).

In their wrangling about authority, the disciples were fairly representative of humanity. But Jesus taught them what authority is really all about. Used rightly, authority is a blessing to those who are under it.

In the ancient world, authority could be anything but a blessing. In fact, in every age of human history, angry and self-centered humans have misused authority as a free ticket to abuse and cruelty.

Today, we have our share of tyrant dictators, corrupt corporate officers and law-enforcement officials, despotic bosses, and abusive spouses, parents and prison guards. Wherever humans have charge of other humans, there is the potential for exploitation and maltreatment.

"Masters," Paul wrote, "provide your slaves with what is right and fair, because you know that you also have a Master in heaven" (Colossians 4:1). God is just and fair. That means at least two things. One is that he will be just and fair with you and me. Another is that you and I need to be just and fair too, because we belong to him.

Deliverance

When Jesus gave authority to the apostles, he gave it to them with an explicit purpose — to drive out demons. Demons were evil spirits who tortured their victims by continual oppression that led finally to taking over their wills completely. These evil spirits saw Jesus as their archenemy — and rightly so. Jesus absolutely opposed their cruelty and subjugation of humanity. One of his stated goals was to drive them out and end their tyranny. Oddly enough, the wicked spirits perceived Jesus as the tormenter, because he would not allow them to continue their oppression of humans.

"We know you are the Son of God," some of them said. "Have you come to punish us before it's time?" (see Matt. 8:29). The evil spirits recognized Jesus' authority, and they knew he would not allow their illicit, gangster-style authority to stand. Jesus gave authority to the apostles to do exactly what he was doing — bringing release to the captives.

Jesus came with all the authority in the universe not to take advantage of humans or to take over the wills of humans, but to deliver. Whether we are talking about release from the cruel domination and repression exercised by evil spirits, or about any release from other forms of oppression, authority is to be used for deliverance — to make things better for those being ruled.

Authority, God style, is for the blessing and furtherance of humans. It is to nurture others, to help them develop, improve and grow. Certainly, authority must sometimes be used for discipline. Even discipline can be a form of deliverance when it is given in wisdom. A heart that is ruled by love knows the difference between correction and cruelty.

Choices

Whenever we have authority, we have choices about how we will use it. We can use it to get our own way. We can use it for revenge or retaliation. We can use it to give favors to friends or family. We can use it to dodge responsibility for our actions. None of this is what Jesus had in mind when he gave authority to the apostles.

Jesus delegated authority so that it could be used to deliver others from bondage and oppression. Like any good gift, though, we can misuse it. We can use authority to get our own way, or we can use it to see that the right thing happens — whether it benefits us or not.

Who is under your authority? Employees? Association or club members? Detainees? Applicants? Family members? Parishioners? Children? Do they view you as a blessing? Or as a demon?

Jesus comes to us with deliverance. Part of that deliverance is that he hears the cries of the oppressed. Another part is that he changes the hearts of those who oppress others. If we are suffering, we can ask our Deliverer for relief. If those under our authority see us more as devilish than as blessed, maybe it's time to ask our Redeemer to change our hearts, too.

A LESSON ABOUT ENVY (MARK 3:20-27)

By J. Michael Feazell

> Then Jesus entered a house, and again a crowd gathered, so that he and his disciples were not even able to eat. When his family heard about this, they went to take charge of him, for they said, "He is out of his mind."
>
> And the teachers of the law who came down from Jerusalem said, "He is possessed by Beelzebul! By the prince of demons he is driving out demons."
>
> So Jesus called them over to him and began to speak to them in parables: "How can Satan drive out Satan? If a kingdom is divided against itself, that kingdom cannot stand. If a house is divided against itself, that house cannot stand. And if Satan opposes himself and is divided, he cannot stand; his end has come. In fact, no one can enter a strong man's house without first tying him up. Then he can plunder the strong man's house. (NIV 2011)

The Bible tells us that Jesus was made like his fellow humans in every way (Hebrews 2:17). In this passage we find that like many of our families, Jesus' family was ready to have him committed. They came down to "take charge" of him, believing him to be out of his mind.

Blindness of envy

Among the reasons Jesus was considered out of his mind, Mark informs us, was that Jesus was running afoul of the authorities. He was banishing demons from people, and the authorities, who apparently weren't, found Jesus' growing popularity most irritating.

It is a little reminiscent of Saul's jealousy over David's military success recorded in 1 Samuel 18. You might think a king would be grateful for the victories of a top general. But not so — Saul saw David as a threat. He feared the people might get the idea that David would make a better king.

The same dynamics seem to be at work between Jesus and the authorities. Jesus was getting too popular. His power over the evil spirits was plain, which made it obvious to everyone that he had the blessing and power of God.

So the authorities saw Jesus not as a blessing, but as a threat. Jesus was better liked than they were. And he was clearly more powerful.

So what to do? Discredit him, of course. But how? Well, let's see — suppose we tell the people that he has power over the demons because he is demon-possessed himself. Yes! That's the ticket! The man is demon-possessed, and not just by any demon, but this Jesus whom you are cheering is possessed by Beelzebul himself!

Truth aside

Truth was not the governing factor. God's will was not a consideration. The joy of those freed from wicked oppression didn't matter. There was only one goal — discredit anyone who makes us feel insecure. Say whatever has to be said.

The accusation, of course, was absurd, and Jesus exposed it as such. "If Satan opposes himself and is divided," Jesus said, "he cannot stand; his end has come."

But Jesus' remark was deeper than merely exposing the silliness of the authorities' accusation. The truth was, Satan's end had come, but not because Beelzebul was kicking out demons through Jesus.

The end of Satan's kingdom had begun because the Son of God had walked onto the stage of history. Jesus continued: "In fact, no one can enter a strong man's house and carry off his possessions unless he first ties up the strong man. Then he can rob his house." Jesus was freeing people from demons because Satan had no power to stop him.

And the authorities knew that. They were not blind. They saw the works of deliverance. But it is possible, even for us, to become so selfishly oriented that we place the preservation of our personal goals above even the hand of God.

Redemption

John wrote, "If we walk in the light, as he is in the light, we have fellowship with one another, and the blood of Jesus, his Son, purifies us from all sin" (1 John 1:7). When our trust is in Jesus Christ (which is the same thing as walking in the light), we have fellowship with one another. This is a fellowship that breaks through the walls of self-centered living. People matter to us.

Jesus told the disciples: "A new command I give you: Love one another. As I have loved you, so you must love one another. By this everyone will know that you are my disciples, if you love one another" (John 13:34-35). Just as light overpowers darkness, so love leaves no place for selfish envy.

Jesus was not a person to the authorities. He was an obstacle, a faceless object to be cleared out of their path. He didn't matter. Have you ever been treated that way? Take heart: Jesus traveled that path before you. He knows what you're experiencing.

Have you ever treated someone else that way? Take heart: Jesus has forgiven you. And if you will receive it, he gives you a heart that can see people as people, not as obstacles in your path. Let's agree to take a look at the relationships in our lives. If there is someone we've been disparaging, maybe it's time to take our concerns to Christ the Redeemer instead of the grapevine.

For reflection

Has someone received a blessing you felt should have come to you? How have you responded? How have you treated that person?

Have you been mistreated recently? How have you coped with it? Have you asked God for his peace (Phil. 4:7)?

A LESSON ABOUT DAMNATION
(MARK 3:22-30)

By J. Michael Feazell

And the teachers of the law who came down from Jerusalem said, "He is possessed by Beelzebul! By the prince of demons he is driving out demons."

So Jesus called them over to him and began to speak to them in parables: "… people can be forgiven all their sins and every slander they utter, but whoever blasphemes against the Holy Spirit will never be forgiven; they are guilty of an eternal sin." He said this because they were saying, "He has an impure spirit." (NIV 2011)

"I think I might have committed the unpardonable sin!" The young man's voice on the other end of the phone was frantic. I tried to rub the sleep out of my eyes and sat up in bed. "Why do you say that?" I asked. "I did it again," he moaned. "And after I had repented so deeply. I don't think I'll ever overcome. I think I'm lost. I feel a horrible dread."

It wasn't the first time we'd had this conversation. This man's persistent struggle with sin had led him to believe that he was under God's curse. If his repentance had truly been sincere, he reasoned, then he would not ever repeat the sin. Therefore, his repentance must not have been sincere, and since he had repented with all his heart, he decided he must not be capable of true repentance.

Another man approached me after a church service one day. "Dr. Feazell," he whispered. "I don't know what to do. I think I've committed the unpardonable sin."

"Let's talk about that," I said. "What did you do?"

He looked at the ground. "I cursed the Holy Spirit."

"How did you do that?" I asked.

"I said, 'Cursed be the Holy Spirit.'"

"Why?"

"I don't know. I was reading the verse where Jesus said that anyone who blasphemed the Holy Spirit would never be forgiven, and I just felt this crazy compulsion to do it. Now I'm scared to death."

I have heard many strange explanations of the unpardonable sin over the years. I have spoken to many people who fear that they might have committed it. But let us understand something — for those who trust in Jesus, no sin is unpardonable.

When Jesus said, "whoever blasphemes against the Holy Spirit will never be forgiven; they are guilty of an eternal sin," he was describing a specific attitude and state of mind that by nature is not true and can never be true of those who trust in him.

Mark explains, "He said this because they were saying, 'He has an impure spirit.'" The teachers of the law had deliberately refused to acknowledge that the works of kindness and mercy that Jesus was displaying among the people were from God. Because of their own jealousy, they had rejected the plain witness of the Holy Spirit that Jesus was sent from God and was doing the works of God. They willingly blinded their eyes to God's own testimony through the Spirit that Jesus had come in his name to bind Satan, destroy his evil works and forgive sins.

God sent the Spirit into the world to bear witness to Jesus Christ, the only name under heaven by which humans can be forgiven and saved. To reject that witness, to despise what God has done to bring about forgiveness of sins, is to reject the forgiveness itself. How can a person be forgiven who refuses to accept forgiveness? How can a person's sins be forgiven if the person rejects the Forgiver of sins?

Are you worried that you might have committed the unpardonable sin? The very fact that you are worried about it is proof that you have not committed it. The unpardonable sin is unpardonable only because it is the sin of refusing to come to Jesus to be forgiven. It is the Holy Spirit who leads us to Jesus Christ. The blasphemy Jesus refers to in this passage is the rejection of the Spirit's witness to him as the Son of God and Savior of the world.

So relax. Trust in Jesus, and rest secure in him. He forgives all sins of every kind, even repeated sins and compulsive sins. And he teaches us through the Holy Spirit, who is his witness, to renounce sin and to live uprightly in him. Remember this: Jesus Christ came into the world to save sinners. For those who come to him, no sin is unpardonable.

For reflection

What sin are you afraid God might not forgive you for? Have you talked to him about it?

A LESSON ABOUT HARD HEARTS
(MARK 4:10-13)

By J. Michael Feazell

> Again Jesus began to teach by the lake.... The Twelve and the others around him asked him about the parables. He told them, "To those on the outside everything is said in parables so that, 'they may be ever seeing but never perceiving, and ever hearing but never understanding; otherwise they might turn and be forgiven!'" (Mark 4:1, 10-13, NIV 2011)

At first glance, this passage seems to say that Jesus taught in parables specifically for the purpose of preventing people from understanding what he was talking about. A closer look, however, reveals just the opposite.

Master teacher

Jesus was not deliberately trying to prevent his listeners from understanding what he was talking about. He was doing just the opposite—using parables as a means of relating the invisible kingdom of God to everyday, visible, real life examples and situations the common person could easily relate to.

Parables were a teaching method quite familiar to Jewish teachers and audiences. They were tools for making things easier to understand, not more difficult. In the hands of Jesus, the great master teacher, these tools would have been even more effective. He came to bring good news to the poor, not confuse them with stories impossible to comprehend.

Faithful

The key to understanding this passage lies in the scripture Jesus quoted to make his point to the disciples about the use of parables. He was quoting Isaiah 6:9-10, a passage that chided Israel's blindness and deafness to God's love. The translation is easily misunderstood unless the context of Israel's struggle with God throughout its history is taken into consideration.

The Septuagint, the Greek translation of the Hebrew Scriptures, noted this problem, and took care to include the sarcastic tone of the wording in its translation. The Septuagint, we should note, was the foremost translation of Jesus' day. In his commentary on Mark, William Barclay paraphrased Jesus' intent this way: "Do you remember what Isaiah once said? He said that when he came with God's message to God's people Israel in his day they were so dully un-understanding that you would have thought that God had shut instead of opening their minds; I feel like that today" (*The Gospel of Mark*,

Westminster Press, 1975).

Israel, as God's own people, had already failed to keep their covenant with God and had ended up a conquered people and an occupied nation, first by the Babylonians and eventually by the Romans.

But God promised to be faithful to his covenant regardless of Israel's unfaithfulness (compare Malachi 4:6). He promised to redeem them in spite of themselves (compare Hosea 11:8-11), and he would do it through the Messiah, the Anointed One, who would be sent to redeem the people and bring them back to God.

But God knew that in the hardness of their hearts, they would also reject their own Messiah. As John wrote in the fourth Gospel, "He came to that which was his own, but his own did not receive him." But even that would not stop God from redeeming his people, and through them, the whole world.

In their rejection of Messiah, Israel's sin against God would reach its full measure. They would kill their Savior, but God would raise him from the dead, and his death and resurrection would become the very means by which God would transform the hearts of not only Israel, but also the gentiles.

New heart

Jesus was saying that stubborn, hard-hearted people cannot understand the things of the kingdom of God even when they are taught in the plainest possible language. It takes a new heart, a heart only God can give (compare Ezekiel 36:26).

Sin alienates us from God, and since we are all sinners, we are all alienated from God — not because he rejects us (he is eternally faithful), but because we reject him. In our alienated state, we are incapable of reconciling ourselves to God. We neither know God nor want him meddling in our lives. Even our concept of God is askew; we think of him as a great butler in the sky who is not worth his salt unless he does everything we ask, or as an angry super-being who is always ready to dish out punishments.

Unless God himself takes the initiative to reconcile us to him, we remain helpless, with no future beyond death. That is exactly what he has done in Jesus Christ. In Jesus we learn exactly what God is like, because Jesus Christ is the exact representation of the Father (Hebrews 1:3; see also Colossians 1:19-20).

Gift

We learn through Jesus that God is merciful, patient and full of grace. God is not against humanity; he is for it. "For God did not send his Son into the world to condemn the world," Jesus said, "but to save the world through him. Whoever believes in him is not condemned..." (John 3:17-18). Through Jesus, our minds are released from the bondage of sin, and we are freed to put our trust in our Creator and Redeemer.

No one understands the things of God apart from the grace he has made manifest in Jesus Christ. "The secret of the kingdom of God has been given to you" (Mark 4:11), Jesus told the disciples. Yet before his ascension, even they did not understand the parables, because their hearts were still hard, too. The Holy Spirit, who leads us into all truth, especially the truth of the gospel, soon melted their stony hearts into hearts of flesh, just as God had promised through Ezekiel.

God never forces us to love him, for love forced is not love at all. Instead, God frees our minds and hearts from all the barriers, rooted in sin, that would otherwise stand in the way. "His divine power has given us everything we need for a godly life," Peter would later write, "through our knowledge of him who called us by his own glory and goodness." (2 Peter 1:3).

Freedom, however, is worthless unless it is exercised. That will be the topic of our next lesson, as we look at the parable of the sower.

A LESSON ABOUT SATAN (MARK 4:14-15)

By J. Michael Feazell

> He taught them many things by parables.... The farmer sows the word. Some people are like seed along the path, where the word is sown. As soon as they hear it, Satan comes and takes away the word that was sown in them (Mark 4:1, 14-15, NIV 2011).

The parable of the sower is the first parable given in the book of Mark. In it, Jesus compares the ways people receive the gospel with the ways sown seeds grow. His first example is that of freshly sown seeds being devoured by birds before they have time to take root. Just as birds eat some of the seeds, so Satan comes to take away the word of truth that some people have received.

A few things to note. First, Satan doesn't come to take the truth away from everyone who receives it. Second, we are not told why Satan comes to some and not others. Third, people are not actually seeds and Satan is not actually a bird; it's only an analogy. The fact that Satan takes away the truth one time, doesn't mean he can do it every time.

It is important to know that Satan is not all he's cracked up to be. He's definitely more powerful than us humans, but he is no match for Jesus Christ.

God vs. Satan

Have you ever seen a gospel tract depicting a battle between Satan and God for the souls of humans? Sometimes they are in comic book form, showing a demon sitting on one shoulder of a person and an angel on the other shoulder. All rests on the person's decision, and the two spirits do all they can to sway the person to their side. It belongs in a comic book, because it is a parody of the truth. Satan is not on a par with God, as though he has the power to prevent God from his redemptive purpose for humanity.

In other words, there is no battle between God and Satan for your soul. That battle, such as it was, was won before the foundation of the world and was made plain to the world in the life, death and resurrection of Jesus.

When a person is the best at doing something, you might say, "She could do that in her sleep." Well, Jesus not only could defeat Satan in his sleep, he defeated him in his death. Satan is a lame duck ruler. His days as corrupt, bully "prince of this world" (John 12:31) are numbered. He doesn't have the last word; Jesus does. And Jesus' word for humans is "Yes."

Satan is our enemy, to be sure. Peter tells us that he "prowls around like a roaring lion looking for someone to devour" (1 Peter 5:8). We are no match for a lion, roaring or not, and we are no match for the devil. But Jesus is.

Jesus has already de-fanged and de-clawed this "lion." So Peter goes on to say, "Resist him [the devil], standing firm in the faith...." (verse 9).

Peter is talking about faith in the Son of God. When we stand with Jesus, trusting him, we stand also in his victory over the devil.

Not a quitter

"As soon as they hear it, Satan comes and takes away the word that was sown in them" (Mark 4:15). But what happens next? Does Jesus throw up his hands, sigh heavily and shake his head in defeat? Does he say, "Well, you got me on that one, Satan."

In the parable, Satan takes away the word that was planted in the person. We are not told in the parable what the sower does about that. But we are told in the Bible that God does not change in his covenant faithfulness to redeem lost humans. "I the Lord do not change," he told Israel, "so you, the descendants of Jacob, are not destroyed" (Malachi 3:6).

Jesus said, "For God so loved the world that he gave his one and only Son, that whoever believes in him shall not perish but have eternal life. For God did not send his Son into the world to condemn the world, but to save the world through him" (John 3:16-17).

Jesus is a sower who does not give up. The fact that Satan might take away the word from a person doesn't mean that Jesus won't sow in that place again. Sometimes, in fact, he might sow in such a place through you.

A LESSON ABOUT SEEDS (MARK 4:16-20)

By J. Michael Feazell

Others, like seed sown on rocky places, hear the word and at once receive it with joy. But since they have no root, they last only a short time. When trouble or persecution comes because of the word, they quickly fall away. Still others, like seed sown among thorns, hear the word; but the worries of this life, the deceitfulness of wealth and the desires for other things come in and choke the word, making it unfruitful. Others, like seed sown on good soil, hear the word, accept it, and produce a crop—some thirty, some sixty, some a hundred times what was sown." (NIV 2011)

When sowers in Jesus' day would sow their seeds, some of the seeds would naturally wind up in places unfavorable to growth, while most of the seeds wound up in good soil. Jesus used the result of the seeds in the various kinds of terrain to illustrate the behavior of people with the gospel. He speaks of rocky places, thorny places and good soil.

It is important to note that the parable does not say that God sows people on rocky places; it says that the way some people receive the gospel is like seed sown on rocky places. It is a comparison, an illustration of how some people deal with the gospel. It is not a justification for viewing God as deliberately making it impossible for some people to embrace the gospel.

People who abandon the word of God in the face of persecution are like seeds that grow on rocky places and therefore have little root. In a similar manner, people who let the word of God take a back seat to the worries of life and the pursuit of wealth are like seeds that get choked among thorns and shrivel.

In contrast, people who hear the word of God and accept it and produce the fruit of it are like seeds that germinate in good soil where there are no impediments to healthy growth.

Listening to Jesus

People, however, are not actually seeds, and God does not actually cast people into situations that prevent them from accepting the gospel. Jesus' parables should not be pushed beyond the point that Jesus intended them to make.

Seeds don't think. They don't make choices. They don't have the ability to ask God for help. The point of the parable is not to tell us that we are hapless seeds doomed to whatever fate might chance to befall us because of the sower's indiscriminate scattering. The point of the parable is that we should take steps to prevent ourselves from acting like helpless seeds.

When we find ourselves letting the cares of this world put the gospel on the back burner of our lives, then Jesus wants us to take note and make a change. He wants us to deepen our spiritual roots, to chop up the spiritual thorns in our lives. He wants us to nestle into the good soil of spending time in his word, of taking our issues, our hopes, our fears and our triumphs to him in prayer. He wants us to put the word of God to use in what we choose to do, to let the gospel flow out from us in kindness, mercy and peace.

It is easy to use the parable of the sower as a tool to judge others, to look down on people we think are weak in the faith and bound to fall away from the word of God. It is harder, but far more useful, to let the parable of the sower teach us and admonish us to keep an eye on our hearts, to make sure that greed, pride and anxious care about possessions and self-importance are not easing into the driver's seat in our lives.

Are you looking for a New Year's resolution? How about this one: Hear the word, accept it and love others as Jesus loves us. That's the lesson of the parable of the sower.

A LESSON ABOUT MEASUREMENT
(MARK 4:21-25)

By J. Michael Feazell

He said to them, "Do you bring in a lamp to put it under a bowl or a bed? Instead, don't you put it on its stand? For whatever is hidden is meant to be disclosed, and whatever is concealed is meant to be brought out into the open. If anyone has ears to hear, let them hear."

"Consider carefully what you hear," he continued. "With the measure you use, it will be measured to you—and even more. Whoever has will be given more; whoever does not have, even what they have will be taken from them." (NIV 2011)

On the list of frustrating things, heavy traffic ranks pretty high. And drivers who don't signal, don't look, won't move over, cut people off, speed, tailgate, go too slow, or drive incredibly noisy or incredibly large vehicles rank among the world's most frustrating people.

I find it surprisingly easy to condemn drivers — other drivers, that is. I find it just as surprising how easy it is to *forgive* my own driving mistakes. I wish I could say this phenomenon only pertained to driving. But the truth is, I find it far easier to forgive myself for just about anything than to forgive the same mistakes in others.

Jesus casts the spotlight on this all too human tendency when he says, "With the measure you use, it will be measured to you — and even more." At first glance, this might seem to be a simple matter of cause and effect: you forgive and then your act of forgiveness will merit forgiveness for you. But to understand Jesus' statement on those legalistic terms would be a mistake.

Jesus makes a similar point in Matthew 18:35, when he says, "This is how my heavenly Father will treat each of you unless you forgive your brother or sister from your heart." It might be easy to assume from this statement that God forgives us on the basis of our forgiveness of others. But that would be a false assumption. God forgives us on the basis of Jesus' perfect sacrifice on our behalf and in our place.

In these statements, Jesus is not prescribing a new form of legalism; he is describing the nature of hearts that trust in him. For example, when we trust in Christ, we no longer have anything to hide. The day will come, of course, when nothing remains hidden (verses 21-23), and that is true whether we trust in Christ or not. But for those who do trust him, that day is in effect already here — they have nothing to hide from him.

But the reason they have nothing to hide from Jesus is not that they are suddenly sinless. It is that they trust him to love them unconditionally and to forgive their sins, sins that they are no longer afraid to show him.

In the same way, those who trust Christ are free from the craving to measure others with the stern rod of selfishness. Because they trust Christ, they can commit their fears and anxieties to him, which frees them from the need to get even or get back at others. In other words, they know they are measured by Christ's rod of grace, which takes the starch out of their natural tendency to condemn others.

Whether it's in traffic, at the courthouse or around the dinner table, we're no longer slaves to our raw impulses—we are free to forgive others as God, for Christ's sake, forgave us, and as Christ lives in us, we do.

What Jesus says in verse 25 is a condemnation only to those who don't trust him—their selfish measuring rod is the only standard they know and the only one they understand. But for those who trust the Redeemer, there is only one measure — the ever-unfolding heights and depths of the love of Christ.

I'm learning not to listen to my knee-jerk reactions to miserable drivers. I'm learning to mutter, "God bless him" instead of ... something else. It's not only a good reminder of who I am in Christ, it's a hazy reflection of the heart of Christ which, by his grace, dwells in me.

A LESSON ABOUT LESSONS
(MARK 4:30-34)

By J. Michael Feazell

Again he said, "What shall we say the kingdom of God is like, or what parable shall we use to describe it? It is like a mustard seed, which is the smallest of all seeds on earth. Yet when planted, it grows and becomes the largest of all garden plants, with such big branches that the birds can perch in its shade."

With many similar parables Jesus spoke the word to them, as much as they could understand. He did not say anything to them without using a parable. But when he was alone with his own disciples, he explained everything. (NIV 2011)

What is the smallest seed in the world?

If you said, "The mustard seed," you wouldn't be alone. That's a pretty common belief among Christian Bible readers. But, as surprising as it may seem, it's not true.

"Wait just a minute," you might be tempted to say. "Doesn't the Bible say that the mustard seed is the smallest seed in the world?"

No, it doesn't. I used to think it did, just as many people still do.

Missing the point

A little study into horticulture will show that the mustard seed is not the smallest seed in the world. Poppy seeds, for example, are smaller than mustard seeds, as shown in the photo at left. For some people, those are fighting words, because they think it means that someone is calling Jesus a liar.

But Jesus did not say that the mustard seed is the smallest seed in the world. Jesus was giving a parable, and just as it has always been with his parables, the typical human response is to miss the point.

The point of the parable is not mustard seeds; the point is the kingdom of God. Mustard seeds are only part of the stage decoration Jesus used in getting across the point he was making about the kingdom. Parables use imaginary scenarios involving mundane things to make a point about something else — something spiritual and unseen.

Parables are not literal, historical stories. That's what makes them parables. They are imaginary stories created to help listeners or readers understand a deeper concept about something else. The teller expects his listeners to know that parables should be understood as beginning with: "Imagine this."

In Jesus' case, he told parables to give insight into the kingdom of God. In this parable of the mustard seed, he is asking the listeners to imagine a mustard seed that is smaller than all other seeds, but then that tiny, insignificant seed grows into something so big that it can provide shelter for the birds.

Jesus was not saying that mustard seeds are the smallest seeds in the world. He was saying that the kingdom of God can be likened to a mustard seed, an imaginary one (remember, it's a parable), that is the smallest seed you could possibly plant, but then it grows to become the largest plant in the whole garden. He was talking about the kingdom of God, not giving a science lesson.

Miraculous and amazing

Jesus wanted us to know that the advance of the kingdom of God begins in a small, practically unnoticed way with a baby born in a stable to a poor woman in an occupied country. That baby grows up to be rejected and despised by the leaders of his own people and crucified like a criminal on a Roman cross. But despite that weak, apparently insignificant beginning, he was raised from the dead and seated at the right hand of God the Father as Savior and Lord, both Creator and Redeemer of all the universe (compare Colossians 1:15-20).

Speaking of both his death and his resurrection, he said, "But I, when I am lifted up from the earth, will draw all men to myself" (John 12:32). From smallest seed to sheltering tree.

Look for the lesson

Jesus built his parables around common, ordinary things that people knew about. Farming, business, poor people, rich people, powerful people, weak people. But parables have a point, a lesson, that goes beyond the mere details of the story. And the lesson is usually made through a surprising twist, an unusual aspect that lifts the details of the story from the ordinary to the amazing.

No wonder Jesus used parables. The kingdom of God and the grace of God are amazing. But if we spend our time trying to turn the details of Jesus' parables into science and history textbooks, we will miss the lesson.

After reading *Animal Farm,* would we argue over whether pigs could really talk? After reading *Les Miserables,* would we scurry to French prison records to find whether there really was a Prisoner 24601? Do we get hung up on whether it was scientifically possible for things to turn to gold when King Midas touched them? Or do we simply think about the stories, ponder the analogies and learn the lessons?

Jesus told stories, good ones, that illustrated important aspects of the kingdom of God. Truth has to do with communicating a true message, and often that is done with creative stories, analogies, metaphors, similes, poems and songs. And Jesus was a master at it.

Imagine that.

A LESSON ABOUT STORMS (MARK 4:35-41)

By J. Michael Feazell

> That day when evening came, he said to his disciples," Let us go over to the other side." Leaving the crowd behind, they took him along, just as he was, in the boat. There were also other boats with him. A furious squall came up, and the waves broke over the boat, so that it was nearly swamped. Jesus was in the stern, sleeping on a cushion. The disciples woke him and said to him, "Teacher, don't you care if we drown?"
>
> He got up, rebuked the wind and said to the waves, "Quiet! Be still!" Then the wind died down and it was completely calm.
>
> He said to his disciples, "Why are you so afraid? Do you still have no faith?"
>
> They were terrified and asked each other, "Who is this? Even the wind and the waves obey him!" (NIV 2011)

The crises of life have often been compared to stormy seas. They come upon us whether we like it or not. They terrify us. They knock us around and threaten to destroy all our stability and security. We don't know whether we can survive them. And we don't know how long they will last. At least, that's how a storm at sea would be for most of us. For Jesus, it was just a chance to grab 40 winks.

As Mark tells the story, the disciples were terrified that the boat was going to break up and everyone would die. But Jesus was asleep (on a cushion no less, Mark notes, adding to the contrast between Jesus' tranquility and the disciples' panic), apparently oblivious to their pending doom. They roust him and cry, "Teacher, don't you care if we drown?" (v. 38). Of course, Jesus quiets the storm with a word, but then he chides the disciples: "Why are you so afraid? Do you still have no faith?" (v. 40).

Some of the lessons in the story are obvious. Jesus has power over the storms of life, experiences them alongside us, loves us, saves us from them and wants us to trust him more than we do.

Let's look at a lesson that

might not be so obvious. Storms don't worry Jesus. He's right there with us during them, but he's perfectly calm about them. He isn't terrified; he isn't impatient; he isn't worried. In fact, he's so calm, he's asleep. To us, he seems to be asleep at the switch. We wonder why on earth he doesn't get up and do something. We start to wonder whether he even knows the trouble we're in. Whether he cares. Whether he even can do anything about it. Whether he's really all he's cracked up to be.

Like the disciples, we believe he's there. In the disciples' case, they could actually see him lying there asleep. We don't have that luxury. We believe he's there, but most of the time he seems just as asleep as he was during the storm that day on the Sea of Galilee. The psalmist had the same lament in Psalm 44:23-24: "Awake, Lord! Why do you sleep? Rouse yourself! Do not reject us forever. Why do you hide your face and forget our misery and oppression?"

Maybe that's why Mark included this story. The not-so-obvious lesson is that Jesus was just as much in control, and the disciples were just as safe in his hands, while he was asleep as while he was awake. Most of the time, life seems like a relentless voyage from one storm to the next. At least it does for me, and I expect it's the same for you. One thing I've learned about myself is that during storms I'm usually a scared rabbit just like Jesus' disciples were.

But I'm also learning that I can take heart in knowing that Jesus isn't scared, and he isn't depressed. He might be asleep, or he might not be, but either way, like the song says, "He's got the whole world in his hands." Even if he doesn't wake up and quiet the storm, I'm safe with him. And if he does wake up and quiet the storm, he's probably going to say: "Why are you so afraid? Do you still have no faith?"

And I can live with that.

Reflection

- Does it sometimes seem that God is ignoring you when you need him most?
- Has a trial you've gone through made you stronger spiritually?
- Do you feel that Jesus should keep you from going through trials?
- When was your faith most tested?
- Why does God let us suffer trials if he loves us?

For further reading:

Where Is God When It Hurts? by Philip Yancey

JESUS IS COMING (MARK 5:1-18)

By J. Michael Feazell

> They went across the lake to the region of the Gerasenes. When Jesus got out of the boat, a man with an impure spirit came from the tombs to meet him. This man lived in the tombs, and no one could bind him anymore, not even with a chain. For he had often been chained hand and foot, but he tore the chains apart and broke the irons on his feet. No one was strong enough to subdue him. Night and day among the tombs and in the hills he would cry out and cut himself with stones.
>
> When he saw Jesus from a distance, he ran and fell on his knees in front of him. He shouted at the top of his voice, "What do you want with me, Jesus, Son of the Most High God? In God's name don't torture me!" For Jesus had said to him, "Come out of this man, you impure spirit!"
>
> Then Jesus asked him, "What is your name?"
>
> "My name is Legion," he replied, "for we are many." And he begged Jesus again and again not to send them out of the area.
>
> A large herd of pigs was feeding on the nearby hillside. The demons begged Jesus, "Send us among the pigs; allow us to go into them." He gave them permission, and the impure spirits came out and went into the pigs. The herd, about two thousand in number, rushed down the steep bank into the lake and were drowned.
>
> Those tending the pigs ran off and reported this in the town and countryside, and the people went out to see what had happened. When they came to Jesus, they saw the man who had been possessed by the legion of demons, sitting there, dressed and in his right mind; and they were afraid. Those who had seen it told the people what had happened to the demon-possessed man—and told about the pigs as well. Then the people began to plead with Jesus to leave their region.
>
> As Jesus was getting into the boat, the man who had been demon-possessed begged to go with him. (NIV 2011)

Some people feel sorry for the pigs in this story — a poor, innocent herd of snorting and grunting swine minding their own piggy business on the hillside, and Jesus lets a bunch of evil spirits enter them and run them off a cliff to their deaths in the sea.

I don't feel sorry for the pigs. I didn't feel sorry for the halibut I ate for dinner last night either. That halibut sacrificed its life so that I could have some protein. I don't know how many beasts, birds, fish, trees and plants have likewise died so that I, by eating them, wearing them or otherwise using them, might live. The herd of pigs that night on the shore of the Sea of Galilee died instead of the child of God whom Jesus traveled across the dark and stormy water to save (see Mark 4:35-41).

No match for Jesus

The man's demons, so powerful he describes them in terms of a Roman legion of 6,000 warriors, made the man torture himself (Mark 5:5). They caused him to be ostracized and chained (verses 3-4). They caused him unrelenting anguish and misery; but they could not destroy him.

Evil spirits these were, hateful and cruel, bent on destruction of whatever they possessed. The instant they entered the pigs, these demons destroyed them. But they could not destroy the one man they possessed.

Under the old covenant, the one Hebrews 10 says was fulfilled in Christ, pigs were ritually unclean, and as such were not even to be touched, much less eaten, by children of the covenant. Jesus, in effect, "sacrificed" a whole herd of swine for the sake of this one tormented man living among the tombs. To Jesus, the deliverance and restoration of one human being is worth whatever sacrifice it takes, even Jesus' own torture and death on a wood cross at Golgotha.

How long had this man lived in the graveyard under the unforgiving power of this legion of demons? We aren't told. But we do know this: Jesus was coming. In Mark's story, the only reason Jesus crossed the Sea of Galilee that evening—bringing the disciples through a storm they feared would kill them all, but which Jesus calmed with a word — was to deliver that poor man from his bondage.

Jesus is coming

What are your demons? What has you in self-destructive bondage? Know this: whatever your devils may be, they do not have the power to finally destroy you. Jesus is coming, he's coming for you, to set you free. Not even death can stop him — his or yours; he conquered death itself. He can free you from anything.

The song says, "Put your hand in the hand of the man who calmed the waters…" Maybe that's what the Gerasene demoniac wanted to do when he ran to Jesus after seeing him from afar (Mark 5:6). But all he could do was fall on his knees and let the demons do the talking (verse 7). It didn't matter. Jesus came to save him, regardless of the odds, regardless of the depth of the pit the man was in, regardless of the man's inability, because of the demons, to ask Jesus to save him.

Jesus freed him and banned his demons forever by way of the pigs drowned in the sea, symbols of the uncleanness and the end of the demons, as well as of the personal sacrifice of Jesus, who took the uncleanness of the world upon himself and cleaned it — that you and I might live free in him.

It has been said that most people have a hard time relating to the story of the Garasene demoniac, but that drug addicts relate to it easily. That makes sense. I think that anyone who takes sin seriously, like Jesus does, relates easily to this story. Like the demoniac, howling away in the dark from the tombs, even when our sinfulness darkens our hearts, somewhere deep inside we know our need, and we know Jesus is the one who has come to set us free.

A LESSON ABOUT HOPE (MARK 5:21-43)

By J. Michael Feazell

Then one of the synagogue leaders, named Jairus, came, and when he saw Jesus, he fell at his feet. He pleaded earnestly with him, "My little daughter is dying. Please come and put your hands on her so that she will be healed and live." So Jesus went with him.

A large crowd followed and pressed around him. And a woman was there who had been subject to bleeding for twelve years. She had suffered a great deal under the care of many doctors and had spent all she had, yet instead of getting better she grew worse. When she heard about Jesus, she came up behind him in the crowd and touched his cloak, because she thought, "If I just touch his clothes, I will be healed." Immediately her bleeding stopped and she felt in her body that she was freed from her suffering.

At once Jesus realized that power had gone out from him. He turned around in the crowd and asked, "Who touched my clothes?" (NIV 2011)

I hate crowds. I hate the jostling, the noise, the sense of being herded in directions I might not want to go and the frustration of proceeding at miserably tedious speeds. It's no wonder that Jesus disciples' were a bit sarcastic when he once asked the crush of bodies knocking him around in a Judean crowd, "Who touched my clothes?"

As it happened, Jesus was in this crowd only because he was on his way to heal the feverish daughter of a synagogue ruler who pleaded that Jesus have mercy on his dying child. Mark likes to tell his stories about Jesus like sandwiches — one story sandwiched in the middle of another—kind of like Jesus was sandwiched in this crowd.

"You see the people crowding against you," his disciples answered, "and yet you can ask, 'Who touched me?'"

Yes, that's exactly what Jesus could ask. He could ask because he'd felt something quite different from the normal collisions of shoulders and elbows and sandals and hips and thighs. He'd felt that "power had gone out from him" (verse 30). He'd sensed that someone had touched his clothes with a definite purpose in mind, a definite need, and that this person had done so believing that through this act God would give deliverance.

And indeed God had. Mark fills in the story for us, even though at the time the disciples were in the dark about what had happened. It seems that a woman had been suffering from debilitating menstrual hemorrhaging for 12 years.

This woman had spent everything on doctors to try to find a cure, and they had done nothing but make her problem worse. Now she was out of options, but that's when she heard that Jesus was coming to town. She decided that if she could just touch his clothes, she would be healed. So she bored her way through the sweaty bodies, came up behind Jesus, and touched his cloak. Instantly, the bleeding stopped and her suffering was over.

The mustard from Mark's sandwich of two stories begins to leak over onto both slices of bread at this point. Jairus, the synagogue ruler, was not afraid to walk right up to Jesus, fall at Jesus' feet, and plead for the daughter he loved. But the sick woman was different. She was just as determined and just as believing as Jairus in Jesus' power to save. But she was too afraid to approach this mysterious man of God head on. Unlike Jairus, she sneaked up behind Jesus, flicked a finger across the wrinkles of his robe and sunk back into the anonymity of the crowd.

But despite her fear, despite her low opinion of herself, maybe because of her status as a woman, but even more likely because of her status as unclean because of the purity laws about menstrual flow, Jesus noticed her. And he called her to him. And he called her daughter.

Meanwhile, Jairus' daughter died, and the messengers of this news told Jairus not to bother Jesus any more about it — after all, it was too late. But Jesus ignored them. He went straight to Jairus' house and despite the scorn and disbelief at his statement that the girl was not dead, but only sleeping, he took her by the hand and gave her back her life and Jairus back his daughter.

Jesus doesn't care who you are. He doesn't care if you're timid and shy, young or old, a leader or an outcast. He knows you, loves you, cares about your needs and fears and crises, and is ready to help. He listens to your up-front, head-on pleas and he senses hopeful hearts at the back of the line and behind the door. Your personality, your temperament, your status, nor even (especially) your sinful history can erect a barrier he can't bring down like the walls of Jericho.

What's your need? What's your crisis? What's your fear? Take it to Jesus. Take it to him in whatever way works for you. He loves you. He's on your side. And he's waiting.

A LESSON ABOUT FAITH (MARK 6:1-6)

By J. Michael Feazell

> Jesus left there and went to his hometown, accompanied by his disciples. When the Sabbath came, he began to teach in the synagogue, and many who heard him were amazed.
>
> "Where did this man get these things?" they asked. "What's this wisdom that has been given him? What are these remarkable miracles he is performing? Isn't this the carpenter? Isn't this Mary's son and the brother of James, Joseph, Judas and Simon? Aren't his sisters here with us?" And they took offense at him.
>
> Jesus said to them, "A prophet is not without honor except in his own town, among his relatives and in his own home." He could not do any miracles there, except lay his hands on a few sick people and heal them. He was amazed at their lack of faith. (NIV 2011)

When the prophet Samuel was looking for the right man to anoint king over Israel, God sent him to the house of Jesse. Jesse's grandmother was the Moabitess, Ruth, and his great-grandma was the infamous woman of Jericho, Rahab. An unlikely family in which to find the most famous king of Israel. But if that were not enough, when Jesse brought out his eldest and most accomplished son to meet Samuel, God said, "No, Sam, that's not him."

Samuel went through seven of Jesse's boys, and God turned thumbs down on every one. Perplexed, Samuel asked Jesse, "Are you sure that's all your kids?"

"Yeah," Jesse said. "That's it. Well, except for David, of course, but there's no way he's the one you're looking for. He's nothing but a sheep kid. He's out there with the sheep now—definitely not king material."

All Jesse's boys nodded and a couple snickered. "Definitely not king material."

"Listen, Samuel," Jesse said. "These are all fine boys here. Why don't you ask the Lord again, because you can bet your sandals that if one of my boys is going to be king, it'll be one of these. David's nothing special, and frankly, things are better around here when he's off with the sheep."

Samuel shook his head, eyeing the imposing lineup of Jesse's boys. Tall, good looking, and probably good warriors, he figured. Why does the Lord always have to pick the low enders? He smiled. He himself was a bit of an unlikely choice too, come to think of it. If it hadn't been for his mom's crazy vow, he might have been a normal kid instead of growing up in the tabernacle cleaning linen and hauling water for old Eli.

"No, the Lord says it's none of this bunch. You'd better go fetch this David out of the pasture." He shrugged. "With the Lord, you never know. I had to pull Saul out from behind a pile of grain sacks, you know. The kid was shaking like an olive leaf."

With a laugh, the prophet added: "The Lord doesn't see people the way we do. He's not into looks and all that folderol."

You know what happened. David's brothers must have been a little miffed that little brother David was anointed king instead of one of them. Maybe they felt a little like the sons of Jacob, who resented the way their dad made over spoiled little Joseph as if the older kids were little more than glorified ranch hands.

It was no different with Jesus. How can somebody you grew up with, somebody you might have watched grow up, somebody whose habits and idiosyncrasies often got on your nerves, suddenly start acting as though he thought he was somebody? Just who in Galilee does this guy think he is?

Woody Allen once said, "I wouldn't want to belong to any club that would have me as a member." Or maybe it was Mark Twain. Or Groucho Marx. Or all of them. Anyway, the people of Nazareth must have had a similar policy: "Anybody from around here has got to be a loser; just look at us. No, we don't care if he can do miracles, this guy has got to be a fraud."

So Jesus said his famous line: "A prophet is not without honor except in his own town, among his relatives and in his own home" (Mark 6:4). You might not remember it quite like that, but don't forget the King James Version is nearly twice as old as the United States; a little modern English is good for the soul. Jesus said it in Aramaic, anyway, and none of us would make that out, even if we've studied it, because understanding someone's pronunciation from 2,000 years ago is different from reading it today.

But we digress. The lesson we're drawing out of this passage is that we're a whole lot more enamored with impressive strangers than we are with the people we already know all too well. That helps account for sexual affairs, you know. It's all in the mystery. If you really knew the goofball you were shacking up with for the night the way his or her relatives and friends do, you'd stay a million miles away. But alas, we have more respect for people we don't even know than for those we do.

It was in Nazareth, where Jesus grew up, that he could heal only a few people. Why? Because they didn't believe he could possibly be a healer. They could not accept one of their own as being somehow greater than they were, even if it meant foregoing the healing he could have brought them. Faith and humility don't travel without each other. Trusting Jesus means seeing yourself in need of him. Knowing your need for him generates trust in him. He's in town, your town, right now. Trust him with your burdens. Let him give you rest. It's you he's come to see.

A LESSON ABOUT INSTRUCTIONS
(MARK 6:7-12)

By J. Michael Feazell

Calling the Twelve to him, he began to send them out two by two.... (NIV 2011)

The first time Jesus sent out the disciples, he gave them some pretty specific instructions: Go two by two, take a staff (presumably a shepherd-style staff, not an office staff), but don't take anything else — no food, no satchel, no money. Wear sandals, but don't take a change of clothes. When you get to a town, stay in the first house you enter until you leave that town. And if anybody doesn't welcome you or listen to you, shake the dust off your feet on your way out of town.

Strange stuff. Apparently they followed the instructions, and apparently they had a good trip — they drove out a lot of demons and healed a lot of sick people by anointing them with oil.

But why the unusual instructions?

Some people think those instructions should still be followed today. Not many people, thank God, but there are some who prey on unsuspecting generous people, citing this passage as their badge of authority to move in and leech off somebody by masquerading as a "servant of God." Don't listen to such people—they're con artists, not evangelists or prophets or whatever else they might call themselves.

So what did Jesus have in mind with these strange rules for this first "disciplic" excursion? Mark is brief, just giving the facts, but not the background. His first readers probably knew what was behind these instructions, but a couple of thousand years down the road we have to piece it together from what we know of the religious and social customs of first-century Judea.

Two by two

The command to go two by two might reflect Deuteronomy 17:6 and 19:15, where Israel was taught that at least two witnesses were needed to establish the truth of a matter — in this case, the veracity of Jesus' ministry.

They were to take no food, satchel or money. It might be that Jesus simply wanted to illustrate the fact that his followers were to trust God for their needs. Or it might be that he wanted to show that his followers were not like certain speakers of the day who traveled into towns with a collection bag to gather money. Or maybe the idea is that they were to travel light to symbolize the urgency of their mission.

Beyond that, it gets pretty murky. They were to take a staff, or walking stick. We could invent a meaning for the walking stick, but it would be our invention. For example, we could say that the disciples would be shepherds of the flock one day, and the staff symbolizes that. But we would be guessing.

Shaking the dust

Why sandals? We're not told. The shaking of dust from the feet might be easier to understand. According to tradition, when a Jew returned to Judea from visiting a foreign country, he was to shake the dust off his feet, thereby keeping the land unpolluted from the dust of gentile lands. The disciples were to shake the dust off their feet as a witness against any Jewish towns that refused them, maybe symbolizing that such a town was cutting itself off from Israel by refusing Jesus.

Whatever the reasons behind them, these instructions were not intended to be the norm for all mission style work from then on. They were unique instructions for a unique band of men on a unique mission, unique even for them. The commands were specific to that particular mission, and they probably had something to do with presenting a symbolic testimony to Jesus as Messiah, even though we're not directly told that.

The Bible is full of instructions that we should follow, but it is also full of stories about instructions that were given to particular people for particular reasons in their particular times.

Naaman, an Aramaic general who suffered from leprosy, was told by Elisha the prophet to dip in the Jordan River seven times to cure the disease (2 Kings 5). Should we go jump in the river to heal our skin problems? The Israelites were told to go outside the camp with a shovel to relieve themselves (Deuteronomy 23:12-13). Should we avoid toilets and drive out of town when we need to relieve ourselves?

It's a good idea to look at the principles behind a particular instruction as a way of helping us determine whether and how to apply that instruction to ourselves in our day. Some biblical instructions might not apply to us at all. Others might need to be applied in ways that are appropriate for our day and circumstances, rather than the specific ways they were applied in biblical stories.

Jesus said that what marks us as his true disciples is that we love one another (John 13:35). Now there's an instruction that means exactly the same thing today as it did when it was first given. Wouldn't it be great if we gave that one the most attention?

A LESSON ABOUT GUILTY CONSCIENCES
(MARK 6:14-29)

By J. Michael Feazell

But when Herod heard this, he said, "John, whom I beheaded, has been raised from the dead!" (NIV 2011)

Herod Antipas was a man with blood on his hands. Of all his accomplishments, great and small, during his 33-year reign as tetrarch (he was not actually a king), he is best remembered for his murder of John the Baptist.

Maybe it's only when past deeds come back to haunt us that our consciences truly come to life. Most people spend their lives covering up their dark side, keeping their skeletons securely locked away in hidden closets under the back stairs of their minds.

Hiding from our sins

It's a sin management thing. Keeping the shame and horror of our sins out of sight and out of mind allows us to function in the light as normal, decent human beings.

It allows us to live with ourselves. But there's always that nagging fear that we have to keep pushing back into the shadows—the fear that somehow, some day, one of those skeletons is going to come to life, crash its way out of the closet, walk up to us in the middle of a crowd and wag its boney finger accusingly in our face.

That's what Herod thought had happened. He had never successfully managed to keep the memory of John's murder chained silently beyond the boundaries of his struggling conscience. Of all the people he had executed, certainly most of them enemies and criminals, this was the one he actually regretted.

It wasn't a political assassination or an act of revenge or even retribution. It was a simple act of cowardice, of embarrassment. He had made a boast in front of two women and was ashamed to take it back. So he murdered the one bright spot in his otherwise decadent, self-indulgent life. Why not? He had bowed to the ruthless demands of his wife, Herodias, before. It was easier that way. One more time shouldn't matter so much. But it did.

Clean conscience

What Herod didn't know was that the man he feared was John the Baptist raised from the dead was actually Jesus the Messiah, the King of the Jews whom his father had tried to murder 30 years earlier in the massacre of the babies in Bethlehem.

But you and I do know. And we know that Jesus can clean out all the skeletons in all our closets — if we want him to.

When we trust our lives to Jesus, we no longer have to manage our sins by hiding from our consciences. Jesus cleans our guilty consciences (see Hebrews 10:22), and God erases our sins from his memory.

Why suffer the misery of a guilty conscience when we don't have to? Isn't it time to unlock the closets for our Savior?

FEEDING 5,000 AND
WALKING ON WATER (MARK 6:30-52)

By Michael Morrison

"The apostles gathered around Jesus, and told him all that they had done and taught" (6:30, NRSV throughout this chapter). Jesus sent them out two by two in 6:7-13, and verse 30 is the tail end of one of Mark's literary sandwiches. Jesus sends out the disciples on their mission, then we are told of how John the Baptist was killed, and this verse tells us that they reported to Jesus how their mission trip went. If we read the two accounts as a whole, we are reminded that carrying out Jesus' mission may carry the ultimate price: martyrdom. Matthew's version makes that more explicit; but here there is only a subtle hint.

They had a successful mission, and yet they are confronted with sobering news about John the Baptist. So Jesus "said to them, 'Come away to a deserted place all by yourselves and rest a while.' For many were coming and going, and they had no leisure even to eat" (6:31). The crowd was besieging them, and they needed some time to relax and recover.

So they went by boat: "And they went away in the boat to a deserted place by themselves." But verse 33 tells us that the only down time they got was while they manned the oars: "Many saw them going and recognized them, and they hurried there on foot from all the towns and arrived ahead of them." I'm not sure how the logistics work here – the people were able to see where the boat was headed, and they walked around the shore faster than the boat could go in a straight line.

Jesus could have seen all the people before he landed, but verse 34 tells us that he landed anyway: "As he went ashore, he saw a great crowd; and he had compassion for them, because they were like sheep without a shepherd; and he began to teach them many things." Jesus is taking on the role of a shepherd-king. The Old Testament prophets had lamented that the people were not being taken care of by their leaders, so Jesus responds by teaching them. They didn't need a military leader – they needed a teacher.

But the main function of these verses is to set the scene for the miracle that follows. "When it grew late, his disciples came to him and said, 'This is a deserted place, and the hour is now very late; send them away so that they may go into the surrounding country and villages and buy something for themselves to eat'" (vv. 35-36). It seems to me that when the hour is late, the people need to go home and sleep, not just eat. But the disciples were concerned about food. Maybe *they* were the ones who were hungry.

"But he answered them, 'You give them something to eat.'" Remember, Jesus had just sent them out on a teaching mission, and they had success. Jesus wants them to continue to be extensions of his ministry, and to be shepherds of the people. But they didn't seem to get the hint. "They said to him, 'Are we to go and buy two hundred denarii worth of bread, and give it to them to eat?'"

That may be a reasonable question, but I doubt that they had the money, and I doubt that village shops would actually have that much bread for sale. It was not a genuine question. It would be like us saying, "What do you want us to do, go down to the 7-11 and buy $5,000 dollars worth of bread? We don't have that much money with us, and the 7-11 wouldn't have that much bread."

Nevertheless, Jesus tells them what to do: "He said to them, 'How many loaves have you? Go and see.' When they had found out, they said, 'Five, and two fish.'" That's all they could scrounge up. (Only John tells us that the food actually came from a boy.)

"Then Jesus ordered the disciples to get all the people to sit down in groups on the green grass." Mark is the only one who tells us that the grass was green (which shows that it was springtime, but that is not important to the meaning conveyed by the story).

"So the people sat down in groups of hundreds and of fifties. Taking the five loaves and the two fish, Jesus looked up to heaven, and blessed, and broke the loaves..." Did he bless God, or bless the loaves? Grammatically, it's not clear.

Jesus "gave them to his disciples to set before the people; and he divided the two fish among them all." This was not "everyone come and get your own" – the disciples were to be the agents of distribution. And everyone ate as much as they wanted, and presumably put a few pieces in their pockets, too, but there was still a lot left over. But they didn't throw away the scraps – the disciples "took up twelve baskets full of broken pieces and of the fish. Those who had eaten the loaves numbered five thousand men." Matthew tells us that there were also women and children. Either way, it's more than twice the population of Capernaum!

Why would the disciples carry that many baskets with them? I suspect that "baskets" here is functioning as a unit of measurement. The point is that they each ended up with a lot of food.

How did it happen? Mark doesn't tell us. Nor do we know if the people perceived a miracle at all. The miracle was done not to impress people, but to impress the disciples, and to give them a role in Jesus' ministry.

It's a nice miracle, but what's the point? There is a contrast here between the feast given by Herod Antipas, and the feast given by Jesus. One was an exercise in self-indulgence, status, and murder; the other was an occasion of generosity. Jesus is the better shepherd, who actually cares about the sheep, more like Moses, who fed the people in the wilderness. (That's why the bread is given more attention than the fish are.)

Walking on water

Right after this miracle, Matthew, Mark and John tell us about Jesus walking on the water. This is what Mark 6:45 says about it: "Immediately he made his disciples get into the boat and go on ahead to the other side, to Bethsaida, while he dismissed the crowd." In other places, Jesus had trouble with the crowds pressing in on him, but here it seems that he was able to disperse the people all by himself. We aren't supposed to worry too much about logistical details like that – Mark is simply setting the story up.

"After saying farewell to them [the crowds?], Jesus went up on the mountain to pray. When evening [nightfall? – John says it was dark] came, the boat was out on the sea, and he was alone on the land. When he saw that they were straining at the oars against an adverse wind…" I'm not sure how well he could have seen a small boat out in the lake when there was a strong wind that would kick up big waves. But even from the shore, he could have figured out that the wind was blowing the wrong way, and if he could see the boat at all, he would know that they hadn't made much progress.

So he goes in for a closer look: "He came towards them early in the morning, walking on the sea. He intended to pass them by." That's a strange comment, it seems to me (and Matthew apparently thought so, too, because he didn't include it). Why did Jesus want to "pass them by"? Maybe Mark means *as if* he were going to pass them by – that is, Jesus wasn't walking directly toward the boat.

"But when they saw him walking on the sea, they thought it was a ghost and cried out; for they all saw him and were terrified." I don't know what it is about ghosts that make people scared (what do ghosts actually *do* to people??), but I suppose that if I saw something like this, I'd be a bit anxious, too. However, people back then believed that ghosts could NOT walk on water. In Greek mythology, the dead stayed in the realm of the dead because they could not walk on water. They had to pay money to a boatsman to get across the River Styx; they could not walk across.

Jason Combs writes, "Gods and divine men walk on water; ghosts do not. But when the disciples see Jesus walking on water, they believe the impossible [a ghost on water] rather than the obvious [Jesus is divine]." (Jason Robert Combs, "A Ghost on the Water? Understanding an Absurdity in Mark 6:49-50," *Journal of Biblical Literature* 127 (2008): 358.) The thick-headed disciples fail again to see who Jesus really is.

"But immediately he spoke to them and said, 'Take heart, it is I; do not be afraid.' Then he got into the boat with them and the wind ceased." Another calming of the storm! Not surprisingly, "they were utterly astounded," But the *reason* that Mark gives is surprising: "for they did not understand about the loaves, but their hearts were hardened." Matthew and John do not have this criticism of the disciples.

I think that walking on water, and suddenly calming a strong wind, would have astounded *anybody*. But Mark tells us that they were astounded because they did not understand about the loaves. It's as if they were reacting to the wrong miracle – a bit of a time lag in their mental processing.

What is the connection? Just because Jesus can multiply bread does not mean that he can walk on water – or does it? Perhaps the thought is that if Jesus can multiply bread, then he is divine, and *nothing* is beyond his ability; the disciples should not be surprised *no matter what*. They did not understand who Jesus was, because their hearts were hard, and God had not yet revealed everything to them. But we do have to give them some credit: they continued to follow Jesus.

EVERYONE MUST DIE!
A STUDY OF MARK 8:27-38

By Michael Morrison

Jesus did most of his ministry in the Jewish areas of Galilee and Judea. But on at least one occasion, he traveled north of Galilee. He used the retreat to debrief his disciples, to discuss his mission, and to teach a fundamental lesson about what it means to be a disciple.

Peter identifies Jesus as the Messiah (verses 27-30)

"Jesus and his disciples went on to the villages around Caesarea Philippi" (NIV 2011 throughout this chapter). This was about 25 miles north of the Sea of Galilee. "On the way he asked them, 'Who do people say I am?'" He already knew what the people thought, but the question led to an important teaching point.

"They replied, 'Some say John the Baptist; others say Elijah; and still others, one of the prophets.'" Some people thought that Jesus preached in the style of John; others that he was like Elijah, or some other prophet.

"'But what about you?' he asked. 'Who do you say I am?'"

Peter said what the others probably thought but were afraid to say: "You are the Messiah." They had seen him cast out demons, heal the sick, walk on water, and feed 5,000 people. Peter concluded, You are the man God will use to rescue us.

Peter's response was correct. But "Jesus warned them not to tell anyone about him." On several occasions, Jesus wanted his identity kept a secret (Mark 1:25, 34, 44; 3:12;5:43; 7:36). Large crowds were already a hindrance to his ministry (1:33, 45; 5:24). Further, Jesus did not want the rulers to see him as a political rival.

Jesus wanted his disciples to be quiet about his identity because what *they* meant by the word "Messiah" was quite different from what Jesus actually was. Peter had the right word, but a seriously flawed concept of what the Messiah would do. This is the next thing that Jesus teaches them.

Jesus predicts his death (verses 31-33)

For the first time, Jesus predicted his own death: "He then began to teach them that the Son of Man must suffer many things and be rejected by the elders, the chief priests and the teachers of the law, and that he must be killed and after three days rise again."

"The Son of Man" is a reference to Daniel's vision of "one like a son of man" who was given a kingdom (Daniel 7:13). When the angel interpreted the vision, he said the kingdom would be given to the persecuted *saints* (7:18-27). The "son of man" represented all the saints. Jesus saw himself as this person who represented the persecuted people of God. He would accept the kingdom on their behalf — and be persecuted on their behalf.

Jesus also saw himself as the fulfillment of Isaiah's prophecy of a servant who would suffer on behalf of his people (Isaiah 53); Isaiah and Daniel were describing the same person.

This was not what most Jews thought — most people assumed that the Messiah would be a victorious king, not a suffering servant. So Jesus taught here that the "son of man" would be rejected by the Jewish authorities, killed on behalf of his people, and then rise again.

In some of his teachings, Jesus spoke in parables that hid part of the meaning (Mark 4:11); this time, however, "he spoke plainly about this." But this new revelation was so *contrary* to expectations, that "Peter took him aside and began to rebuke him."

One minute, Peter declares Jesus to be the leader God sent to his people. The next minute, Peter is contradicting his God-appointed leader! This is an emotional reaction. What Jesus said deeply disturbed Peter's idea of what the Messiah would do — and what he would do for Peter himself.

The disciples expected to receive certain benefits for following Jesus. They had left family, jobs and homes, and it was natural that they wanted a reward (Matthew 19:27). Some wanted to be the greatest in the kingdom (Mark 10:37). They were thinking that the kingdom of Jesus would be similar to the kingdoms of this world, where the king's closest friends got the most benefits.

Peter was looking forward to being the chief of staff, the secretary of state, or someone important in the new government. But Jesus had just taken his high hopes and smashed them.

Peter had the presence of mind to take Jesus aside and "correct" his teacher privately. Repent of this defeatist attitude! We won't let it happen — we'll take up swords and protect you!

We do not know if the other disciples could hear what Peter and Jesus said. But Jesus' reply was said with them in mind: "But when Jesus turned and looked at his disciples, he rebuked Peter. 'Get behind me, Satan!' he said." Jesus calls Peter Satan, the Hebrew word for "adversary." Peter is opposing God's plan. (If Satan had actually been there, Jesus would have rebuked Satan. But the text clearly says that Jesus rebuked Peter.)

You have called me your leader, and I am, Jesus might have said. So get behind me and *follow*— don't try to get in front and lead. You don't even know where you are going. "You do not have in mind the concerns of God, but merely human concerns."

Peter was thinking about the things that ordinary human beings think about. He wanted what his friends and neighbors did: freedom from foreign oppression, safety, security, money, and a reward for the risk and the work.

But God has something a lot more important in mind than that. He can see an enemy that is stronger than Rome, an enemy that must be conquered by suffering and death, not by replacing Roman overlords with Jewish ones.

Take up the cross (verses 34-37)

The lesson Jesus wanted to teach Peter was needed by everyone. So Jesus "called the crowd to him along with his disciples and said: Whoever wants to be my disciple must deny themselves and take up their cross and follow me."

If you want to learn from me, he said, you must put aside your desires for fame and fortune, and be willing to die. You must be willing to follow me into death, if that's where it ends up. I am not looking for people who simply want to benefit themselves. The world already has enough of those people.

And why should people be willing to give up their lives? "For whoever wants to save their life will lose it, but whoever loses their life for me and for the gospel will save it." If your priority is on saving your life, you will be a loser, because you *will* die.

But if you are willing to lose your life for Jesus, and die for his kingdom, then you will save your life. Jesus is talking about life *after* you die, and that is the perspective we all need.

If we focus on life in this age, we will lose it. But if we focus on Jesus and his message, we will have a better life in the age to come. The losses are temporary, but the rewards are eternal.

"What good is it," Jesus asks, "for someone to gain the whole world, yet forfeit their soul?" No matter whether you are thinking about military conquest or financial gain, what good would it do you, even if you have the maximum success possible? You are still going to die. (The Greek word translated "soul" can refer to life in this age.) There is an enemy here, an oppression that is far worse than Rome.

"What can anyone give in exchange for their soul?" Even if you had the whole world, you could not buy your life back. So why struggle for such a temporary victory?

What we need is a Messiah who conquers death itself — and that can be done only by someone who enters death and emerges victorious on the other side. We need a Messiah who dies and returns to life.

Jesus summarizes by pointing to the day of reward: "If anyone is ashamed of me and my words in this adulterous and sinful generation, the Son of Man will be ashamed of them when he comes in his Father's glory with the holy angels."

If we cannot accept the sort of Messiah that Jesus actually is, if we cannot accept what he teaches, then Jesus will be disappointed about the priority we chose. He is offering us an endless age of divine glory; tragically, some are seeking first a short-lived life in a very troubled world. He does not reject us permanently, just as he did not reject Peter, but he will lament that we chose such a small reward.

The Greeks had a word for it: Χριστός

Hebrew had a word for it, and when the Old Testament was translated into Greek, Greek-speaking Jews found a word for it, too. It starts with the Hebrew word *mashah,* which means to spread a liquid, or anoint with oil. An anointed person was called *mashiach,* an anointed one; it was most often used in reference to Jewish kings, but was also used for Cyrus, a Persian king.

When the Jews were in exile and looking forward to the restoration of the Davidic line of kings, they set their hopes on the anointed one, the *mashiach* who would restore the nation.

Similarly, the Greek word starts with *chriō,* meaning to anoint with oil. In secular Greek the adjective *christos* always referred to things that were "rubbed on," and never to people. But the Jews applied this word to their hopes for a messianic leader, and Christians applied it to Jesus. Jesus is the Christ, the Anointed One.

THE TRANSFIGURATION:
SNEAK PEEK AT THE RESURRECTION:
A STUDY OF MARK 9:1-13

By Michael Morrison

The disciples are discouraged — even dismayed. They thought they were following a Messiah into a glorious kingdom. But then Jesus told them that he was going to his death.

Where was the glory they hoped for, the kingdom that Jesus seemed to promise? Jesus needed to offer the disciples some hope for the future, and this is what comes next in the story.

The kingdom in power and glory (verses 1-4)

Jesus told his disciples, "Truly I tell you, some who are standing here will not taste death before they see that the kingdom of God has come with power" (NIV 2011 throughout). Jesus assures them that the glory of the kingdom will indeed come — and it will be seen before the disciples die.

The disciples had already seen some of the power of God's kingdom. Whenever Jesus cast out demons and healed the sick, the power of the kingdom was at work (Matthew 12:28). The disciples saw the power of the kingdom on the day of Pentecost (Acts 2:1-4). They saw it in miracles, and in the spread of the gospel all the way to Rome.

But Jesus is referring to something else. His promise is found in Matthew, Mark, and Luke, and in each account, it is immediately followed by the Transfiguration, in which three disciples had the privilege of seeing Jesus in a special glory. In all three Gospels, we are told that the Transfiguration happened about a week after the prediction—the saying and the fulfillment are tied together by this literary technique.

"After six days Jesus took Peter, James and John with him and led them up a high mountain, where they were all alone." Tradition says that this was Mount Tabor, but it is only 2,000 feet high. Mt. Hermon may be a better candidate, since it is the tallest mountain in the area (9,000 feet), and Caesarea Philippi is at the base of Mt. Hermon.

Peter, James and John were the disciples closest to Jesus. They also seem to have been the most ambitious — Peter was the most outspoken, and James and John wanted positions of honor when Jesus came in his glory (Mark 10:37). These three may have needed the most reassurance that something better would come after the persecution.

And they saw it: "There he was transfigured before them. His clothes became dazzling white, whiter than anyone in the world could bleach them. And there appeared before them Elijah and Moses, who were talking with Jesus."

Were Elijah and Moses resurrected, or was this just an "appearance"? Matthew 17:2 says that Jesus' face "shone like the sun." Was it a vision, or was Jesus really changed? We do not know. Why Moses and Elijah? That is more easily answered. Jews respected both of them highly, and they represent high points in Israelite history, corresponding to the Law and the Prophets.

What were they talking about? Luke 9:31 says that they were discussing Jesus' "departure which he was about to bring to fulfillment at Jerusalem." They were talking about his death. Did Elijah and Moses know the manner and purpose of Jesus' death, or were they asking Jesus to explain it to them? Apparently it is not important that we know.

Listen to Jesus (verses 5-8)

If we had been there, we probably would not have understood it any better than Peter did. "Peter said to Jesus, 'Rabbi, it is good for us to be here. Let us put up three shelters — one for you, one for Moses and one for Elijah.' (He did not know what to say, they were so frightened.)"

A week earlier, Peter said that Jesus was the Messiah. Now, he uses the lesser title "Rabbi." Which title is most appropriate? We will soon have an authoritative answer!

Why did Peter talk about shelters? In a state of glory, why would anyone need a shelter? Perhaps Peter was thinking of the Festival of Tabernacles, which many Jews associated with the arrival of the kingdom. Perhaps the shelters were an invitation for the prophets to stay a while.

Something even more astounding happened next. "Then a cloud appeared and covered them, and a voice came from the cloud: 'This is my Son, whom I love. Listen to him!'" The cloud was not just above them — it "covered them" in the sense of covering them up, as a dense fog, blocking their view.

And God tells us what is important: Jesus is the Son of God, loved by God, speaking the words of God. Even when the greatest prophets from Israel's history are present, the disciples should listen to Jesus. Jesus is greater even than Moses and Elijah, and therefore greater than the Law and the Prophets. If he says that he is going to be their Messiah by dying in Jerusalem, then they should pay attention to what he says.

"Suddenly, when they looked around, they no longer saw anyone with them except Jesus." Peter had hoped to prolong the moment, but it was over.

The event was not to get them in touch with past prophets, but for them to be more dedicated to the leader they had, because he was more than a prophet — he was the Son of God, and God had just validated the path that Jesus was on.

The glory they saw in Jesus no doubt encouraged them that the glorious kingdom would be a reality. But it was not just a future reality. Jesus had been the beloved Son of God all along, and his disciples should accept his teachings, even if they are the opposite of what they wanted and expected. Since he is the beloved Son of God, the disciples could be sure that glory would follow, even if dark days lay in the immediate future.

The Transfiguration also shows that God's kingdom transcends human kingdoms. God's reign is not just a bigger and better empire, and the leaders in the kingdom are not just kinder and stronger versions of Roman or Judean kings. The transformed face and clothes of Jesus show that it is *far different;* it is not just a continuation of normal history.

Indeed, when the disciples catch even a small glimpse of the glory, they are frightened and don't even know how to speak intelligently. They had only a glimmer of understanding of what the kingdom really is.

So what should the disciples do?

They should listen to Jesus, get behind Jesus and follow him. They should not take matters into their own hands, because their efforts are as useless as making shelters for glorified beings.

But what about Elijah? (verses 9-13)

"You had to be there," the saying goes. But in this case, it didn't do a lot of good to "be there." "As they were coming down the mountain, Jesus gave them orders not to tell anyone what they had seen until the Son of Man had risen from the dead. They kept the matter to themselves, discussing what 'rising from the dead' meant."

Jesus had predicted his own death and resurrection, but the truth was so contrary to what the disciples expected that they couldn't understand the plainest of words. It was only after Jesus rose from the dead that they could begin to understand — but until that understanding came, they would not be able to tell the story right. So Jesus told them to keep it a secret until the time was right.

The Transfiguration gave them a glimpse of the glory that Jesus had, and the glory that he would share with all who took up the cross to follow Jesus into the valley of the shadow of death.

THE FIG TREE AND THE TEMPLE
IN MARK 11:12-16

By J. Michael Feazell

Jesus' cursing of the unfruitful fig tree presents Christians with a dilemma unique in the Gospels. A cursory reading of the text portrays Jesus as acting quite out of character, using his divine power in selfish anger to curse a mere tree because it did not act contrary to nature by providing him fruit out of season to satisfy his hunger. Many ideas have been brought forward in an effort to explain the apparent anomaly of Jesus' behavior in the fig tree incident. These range from flatly rejecting the authenticity of the account to blaming the confusion on a problem of "misplaced clauses habitual with Mark" (Cotter 66).

I believe the account is best understood, however, when it is taken just as it is written, and when it is interpreted in light of: 1) Mark's overall goal of declaring the identity and authority of Jesus and 2) the significance of the fig tree in Jewish and Roman culture. In this paper, I will suggest that Mark intentionally designed the account as it stands for the purpose of intensifying the meaning of Jesus' identity and authority, as well as declaring the fate that awaited Jerusalem.

The account of the cursing of the fig tree (11:12-14, 20-26) is interrupted by the description of Jesus' cleansing of the temple (15-19). This a-b-a structure makes evident the connection between the fig tree and the temple (Lane 400). It is instructive to note, however, that even this structure is sandwiched between another—two accounts pointing directly to Jesus' identity and authority (Hooker 261): Jesus' triumphal entry into Jerusalem on the colt, declared as the one who comes in the name of the Lord (11:1-11) and the questioning of his authority by the chief priests, the scribes and the elders (11:27-33). The entire chapter, then, forms an elaborate a-b-c-b-a structure, a carefully constructed pericope that leads the reader to a greater understanding of Mark's central issue: the identity and authority of Jesus.

First, Jesus is identified and hailed as the one who comes in the name of the Lord, who ushers in the kingdom of the Messiah, the son of David (1-11). Next, Jesus instructs his disciples, using the figure of the fig tree, about what will befall the nation that has rejected its king (12-14). He then enters the temple and cleanses it, acting within his authority as Messiah, and the chief priests and the scribes reject him and begin looking for ways to kill him (15-19). Next, Jesus and his disciples pass by the fig tree on the way back to Jerusalem and find that Jesus' declaration that no one would eat fruit of it again had become reality, which leads to instruction about faith, prayer and forgiveness (20-26). The structure of this pericope is then concluded by the account of the chief priests', scribes' and elders' refusal to accept Jesus' authority (27-33). Chapter 11, therefore, is consistent with the overall focus of the Gospel of Mark: the identity and authority of Jesus. With Mark's structure in mind, we will now proceed to analyze the cursing of the fig tree, beginning in verse 12.

As Mark sets up the story, he points out several facts. It was the day after the triumphal entry into Jerusalem (12). Jesus and his disciples were walking from Bethany (12), where they had spent the night (11), toward Jerusalem (15). Jesus was hungry (12). He saw a fig tree in leaf in the distance. He went to it to see if it might have any fruit, but found only leaves (13). Then Mark adds the confounding clause, "for it was not the season for figs" (13d, NRSV in this chapter). This is the troubling element for many who find this passage difficult. If Jesus' purpose in approaching the fig tree were simply because he was hungry, as Mark intimates, and it was not even the season for figs, which Jesus must have known before he even approached the tree, then how can he be justified in saying to it, "May no one ever eat fruit from you again" (14)? Before we consider the answer to that question, we need to take note of additional facts provided by Mark.

When Jesus made the statement to the tree, Mark notes that "his disciples heard it" (14c). Picking up the story in verse 20, after the cleansing of the temple, we find that the fig tree had not only withered away, but had withered away to its roots (20). We are also told that Peter "remembered," and that he called Jesus' attention to the withered tree, saying Jesus had "cursed" it (21), even though the word "curse" was not used in verse 14. Then, without apparent transition, Mark says Jesus "answered" them (though no question is posed) by giving instruction about faith that can remove mountains (22-26)—another enigmatic passage for many Christians, which we shall comment about later.

Let us now consider how the facts provided by Mark serve to clarify the meaning of what would otherwise be a troubling passage. First, we need to note that "his disciples heard it" (14c). The presence of this statement indicates that Jesus' pronouncement on the tree was a teaching situation. Jesus' words were intended to instruct his disciples, and the incident, therefore, was intended to provide the opportunity to teach them and the reader. In contrast, we find Jesus again teaching immediately after he cleansed the temple (17), and Mark tells the reader that "when the chief priests and the scribes heard it, they were looking for a way to kill him" (18). Mark often provides a reaction to Jesus' actions and instruction —astonishment (10:51), grief (10:22), inability to understand (9:32), etc. In this case, the response from those who "heard it," unlike his disciples in 14c, is to reject Jesus and look for ways to kill him.

Once we recognize that the fig tree incident is recorded as a teaching situation, the lesson of which is given in the events and sayings of Jesus in the following verses, the reasons for Mark's letting the reader know that Jesus was hungry (12), that he knew the distant fig tree was in leaf (13), and that it was not the season for figs (14), begin to come into focus. The fact that Jesus was hungry provides not only the immediate reason to approach the tree (a fact essential to the narrative — approaching a fruitless tree only to be disappointed would be meaningless unless someone was hungry), it is also vital to the prophetic declaration Jesus was to make. Many scholars agree that Jesus would have had in mind such passages as Jeremiah 8:13: "When I wanted to gather them, says the LORD, there are no grapes on the vine, nor figs on the fig tree; even the leaves are withered, and what I gave them has passed away from them." The fact that Jesus was hungry and approached the fig tree looking for fruit illustrates his identity and authority as the Judge of Israel who finds that the nation, despite its "leafy" appearance, has not produced the fruit God desired.

Another view of why Mark points out that Jesus was hungry is suggested by A. de Q. Robin in connection with Micah 7:1-6:

> It is quite conceivable that seeing the fig tree brought this Micah passage to the mind of Jesus and in accordance with the Rabbinic practice of indicating a passage of scripture by quoting its opening words, he was heard by the disciples to say: "My soul desires the first ripe fig." This could quite easily lead to the misunderstanding that he was hungry, when in fact he was commenting on the state of the nation and its leaders, before pronouncing the judgement of God upon them first in the symbolical action of cursing the fig tree, then in the cleansing of the Temple. (280)

There is no question that Jesus had in mind the fig tree as a symbol of the nation and its leaders in accordance with the Old Testament prophets, nor that Jesus did, on occasion, indicate a passage of Scripture by quoting its opening words (as in Mark 15:34), but I would expect to find in the text the actual quotation of the opening words if that is what Mark intended. Although I agree with Robin's assessment of the meaning of the passage, I do not find it necessary to conclude that there was a "misunderstanding that he was hungry." Rather, I see the fact that Jesus was hungry as necessary to the unfolding of the lesson he was about to teach, and with Robin, as symbolic of God's desire to find fruit on his beloved, but stripped "tree," Israel.

Likewise, then, the fact that "it was not the season for figs" (13d) becomes essential to the sense of the passage. Jesus was not out to condemn a nonbearing *tree;* he was pronouncing judgment against the religious barrenness of the *nation.* The tree is not in trouble, the nation is. The tree has not rejected its Messiah, the nation has. The tree is being used as a *symbol,* not the object itself, of the judgment. If it had been the season for figs, then the tree would have itself borne certain responsibility, and its judgment would have applied as much to itself as to the nation, watering down the force of the symbolism. But Jesus is not interested in judging fig trees. The focus is, rather, on the nation, the temple, the Jewish leadership. Therefore, Mark makes plain that it was not the season for figs. (Matthew does not include the clause, "it was not the season for figs." This is easily explained by the fact that Matthew's Judean readership would know that spring is not the season for figs (Cotter 63), something that would not necessarily be evident to all of Mark's readers.) I believe William Lane is correct when he asserts the following:

> If the incident occurred in the period approaching Passover, the parenthetical statement in verse 13c is incontrovertible and suggests that Jesus had no expectation of finding edible figs. Events have meaning beyond their face value; they become significant as they are interpreted. The unexpected and incongruous character of Jesus' action in looking for figs at a season when no fruit could be found would stimulate curiosity and point beyond the incident to its deeper significance (400).

The fact that it was not the season for figs, then, should not make Jesus appear unreasonable, as some have assumed; rather, it underscores the point of the passage: the nation has not borne fruit — its spiritual leaders are incapable of recognizing the Messiah, the temple is a den of robbers and not a house of prayer for the nations — and the Judge has arrived to pass sentence. As Cole observes, "Like tree, like temple, like nation; the parallel is exact" (177).

To gain a deeper insight into the prophetic symbolism of Jesus' action, we must now turn briefly to the significance of the fig tree in Jewish and Roman culture. As William Telford's extensive research demonstrates, the fig tree held a special place in both Jewish and Graeco-Roman culture (Telford 277). Its fruit, whether fresh, dried, or pressed into cakes was highly esteemed. Its leaves and other parts provided medicines. Its sap was used in the production of cheese. It gave shade, and its blossoming was a sign that winter was over.

Perhaps of greatest significance, however, in Jesus' selection of a fig tree as the symbol of Israel's judgment are three other factors: First, in Greco-Roman culture the fig tree was associated with various deities, primarily the tree god Dionysus (284). Jesus' destruction of the fig tree, then, besides demonstrating his identity and authority as Judge of the nation of Israel (which is the primary purpose of the miracle) would have also demonstrated his superiority over the gods of the empire (289).

Second, in Greco-Roman culture, the sudden withering or blossoming of any tree was considered a powerful omen of coming destruction or blessing (296). The withering of a fig tree outside the city of Jerusalem would likely have been seen, especially by Mark's gentile readers, as "a portent of disaster for that city" (300).

Third, as referred to above (and certainly the most significant factor of the three), the fig tree was regarded in the Jewish Scriptures as symbolic of the nation of Israel. Lane summarizes:

> The prophets frequently spoke of the fig tree in referring to Israel's status before God (e.g. Jer. 8:13; 29:17; Hos. 9:10, 16; Joel 1:7; Micah 7:1-6), while the destruction of the fig tree is associated with judgment (Hos. 2:12; Isa. 3:4; cf. Lk. 13:6-9). In this context the fig tree symbolizes Israel in Jesus' day, and what happens to the tree the terrible fate that inevitably awaited Jerusalem (400).

The cursing of the fig tree, then, is not a strange and unexplainable aberration in Jesus' character, nor in Mark's Gospel, but a powerful and culturally meaningful pronouncement of judgment against the people who should have borne fruit by accepting their Messiah, but instead had rejected him.

The account of the cleansing of the temple (15-19) illustrates the extent to which the Jewish leadership had gone in losing contact with God's purpose for the temple and for his people Israel. Jesus quotes Isaiah 56:7, pointing out that the temple is to be a house of prayer for all peoples (17). Yet, the High Priest had instituted the practice of selling sacrificial animals and ritually pure items in the Court of the Gentiles, a practice which made it impossible for the gentiles to worship there (Lane 404-407). Furthermore, the general corruption of the High Priesthood and the religious leadership is evidenced by the fact that they responded to Jesus' zeal for the sanctity of the temple by deciding to kill him (18)—the supreme declaration of their refusal to accept his identity and authority.

That the issue at stake is acceptance or rejection of Jesus as Messiah is again highlighted by Jesus' discourse on faith, prayer, and forgiveness in verses 22-26. Peter remembers Jesus' declaration against the fig tree and calls Jesus' attention to it (21). Mark then writes, "Jesus answered them, 'Have faith in God'" (22), though no specific question had been posed. The question, however, is implied: "What is the meaning of this?" (There is no need here to answer the question, "How did you do that?" although what follows also answers that question. Jesus is not explaining how to curse fig trees, he is explaining what should be learned from this event.) Jesus' answer is simply the encouraging admonition: "Have faith in God." He points them to "quiet confidence in the power and goodness of God" (Lane 410). This is what the chief priests and the scribes, by contrast, did not have. They were prepared to kill the Messiah. But those who accept the identity and authority of Jesus are the ones who have faith in God. In fact, to have faith in God *is* to accept the identity and authority of Jesus.

Jesus' words in verses 23-24 must be understood in light of verse 22 (rather than as a *carte blanche* for personal willfulness, as they are sometimes misinterpreted). Whatever is asked in faith, without doubting, will be granted, so long as it is within the context of God's goodness and sovereignty. Even more, these verses should be understood in light of the entire chapter, and in light of Mark's entire Gospel. Mark is emphasizing the identity and authority of Jesus, and the monumental consequences of accepting or rejecting him. Although some scholars prefer to see "this mountain" (23) as referring to the Mount of Olives (Gundry 649; Lane 410), it would be consistent with the point of the passage if it refers to the temple mount, as asserted by Hooker:

Whatever its origin, the inclusion of the saying at this point suggests that Mark is now interpreting it of the temple mount. In contrast to Jewish expectation that at the Last Day "the mountain of the house of the Lord" would be exalted and "established as the highest of the mountains" (Micah 4:1), Jesus now pronounces judgment on it and declares that it will be submerged in the sea. The sea was the place of destruction (cf. 5.13; 9.42) (270).

Through faith in Jesus, acceptance of his identity and authority, believers enter into his victorious power, and nothing consistent with the perfect will of God is impossible for them. Though it is impossible to be reconciled to God by one's own effort, through faith in Jesus all things are possible, even reconciliation to God. It is only through faith in the power and authority of Jesus, the One who comes in the name of the Lord, that prayer in accord with the will and purpose of God can be offered in unwavering assurance. The importance of forgiveness then becomes plain (25). Faith in Jesus requires a heart of humility that forgives its neighbor, not the hateful and unforgiving heart of the chief priests and scribes. (Verse 26, while consistent with the thought, is not considered part of the original text, and is not included in the NRSV.)

The destruction of the fig tree stands as a continuing testimony to any nation, institution, church or person that God demands fruit of his creation. All blessings, resources or advantages any human or group of humans possess have been granted by God. God, like the master who gave the talents

(Matt. 25:14-30), expects what he has given to be put to use in his service to bring honor and glory to him. But the lesson of the withered fig tree is not merely that God expects fruit. The vital, overarching concern here is that God expects *belief.* He expects faith in the one he has sent, and this life-changing faith *is the fruit for which he is looking!*

The central issue is twofold: 1) no fruit can be borne unless one recognizes and accepts Jesus Christ as Lord and Master and 2) to accept Jesus Christ *is* to bear fruit for God. The leadership of Israel was barren, like the fig tree, because they refused to believe. For any variety of reasons, primarily their desire to hold on to what was most valuable to them, they would not accept the identity and authority of Jesus as Messiah and Lord. Unlike the fig tree, which was incapable of bearing fruit out of season, those who know the Lord *can and will bear fruit in and out of season.* The impossible becomes possible through faith in the One who comes in the name of the Lord. The mountains of institutionalized worship, of fruitless reliance on systems, formulas, and traditions of human origin to bring about righteousness melt away before the sheer power of faith in what God does in Jesus Christ.

Believe in the Lord, and we become "fig trees" that bear fruit we could never have borne of ourselves. Sins are forgiven, redemption becomes reality, and we pass from the kingdom of this world into the kingdom of God only when we forsake everything and believe in him, when we take up our cross and follow him.

The only thing that awaits those who will not accept his authority, who will not believe in him and follow him, is judgment — complete destruction, "from the roots." Conversely, what awaits those who believe in him, who forgive as they are forgiven, who, only through faith in him, are able to remove all obstacles and barriers to true life, is eternal communion with God and all the saints — from every nation — gathered in triumphal joy in the spiritual temple that shall never need cleansing.

Bibliography

Barclay, William. *The Gospel of Mark.* Vol. 2 in *The Daily Bible Study Series.* Rev. ed. 18 vols. Philadelphia: Westminster, 1975.

Birdsall, J. Neville. "The Withering of the Fig-Tree (Mark xi. 12-14, 20-22)." *The Expository Times.*73 (1962); 191.

Cole, R. Alan. *Mark.* Vol. 2 in *The Tyndale New Testament Commentaries.* Gen. Ed. R. V. G. Tasker. 20 vols. Grand Rapids: Eerdmans, 1976.

Cotter, Wendy J. "For It Was Not the Season for Figs." *The Catholic Bible Quarterly.* 48 (1986): 62-66.

Gaebelein, Frank E., ed. Vol. 8 in *The Expositor's Bible Commentary.* 12 vols. Grand Rapids: Zondervan, 1984.

Gundry, Robert H. *Mark: A Commentary on His Apology for the Cross.* Grand Rapids: Eerdmans, 1993.

Guthrie, Donald. *New Testament Introduction.* Downers Grove: InterVarsity, 1970.

Hooker, Morna D. *The Gospel According to St. Mark.* Vol. 2 in *Black's New Testament Commentary.* London: A & C Black, 1991.

Hull, Jr., Roger. "The Cursing of the Fig Tree." *Christian Century.* 84 (1967); 1429-1431.

Lane, William L. *The Gospel According to Mark.* Vol. 2 in *The New International Commentary on the New Testament.* 18 vols. Grand Rapids: Eerdmans, 1974.

Powell, Mark Allan. *What is Narrative Criticism?* Minneapolis: Fortress, 1990.

Robin, A. de Q. "The Cursing of the Fig Tree in Mark XI. A Hypothesis." *New Testament Studies* 8 (1962); 276-281.

Stanton, Graham H. *The Gospels and Jesus.* New York: Oxford University Press, 1989.

Telford, William R. "More Fruit from the Withered Tree." *Journal for the Study of the New Testament.* 48 (1981); 264-304.

A TASTY SANDWICH (MARK 11)

By Joseph Tkach

Have you ever picked up one of those small, multi-layered sandwiches at a buffet and been surprised at how tasty it was? A Bible story can be like that—perhaps a bit confusing at first with its multiple layers, yet surprisingly tasty and nourishing once you get into it. There's a story like that in Mark chapter 11. The first layer goes like this:

> As they were leaving Bethany, Jesus was hungry. Seeing in the distance a fig tree in leaf, he went to find out if it had any fruit. When he reached it, he found nothing but leaves, because it was not the season for figs. Then he said to the tree, "May no one ever eat fruit from you again." And his disciples heard him say it. (Mark 11:12-14)

Why did Jesus do that? It seems at first glance a rather unreasonable thing to do. It wasn't the season for figs—so why blame the tree? Was the pressure of the last weeks of his earthly ministry getting to Jesus? No, he knew exactly what he was doing. He didn't mutter this under his breath—as verse 14 indicates, he made sure his disciples heard.

Mark then adds another layer to this "tasty sandwich":

> On reaching Jerusalem, Jesus entered the temple courts and began driving out those who were buying and selling there. He overturned the tables of the money changers and the benches of those selling doves, and would not allow anyone to carry merchandise through the temple courts. And as he taught them, he said, "Is it not written: 'My house will be called a house of prayer for all nations'? But you have made it 'a den of robbers.'" (Mark 11:15-17)

What Jesus did here was a public relations nightmare! Approaching the city the day before, the multitudes greeted him as a conquering hero. This was a particularly sensitive time of year, and the occupying Romans were on the lookout for trouble. Jesus had "flown under the radar" in his triumphal entry, so the sensible thing for him to do now would have been to keep his head down. Instead, he causes a major incident in the most sensitive spot imaginable—the Temple. He charges it with being unfruitful in prayer for the nations.

This shocking proclamation exposes the corruption and hypocrisy of Israel's religious elite. Jesus is accusing them of abandoning Israel's mission to be a light to the nations, and attempting to keep God's blessing for themselves. Jesus is asking for trouble!

Then Mark adds another layer:

> The chief priests and the teachers of the law heard this and began looking for a way to kill him, for they feared him, because the whole crowd was amazed at his teaching. (Mark 11:18)

Jesus' prophetic word was sure to provoke a showdown with the religious elite. But it wasn't quite time yet. So...

> When evening came, Jesus and his disciples went out of the city. (Mark 11:19)

Jesus' cursing of the fig tree was not about the tree. It had no fruit through no fault of its own. That would be clear to all. He was using the incident with the tree to illustrate a far more important lesson. But it was not a lesson that the disciples grasped at the time, as we see in the last layers of the story:

> In the morning, as they went along, they saw the fig tree withered from the roots. Peter remembered and said to Jesus, "Rabbi, look! The fig tree you cursed has withered!" (Mark 11:20-21)

Jesus' reply to Peter might seem rather unsatisfying—perhaps even condescending:

> "Have faith in God," Jesus answered. "Truly I tell you, if anyone says to this mountain, 'Go, throw yourself into the sea,' and does not doubt in their heart but believes that what they say will happen, it will be done for them." (Mark 11:22-23)

Let's review what Jesus is saying here in context. He is not giving advance notice of a breakthrough in civil engineering. This lesson is no more about the mountain than the other was about the fig tree. In the ancient world, "mountains" often symbolized empires and kingdoms. Casting them into the sea symbolized their judgment—being thrown into a place of destruction (Mark 9:42). This was likely baffling to the disciples, because what Jesus predicted did not happen immediately. The disciples were weak in faith, and so the one who "does not doubt" here is Jesus. He has no doubts that his Father will bring this to pass—that he will judge the Jewish religious elite and the Roman overlords who refuse to bow to Jesus' lordship. Eventually, they will be thrown down.

The point here is that the kingdom that Jesus is inaugurating by the authority of his words and deeds stands over all other authorities, religious or secular. His rule and reign has begun and he knows that it will reach its fullness over time. Jesus' words of judgment—sorting out what is what—will come to pass, even if there is a delay, just as there was between the words Jesus spoke and the effects seen upon the fig tree. This delay does not diminish the effectiveness and certainty of his authoritative word. In that regard, remember the prophecy of Micah:

> In the last days the mountain of the Lord's temple will be
> established as the highest of the mountains; it will be exalted above
> the hills, and peoples will stream to it. (Micah 4:1)

These "last days" have been unfolding for a long time. The Temple was
destroyed by the Romans in AD 70 and then, by AD 476, the Roman Empire
ceased to exist. Yet we still await the ultimate consummation of the last days,
which will occur at Jesus' return in glory. The kingdom Jesus inaugurated
2,000 years ago eventually will completely overthrow all opposition, whether
religious or secular. But, according to our Lord's way, this overthrow comes
gradually, and not through cruelty, force or intimidation.

Instead, the kingdom advances through the pronouncement of the Lord's
word by his people who, themselves, live by faith in that word. Opponents
to Jesus' kingdom reign are thus conquered "from the roots," over long
periods of time and in ways generally not immediately seen. For these
vanquished foes, rather than revenge, there is forgiveness, love and mercy.

The time span between the inauguration and consummation of the
kingdom involves a process of judgment that leads to peace—a peace that
the world is unable to understand, for it goes against the grain of human
nature (John 14:27). Those whom Jesus chose to join him in the next stage
of his ministry needed to understand, as do we. We await the fullness of the
kingdom with patience and a hope that will not be disappointed.

With concluding words from Jesus, Mark adds a final and rather
surprising layer to this tasty sandwich:

> Therefore I tell you, whatever you ask for in prayer, believe that
> you have received it, and it will be yours. And when you stand praying,
> if you hold anything against anyone, forgive them, so that your Father
> in heaven may forgive you your sins. (Mark 11:24-25)

Here is the unexpected, perhaps shocking, way the kingdom unfolds.
Through clarifying judgment, over time, all opposition to the kingdom is
overcome as it is exposed for what it is: *nothing* compared to the rule and reign
of God in Christ, which alone gives life eternal.

As believers, we pray for and thus welcome this unfolding judgment—
not through revenge or condemnation, but by extending the Lord's
forgiveness to all. This we do because our concern is that deception be lifted
and all enter God's glorious kingdom, receiving God's forgiveness as his
redeemed children. Because we have received that forgiveness, we have
passed through the Lord's loving and freeing judgment, which led to our
repentance. And now we wish for others to gain what we have received.
Ultimately, God's judgment, delivered to us in Jesus Christ, is a word of
compassion and salvation. And that is a tasty sandwich indeed!

EXPLORE THE GOSPELS: LUKE

By Jim Herst

The Gospel of Luke and the Acts of the Apostles are the two parts of a work addressed to Theophilus (compare Luke 1:1-4 with Acts 1:1-2). The author of Acts apparently accompanied Paul on some of his journeys – note the "we" in Acts 16:10-17;20:5-15; 21:1-18; 27:1–28:16. A comparison of Acts with Paul's epistles indicates that Luke the physician was the author of Acts and the third gospel.

Theophilus was frustrated. He was a wealthy man and had a responsible position in society. Others might have thought he "had it made." But Theophilus lived up to his name, which meant "lover of God." He was still looking for the truth.

Although he was a Gentile, he was fascinated by the religion of the Jews. He had recently come into contact with an unusual sect, who on the one hand seemed to be Jewish, and yet were rejected and even hated by them.

These people were known as Christians, after their leader, Christos. Something about Christos' radical teachings fascinated Theophilus. In spite of his education and position, he was at heart a humble man. Christos seemed also to have been humble, even though his followers claimed that he was God.

Christos had been dead – executed as a criminal – several decades ago, but he was already a legend. His followers claimed he had worked miracles, walked on water, and had even raised the dead. He could easily have become rich and famous, but he chose to live and work among ordinary people. He considered everyone – even the lowliest outcasts and misfits – worthy of respect.

But were these stories true? Christos and his revolutionary way of life fascinated the gentle Theophilus, but before he could commit himself to it he needed to know more. But how? Were Christos' devoted disciples, who even seemed ready to die for him, reliable? They were mostly uneducated. Some were even slaves! Were their stories to be trusted? Well, he did know someone he could trust. This man was a Christian, and an educated person like himself. He was known as Luke, the beloved physician. He had not known Christos personally, but he was a meticulous scholar.

Luke, knowing that Theophilus needed a careful explanation of the factual basis for the Christian beliefs, sent him a carefully written manuscript. It began:

So many others have tried their hand at putting together a story of the wonderful harvest of Scripture and history that took place among us, using reports handed down by the original eyewitnesses who served this Word with their very lives. Since I have investigated all the reports in close detail, I decided to write it out for you, most honorable Theophilus, so you can know beyond the shadow of doubt the reliability of what you have been taught.

Fascinated, Theophilus settled down to study the manuscript – the first person to read what we now know as… The Gospel According to St. Luke.

Maybe this is not exactly the way it happened. But something like this prompted Luke, the "beloved physician" to put pen to papyrus and write a definitive account of the life of Jesus Christ. The result was a thoroughly researched and beautifully written narrative of what Jesus was like and what he did.

Luke's Gospel is not a dry theological treatise. He was excited by what he had discovered, and he wanted to share that excitement and joy with his readers. "Gospel" is an old English word meaning "good news." No one has conveyed that good news better than the "beloved physician."

What's in a name?

The Gospel of Luke and the Acts of the Apostles are the two parts of a work addressed to Theophilus (compare 1:1-4 with Acts 1:1-2). The author of Acts apparently accompanied Paul on some of his journeys – note the "we" in Acts 16:10-17; 20:5-15; 21:1-18; 27:1 – 28:16. A comparison of Acts with Paul's epistles indicates that Luke the physician was the author of Acts and, hence, of the third Gospel.

Outline of Luke

Luke tells the story of Jesus' life and ministry.

1. The preparation (1:1–4:13)

The events preceding Jesus' ministry can be divided into three sections:

- 1:1-4 The prologue, where Luke explains his purpose in writing his gospel.
- 1:5–2:52 Jesus' birth and early years. Luke shows parallels between the annunciation and birth stories of John the Baptist and Jesus.
- 3:1–4:13 The ministry of John the Baptist and the preparation for Jesus' ministry, baptism and his victory over Satan.

2. Jesus' Public Ministry (4:14–21:38)

- 4:14–9:50 Jesus' ministry in Galilee: preaching in the synagogues and performing miracles, which helped the people but began to bring him into conflict with the religious authorities.

- 9:51–19:27 "Jesus resolutely set out for Jerusalem" and is eventually welcomed triumphantly. Throughout this section, Luke mentions several times that Jesus is on a journey (9:52-53, 56; 10:1, 38; 13:22, 31-33; 14:25; 17:11, 18:31, 35; 19:1, 11, 28). (However, it is historically likely that Jesus made several trips back and forth from Galilee to Jerusalem; Luke presents it as a single journey to reflect the theological truth that he was destined to die in Jerusalem and he never wavered from his goal). This section contains many parables unique to Luke's Gospel:
  - The good Samaritan (10:29-37)
  - The friend at midnight (11:5-8)
  - The rich fool (12:13-20)
  - The returning master (12:35-38)
  - The barren fig tree (13:6-9)
  - The wedding banquet (14:7-14),
  - The great banquet (14:15-24)
  - The lost coin (15:11-32)
  - The shrewd manager (16:1-9)
  - Lazarus and the rich man (16:19-31)
  - The unjust judge (18:1-8)
  - The Pharisee and the tax-collector (18:9-14).

3. Jesus' ministry in Jerusalem 19:28–21:38

- His triumphant entry, a lamentation over the city (19:41-44)
- The 'cleansing' of the Temple (19:41-48)
- His teaching on "tribute to Caesar" and the temple tax (21:1-38)
- His prophecy of the destruction of the temple and the city of Jerusalem itself (21:1-38).

4. Jesus' suffering, death and resurrection. 22:1–24:53

The passion narrative portrays Jesus' suffering, death and resurrection. Luke includes three of Jesus' sayings on the cross not found in the other accounts (23:34, 43, 46), including a plea for God to forgive those who were crucifying him (23:34).

How to read this book

In some ways, the best way to read Luke is to study it and Acts as a continuous work, written by the same author. For example, knowing how important the Holy Spirit is to the story in Acts helps us appreciate its role before and at Jesus' birth (1:15, 35, 41, 67; 2:25-26) and in guiding his ministry (3:22; 4:1, 18).

Luke-Acts, as the work is called by scholars, has a more historical emphasis than the Gospels of Matthew, Mark and John. As in the historical books of the Old Testament, God is the main character in Luke-Acts – his unseen hand guides events to fulfill his purpose. But Luke also places these events into "the context of world history. He connects it not only to the story of Israel but also to the larger *oikoumene,* the civilized world of Hellenism. Thus he alone of the evangelists provides chronological references for key events (see Luke 1:5; 2:1-2; 3:1-2; Acts 18:12)" (Luke Timothy Johnson, *The Gospel of Luke,* Sacra Pagina series, vol. 3, pp. 5-6).

Luke, an educated man, wrote in very good Greek. Where the parallel accounts merely transliterate a Hebrew or Latin word, Luke often uses a Greek word instead. Luke explains to his largely gentile audience how God's promises to Israel in the Old Testament came to be fulfilled in Jesus Christ, and how the gentile mission came to be included in those promises.

Learning about Jesus Christ

Although Luke, like the other evangelists, acknowledges Jesus' divine status, he is careful to stress his humanity as well. Luke portrays the Jesus who entered history as a human being. Only Luke's record of Jesus' genealogy goes back to Adam (3:23-38). Only Luke records:

- Jesus' circumcision (2:21)
- His presentation at the temple (2:22-38)
- His growth as a child (2:40)
- His meeting at age 12 with the religious leaders in the temple (2:28-38)
- His continued development "in wisdom and stature" (2:52). These precise details establish Jesus as a person in history.

Luke again stresses the humanity of Jesus in his full account of the temptation scene (4:1-13). He also paints Jesus against the background of pious Judaism. He mentions Jesus' custom of attending synagogue on the Sabbath (4:14-16, 31, 44) and that he was frequently the guest of Pharisees (7:36; 14:1).

Luke tells us, "Jesus often withdrew to lonely places and prayed" (Luke 5:16). Only Luke records Jesus praying at certain crucial periods in his life: at his baptism (3:21), before calling his disciples (6:12), before Peter's pivotal confession of Jesus as Christ (9:18) and before the transfiguration (9:28). These prayers highlight Jesus' human need to pray to God.

Other topics

- **Women:** Luke-Acts shows us that, both during Jesus' ministry and in the early church, several women were among the most dedicated of his followers. D. L. Bock comments:

  > Luke features the responsiveness of women (7:36-50; 8:1-3; 8:48; 10:38-42; 13:10-17; 24:1-12). Often it is not just a women but a widow who is cited, since she represented the most vulnerable status within society (2:37; 4:25-26; 7:12; 18:3, 5; 20:47; 21:2-3). Whether in parable or by example, these women show that they are sensitive to the message of Jesus. Though on the fringes of first-century society, they are in the middle of Luke's story. Often they are paired with men (2:25-28; 4:25-27; 8:40-56; 11:31-32; 13:18-21; 15:4-10; 17:34-35; Acts 21:9-10), a feature suggesting that the gospel is for both genders. (*Dictionary of Jesus and the Gospels,* p. 506)

- **Prayer:** The early church experienced dramatic answers to prayer on several occasions (Acts 4:31; 8:1517; 9:40; 12:5-11). Luke shows that the practice of prayer is rooted in Jesus' example (5:16). Luke also

  > includes parables which teach so much about prayer, the friend at midnight (11:5 ff.), the unjust judge (18:1ff.), the Pharisee and the tax-collector (18:10ff.). In addition Luke records some exhortations to the disciples to pray (6:28; 11:2; 22:40, 46), and he has a warning against the wrong kind of prayer (20:47). (Leon Morris, *The Gospel of Luke,* Tyndale New Testament Commentaries, p. 50)

- **Wealth:** Luke has many statements relating to the affluent and the influential. They direct the rich to help the poor, and show the proper use of money generally: "[Luke] has the parable of the two debtors (7:40-43); of the rich fool (12:16-21); of the rash builder of the tower (14:2830); of the unjust steward and his astute financial manipulations (16:1-9); of the rich man and Lazarus (16:19-31); of the servants and the pound (19:11-27)" (William Barclay, *Introduction to the First Three Gospels,* p. 219).

What this book means for you

Luke portrays a Jesus Christ who defined his mission as follows: "The Spirit of the Lord is on me, because he has anointed me to preach the good news to the poor. He has sent me to proclaim freedom for the prisoners and recovery of sight for the blind, to release the oppressed, to proclaim the year of the Lord's favor" (4:18-19). Jesus brought good news to everyone, including the poor and oppressed, to all groups who were despised and marginalized by society in first-century Israel. Through the church, he brings the same good news for our society today. Luke's Gospel emphasizes that through Jesus Christ, salvation is available to all, freely and without prejudice.

Only Luke's Gospel records the parable of the good Samaritan (10:30-37) and the story of the Samaritan who expressed gratitude to Jesus for being healed (17:11-19). These incidents foreshadowed the entrance of the Samaritans into the church of God (Acts 8:4-25).

In Luke, despised tax collectors become examples of repentance and discipleship – in parable and in reality (3:12; 5:27-32; 18:9-14; 19:2-10). Jesus forgives and praises a sinful woman (7:36-50) and promises paradise to a repentant thief (23:43). Repentance and forgiveness of sins are to be preached in Jesus' name to all nations (24:47). "All [humanity] will see God's salvation" (3:6). All we have to do is ask! (11:13)

We know you will enjoy this beautifully written account of the life of Jesus. Why not read, or re-read the Gospel of Luke? If you take one chapter a day, it will only take three and a half weeks for you to discover for yourself this awesome message of hope.

SPECIAL REPORT:
WHAT YOU HAVE HEARD IS TRUE!

By Michael Morrison

About 30 years after Jesus Christ, a wealthy man named Theophilus became interested in following Jesus. Some of the stories he heard about Jesus seemed too strange to be true. So he asked an investigator to get the facts about what Jesus had really done and taught.

This special investigator learned as much as he could about Jesus' life, work and teachings. He then wrote an organized documentary about Jesus. We call it the Gospel of Luke.

Luke's writing technique

Luke tells us how he went about his task: "I made a careful study of everything and then decided to write and tell you exactly what took place. Honorable Theophilus, I have done this to let you know if what you have heard is true" (Luke 1:3-4, Contemporary English Version throughout).

In addition to being inspired by God to write this Gospel, it's clear that Luke did his research, probably traveling to Judea and interviewing Christians who had known Jesus. Luke learned that Jesus took special interest in the less-respected members of society.

Luke's writing style suggests that he had an upper-middle-class education. Theophilus, judging by the title "Honorable," may have been a wealthy government official. The name *Theophilus* means "lover of God," so anyone who loved God would feel welcome to read Luke's report.

Luke wanted Theophilus to know about Jesus' interest in disadvantaged people. Like Luke, Theophilus would be surprised and intrigued at how Jesus regarded poor people, for example.

- **The poor:** Many Jewish religious leaders assumed that poor people were religiously inferior — that God wasn't blessing them because they weren't living right. But Luke showed that Jesus went out of his way to remind everyone that he had a message for the poor: "The Lord's Spirit has come to me, because he has chosen me to tell the good news to the poor" (Luke 4:18). On another occasion, "Jesus looked at his disciples and said: God will bless you people who are poor" (Luke 6:20). What would a wealthy man think of that?
- **The rich:** Jesus included both the poor and the wealthy in his work. But his message to the rich had a different focus: "You rich people are in for trouble," he said (verse 24). But Luke reported that Jesus

Christ didn't criticize the rich because they had money. It was their attitude that was most important. Jesus warned the rich to trust in God, not in wealth (Luke 12:15-21).

"You cannot be the slave of two masters…. You cannot serve God and money" (Luke 16:13). "It's terribly hard for rich people to get into God's kingdom" (Luke 18:24).

A wealthy man could be disturbed by such words. But he would see near the end of the report that God can save even a rich man. The cost? A complete change in his attitude toward money.

Luke had heard about, perhaps even interviewed, a wealthy tax collector named Zacchaeus, who told Jesus he would give half his money to the poor. Jesus was pleased. "Today you and your family have been saved, because you are a true son of Abraham" (Luke 19:9).

- **Women:** Jewish teachers of that time usually considered women to be inferior. But Luke learned that Jesus treated women as individuals worthy of individual attention. Jesus recognized their faith and their feelings.

To illustrate this, Luke included several stories about women in his report. He began with Elizabeth, the mother of John the Baptist, and Mary the mother of Jesus. Anyone who thought women were inferior would have been surprised. In Luke's report, the first person on whom the Holy Spirit came was Elizabeth (Luke 1:41). The first to be called "blessed" was Mary (verses 28, 42).

And in a more personal touch, Luke described Mary's worry when she thought her young son was lost in Jerusalem (Luke 2:48). She "kept on thinking about all that had happened" (verse 51).

In his research, Luke found that women helped pay the cost of Jesus' ministry: "Joanna, Susanna, and many others had also used what they owned to help Jesus and his disciples" (Luke 8:3). Joanna, he noted, was the wife of a government official. Luke knew that Theophilus (who may have been a government official himself) would be interested.

Another story Luke reported was about Jesus teaching in the home of Martha. Martha was busy with housework, but her sister Mary was listening to Jesus. Martha complained to Jesus: "Doesn't it bother you that my sister has left me to do all the work by myself?" (Luke 10:40). But Jesus reminded her that Mary had chosen to do the more important thing (verses 41-42). The teachings of Jesus were important for women as well as for men. (For more about Luke's interest in women, see a later chapter.)

- **The disabled:** Many people of Theophilus' day assumed that handicaps were evidence of sin (John 9:2). But Jesus had special compassion for the disabled and took care of their needs: "Blind people are now able to see, and the lame can walk. People who have leprosy are being healed, and the deaf can now hear," reported Luke (Luke 7:22).

- **Non-Jews:** Jews in Jesus' day often looked down on non-Jews. After all, weren't the Jews God's chosen people? And weren't the other nations good-for-nothing idol worshipers? But Luke showed that Jesus had an interest in non-Jewish peoples, and that this was an unpleasant surprise to many Jews of Jesus' day.

  Jesus began his ministry by reminding everyone that, God's prophets had served people of other nations (Luke 4:25-27). This made the Jews so angry that they tried to kill Jesus (verses 28-30).

  Jesus' attitude toward other ethnic groups was also shown in the parable of the good Samaritan (Luke 10:30-37). Jews despised Samaritans, but Jesus dared to use one as a good example. Jesus broke through social barriers and practiced religious equality.

- **Sinners:** Many Jewish leaders looked down on those who did not observe their strict rules. They assumed that the common people, the crowds, were so far from God that it was pointless to try to teach them (John 7:49).

  But Jesus preached to the crowds, and they loved him for it (Luke 5:15). He gave them the good news that God would not neglect them, that they were valuable to him. He said: "I didn't come to invite good people to turn to God. I came to invite sinners" (verse 32).

Luke learned that Jesus spent time with all classes of people. He attended banquets with tax-collectors (who were assumed to be cheats and traitors). But the religious leaders criticized Jesus for the company he kept. "Jesus eats and drinks too much!" they said. "He is even a friend of tax collectors and sinners" (Luke 7:34).

Luke described an incident that occurred when Jesus was dining at the home of one of his critics: "When a sinful woman in that town found out that Jesus was there, she bought an expensive bottle of perfume. Then she came and stood behind Jesus. She cried and started washing his feet with her tears and drying them with her hair. The woman kissed his feet and poured the perfume on them" (verses 37-38).

This must have astonished everyone who saw it. A Jewish teacher allowing himself to be touched by a woman? And not just any woman, but a woman everyone knew to be "sinful"! And not just touched, but anointed with expensive perfume and caressed with a woman's hair, which was normally kept hidden. Scandalous!

But Jesus understood the deep emotion that had prompted her act of adoration. "All her sins are forgiven, and that is why she has shown great love. But anyone who has been forgiven only a little will show only a little love," he told his self-righteous host (verse 47). Jesus then told the woman, "Your sins are forgiven.... You are now saved" (verses 48, 50).

Hope for the humble

Luke showed Theophilus how Jesus reached out to those less respected in first-century Jewish society. Jesus loved everyone, regardless of their station in life. Even his enemies knew it: "You treat everyone with the same respect, no matter who they are" (Luke 20:21).

Anyone can be blessed by God no matter how lowly he or she may seem to be. As Jesus said, "The people who are really blessed are the ones who hear and obey God's message!" (Luke 11:28).

To emphasize this, Luke used the terms *repentance, forgiveness* and *salvation* more often than other Gospel writers did. His report encouraged sinners to turn to God, knowing they would be accepted by him.

Luke recorded the story Jesus told to "some people who thought they were better than others and who looked down on everyone else." Two men were praying, Jesus said. The Pharisee prayed, "I am really glad that I am not like that tax collector over there." The tax collector, on the other hand, "was so sorry for what he had done that he pounded his chest and prayed, "God, have pity on me! I am such a sinner.""

Jesus then said, "It was the tax collector and not the Pharisee who was pleasing to God. If you put yourself above others, you will be put down. But if you humble yourself, you will be honored" (Luke 18:9-14).

Time after time, Luke showed that God wants all people, no matter what their social or religious status, to come to him in repentance and humility. And he will joyfully accept every sinner who turns to him (Luke 15:7, 10).

What a message! God loves rich and poor, saint and sinner, women as well as men. It had seemed too good to be true. But it *was* true, and *is* true. Luke had checked it carefully, and sent the good news to Theophilus — and to us today.

OPEN LETTER TO A WEALTHY MAN

By Michael Morrison

"Sell everything you have and give to the poor," said Jesus to a rich man (Luke 18:22). Jesus' demand is shocking. Is there something wrong with owning things and having money? Did Jesus make similar demands of all his disciples?

We learn answers in Luke's Gospel. Both Luke and some of his readers had reason to be especially interested in Jesus' teachings about money. Luke had come from the wealthier part of society — his literary skills reflect an education available primarily to families who could afford private schooling.

Theophilus, the recipient of Luke's Gospel, was probably among the wealthiest members of society. Luke addresses him as "most excellent," a title of honor given to officials of high rank. Luke names him as the patron of his book, implying that Theophilus was wealthy enough to own a library and underwrite publication of a book. Theophilus, who had enough faith in Jesus to finance Luke's book, had ample reason to be interested in Jesus' teachings about money. Perhaps for such reasons we see more about finances in Luke than we see in the other Gospels.

Woe to the rich

The Gospel begins with a warning for the rich: God puts down the mighty and sends away the rich; he exalts the low and fills the hungry (1:52-53). Readers soon learn that Jesus' gospel is targeted to the poor (4:18; 7:22). The rich are told to give to the poor (3:11). Peter, James, John and Levi "left everything" to be disciples of Jesus (5:11, 28).

The sermon on the plain is particularly shocking with its radical demands: The poor are to be blessed, but there is woe for the rich (6:20, 24). People should give and lend sacrificially —"to everyone who asks" (6:29-35). Though the reader might make some allowance for exaggeration or further clarification, the demands are nevertheless startling and thought-provoking. Luke did not report this so poor Christians would make demands of rich ones. Rather, he wrote this to all who had money, exhorting them to be generous.

But Jesus was not consistently critical of the rich. He ate with Levi and other tax collectors in a great feast (5:29). Levi was able to give a banquet after he had supposedly "left everything." This discrepancy between what is said and done suggests that at least some of the statements about wealth are hyperbolic or exaggerated —a possibility we must consider for other statements. When the account says they "left everything," it does not mean they abandoned everything they owned and accepted destitution. Rather, it seems to mean they quit what they were doing — they changed their profitable career to that of being a disciple.

Jesus was criticized for attending Levi's banquet —not because of the lifestyle of wealth, but for associating with "sinful" tax collectors (5:30; 7:34). Later, he stayed at the house of Zacchaeus, a rich tax collector (19:2-5). Jesus healed the slave of a centurion who was wealthy enough to build a synagogue (7:2, 5, 10). Jesus included both the poor and the rich in his ministry.

Parable about a creditor

While Jesus was eating with Pharisees, a woman anointed his feet with perfumed oil (7:36-37). Though such perfume was expensive, Jesus was not criticized for the waste of wealth, at least not in the way that Luke reports the story, but for allowing a sinful woman to touch him (7:39). Jesus used the opportunity to tell a parable paralleling a financial matter and a spiritual principle. The creditor, in a role corresponding to God and Jesus, forgave debts, corresponding to forgiving sins (7:41-42). Later, Jesus even implied that God forgives our sins if we forgive those who owe us money (11:4). Creditors should forgive; debtors are encouraged to pay up quickly (12:58).

The parable of the creditor shows that the appropriate response to forgiveness is love (7:47) or, by example of the woman, the use of financial assets to serve Jesus. Also, the parable incidentally notes that one can gain friends by forgiving debts, a lesson also illustrated by the parable of the shrewd steward (16:1-9).

Jesus' own examples

How did Jesus himself live? His parents seem to have been lower middle class, judging by their offering of two doves (2:24) and by the occupation of carpentry. Jesus once said he had nowhere to put his head (9:58), but that seems to have been a hyperbole appropriate to an itinerant stage in his ministry right after he had been refused housing (9:52-53). Elsewhere, Jesus stayed in houses, such as that of a rich man (19:2-5) or of a woman (10:38), and ate at banquets.

Jesus himself is not shown giving money, and he turned away a man who, in effect, asked for money (12:13-15). Jesus didn't even try to determine whether the man had a legal right to the money; he simply used the occasion to warn about greed (12:15-21). Jesus gave food to the 5,000, but this was clearly not his usual practice.

When Jesus sent out the 12 disciples, he told them to take no money with them (9:3; 10:4). This instruction would not have been needed if that had been the practice of the group all along. Further evidence that the group normally carried money is the fact that the disciples wondered whether they should buy food for the 5,000 (9:13). One source of their money was the women who traveled with them (8:3). When Jesus told the 12 to travel without money, it was for a short journey, and for a lesson in faith, not a normal practice. Sympathetic listeners would provide food and shelter (9:4; 10:7). For the disciples' later ministry, they were told to carry some money (22:36). A life of faith does not require a life of destitution.

Wealth — an enemy of faith

But it is clear that riches can be an enemy of faith. Jesus warned that riches could "choke" a disciple and cause him to be spiritually unfruitful (8:14). Those who exalt themselves (a tendency of the rich) are warned that they will be humbled (11:43; 14:8-11; 18:14). Jesus warned against banqueting that diverted attention from spiritual necessities, in parable (12:45), in Old Testament examples (17:27-28) and in direct admonition (21:34). When Christ returns in glory, we are not to worry about our goods (17:31). A parable described rich men as too preoccupied to attend the kingdom's inaugural banquet (14:18-19). Jesus chided Martha for allowing physical things, apparently even humble ones, to divert her attention away from discipleship (10:41).

Jesus taught that the wealthy should not trust in their wealth (12:15-21), and the poor should not have anxiety about their needs (7:22-25; 12:29). Faith is needed by both rich and poor. Life does not consist of possessions; that is not what life is about (12:15). Instead, we are to look to God each day for the physical needs of the day (11:3). If our allegiance is toward God rather than physical things (16:13), he will supply our needs (12:29-31). Day-to-day dependence on God requires faith. This is one lesson the disciples learned in their journeys without money (22:35).

At another dinner, Jesus scathingly criticized the Jewish religious leaders, including their use of money. They tithed faithfully but neglected justice (11:42a). They should have done both (11:42b) by giving alms to the poor (11:41). When they give dinners, they should invite the poor and the disadvantaged (14:12-13), reflecting the kingdom of God's invitation to the poor and disadvantaged (14:21).

"Sell your possessions," Jesus told his disciples after telling them to have faith rather than anxiety, "and give to the poor" (12:33). But we see no record of the disciples actually giving everything away. Indeed, we see later that they are told to carry a moneybag (22:36); the women spend money on spices and perfumed oils rather than giving it away (23:56), and they seem to have a house to stay in (24:33).

We must understand Jesus' command in 12:33 as an exaggeration for teaching purposes — not intended to be taken to literal extreme (much as we do not expect disciples to be perpetually girded and their lamps perpetually burning — 12:35). Jesus' point is not a requirement for poverty — it is a startling demand for faith and allegiance to God.

Treasures in heaven

Since wealth is a powerful tool of self-exaltation, it tempts anyone who has it. But as we use wealth for others instead of just for ourselves, we gain "treasure in heaven" (12:33; 18:22-23). This spiritual treasure comes from the heart (6:45). By using possessions for others, we counteract mammon's temptation and reinforce our desire to seek God's kingdom (12:34, 31). If we give generously, we will be rewarded generously (6:38) at the resurrection of the just (14:12-14).

Jesus told the rich to give to the poor. But what about gifts to God or his ministry? Such gifts are also commendable: Jesus told a healed leper to make an offering (5:14). We are to be "rich toward God" (12:16-21). Jesus commended the widow who put two pennies into the temple treasury (21:2). We should give to God "what is God's" (20:22-25). Jesus upheld the practice of tithing (11:42), but noted that it could not justify anyone (18:12). When we do only that which is commanded, we are "unworthy servants" (17:10).

A question of allegiance

Luke 16 contains several teachings about wealth, including the parable of the shrewd steward, which concludes with some sayings that imply that we should be faithful in our use of money (16:10-12). "No servant can serve two masters.... You cannot serve both God and Money" (16:13). Jesus' statement, succinctly describing the tendency of money to vie for our allegiance, challenges us to purify our priorities.

The Pharisees, "who loved money," criticized Jesus again, and Jesus said, "What is highly valued among men [in this context, money] is detestable in God's sight" (16:14-15). Anything that diverts our allegiance from God is an abomination.

Next comes the parable of Lazarus and the rich man. The beggar was carried "to Abraham's side"; the rich man went to torment in Hades (16:22-

25). Why was he tormented? The parable associates his torment with his enjoyment of wealth in this life (16:25). This is of course not intended to be a precise prediction of the afterlife or of eternal rewards, but it is part of the picture about wealth being painted by Luke as he relates the story.

"How hard it is for the rich to enter the kingdom of God!" said Jesus in one of his most famous sayings. "It is easier for a camel to go through the eye of a needle than for a rich man to enter the kingdom" (18:24-25). He said this right after a rich man had refused Jesus' command to "sell everything you have" (18:22-23). "Any of you who does not give up everything he has cannot be my disciple" (14:26-33). We must renounce any undue influence it might have on us; it must not diminish our allegiance to Christ.

We have already seen that extreme destitution was not the life-style of Jesus or his disciples. Jesus was making a point about allegiance, not poverty. If there is a conflict between following Jesus and making or saving money, we must forsake money, or even our family or our own lives (9:23-24; 14:26), and we will be rewarded in the age to come (18:29-30).

Wise use of wealth

God, as Creator, has a prior claim to everything we might have. We have enormous debts to him, debts he has graciously forgiven. His grace toward us has been extravagant; his claims on us are likewise extravagant: everything we own. We have no reason to cling to any of it. Yet God, the giver, gives us varying amounts of wealth. What are we to do with it?

Jesus' parables often focus on a right use of possessions. Jesus criticized both stockpiling (12:16-21) and waste (15:13; 16:1). The Samaritan is praised for giving money as well as help (10:35). The faithful steward is to give food to his fellowservants (12:42). "From the one who has been entrusted with much, much more will be asked" (12:48). The fig tree was expected to bear fruit (13:9); the vineyard was rented out with the expectation of productivity and payment (20:9-16). Christian leaders are expected to serve others, and they will be rewarded in God's kingdom (22:25-30).

In the parable of pounds, servants were given money with which to do business. If they increased their master's money, they were rewarded (19:13-26). "To everyone who has, more will be given, but as for the one who has nothing, even what he has will be taken away." [The modern equivalent of this proverb is, "The rich get richer and the poor get poorer." Jesus was using the proverb in a different context, that of future reward for earthly faithfulness.]

In contrast to some modern social critics of wealth, Luke only tangentially addresses the method by which people have become wealthy. John the Baptist (rather than Jesus) suggests that wealth may be ill-gotten (3:13-14); a tax collector admits the possibility but implies that he is innocent (19:8). Jesus accuses the scribes of devouring widows' houses, presumably profiting from the widows' losses (20:47). Jesus drove traders out of the temple (19:45), but there is no stated connection between their trading and wealth. The Pharisees are criticized for not giving alms and neglecting justice (11:41-42), but there is no suggestion that they became wealthy by being immoral. Perhaps the implication for the reader is that the past does not matter as much as the use of wealth in the present.

Good role models

Near the end of Luke's Gospel come two distinctly positive role models for wealthy men. First, Zacchaeus, a rich tax collector, volunteered to give half his fortune to the poor and to repay with penalty if he had taken anything dishonestly. Jesus did not demand the other half of the man's goods. Instead, he said, "salvation has come to this house" (19:2-10).

Last, Joseph of Arimathea, a member of the council, a good and righteous man, who was looking for the kingdom, buried Jesus in a new tomb (23:50-53). Luke does not say he was rich, but it seems to be implied. Theophilus, or any other wealthy reader, might be able to identify with Zacchaeus and Joseph.

Christianity is not a religion exclusive to the lower class; it is a reasonable and respectable way of life that men of intelligence and wealth may accept. Jesus welcomed the poor; he also welcomed the rich, and of each he demanded allegiance and faith and obligation to serve one another.

LUKE'S LEGACY TO WOMEN

By Sheila Graham

"Hail, thou that art highly favoured, the Lord is with thee: blessed art thou among women" (Luke 1:28, King James Version). How many times have we heard these familiar words of the archangel Gabriel repeated, especially every year around the time of Christmas.

You may have repeated these Old English words yourself as a child, dressed in a white robe with wobbly angel wings and a lopsided halo as you portrayed Gabriel in a nativity play.

Only in Luke

Did you know that the biblical story of Gabriel's announcement to Mary that God had chosen her to be the mother of the Messiah is recorded only in the Gospel of Luke?

Without the inspired writings of Luke, we would also not know about the miraculous conception of Elizabeth, mother of John the Baptist; the story of the prophetess Anna; the virgin Mary's song of praise: the story of the woman anointing Jesus' feet with her tears and costly oil; and of the women disciples, along with men, who accompanied Jesus in his travels and helped support his ministry.

What a legacy the third evangelist has left Christians. Luke has a special interest in women. Only he tells us of the prominence of women in Christ's ministry. As Ben Witherington III writes: "It is Elizabeth and Mary, not Zechariah and Joseph, who are first to receive the message of Christ's coming, who are praised and blessed by God's angels, and who are first to sing and prophesy about the Christ child. Luke presents these women not only as Witnesses to the events surrounding the births of John and Jesus, but also as active participants in God's Messianic purposes" (*Women in the Earliest Churches,* page 134).

Of course, Luke was not a feminist. His purpose was to show how God had turned society upside down. The rich and complacent were rejected by God while the poor and repentant were accepted.

"Luke's portrayal of Mary is emblematic of how God reverses the poverty and powerlessness of the human condition. And throughout his narrative, Luke pays particular and positive attention to the role of women. The theme of reversal is expressed as well by the inclusion within the people of God of Samaritans and Gentiles" (Luke Timothy Johnson, *The Gospel of Luke,* Sacra Pagina series, page 22).

The beloved physician

Apparently, Luke was the only New Testament writer who was a gentile. According to Paul, he was a physician and seems to have been in contact with Paul during Paul's last years in prison (Colossians 4:14).

No doubt Luke used his friendship with Paul as a primary resource as he prepared to write Acts, his account of the first decades of the New Testament church.

God inspired Luke the historian to include in his works stories of women that were not a part of the other New Testament writings. For how could we otherwise know how prominent women were in the early church without Luke telling us of the faith of women, of the healing of women, of women's role as disciples, of women's part in the birth, death and resurrection of Jesus Christ?

Women in discipleship is one of Luke's themes. He not only reports about the female followers of Jesus Christ, but specifically names them.

"After this, Jesus traveled about from one town and village to another, proclaiming the good news of the kingdom of God. The Twelve were with him, and also some women who had been cured of evil spirits and diseases: Mary (called Magdalene) from whom seven demons had come out; Joanna the wife of Cuza, the manager of Herod's household; Susanna; and many others. These women were helping to support them out of their own means" (Luke 8:1-3).

Mary and Martha

In Luke's story of Mary and Martha, he records Christ's emphasis on women putting their spiritual responsibilities ahead of their physical ones.

Jesus and his disciples were visiting the home of Martha and Mary in Bethany, a small town about two miles east of Jerusalem. With such a large group to feed, Martha was understandably concerned that the preparations for the meal were successfully completed.

You can imagine the scene. Martha was rushing about, trying to do several things at once to prepare to feed this large group of people in her home. Her sister Mary, in the meantime, sat with the men listening to Christ talk, oblivious to or perhaps ignoring Martha's frustrated glances her way.

Martha's next action shows how close this family was to Jesus. Martha openly complained that her sister, Mary, was not helping her prepare the meal. Please tell her to help me, Martha said to Christ.

Instead, Jesus Christ gently rebuked her: "'Martha, Martha,' the Lord answered, 'you are worried and upset about many things, but only one thing is needed. Mary has chosen what is better, and it will not be taken away from her'" (Luke 10:41-42).

Surprising words in a culture where women's primary task was to take care of domestic concerns rather than study God's Word.

The importance of spiritual concerns, of having a relationship with God is emphasized again in Luke's report of a woman calling out to Jesus: "'Blessed is the mother who gave you birth and nursed you.' He replied, 'Blessed rather are those who hear the word of God and obey it'" (Luke 11:27-28).

Women in the book of Acts

Although women are not depicted as often in Luke's book of Acts as in his Gospel account, in Luke's portrayal of the theme of the last becoming first and the first becoming last is the example of the seven men chosen to distribute food to the gentile widows.

Witherington comments on this story from Acts 6:1-7: "Stephen and Philip, both prominent preachers and teachers of the Word, are among the seven chosen to supervise the food distribution to the widows. Thus, leading men are chosen for a task that normally a male servant would fulfill in a [Judean] Jewish setting, or a woman would fulfill in a Hellenistic or Roman setting. In the eyes of the Hellenists, for a prominent man to fulfill such a task would be demeaning and a reversal of roles with a man doing a woman's or servant's work" (*Women and the Genesis of Christianity*, page 212).

Luke showed by this and many other examples that service to others was not to be looked down on and delegated as "woman's work," but was an integral part of being a Christian for both men and women.

First European convert

In Acts, Luke goes on to tell us that a woman was Paul's first convert in Europe. In the remarkable story of the Macedonian woman Lydia, Luke shows Paul beginning a local church with women converts.

But before we read Luke's story, notice in Acts 16:9-10 that while in Troas Paul has a vision of a man of Macedonia begging him to come there to help the Macedonians.

The apostle Paul concludes that God has called him to preach the gospel to the Macedonians and sets sail for that region. Imagine Paul's surprise when his "man of Macedonia" turns out to be a woman!

Paul no doubt raised an eyebrow when he found only a group of women to speak to when he first arrived in Macedonia. "On the Sabbath we went outside the city gate to the river, where we expected to find a place of prayer.

We sat down and began to speak to the women who had gathered there."

Luke continues: "One of those listening was a woman named Lydia, a dealer in purple cloth from the city of Thyatira, who was a worshiper of God. The Lord opened her heart to respond to Paul's message" (Acts 16:13-14). Luke goes on then in the same chapter to tell of the conversion of a man, Paul's jailer (verses 29-34).

"Luke's intention is once again to convey a certain male-female parallelism in order to stress the equality of man and woman in God's plan of salvation, and their equal importance to the new community" (Witherington, *Women and the Genesis of Christianity*, page 215).

A new life

All Christians have a new relationship with God. Through Christ, we — both male and female — have become God's own children and one in Jesus Christ.

"You are all sons of God through faith in Christ Jesus, for all of you who were baptized into Christ have clothed yourselves with Christ. There is neither Jew nor Greek, slave nor free, male nor female, for you are all one in Christ Jesus" (Galatians 3:26-28).

Christ is calling all to repentance and a new way of life. Those of you who are women, Jesus Christ calls you equal in his sight, and heirs to all of his promises. And, as you humbly follow him, Christ will use you in his service.

Let's thank God for caring for women so much that he inspired Luke to record these accounts of Christian women in the New Testament. What a legacy he has left us, and what a responsibility.

THE PROMINENCE OF WOMEN
IN THE GOSPEL OF LUKE

By Michael Morrison

Women were prominent in Luke's portrayal of Jesus' life.

Elizabeth, mother of John the Baptist:

- Elizabeth was the mother of John the Baptist, whose work paved the way for Jesus (Luke 1:5-7).
- After Elizabeth conceived (verse 25), her unborn baby jumped when Mary visited (verses 41-44).
- Elizabeth said that her son's name was John (verses 57-60).

Mary, mother of Jesus:

- An angel told Mary she would be the mother of Jesus Christ (verses 26-38).
- Mary offered a poem of praise, the Magnificat (verses 46-55).
- Mary gave birth (2:5-7) and thought about the wonderful things said about Jesus (verse 19).
- Mary was blessed by Elizabeth and Simeon (1:42; 2:34-35).
- Mary did not understand, but treasured Jesus' sayings (2:50-51).
- Mary kept in contact with Jesus during his ministry (8:19).

Women healed by Jesus:

- Jesus healed Simon Peter's mother-in-law (4:38-39).
- He healed a 12-year-old girl (8:41-42, 49-56).
- He healed a woman with a 12-year infirmity (verses 43-48).
- He healed a woman who had been crippled 18 years (13:10-17).

Women as good examples:

- A sinful woman anointed Jesus and was forgiven (7:37-50).
- Mary listened while Martha worked (10:38-42).
- A woman in a parable found a lost coin (15:8-10).
- In another parable, a widow kept going to a judge to obtain justice (18:1-5).
- A poor widow gave two small coins to the temple (21:1-4).

Other roles of women:

- Anna, a prophetess, blessed the child Jesus (2:36-38).

- Women, part of Jesus' traveling party, helped pay his way (8:1-3).
- An anonymous woman blessed Mary (11:27-28).

Witnesses to the resurrection:

- Women were among those who observed the crucifixion (23:27, 49).
- Women prepared spices to anoint Jesus' body (verses 55-56).
- Women were the first to find Jesus' tomb empty (24:1-3).
- Angels told the women that Jesus had risen (verses 4-8).
- Women were the first to tell the other disciples (verses 9-11).
- Although first-century culture usually minimized the importance of women, Luke portrayed women as good examples in the early church.

LUKE'S "ORDERLY" ACCOUNT – AN EXAMINATION OF BIBLICAL PRECISION

By Michael Morrison

Luke tells us that his book is an "orderly" account of the story of Jesus Christ (Luke 1:3, NIV). What is the nature of Luke's order?

The Greek word is *kathexes,* which is also used in Luke 8:1 (where it is translated "afterwards"), Acts 3:24 ("on"), Acts 11:4 ("precisely") and Acts 18:23 ("from place to place"). The word refers to sequence — chronological, geographical or logical. Let's look first at the context of Acts 11:4.

Acts 10 and 11

After the visions of Peter and the conversion of the gentile Cornelius, some believers in Jerusalem criticized Peter. So Peter "explained everything to them precisely [*kathexes*] as it had happened" (Acts 11:4). His explanation, however, is not strictly chronological.

Peter begins the story with his vision (11:5), although Luke has already told the reader that two other events happened earlier: Cornelius had a vision and sent two servants to Joppa (10:1-8). But in Peter's orderly account, he does not mention the servants until the point in the story that he learned about them (11:11). Although the servants told Peter about Cornelius' vision of an angel (10:22), Peter does not mention that. According to Peter's account, he does not learn about the angel until Cornelius himself tells him (11:13).

What Peter says is not false — it is orderly and true — but it is not strictly chronological. Acts 10 gives one perspective, Acts 11 another.

Gentiles in the church

One incident that *may* be reported out of chronological sequence is the conversion of gentiles. Many people think that Cornelius (Acts 10) was the first gentile Christian. But Acts 2:11 tells us that gentile proselytes to Judaism were part of the Pentecost audience, and presumably some of them became Christians. Because proselytes were circumcised, no one questioned whether they could be in the church.

Acts 8 tells us about the conversion of Samaritans, who were regarded as gentile by some Jews but not by all Jews. Acts 8 also describes the conversion of an Ethiopian eunuch, but it does not tell us whether he was Jewish. The account stresses his status as a eunuch. Both Samaritans and eunuchs were on or outside Jewish margins of acceptability.

Acts 10 describes the conversion of Cornelius, who we are clearly told was a gentile who worshiped God (10:1-2). Cornelius and his group received the Holy Spirit, spoke in tongues and were baptized (10:44-48). This incident helped Peter and the Jerusalem church realize that God was saving gentiles (10:45; 11:18). Gentiles did not have to convert to Judaism first — they did not have to be circumcised.

Acts 11 then moves to the city of Antioch, and *it also moves back in time* by mentioning the persecution following Stephen's martyrdom (11:19; 8:1, 4). Thus Luke avoids specifying the exact sequence.

As Christians moved away from persecution, they told others the gospel message (11:19). Most of them spoke only to Jews, but some spoke to gentile Greeks, too (11:20). Some of these may have been converted before Cornelius. But there is no report of controversy. As later sections of Acts show, the Antioch church was more open-minded about gentiles. God did not need to give visions and miracles to convince the Antioch Christians that gentiles could be saved.

Luke has organized the story by showing expansion from a Jewish center, to Jews on the fringes, to gentiles near Judaism, and finally he reports the gospel going to gentiles with no previous connection to Judaism.

The commission of Paul

Luke gives three perspectives on the conversion or commission of Paul. Paul was named Saul at the time, but I will use the better-known name Paul. Some people do not like to call his experience a conversion, since he did not decide to leave one religion and join another. Rather, even decades later he considered himself a Pharisee (23:6). However, the Holy Spirit changes a person so much that it is appropriate to call Paul's change a conversion. He certainly had a change of mind and a change of direction in his life.

But it may be best to call Paul's experience a call rather than a conversion because his experience is not typical of a conversion. It does not set a pattern that other believers must experience. The significance of Paul's Damascus Road experience is far beyond conversion. It was a call to ministry, a commission to be an apostle to gentiles.

The first story is told by Luke in Acts 9:1-30; the second by Paul, speaking to a crowd in Jerusalem (22:3-21); the third by Paul, speaking to King Agrippa (26:9-20). It is instructive to compare these stories, because this will reveal some of Luke's method of "ordering" his narrative.

Comparing the three accounts is similar to comparing the three synoptic Gospels, except that in this case we are clearly discussing only one event, described by the same writer, who in each case knew the same facts.

Nevertheless, there are several significant differences in the way the story can be told — different ways of reporting who said what when.

The story begins with Paul persecuting Christian Jews in Jerusalem (9:1; 22:4; 26:10-11). He requested authority to persecute Christians in Damascus (9:2; 22:5; 26:12). About noon (22:6; 26:13), as Paul neared the city (9:3; 22:6), a bright light from heaven flashed around him (9:3; 22:6) and his companions (26:13).

Paul tells us that he and his companions all fell to the ground (22:7; 26:14). But Luke, even though he knew Paul's story, tells us that Paul's companions stood (9:7). One way out of this apparent contradiction is to suppose that they all fell down but immediately scrambled to their feet in the blinding light. Or perhaps we might suppose that "stood speechless" is an idiom that has nothing to do with posture, but simply means "didn't move or talk."

No matter what the speculative solution, it illustrates the flexibility that an ancient history writer had in retelling the story. Luke did not feel a need to explain the difference between falling down and standing speechless, because that detail was not essential to the significance of the story. It shows us that we also need to focus on significance, not on irrelevant details. It would be a mistake to focus on a word that was not important.

Paul's companions "heard the sound" (9:7) but "did not understand the voice" (22:9). The NIV obscures what in Greek is an apparent contradiction. Acts 9:7 says they heard the *phone;* 22:9 says they did not hear the *phone. Phone* can mean either voice or sound, and *akouo* can mean either hear or understand, so the NIV used different translations to avoid a contradiction. But in Greek, the apparent contradiction remains. Luke was inspired to use contradictory phrases within his own book. He did not explain it; it was not relevant to his purpose.

Paul's companions saw the light (22:9) but did not see anyone (9:7). But the way Acts 9 presents the story, it looks like Paul didn't see anyone, either. We are simply told that when he opened his eyes, he saw nothing. It is only later in the story that we are told, by Ananias, that Paul had seen Jesus (9:17; cf. 9:27; 22:14). We might conclude from Acts 9 that Jesus appeared like a bright light. If we ask whether Paul's companions saw the same light, we would be dealing in the irrelevant. It does not matter what they saw or heard. The minor differences remind us to be cautious about reading too much into specific details that are not relevant to the main point. Omissions are likely.

A greater difference is found in the presentation of Paul's commission. Was he told to go to Damascus to get his commission (9:6; 22:10), or was he told right away what it was (26:16-18)? In 9:15-16, the commission is give from the Lord to Ananias. In 22:14-15, it is from Ananias to Paul. It is easy to see that both may be true. But in 26:16-18, it is from the Lord to Paul — Ananias isn't even mentioned! It seems that Paul has abbreviated the story for the benefit of King Agrippa. The importance is in the commission, not in the sequence of messengers or the location.

In all these commissions, Paul is sent to gentiles and Jews. In 9:15, Paul is simply to carry Jesus' name (Acts 9 emphasizes the *name* of Jesus). In 22:15, he is to be a witness of his experience. In 26:16-18, he is not only a witness but also a preacher of forgiveness and sanctification by faith. Acts 9 reports him as preaching primarily that Jesus is the Christ, the Son of God (9:20, 22); Acts 26:20 says he preached repentance. Apparently Luke considered these to be synonymous messages; we would err if we made too much of the differences in terminology — not only here but also elsewhere — not only in Luke but also in other biblical writers. We must allow for literary variation and differing emphases.

Acts 9:10-16 tells us about the vision of Ananias — a vision other accounts omit. Acts 9:12 tells us of a vision Paul had, a vision not otherwise described. Acts 22:17-21 tells us of yet another vision. Nowhere in Acts are we told about three years in Arabia and Damascus or the 14 years that went by before Paul went to Jerusalem again for the apostolic conference (cf. Galatians 1:15-2:1).

Most of these differences are simply omissions, not contradictions. But they show that we cannot assume that any version of *any* story includes all the details *we* think are relevant. Nor can we assume it is in strictly chronological order or that every passage of time is chronicled. The variations show the flexibility with which an inspired historian could tell the story.

Discrepancies in prophecies

We saw above that Luke didn't mind putting an apparent contradiction in his history. We see another example in Acts 20:22; 21:4. The first verse says that the Holy Spirit compelled Paul to go to Jerusalem; the second verse says the Spirit inspired some Christians to urge Paul not to go. Is the same Spirit giving contradictory direction?

In 21:11, we see another discrepancy — Agabus was inspired to predict that the Jews would bind Paul. It would be easy for modern interpreters to see this prophecy as clearly predicting who would do the binding. But as the account develops, we find that the Roman soldiers were actually the ones who bound Paul (21:33). Instead of the Jews handing over Paul to the gentiles (21:11), Paul was actually rescued by the gentiles (21:32). The prophecy was fulfilled in principle, in the end result, but not in the literal details of sequence. It would be a mistake to insist that all prophecies must be literally fulfilled.

Paul creates a prophetic discrepancy, too. In 27:10, he predicted that the voyage would bring great loss of life; in 27:22 he modifies this by saying that no lives will be lost. Why does Luke record a prophecy that he knows will be rescinded? His reasons may not be clear to us, but it is clear that we cannot hold Luke to a standard of accuracy that was never part of his intention.

These minor discrepancies do not negate the inspiration of the Bible. God, who cannot lie, caused these differences to be recorded in the canon. They warn us to be careful when examining biblical details. They were not intended to have the precision we sometimes want to ascribe to them. It is a mistake to press the details beyond the intention of the author.

Gospel of Luke

Let us now look briefly at the Gospel written by Luke. He begins Jesus' ministry in Luke 4:14. After two summary verses about Galilee, Luke tells us about an incident in the Nazareth synagogue (verses 16-30). But we should not conclude from this that Jesus' sermon in Nazareth came early in his ministry. (Matthew 4:12-13 begins Jesus' ministry by noting that Jesus went *away* from Nazareth.) Luke 4:23 mentions that he had *already* done notable works in Capernaum.

Luke had a literary reason to begin the story with Nazareth — the incident is a miniature of Jesus' entire ministry, from his mission statement, the initially favorable reaction, his expulsion and an attempt to kill him. The Nazareth story sets the scene for the other events in Jesus' ministry.

Various other events in Luke's story are in a different order than we find in the other Gospels. The healing of Peter's mother-in-law comes early in Luke (4:38-39) but midway in Matthew (8:14). Jesus calls four disciples after that in Luke (5:1-11) but beforehand in Matthew (4:18-22) and Mark (1:16-20, 29-31). Which sequence is correct?

We cannot assume that *any* narrative sequence necessarily indicates a chronological sequence — even if temporal connectives such as "then" or "immediately" are sometimes used. Although the reported events happened, they did not necessarily happen in the sequence they are reported in.

One of the narrative techniques Luke uses is to organize many of the stories in the context of a trip from Galilee to Jerusalem. In Luke 9:51, "Jesus resolutely set out for Jerusalem." Luke 13:22, 18:31 and 19:28 say that Jesus was still on his way to Jerusalem and imply that everything between 13:22 and 19:28 happened on this one trip. But that is reading too much into Luke's geographic notes. Several of the intervening events are set in Galilee or Jerusalem by Matthew or Mark.

Luke presents it all as a journey because Jesus' ministry was, figuratively speaking, a one-way trip to death in Jerusalem. Luke doesn't tell us when Jesus went back to Galilee and began his journey toward Jerusalem again. What Jesus said and did is important — but when and where is not as important.

Jesus healed a blind man near Jericho, for example. Was it while he was going in (Luke 18:35) or while going out (Mark 10:46)? It is possible that Jesus healed one blind man while entering and another while exiting, but it seems unlikely that both men would use the exact same words, "Jesus, Son of David, have mercy on me." Perhaps Jesus went out the city gate, heard the man calling, and then went back in to heal the man — thus Jesus was exiting and entering at the same time. Or perhaps he was leaving old Jericho and entering the newer city. Hypothetical reconstructions can weasel out of a contradiction, but they sometimes seem overly ingenious — and they certainly are not the focus of the inspired writers.

Matthew says that there were two blind men at Jericho, both healed while Jesus was going out (Matthew 20:29-30). So was there one man, two, or three? Why don't Mark and Luke tell us that Jesus healed more than one? Such details are extraneous — the main point is that Jesus healed blindness, and that even a blind man could be inspired to recognize him as the Son of David, the Messiah.

This is not to say that the Gospels are totally inaccurate about time and space. Most of the sequence and settings are probably accurate. But a few exceptions occur, which means we must be cautious about constructing a modern history of Jesus that is concerned about the details that the writers were not inspired to be concerned about. The big picture is more important than the details.

Consider Peter's confession of Christ, for example. What did Peter say? "You are the Christ, the Son of the living God" (Matthew 16:16). "The Christ of God" (Luke 9:20). We could say that Peter said *both* of these phrases, but it seems an unlikely and unnecessary redundancy. Another legitimate possibility is that Matthew or Luke was inspired to translate Peter's Aramaic words with a dynamic equivalence appropriate for the original readers. The significance is conveyed — not necessarily the precise words. We see a similar equivalence in John's account, where Peter's recognition of Jesus is phrased, "You are the Holy One of God" (John 6:69).

The ascension

Luke's ascension stories provide a brief example about jumping to chronological conclusions. Luke 24:1-12 is dated on the Sunday after the crucifixion; 24:13-32 is dated "that same day." Verses 33-44 are a few hours later — probably Sunday evening. Verses 45-49, introduced by "then," probably refer to Sunday evening, too.

Verses 50-53 describes the ascension, without any indication of *any* passage of time, or any trips to Galilee. If this were the only account we had, we might assume that Jesus ascended that same Sunday night. In this case, however, we have other accounts, including one written by Luke himself, that inform us otherwise.

In other cases, we do not have parallel accounts that expand our information. It is dangerous to assume that a parallel account, if found, would not inform us about a change in location or a long delay. We cannot assume that "then" means "the very next event" or assume that one event followed right after another. Even though the writer may say nothing about it, weeks may have passed. The Gospel writers wanted to tell us what happened, but in most cases the *when* was not important enough to be worth specific mention.

Chronological precision apparently wasn't necessary or expected in Luke's "orderly" account — and we cannot assume it in *any* of the Gospels. We could use a harmony of the Gospels to construct a chronology, but that in itself could not prove that our result was accurate. The inspired writers had some flexibility in details as they told the stories for different audiences and purposes. So we must be cautious about using such details for purposes they were not intended for.

These observations encourage us to focus more on the big point than on the details — more on the theological purpose of each passage and less on the chronology and geography. Those timeless truths had historical roots (and it is important that they do), but it is rarely important to specify precisely when and where the events happened.

Instead of focusing on details that have little relevance to Christian life today, we need to focus on spiritual principles and timeless truths. Thus our time would be well spent — certainly a positive result.

ANNOUNCING THE KING:
A STUDY OF LUKE 1:1-38

By Michael Morrison

Luke begins his book about Jesus with a preface that describes his research methods. His introduction (all one sentence in Greek) is similar to the beginning of Greek historical works:

> Many have undertaken to draw up an account of the things that have been fulfilled among us, just as they were handed down to us by those who from the first were eyewitnesses and servants of the word. Therefore, since I myself have carefully investigated everything from the beginning, it seemed good also to me to write an orderly account for you, most excellent Theophilus, so that you may know the certainty of the things you have been taught. (Luke 1:1-4)

Luke does not say that there is anything wrong with previous accounts, which were written by reliable eyewitnesses, but he wants to add his research to strengthen the faith of his readers. "I have checked it out," he says, "and it is true. I'll give you the details."

Ancient writers sometimes dedicated their books to a patron who paid the cost of making copies of the book. Theophilus may be such a sponsor, a person interested in Christianity. Since his name means "lover of God," any reader who loved God would be invited to read. Luke presents his book as a historically accurate account of "the things that have been fulfilled among us."

An announcement to Zechariah

Just what are those things? Luke hasn't yet told us. He begins by putting us into the flow of history—a story of God's people: "In the time of Herod king of Judea there was a priest named Zechariah, who belonged to the priestly division of Abijah; his wife Elizabeth was also a descendant of Aaron" (v. 5). Luke is writing at least 60 years after these events, but his details suggest that he has done enough research to find the facts. The priests were divided into 24 divisions; each served two one-week periods each year.

"Both of them were upright in the sight of God, observing all the Lord's commandments and regulations blamelessly. But they had no children, because Elizabeth was barren; and they were both well along in years" (vv. 6-7). Being childless was a disgrace in that society, and some people might assume from it that Zechariah and Elizabeth were not pleasing God. But Luke assures us that they were righteous in every way.

Now that he has introduced the characters, he tells the story:

> Once when Zechariah's division was on duty and he was serving as priest before God, he was chosen by lot, according to the custom of the priesthood, to go into the temple of the Lord and burn incense. And when the time for the burning of incense came, all the assembled worshipers were praying outside. Then an angel of the Lord appeared to him, standing at the right side of the altar of incense. When Zechariah saw him, he was startled and was gripped with fear. (vv. 8-12)

A priest could offer incense in the temple only once in his lifetime, and some never had that honor at all. Zechariah may have been nervous at his responsibility, and the sudden appearance of the angel frightened him. The angel told him:

> Do not be afraid, Zechariah; your prayer has been heard. Your wife Elizabeth will bear you a son, and you are to give him the name John. He will be a joy and delight to you, and many will rejoice because of his birth, for he will be great in the sight of the Lord. He is never to take wine or other fermented drink, and he will be filled with the Holy Spirit even from birth. Many of the people of Israel will he bring back to the Lord their God. And he will go on before the Lord, in the spirit and power of Elijah, to turn the hearts of the fathers to their children and the disobedient to the wisdom of the righteous—to make ready a people prepared for the Lord. (vv. 13-17)

Zechariah had apparently given up hope for a son, but he probably still prayed for God to rescue his people. So the angel tells him the first step in the salvation of Israel: Zechariah will have a son—not just any son, but one who is "great in the sight of the Lord." As part of his special role set apart for God, he would avoid wine (a rule that Nazirites also followed, but John was probably not a Nazirite). He would be a great prophet, turning the people back to God, fulfilling the prophecies of Malachi 4:5-6 and Isaiah 40:3. After a gap of several centuries, God would again inspire one of his servants to speak to the nation.

How can I be sure?

But Zechariah was reluctant to believe it. He asked: "How can I be sure of this? I am an old man and my wife is well along in years" (v. 18). The angel then gave him reasons to believe—first, that the message was from God, and second, that a miracle would happen to Zechariah himself:

"I am Gabriel. I stand in the presence of God, and I have been sent to speak to you and to tell you this good news. And now you will be silent and not able to speak until the day this happens, because you did not believe my words, which will come true at their proper time" (vv. 19-20). Zechariah was righteous, but he asked for evidence, so God gave him some he could not deny. God keeps his promises, whether they are to a nation or to an individual.

"Meanwhile," Luke tells us, "the people were waiting for Zechariah and wondering why he stayed so long in the temple. When he came out, he could not speak to them. They realized he had seen a vision in the temple, for he kept making signs to them but remained unable to speak" (vv. 21-22). The priest who offered incense was also supposed to give a blessing, but Zechariah could not.

However, Zechariah kept his commitment, staying in Jerusalem as long as his priestly division was supposed to serve, and then he went home. Elizabeth became pregnant, but kept her pregnancy secret for five months (vv. 23-24). And she rejoiced: "The Lord has done this for me," she said. "In these days he has shown his favor and taken away my disgrace among the people." She went from disgrace to favor.

An announcement to Mary

The next event Luke tells us about happened "in the sixth month"—in the sixth month of Elizabeth's pregnancy. He introduces the characters: "God sent the angel Gabriel to Nazareth, a town in Galilee, to a virgin pledged to be married to a man named Joseph, a descendant of David. The virgin's name was Mary" (vv. 26-27). She was probably a teenager, with a legally binding commitment to marry Joseph. Joseph may have been much older; we do not know.

Gabriel went to Mary (we do not know how he appeared) and said: "Greetings, you who are highly favored! The Lord is with you" (v. 28). This was an odd greeting, Mary thought, and she "was greatly troubled at his words" (v. 29). She was just an ordinary girl; why should she be given this honor? So Gabriel said:

Do not be afraid, Mary, you have found favor with God. You will be with child and give birth to a son, and you are to give him the name Jesus. He will be great and will be called the Son of the Most High. The Lord God will give him the throne of his father David, and he will reign over the house of Jacob forever; his kingdom will never end. (vv. 30-33)

The angel announced that Mary would have a child, the Son of God, the son of David, a ruler forever. In other words, the Messiah. What a breathtaking announcement! (This is commemorated in March in traditional Christian calendars as the Feast of the Annunciation.) She was to name him Jesus, which means "The Lord is salvation."

This is not a vague prophecy that in some distant future Mary would become pregnant and have a son. That wouldn't be much of a prediction, since almost all women had that experience. Mary understood that she would become pregnant right away. "How will this be," Mary asked the angel, "since I am a virgin?" (v. 34).

Mary's question sounds similar to Zechariah's, but Gabriel did not rebuke her for skepticism. Perhaps an old priest was supposed to have more faith than a teenage girl, or perhaps Mary simply had more faith. To answer her question, Gabriel basically repeated his prophecy, and gave Mary a sign by revealing Elizabeth's pregnancy. Gabriel answered:

The Holy Spirit will come upon you, and the power of the Most High will overshadow you. So the holy one to be born will be called the Son of God. Even Elizabeth your relative is going to have a child in her old age, and she who was said to be barren is in her sixth month. For nothing is impossible with God. (vv. 35-37)

God's Spirit will cause you to be pregnant, he said, which is why your son will be the Son of God. And if you want further evidence of a miraculous pregnancy, go ask your relative Elizabeth. (We do not know how they were related.) If God can cause an elderly woman to become pregnant, he can also cause a young woman, even a virgin, to become pregnant. He will keep his promise.

Mary's response is a model for all of us: "I am the Lord's servant," she said. "May it be to me as you have said" (v. 38). Her attitude is a great example for all of us. She was willing, even though women who became pregnant before marriage were not treated well in that society. She would go from favor to disgrace—and she did not yet know the heartache involved in being the mother of the Messiah.

Things to think about

- Have I carefully investigated the facts about Jesus? (v. 1)
- What prayer would I most like God to answer for me? (v. 13)
- Is my heart turned toward my children? (v. 17)
- Do I consider myself "highly favored" by God? (v. 28)
- Am I as willing as Mary to let God work in my life? (v. 38)

TWO SONGS OF PRAISE:
A STUDY OF LUKE 1:39-80

By Michael Morrison

After the angel Gabriel told Mary that her relative Elizabeth was pregnant in old age, "Mary got ready and hurried to a town in the hill country of Judea, where she entered Zechariah's home and greeted Elizabeth" (Luke 1:39-40). Gabriel had told Mary that Elizabeth was pregnant (v. 36), so Mary quickly made the three-day journey to Judea. Elizabeth's pregnancy was evidence that what the angel said about Mary was also true. One miraculous pregnancy was a sign of the other, just as the first son would prepare the way for the work of the second.

"When Elizabeth heard Mary's greeting, the baby leaped in her womb, and Elizabeth was filled with the Holy Spirit" (v. 41). Elizabeth was inspired to understand a supernatural significance to this reaction, and even before Mary gave her the news, she knew Mary would have a child: "Blessed are you among women, and blessed is the child you will bear! But why am I so favored, that the mother of my Lord should come to me? As soon as the sound of your greeting reached my ears, the baby in my womb leaped for joy. Blessed is she who has believed that what the Lord has said to her will be accomplished!" (vv. 42-45).

Elizabeth counted it an honor to be visited, for she recognized that Mary's child would be her Lord. It was a joyful occasion, for the Savior was coming to the people who had waited for so long. Both Elizabeth and Mary are good role models for Christians today. Anyone who believes that the Lord keeps his promises will be blessed.

God inspired Elizabeth to praise and encourage Mary's faith, that her child would, as the angel promised, be the Son of God, ruling over the children of Israel forever (vv. 32-33).

Mary's song of praise

Mary's response is a hymn of praise, arranged with the parallel thoughts that characterize Hebrew poetry, such as Hannah's prayer in 1 Samuel 2. Mary's song is traditionally called the Magnificat (the first word of the Latin translation):

> My soul glorifies the Lord
> and my spirit rejoices in God my Savior. (vv. 46-47)

In this verse, the second line repeats the thought of the first—"my soul" and "my spirit" are similar, and "glorifies" and "rejoices in" are similar ideas. But the second line adds a new thought at the end: Not only is God the Lord, he is also the Savior. Mary then gives a reason for rejoicing: God has rewarded her humility:

> for he has been mindful
> of the humble state of his servant.
> From now on all generations will call me blessed,
> for the Mighty One has done great things for me—
> holy is his name. (vv. 48-49)

Mary, seeing the evidence in Elizabeth, knows that God has already done what he promised to Mary, that she would be the mother of the Messiah. Mary says that God has helped her, and everyone will know of her blessing. She then reverses the flow by saying again that God has helped her, and praising God, returns to the thought that she started her poetry with. (This mirror-like arrangement is called a chiasm.)

Mary then expands her praise to include everyone who trusts in God, contrasting God's blessings for the humble with his opposition to the proud:

> His mercy extends to those who fear him,
> from generation to generation.
> He has performed mighty deeds with his arm;
> he has scattered those who are proud in their inmost thoughts. (vv. 50-51)

To those who worship God, he gives mercy, but those who do not care about God are brushed aside with mighty deeds. A similar contrast is seen in verses 52-53, with another balanced structure—the rich, the poor; the poor, the rich:

> He has brought down rulers from their thrones
> but has lifted up the humble.
> He has filled the hungry with good things
> but has sent the rich away empty.

God works in a great reversal, bringing the mighty down and exalting the poor and the weak. God did not send his Son into the palaces of royalty, but he honored the working poor of Galilee. Salvation comes not from human power, but must depend on the intervention of God. Mary represents all who trust in God to do what he has promised.

Mary concludes by mentioning God's promise to the ancestors of the nation:

> He has helped his servant Israel,
> remembering to be merciful
> to Abraham and his descendants forever,
> even as he said to our fathers. (vv. 54-55)

The birth of John

The next significant event in Luke's story is the birth of John. "When it was time for Elizabeth to have her baby, she gave birth to a son. Her neighbors and relatives heard that the Lord had shown her great mercy, and they shared her joy" (vv. 57-58).

They did not name the baby until the eighth day, when he was circumcised, and there was a community celebration. Although boys were often named after their grandfathers, the neighbors and relatives thought it would be appropriate to name the boy after his elderly father: "On the eighth day they came to circumcise the child, and they were going to name him after his father Zechariah, but his mother spoke up and said, 'No! He is to be called John'" (vv. 59-60).

"John" comes from the Hebrew *Yohanan,* which means "God is gracious." The neighbors objected to this name, since it wasn't in the family traditions. Zechariah was apparently deaf as well as mute, so "they made signs to his father, to find out what he would like to name the child" (v. 62).

Zechariah "asked for a writing tablet, and to everyone's astonishment he wrote, 'His name is John.' Immediately his mouth was opened and his tongue was loosed, and he began to speak, praising God" (vv. 63-64). Earlier, Zechariah had been made mute after he asked, "How can I be sure of this?" (v. 18). He now had the evidence he wanted, and as the angel promised (v. 20), his speech was restored when God fulfilled his promise.

Luke will soon tell us what Zechariah said, but first he tells us what effect the miracle had on the people: "The neighbors were all filled with awe, and throughout the hill country of Judea people were talking about all these things. Everyone who heard this wondered about it, asking, 'What then is this child going to be?' For the Lord's hand was with him" (vv. 65-66).

Rumors were stirring, Luke tells us. Many people knew that God was doing something among his people. Could it be that God would give them the Messiah they hoped for?

Zechariah's praise

"Zechariah was filled with the Holy Spirit and prophesied" (v. 67). After nine months of enforced silence, in which he no doubt frequently thought about God's faithfulness, he praises God. His song is called the Benedictus, which is the first word of the Latin version.

> Praise be to the Lord, the God of Israel,
> because he has come and has redeemed his people.
> He has raised up a horn of salvation for us
> in the house of his servant David. (vv. 68-69)

Zechariah names John. [Illustration by Ken Tunell]

Surprisingly, Zechariah (a Levite) is not speaking of his own son—just as Elizabeth did, he focused on Mary's unborn child, predicting the son of David. But John, the Levite baby, is nevertheless part of God's preparation for rescuing the Jewish nation. In Hebrew, "horn" was a symbol of strength (perhaps from the strength of horned animals such as oxen), so Zechariah predicts a mighty salvation. He focuses on the Jewish people; he may not have realized (unlike Luke, who knew more of the story) that the Messiah would rescue the Gentiles as well.

Just as Mary did, Zechariah mentions that salvation was predicted, that it was part of the blessings promised to Abraham (Gen. 22:18), and that God was keeping those promises:

> (as he said through his holy prophets of long ago),
> salvation from our enemies
> and from the hand of all who hate us —
> to show mercy to our fathers
> and to remember his holy covenant,
> the oath he swore to our father Abraham:
> to rescue us from the hand of our enemies,
> and to enable us to serve him without fear
> in holiness and righteousness before him all our days. (vv. 70-75)

Zechariah briefly turns his attention to his own son, with an echo of Isaiah

40:3 and Malachi 3:1:

> And you, my child, will be called
> a prophet of the Most High;
> for you will go on before the Lord
> to prepare the way for him,
> to give his people the knowledge of salvation. (Luke 1:76-77)

He then describes the salvation of the Lord—not a military conquest, but a spiritual rescue, bringing light and instruction in the way of peace. In this section, Zechariah uses concepts found in Isaiah 9:2; 60:1-3; and Malachi 4:2:

> through the forgiveness of their sins,
> because of the tender mercy of our God,
> by which the rising sun will come to us from heaven
> to shine on those living in darkness
> and in the shadow of death,
> to guide our feet into the path of peace. (vv. 77-79)

Salvation will come not through force, but through spiritual growth. Through the Lord, the people will be enlightened about salvation, forgiveness, mercy and peace. John's role will be to prepare the way.

Luke now summarizes the next 30 years for John: "The child grew and became strong in spirit; and he lived in the desert until he appeared publicly to Israel" (v. 80). There is a hint of greater things yet to come. The promises made to the people have not been forgotten.

Things to think about

- Do I believe that the Lord will do as he said? (v. 45) Why is it sometimes difficult to trust him?
- What mighty things has the Lord done for me? (v. 49)
- When God intervenes in my life, do I respond with songs of praise?
- How important is the mercy of God to me? (vv. 50, 54, 58, 72, 78) When I praise him, is mercy a frequent theme?
- Do I serve God "without fear," or am I sometimes embarrassed? (v. 74)
- Who is "the rising sun ... from heaven"? (v. 78). Has he guided me in the path of peace? (v. 79)

A SAVIOR IS BORN:
A STUDY OF LUKE 2:1-21

By Michael Morrison

Luke begins his book with dramatic announcements: angelic messages, songs of praise, and miracles. This is only the beginning, for Luke has equally dramatic events to report for the birth of Jesus. First, he sets the scene by telling us why Joseph and Mary went to Bethlehem.

A Roman census

"In those days Caesar Augustus issued a decree that a census should be taken of the entire Roman world. (This was the first census that took place while Quirinius was governor of Syria.) And everyone went to their own town to register" (Luke 2:1-3, NIV 2011 in this chapter). Roman taxation was based on population counts.

Unfortunately, we do not have any Roman records of this census, so we do not know the date. For one thing, the census may not have been done in all regions in the same year. Luke's words could mean "that Caesar decreed that the enrollment, which had previously been going on in some parts of the empire, should now be extended to all parts" (Ben Witherington, "Birth of Jesus," *Dictionary of Jesus and the Gospels,* p. 67). In Egypt, a census was conducted every 14 years.

Luke, writing in the style of a Greek historian, indicates dates by political rulers and events. Quirinius ordered a census in A.D. 6-7 (mentioned in Acts 5:37), but we do not have any evidence that Quirinius was governor when Herod was alive. He was a consul at that time, and may have had a temporary authority over Syria.

If "everyone" went to their own town for this census, it was presumably required (registration by family origin was a Jewish, not a Roman custom), and most likely at a time of the year when people could travel to their respective cities.

"So Joseph also went up from the town of Nazareth in Galilee to Judea, to Bethlehem the town of David, because he belonged to the house and line of David" (Luke 2:4). Many other people would have also been of the line of David, but if they lived in Jerusalem, only five miles away, they could register for the census without having to spend the night in Bethlehem.

"He went there to register with Mary, who was pledged to be married to him and was expecting a child" (v. 5). Joseph and Mary were not yet officially married, but for the census they were counted together. Perhaps Joseph did not want to leave Mary alone in Nazareth, where she might face ridicule and shame. And perhaps they knew, as others did, that the Messiah would be born in Bethlehem (Matt. 2:5; Micah 5:2). The political decree therefore served the purpose of God, who was working behind the scenes as well as in more spectacular ways.

The birth of Jesus

We do not know how long Joseph and Mary stayed in Bethlehem. They probably traveled well before the baby was due. Luke just tells us, "While they were there, the time came for the baby to be born, and she gave birth to her firstborn, a son. She wrapped him in cloths and placed him in a manger, because there was no guest room available for them" (vv. 6-7). Bethlehem was small and off the main road; it may not have had a real inn.

Poor people often did not have a barn for their animals, so they had a manger inside the home. Mary used the manger because the guest room was either not large enough or occupied by others. Luke describes this in a matter-of-fact way, as if nothing was too far out of the ordinary.

> In the vast majority of ancient Near-Eastern peasant homes for which we have archaeological and literary evidence, the manger was within the home, not in some separate barn. The animals as well as the family slept within one large enclosed space that was divided so that usually the animals would be on a lower level, and the family would sleep on a raised dais.... We should probably envision Mary and Joseph staying in the home of relatives or friends, a home which was crowded due to the census.... Mary gave birth to her child perhaps in the family room and placed the baby in the stone manger. (Witherington, 69-70)

The point is that Jesus (although a king) was born in humble circumstances. Even in his family's home town, he was in temporary accommodation, with an improvised bed. One lesson we see here is: "Importance is not a matter of one's environment or the supposed status that things bring. Rather, importance is a function of one's role in God's work" (Darrell Bock, *Luke,* NIV Application Commentary, p. 86).

Shepherds and angels

Luke now brings the supernatural into the story: "There were shepherds living out in the fields nearby, keeping watch over their flocks at night. An angel of the Lord appeared to them, and the glory of the Lord shone around them, and they were terrified" (2:8-9).

Although the Bible usually portrays shepherds in a positive way, society often looked down on them, as they do the homeless today. Shepherds could not keep ceremonial laws, they moved often, and people didn't trust them— they weren't even allowed to testify in court. Due to their occupation, they had not gone to their own town to register for the tax census. (Flocks of sheep were kept year-round near Bethlehem to provide sacrifices at the temple.)

Like most other people, the shepherds were afraid when they saw the angel and the glory of the Lord. But the angel told them: "Do not be afraid. I bring you good news that will cause great joy for all the people. Today in the town of David a Savior has been born to you; he is the Messiah, the Lord. This will be a sign to you: You will find a baby wrapped in cloths and lying in a manger" (vv. 10-12).

The angel announced the good news: the Messiah has been born, he is a Savior for all the people, and this is a reason to have great joy. But most people were totally unaware of the good news. The angel was not sent to everyone—just to a few shepherds who represented all humanity.

It would not be strange to find a newborn baby wrapped in cloths, but it was apparently unusual to find one in a manger. This is the third "sign" (evidence that God was involved) that Luke reports. Bethlehem was small enough that there wouldn't be very many newborn babies in it, and it was apparently small enough that the shepherds could find the baby without supernatural help.

"Suddenly a great company of the heavenly host appeared with the angel, praising God and saying, 'Glory to God in the highest heaven, and on earth peace to those on whom his favor rests'" (vv. 13-14). This short song is called *Gloria in Excelsis Deo,* which is the way it begins in Latin. An army of angels announced peace.

Through the Savior, peace will come not to everyone, but to those God is pleased with (see Matt. 10:34; Luke 12:32). "It is those whom God chooses, rather than those who choose God" (Leon Morris, *Luke,* rev. ed., p. 95). "Jesus comes for all, but not all respond to and benefit from his coming" (Bock, p. 85). Though we were formerly God's enemies, we were reconciled to God, given peace with him, through our Savior. The birth of the Savior is certainly a good reason for praising God!

The news spreads

"When the angels had left them and gone into heaven, the shepherds said to one another, 'Let's go to Bethlehem and see this thing that has happened, which the Lord has told us about.' So they hurried off and found Mary and Joseph, and the baby, who was lying in the manger" (Luke 2:15-16). This apparently all happened on the evening after Jesus' birth.

"When they had seen him, they spread the word concerning what had been told them about this child, and all who heard it were amazed at what the shepherds said to them" (vv. 17-18). So the shepherds became evangelists for a time, telling people about the angels, the singing and the baby. As in previous cases, everything the angel said was true.

People were amazed at the story, but did they believe it? We do not know. Amazement is often short-lived (see Luke 4:22, 28). Mary, however, "treasured up all these things and pondered them in her heart" (2:19). Mary, the model of a good disciple, not only remembered these events, she also thought more about their significance. What manner of Messiah would her child be? The story is just beginning.

So the shepherds returned to their flocks and fields, "glorifying and praising God for all the things they had heard and seen, which were just as they had been told" (v. 20). God had kept his word. The shepherds went back to their work, filled with hope and confidence that deliverance would come.

Meanwhile, Joseph and Mary had to complete the assignment that Gabriel had given them: "On the eighth day, when it was time to circumcise the child, he was named Jesus, the name the angel had given him before he was conceived" (v. 21).

Things to think about

- How would I feel about a couple who were not officially married, yet were living together and the woman was pregnant? (v. 5)
- How would I feel about putting my firstborn child in a feed trough because that was the only place there was room? (v. 7) How often

does God's plan for me involve inconveniences, and how do I react to them?

- How would I react to a heavenly choir singing praises to God because a baby had been born? (vv. 13-14) Does the birth of Jesus bring me joy?
- How well do I tell others about what God has done? (v. 17) Am I amazed? (v. 18) Or could I be totally unaware of what he is doing?
- Do questions cause me to doubt, or do I patiently ponder them? (v. 19)

WHAT CHILD IS THIS?
A STUDY OF LUKE 2:22-52

By Michael Morrison

Luke reports two events between Jesus' birth and the beginning of his ministry. These are not reported out of idle curiosity, however—both events point forward to his importance in God's plan of salvation. Remarkable prophecies were spoken when Jesus was presented to the Lord, and Jesus himself alluded to a special role when he was coming of age.

Presented to God

The Law of Moses required every firstborn son to be redeemed and dedicated to God, since God had spared all the firstborn sons of Israel in the 10th plague on Egypt (Ex. 13:11-16). The Law further specified that, for a son, the mother should wait 40 days and then bring a burnt offering and a sin offering to the sanctuary. She was to bring a lamb and a bird, or if she could not afford a lamb, two birds (Lev. 12:1-8).

Luke tells us that Joseph and Mary were obedient to the Law of Moses:

> When the time of their purification according to the Law of Moses had been completed, Joseph and Mary took [Jesus] to Jerusalem to present him to the Lord (as it is written in the Law of the Lord, "Every firstborn male is to be consecrated to the Lord"), and to offer a sacrifice in keeping with what is said in the Law of the Lord: "a pair of doves or two young pigeons." (vv. 22-24)

Apparently the family could not afford a lamb. It is also interesting that Luke speaks of "their" purification, although the Law spoke only of the purification of the mother. It is ironic that the Law required redemption for the Redeemer, and a sin-offering to purify a divinely caused conception.

It was at this trip to the temple that some significant prophecies were given:

> Now there was a man in Jerusalem called Simeon, who was righteous and devout. He was waiting for the consolation of Israel, and the Holy Spirit was upon him. It had been revealed to him by the Holy Spirit that he would not die before he had seen the Lord's Christ. Moved by the Spirit, he went into the temple courts. (vv. 25-27)

This godly man earnestly wanted God to rescue Israel, and the Holy Spirit spoke to him (as he had spoken to the Old Testament prophets) and caused him to come to the temple at the right time.

When Mary and Joseph brought the baby Jesus to the temple courts for the dedication and purification ritual, Simeon intervened:

> Simeon took him in his arms and praised God, saying: "Sovereign Lord, as you have promised, you now dismiss your servant in peace. For my eyes have seen your salvation, which you have prepared in the sight of all people, a light for revelation to the Gentiles and for glory to your people Israel." (vv. 28-32)

The Holy Spirit revealed to Simeon that this child was the answer to his hopes and faith; although the salvation itself had not been completed, it was sure. God had kept his promise to Simeon. His lifelong desire was coming to pass, and he felt his life was complete. He had seen the answer, and he knew that this child would be the salvation not only of Israel but all the Gentiles, too. He was God's Anointed One, who would be the "light to the Gentiles" (Isa. 42:6).

Joseph and Mary "marveled at what was said about him" (v. 33). Could it be that Joseph and Mary didn't quite believe that this miraculous child would be the Savior of all peoples? Or more likely, Luke tells us this for our benefit, so that we think more deeply about the significance of what was said. We should also marvel at these auspicious words.

After Simeon had blessed Jesus, he also blessed Joseph and Mary. But the salvation of Israel would not be a bed of roses—Simeon also spoke of troubles to come: "This child is destined to cause the falling and rising of many in Israel, and to be a sign that will be spoken against, so that the thoughts of many hearts will be revealed. And a sword will pierce your own soul too" (vv. 34-35).

The Savior of Israel would cause some to rise in God's favor, but would also cause some to fall, because some people would speak against him. They would not like the salvation that he brought, and their thoughts would be exposed as ungodly. They would reject his brand of salvation, thinking that they did not need it. And Mary herself would suffer as a result. We are not yet told how—Luke keeps us in suspense.

The prophetess

Luke also tells us about Anna, who was known to be a prophetess. He does not quote her words, but nevertheless includes her involvement:

> "There was also a prophetess, Anna, the daughter of Phanuel, of the tribe of Asher. She was very old; she had lived with her husband seven years after her marriage, and then was a widow until she was eighty-four. She never left the temple but worshiped night and day, fasting and praying. Coming up to them at that very moment, she gave thanks to God and spoke about the child to all who were looking

forward to the redemption of Jerusalem" (vv. 36-38).

Anna, an elderly model of piety, was apparently inspired to understand that this baby boy was the Savior who would redeem the people of God, and she spread the good news about him. More and more people were learning that the time of salvation has come.

Luke then wraps up this part of the story with some general comments: "When Joseph and Mary had done everything required by the Law of the Lord, they returned to Galilee to their own town of Nazareth. And the child grew and became strong; he was filled with wisdom, and the grace of God was upon him" (vv. 39-40). Luke says nothing about the family's trip to Egypt (Matt. 2:13-23). He simply brings Jesus to Nazareth, his childhood home. There he grew in wisdom, and God was with him.

Jesus in the temple

Jesus' parents, as Law-abiding Jews, went to Jerusalem every year for the Passover (v. 41). When Jesus was 12 (13 was considered the age of spiritual maturity), they went as usual to the Passover festival.

"After the Feast was over, while his parents were returning home, the boy Jesus stayed behind in Jerusalem, but they were unaware of it" (v. 43). (They must have had other children to take care of.) They simply assumed he was in the traveling party, which might have included a large number of friends, neighbors and other children.

"Thinking he was in their company, they traveled on for a day." But probably when he did not join the family at night, "they began looking for him among their relatives and friends. When they did not find him, they went back to Jerusalem to look for him" (vv. 44-45).

After a day traveling north, and one traveling south and a day of searching, "they found him in the temple courts, sitting among the teachers, listening to them and asking them

questions. Everyone who heard him was amazed at his understanding and his answers" (vv. 46-47). Later, people would not merely be amazed at Jesus—they would be angry. But at this point, Jesus was simply amazing. Even his questions showed an unusual depth of understanding for someone his age.

But when his parents finally found him, "they were astonished. His mother said to him, 'Son, why have you treated us like this? Your father and I have been anxiously searching for you'" (v. 48). Mary felt that Jesus had done something wrong. They had trusted him to join the group traveling back to Galilee, but he hadn't.

Perhaps it was an innocent mix-up. Jesus may have tried to find his parents, too, but eventually had to go back to a location where they could find him, and while waiting, he used his time well. We do not know, but Jesus thought they should have known to look for him in the temple. Where he slept, we do not know.

"Why were you searching for me?" he asked. "Didn't you know I had to be in my Father's house?" (v. 49). It was necessary, Jesus said, that he would be doing the work of God. Jesus was referring to his heavenly Father and his divine mission, "but they did not understand what he was saying to them" (v. 50). They knew their child was the Messiah, that he had a special mission, but they did not know the details of how he would do his work. There was a bit of mystery to this child—but Jesus knew what he had to do.

His time had not yet come, so "he went down to Nazareth with them and was obedient to them. But his mother treasured all these things in her heart. And Jesus grew in wisdom and stature, and in favor with God and men" (vv. 51-52).

Things to think about

- Joseph and Mary set a good example of obedience (vv. 22-24). Although the law they obeyed is obsolete, their attitude is still exemplary. Am I as dedicated to God as they were?
- How well do I respect the spiritual service of elderly saints?
- Have I experienced pain as well as salvation from Jesus? (v. 35)
- Do I have a sense of mission like Jesus did? (v. 49) What am I dedicated to?
- Do I grow in favor with God and with other people? (v. 52) Is it sometimes necessary to have less favor?

A NEW LOOK AT THE GOOD SAMARITAN

By Joseph Tkach

The Good Samaritan is one of Jesus' most popular parables. Preachers often use it to encourage people to be unselfish and to be proactive in serving others. But there is more to the story than that. Jesus was doing far more than putting hypocritical religious leaders in their place. Let's take a closer look.

> A man was going down from Jerusalem to Jericho, when he fell into the hands of robbers. They stripped him of his clothes, beat him and went away, leaving him half dead.
>
> A priest happened to be going down the same road, and when he saw the man, he passed by on the other side. So too, a Levite, when he came to the place and saw him, passed by on the other side.
>
> But a Samaritan, as he traveled, came where the man was; and when he saw him, he took pity on him. He went to him and bandaged his wounds, pouring on oil and wine. Then he put the man on his own donkey, took him to an inn and took care of him. The next day he took out two silver coins and gave them to the innkeeper. "Look after him," he said, "and when I return, I will reimburse you for any extra expense you may have."
>
> Which of these three do you think was a neighbor to the man who fell into the hands of robbers? (Luke 10:30-37)

The answer to Jesus' question was obvious. But Jesus was teaching far more than a straightforward lesson in social responsibility. Let's consider the context. Jesus was answering a lawyer who had asked, "What must I do to inherit eternal life?" (verse 25).

This man was a religious lawyer, priding himself in his understanding of all 613 points of the Torah. The religious leaders of Jesus' day were the inheritors of a system that had turned obedience to God into an obstacle course, so strewn with picky dos and don'ts that it left the average person on a permanent guilt trip.

This approach contradicted what Jesus taught, and confrontation became inevitable. The lawyers, along with the Pharisees, Sadducees, scribes and others in religious leadership, were constantly trying to discredit Jesus. There was a motive behind the lawyer's apparently innocent question.

So Jesus answered wisely, "Do what is written in the law. How do you read it?" (verse 26).

The lawyer knew the answer to that. "'Love the Lord your God with all your heart and with all your soul and with all your strength and with all your mind'; and, 'Love your neighbor as yourself'" (verse 27).

"You have answered correctly," Jesus replied. "Do this and you will live" (verse 28).

It was a good answer, as far as it went. But you know what lawyers are like. They are trained to look for some extenuating circumstance that might in some way limit the extent of the law. The lawyer knew that the command to "love your neighbor as yourself" was difficult, in fact, impossible to fulfill. So he thought he had found a loophole.

"And who is my neighbor?" he asked Jesus. That is when Jesus gave his famous parable.

Cast and location

Jesus set his story on the road from Jerusalem to Jericho, a distance of about 17 miles. Jerusalem was where the Temple was located, the center of the Levitical priesthood. The priests were the highest class of the Levites. They were supported by thousands of other Levites who served at lower levels, doing such tasks as keeping the altar fire going, lighting the incense, singing in the Temple chorus and playing musical instruments.

When they were not on duty, many of these priests and temple workers lived in Jericho, which had become a "bedroom community" of Jerusalem. They often traveled this road between Jerusalem and Jericho.

Travel in those days could be hazardous. One stretch of the Jericho road was known as the "Way of Blood," because so many people were robbed and killed there. This was where Jesus set the scene for his parable. People knew exactly where he was talking about.

In Jesus' story, the first to see the victim is a priest, but rather than get involved, he passes by on the other side of the road. He is followed by a Levite, a temple-worker. The Levite does the same—he passes by. Then along comes a Samaritan. A what? Jesus would have caused a stir with that. The Jews of that time did not often hear the words "good" and "Samaritan" used in the same sentence.

The Samaritans were a mix of Jew and gentile, and the Jews did not like them. They had names for Samaritans like "half breeds" and "heathen dogs," and considered them to be spiritually defiled. But in Jesus' story, it is this outcast who stops to help.

Not only does this Samaritan help, but he goes far beyond what most people do. He cleans the victim's wounds with oil and wine. Then he bandages them. People didn't carry first-aid kits back then. He likely would have had to tear up some of his own clothing to make a bandage. Next, he puts the injured man on his donkey and takes him to an inn. He takes two silver coins, a considerable amount in those days, and promises to reimburse the innkeeper for any further expense.

This is an exceptional level of assistance, especially as the victim is a total stranger and someone who is supposed to be a social enemy. But the Samaritan did not let that stand in the way.

With this deceptively simple little story, Jesus impales the lawyer on his own hook. He asks him, "Which of these three do you think was a neighbor to the man who fell into the hands of robbers?" (verse 36).

What can the expert in the law say, except, "The one who had mercy on him."

Then Jesus delivers the knockout blow. "Go and do likewise," he says (verse 37).

Remember, this "teacher of the law" was from a class of people who prided themselves on how carefully they obeyed God. For example, they would not even pronounce God's name, considering it too holy to utter. They would even take a ritual bath to ensure purity before writing God's name. Along with the Pharisees, they were fastidious about observing the law in every detail.

The lawyer had asked what he needed to do in order to inherit eternal life. Jesus' answer was, in effect, "You have to do the impossible."

How could anyone be expected to live up to the standard of the Samaritan in this story? If that is what God expects, even the meticulous lawyer was doomed. But Jesus had chosen his words carefully. He was showing that humans cannot meet the perfect requirements of the law. Even those who fully dedicate themselves to it fall short. Jesus is the only one to fulfill the law in its deepest intent. Jesus alone is the Good Samaritan.

The robbers correspond to sin and the forces of evil, the devil and his dominion. The man who was beaten and robbed is representative of all humanity, helpless, hopeless and left to die.

The priest and the Levite represent the laws and the sacrifices of the old covenant. They are ineffective. The Good Samaritan is the only one who can help. The wine and the oil correspond to the blood Jesus shed for us and the Holy Spirit who dwells in us. (A point that Jesus' original audience could not understand. But from our perspective after the resurrection, we can see new significance in the details.)

The inn could then represent the church, where God puts his people to be spiritually nurtured until he returns for them. Perhaps the innkeeper signifies the elders of the church.

Jesus used the lawyer's question to show how inadequate for salvation even the best human effort is, and how wonderful and sure is his work of redemption for humanity. Jesus, and only Jesus, can rescue us from the "Way of Blood." And he did it by way of blood.

PARABLE OF THE LOST SON

By Michael Morrison

The parable of the prodigal son (Luke 15:11-32) is perhaps better named the parable of the lost son, since it is designed to go with the parables of the lost sheep (verses 3-7) and lost coin (verses 8-10). Some have even called it the parable of the prodigal father, because of the father's extravagance. Even today, after centuries of teaching about God's grace, the father's willingness to forgive his runaway son is shockingly generous.

This is Jesus' longest parable: 22 verses. Let's go through the parable, noting its story, its organization and its lessons. NIV 2011 used throughout.

Historical background and observations

1. Return of the lost son — verses 11-24

A. Departure of the younger son — verses 11-16

"There was a man" — A standard introduction to a parable. "Who had two sons" — The first parable in this chapter had one of 100 getting lost, the second parable one in 10, this one has one out of two becoming lost. The sequence emphasizes the magnitude of the lost son. To lose half your sons would be a tragedy, and regaining half would likewise be a greater cause for rejoicing.

"The younger son" — There's no mention of a wife, so he would probably have been 18-20. His youth isn't emphasized, but younger sons may be more likely to be foolish and older sons more likely to look down on a brother. Figuratively, the older son could represent the Pharisees and the younger one the newly religious Jews Jesus was teaching (verse 1). In the early church, the older son may have been seen as corresponding to the Jews and the younger son to Gentiles.

"Give me my share of the estate" — Inheritances were normally given only when the father died. The son's demand (not a request) for an early distribution was unusual and frowned upon. Traditionally, firstborn sons were given twice as much as other sons, but we don't know if this was always done in Jesus' day. If so, the younger son would have received one third of the estate. The amount isn't stressed. Nor are we told how the property was divided. Such details are ignored because they aren't part of the point.

"Divided his property" — Early distribution of the estate normally meant that the father continued to receive the benefits of the estate as long as he lived. (Hence the father could kill the fatted calf without asking the older son who owned it.) The younger son didn't just receive surplus property; it was part of the father's source of income. (The word for property is bios, meaning "the resources which one has as a means of living" (J. Louw and E. Nida, *Greek-English Lexicon of the New Testament,* volume 1, page 560, 57.18.) If a son sold land, the new owner could not use it until the father died. Again, such details are glossed over because they are not part of the point. "Between them" — The older son also received his share.

"Not long after that" — His departure was probably not surprising. His desire for his inheritance indicated he wanted to strike out on his own rather than continue being part of the family. He was insulting the family as well as injuring it. "A distant country" — A Gentile country. Many Jews lived in Gentile areas. "Squandered his wealth in wild living" — Not only did he waste the money, he sinned in the process. However, his sins aren't specified. Luke doesn't emphasize the sinning as much as he does losing the money. This is consistent with Luke's interest in possessions and poverty. Perhaps the prodigal son was trying to make friends by spending money on them.

"Spent everything…began to be in need" — His poverty is emphasized, not any deficiency in character. Luke is emphasizing his lostness, not his guilt.

"To feed pigs" — He had an unclean occupation, abandoning religious scruples, but still the emphasis seems to be on his poverty (hunger, verse 16) rather than sin.

"He longed to fill his stomach with the pods" — As if he wasn't allowed to eat the carob-tree pods! He wished he could eat them, but he couldn't, because he could not digest them. A servant would have received some pay. Jesus is painting a hypothetical, not an actual story, to emphasize the son's desperate plight. "No one gave him anything" — He received no alms (one of Luke's interests). His former friends did not help him.

B. The son decides to return — verses 17-20

"When he came to his senses" — This pivotal verse changes the direction of the story. "When" (rather than "it so happened that") seems to imply that his sanity was inevitable. "Repentance" is not used. "My father's hired servants" — He contrasts himself, a hired servant of a Gentile, to his father's servants, who had plenty to eat. "Food to spare…starving to death" — Though the setting of the story is sin and repentance (verses 1-2), the story emphasizes financial destitution rather than moral corruption. "Starving" is another exaggeration. If he had been near starvation, he would not have had the strength to be able to travel back home.

"Set out and go" — Literally, "rising up, I will go." Commentators say this was a translation of an Aramaic idiom for go immediately. But "arise" may also hint at a rising in state of life.

"Sinned against heaven" — "Heaven" is a euphemism for God — used perhaps because the father represents God in the story. Specific sins aren't mentioned except in the accusations of the older brother (verse 30). "And against you" — He acknowledged his affront to the family — wasting the family's wealth.

"No longer worthy to be called your son" — This could be in a legal and a moral sense: He had no rights for further inheritance, and his behavior had not been up to family standards. He assumed that his relationship to his father was based on the work that he did. "Make me like one of your hired servants" — He was willing to earn his keep by serving the family (which would have meant serving his older brother, too). "Hired men" is *misthioi*, contract laborers, probably farmhands, not the *douloi,* household bondservants, mentioned in verse 22.

C. Reception by the father — verses 20-24

"While he was still a long way off, his father saw him" — Some commentators say this implies that the father was continually watching for the return of his son. This is conjectural; the text says nothing about watching, nor does it add a word like "when" to imply inevitability. It says: "The son being yet far off, his father saw him." Certainly, the father was extremely willing to seek reconciliation — seeing the son far away shows that (as do later verses), without any need to add the idea of watching.

"Compassion...ran" — These words emphasize the father's enthusiasm. In ancient societies, it was considered undignified for an older man to pull up his robes to run. His actions, representative of God's feelings for repentant sinners, show enthusiastic acceptance, love and joy. Kiss — Perhaps a sign of forgiveness (cf. 2 Samuel 14:33). The son didn't finish his speech, perhaps because he was cut short by his father.

"Best robe...ring" — Both robe and ring may allude to Joseph's promotion to authority (Genesis 41:42). Robes were given to honored guests; the ring was a signet ring, indicating authority. "Sandals" — Servants did not wear sandals; only family members did.

"Fattened calf" — Meat was eaten primarily on festivals, and calves would be fattened for such feasts, so perhaps the celebration here hints at a religious reconciliation. The celebration corresponds to the "rejoice" of the parables of the lost sheep and coin.

"This son of mine was dead" — In what way was he dead? Here are two possibilities: 1) The father heard about the famine, hadn't heard from his son in a long time, and thought he had died. 2) Perhaps he counted him metaphorically dead because he had become as a Gentile. Some Jews conducted funerals for children who married Gentiles. But the father doesn't seem to be the type to disown his son.

2. Conflict with the older son

A. The older son comes home — verses 25-27

So far, this parable has been parallel to the first two parables; the lost has been found and there is rejoicing. Now the older son is introduced for an additional lesson in the parable. In some ways this is two parables in one, both parts ending with the statement about dead and alive, lost and found. Both sons are lost — one who left home (like the sheep that was lost in v. 4) and one who was lost even while at home (like the coin in v. 8). Both the "sinners" and the Pharisees were separated from God — the first ones are visibly lost, the others still live at home — but both are welcomed when they turn to God.

The older son's arrival on the scene is odd; normally a servant would have been sent to get him at the start. But in the parable it is as if the older son found out about the party by accident. Some commentators say this implies the son was out of touch with his father, estranged in attitude or too addicted to work. This seems to read too many details into the story.

The older son is contrasted to the younger: The younger starts the story by leaving home, the older starts by returning. The younger then decides to go home, the older refuses to enter. The younger wants to be his father's servant, the older son resents being a servant. The younger son admits guilt; the older one insists on his own innocence.

The servant (*pais,* a child or servant) describes the younger son as "safe and sound," or in health; this is less dramatic than the father's comment about dead and alive. The servant is matter-of-fact; the father is elated.

B. Complaint of the older son — verses 28-30

The older son "became angry" — in contrast to his father's compassion — and he did not want to go in despite knowing his father's will. His father went out — in contrast to the older son's unwillingness to come in. The father went out, just as he had done for the younger son. "Pleaded with him" — The father eagerly desired for the older son to share his joy. Normally a son would simply do what his father said to do; here the older son is disobedient. The older son had inherited his father's estate, but not his attitude of mercy.

"Look!" — The older son starts abruptly, hinting of disrespect, frustration and impatience. "I've been slaving for you" — The verb is *douleun,* related to *doulos,* servant. His relationship to his father was based on work, not love.

"Never disobeyed" — until now.

"You never gave me even a young goat" — Yet a goat is of lesser value than a calf. But the father would have given a goat if the son had asked (verse 31). The son felt unappreciated and unrewarded; his complaint suggests that he had a long-smoldering resentment. He complained about the extra given to the younger — similar to the workers in the vineyard who complained about a days' wage being given to those who worked only one hour.

"This son of yours" — The older brother doesn't say "my brother"; it is as if he no longer claims him. "Squandered" — Literally, "devoured," an ironic word for a hungry man. "Your property" — This continues the emphasis on physical possessions. The younger son had wasted part of the family estate, failing in his duty to provide for his father. "With prostitutes" — Did the older son really know how his brother had spent the money? Perhaps the waste had begun before the son left home, or perhaps some reports had come back from the far country. Both are possible, but the story says nothing about it. This suggests that the older son was making an unsubstantiated accusation.

C. Response of the father — verses 31-32

"My son" — The usual word for "son" in this parable is *huios;* here it is *teknon,* "child," a term of affection. "Everything I have is yours" — The older son will get the entire inheritance. Some commentators speculate about the legal status of the property rights and whether the younger son could have inherited something, but the parable says nothing about it. Inheritance details are not the point; acceptance or reconciliation is. Older sons inherited twice as much as other sons because they had a responsibility to the family. The older son would have had a duty to take care of a brother who fell on hard times. But the older son was not willing to accept this responsibility; he simply wanted the property.

"We had to celebrate" — The word *edei* is used, meaning "it was necessary." Rejoicing about the return of a lost person isn't just an option; it is a necessity. "This brother of yours" — Not "my son," but "your brother." The father reminded the older son of his family responsibility. The implication is that it is necessary for *him* to rejoice.

What this parable teaches us about God

The context helps us understand the lessons of the parable. Verses 1-2 tell us that sinners and tax collectors were being taught by Jesus. Pharisees then criticized Jesus — not for teaching them, but for eating with them, which was a sign of social acceptance. The Pharisees tried hard to be righteous, and they were disturbed that Jesus accepted people who hadn't been trying hard. Perhaps they were worried that Jesus was making it too easy on people, and his acceptance might encourage others to be lazy.

Jesus then gave the parables of the lost sheep and the lost coin, both illustrating the point that God rejoices about each sinner who repents. "There will be more rejoicing in heaven over one sinner who repents than over ninety-nine righteous persons who do not need to repent" (verse 7). There's no such thing as a person who has no need for repentance, but the Pharisees weren't yet aware of that. There would be rejoicing for them, too, if they would accept it.

The parable of the lost son continues the theme of rejoicing and adds to it. The first half of the parable illustrates rejoicing over a sinner who returned; the second half more directly addresses the situation Jesus faced: criticism about his willingness to be with sinners. Jesus, by telling the parable the way he did, chides those who do not rejoice about the sinners' interest in being taught (figuratively, returning to God).

In the first two parables, the lost were found by searching. But the younger son was found by waiting. The spiritually lost were already coming to Jesus; he didn't need to seek them out. They had been spiritually dead and were now showing interest — they wanted to be taught by Jesus. Jesus received them and ate with them. His reception would have encouraged them to keep the laws they already knew and to continue to listen to him for more instruction in God's way.

But the parable is not just about Jesus in the first century; it is a timeless message about God the Father. He rejoices over (cf. the celebration) and honors (cf. the robe, ring and sandals) every sinner who repents. He doesn't wait for a full and formal apology; he perceives the attitude and comes toward us. This theme of joyful acceptance, similar to that of the first two parables of this chapter, dominates the first part of this parable. This is the lesson illustrated by the father: He is always ready to welcome a returning child.

The parable shows that sinners can confess and return to God. Since God is gracious, sinners can return to him with confidence that he will warmly welcome them. But in the parable, financial destitution is more prominent than moral fault. Unlike the first two parables, the word *repent* is not used; only superficial reasons are given for the son's return. As Jesus spoke to the Pharisees, encouraging sinners to return was not the main issue; the main issue was what to do about sinners who were already willing to return.

Most importantly, the parable shows that God's people should rejoice at a) the willingness of sinners to turn to God and b) the willingness of God to receive them. This is the lesson of the second half of the parable, illustrated by the father's correction of his older son. This theme most directly addresses the setting of the parable, the Pharisees' criticism of Jesus' reception of sinners. The parables of the lost sheep and lost coin and the first half of the parable of the lost son are preparatory to this main point.

These themes are timeless. God rejoices over each person who repents, and so should we. We need not kill a calf for repentant persons (Jesus didn't; the parable illustrates the attitude of rejoicing, not the specific actions we should take). We need to accept repentant sinners to social fellowship (cf. eating with them, verse 2) and religious instruction (cf. allowing them to listen, verse 1). This particular parable does not say we should *seek* outcasts (that is shown better by the parables of lost sheep and lost coin), but that we should be happy when they come to us to be taught.

In effect, Jesus' story shows that it is ungodly to refuse to rejoice about repentance. The Pharisees, by insisting on a too-strict standard of righteousness, were being unrighteous. They, too, needed to repent.

Epilogue

The parable ends without revealing what the older son did. Would the hard-hearted son change his mind and rejoice about his brother's return? For the situation in Jesus' day, either response was still possible — it was up to the Pharisees. Would they rejoice with Jesus? History shows that some did and some did not.

Similarly, the parable does not reveal what the younger son did. Did he abuse his second chance? That also reflects the situation Jesus was in. Would the tax collectors and sinners continue in their repentance? It was not yet known. Nevertheless, it is appropriate — no, necessary — to rejoice at their first change of heart, rather than waiting for some probationary period.

THE PRODIGAL GOD

One of Jesus' best-loved parables reveals far more
about God's love than we might at first think.

By D. Taylor

Most Christians are familiar with Jesus' parable of the prodigal son. Some refer to it as the parable of the lost son. It's found in Luke 15 in the New Testament. This wonderful story has been read by children and adults alike countless times. It never ceases to inspire us—even tug on our heartstrings as the father in the story lovingly accepts his errant son back.

A quick look at this parable reveals the example of a hasty young man who wastes his inheritance with lavish living while living in a foreign land (Luke 15:13). Matters are made worse when a severe famine grips his new homeland (verse 14). Desperate, he hires himself out to a man who lets him feed his pigs (verse 15). Hungry and humiliated, he decides to go home to his father, who receives him with open arms (verses 17-24).

But there is more to the story than this—much more. Perhaps that's why Norval Geldenhuys in *The New International Commentary on the New Testament* calls this story the "'Gospel within the Gospel." To gain an enriched appreciation and understanding of this best-loved parable, let's take a closer look at the Gospel of Luke, chapter 15. Let's allow the story to take us back to the time when Jesus spoke what William Barclay in *The Daily Study Bible Series* calls "'The greatest short story in the world."

Another confrontation

It was another testy meeting between Jesus and the religious leaders of Judea, the Pharisees. In their midst were "sinners" and tax collectors who had gathered to hear what Jesus had to say. Noting the makeup of the crowd that was gathering, the Pharisees and religious teachers began muttering about the kind of company Jesus was keeping, saying, "This man welcomes sinners and eats with them" (Luke 15:1-2).

This wasn't the first time they had criticized Jesus and his disciples for associating with those the Pharisees considered to be off-limits. Sometime earlier, during a banquet given for Jesus by a tax collector named Levi, a group of Pharisees questioned Jesus' disciples. The Pharisees asked, "Why do you eat and drink with tax collectors and "sinners'?" Jesus responded by saying: "It is not the healthy who need a doctor, but the sick. I have not come to call the righteous, but sinners to repentance" (Luke 5:29-31).

Hearing the same criticism later, pictured in Luke 15, Jesus again answered the Pharisees' reproach. This time he chose to elaborate. He began by telling two parables: the first focusing on a sheep recovered after straying from a flock of 100, the second on one of 10 coins that had been lost and later found (Luke 15:3-10). Jesus explained each story's significance: the great joy that takes place in heaven when a person involved in sin repents of his or her lost ways and is restored to a right relationship with God (verses 7, 10).

The third parable was the culmination of his response. For many readers, this third parable focuses on the prodigal son. Perhaps that is the person they can identify with the most. And indeed, in this story Jesus does illustrate a young man who had lived a profligate, wasteful life-style and who comes to his senses.

But the word *prodigal* can mean several things—negative or positive: recklessly extravagant, characterized by wasteful expenditure, lavish, yielding abundantly, luxuriant or profuse *(Webster's Ninth New Collegiate Dictionary)*. The son was extravagant in a negative way, but the father was extravagant in a positive sense.

Christ's parable also gives us a wonderful glimpse of God the Father's tender, compassionate, even lavish love, as exemplified in the role of the father in the parable, for those who turn from their sins. As we examine this father's actions, we can come to see how differently God views things than we do. "'For my thoughts are not your thoughts, neither are your ways my ways,' declares the Lord. 'As the heavens are higher than the earth, so are my ways higher than your ways and my thoughts than your thoughts" (Isaiah 55:8-9).

Freedom of choice

The father of the story complied without any complaint with his son's headstrong wish to receive his inheritance for immediate use (Luke 15:12)— a request that was rarely granted in the Jewish society of Jesus' day. The apparent ease with which the younger son's desire was granted seems to suggest that the father gave his children great latitude in making choices.

Likewise, we too are constantly confronted with choices. It is up to each of us to choose our way in life. This is a privilege our wise, loving Father allows us, on the one hand, even while encouraging us to follow his way on the other. Just as we learn through many of our self-willed choices, the son in the story also came to understand that the way he had chosen did not bring him the happiness he sought (verse 17).

The son rehearsed what he would say to his father when he returned. He had sinned against God and his father, and he was no longer worthy to be his son. He wanted to be made just as one of his father's hired servants (verses 18-19). And so he returned home.

The father saw his son while he was still some distance away, and was moved with compassion (verse 20). Some commentaries suggest that the father had been watching and waiting for his son's return. *The Expositor's Bible Commentary* suggests that the "father's 'compassion' assumes some knowledge of the son's pitiable condition, perhaps from reports" (vol. 8, page 984). This reminds us of what David records about God in Psalm 139:1-16.

Whatever the case, the elderly father did something uncharacteristic for the culture of the day: he ran to meet his son. Then he embraced and kissed him fervently, or many times, as the Greek verb also indicates.

As the son began to repeat the speech he had rehearsed, his father interrupted (Luke 15:21-22). Instead of allowing his son to offer his services as a hired servant—one who, as William Barclay notes, could be dismissed at a day's notice—the father did something remarkable. He called for the "best robe" (a sign of position), a ring for his finger (a sign of authority) and shoes (reserved only for freemen) (verse 22).

The father ordered the fattened calf to be killed and a party to be organized to welcome his son home. "For this son of mine was dead and is alive again; he was lost and is found" (verses 23-24). The father welcomed his son back with great emotion and joy, and restored his son to a position of honor, not to that of a hired servant. It's remarkable that our heavenly Father does the same with us.

When we sin, we separate ourselves from God (Isaiah 59:2). We leave the company of God's family for a world influenced by Satan. Sin consumes us and destroys us—it leads to death (Romans 6:23). But when we repent, our sins are forgiven and we are restored to a right relationship with God —a restoration so complete, it is as if we never left the family (Acts 3:19; Isaiah 43:25).

The older son, upon learning of his brother's return, was angry with his father. After all, hadn't he remained loyal, slaving away for his father? He had never received even as much as a roasted goat in his honor. And "this son of yours" (a not-so-subtle sense of superiority here), who had wasted his inheritance on prostitutes comes home and gets a fatted calf!

How God views repentance

The older son reveals a lot about human nature. When we read the story, most of us have a hard time disputing his reasoning. What's fair about a wasteful son returning home to a banquet while the loyal son who did everything that was asked of him received no such honor?

Jesus reminds us through the father's response that God's ways are not ours (Isaiah 55:8). The father gently acknowledged to his older son that he

355

was aware that he had always been with him, and that everything the father had was his older son's. But they had to celebrate the return of "this brother of yours" (a reminder of the older son's relationship with his brother). It was not just necessary, "it was the right thing. The father had to do it. Joy was the only proper reaction in such a situation" *(The Tyndale New Testament Commentaries,* vol. 3, page 268).

When we repent, God restores us to the full honors due a child of God, regardless of our sins (Acts 3:19: 1 John 2:1-2). This is hard for human beings to grasp. But the lavish mercy and forgiveness of God, made possible by the perfect, willing sacrifice of Jesus Christ, are truly amazing. Indeed, one could say they are *prodigal.* Because if any point stands out in this parable, it is how lavish God is in his forgiveness and mercy.

Throughout this parable, Jesus illustrated to the "sinners" (speaking to each of us) that, just as for the wayward son, the way to repentance was wide open for them. To the Pharisees and religious teachers (also speaking to each of us), Christ showed that the people they looked down on so much, the "sinners" and tax collectors, were part of their family, too, and a slavish obedience to the law brings no spiritual reward in itself (Isaiah 1:11; Ephesians 2:8-9). It is God, by his grace and mercy, who rewards us (Romans 9:14-18).

The father in the story reveals the humanly incomprehensible love that God our Father has for each of us, and the earnest desire he has to forgive us and have a relationship with us. Far from being the story of the prodigal son, Luke 15 is more aptly the story of the prodigal God—one whose lavish, extravagant, luxuriant love for us can only amaze us on the one hand and give us great solace and comfort on the other.

Sources

Barclay, William. *The Daily Study Bible Series,* rev. ed. *The Gospel of Luke.* Philadelphia: Westminster, 1975, pages 203-206.

Gaebelein, Frank E., et al., eds. *The Expositor's Bible Commentary,* vol. 8. Grand Rapids: Zondervan, 1984, pages 982-985.

Geldenhuys, Norval. *The New International Commentary on the New Testament: Commentary on the Gospel of Luke.* Grand Rapids: Eerdmans, 1988, pages 405-413.

Morris, Leon. *The Tyndale New Testament Commentaries,* rev. ed.. *Luke: An Introduction and Commentary.* Grand Rapids: Eerdmans,1989, pages 262-268.

LAZARUS AND THE RICH MAN

By J. Michael Feazell

Let's look at a passage that is often interpreted as proving that all who die without having come to faith are automatically damned. It is the story of Lazarus and the Rich Man, in which Abraham tells the rich man there is a great gulf fixed that keeps those in Hades separate from those who are with Abraham. It is found in Luke 16:19-31. Before the story begins, however, we can back up a few verses to get an idea of whom Jesus was talking to when he told this story and what was the subject that prompted him to tell it.

In verse 14, we read this: "The Pharisees, who were lovers of money, heard all this, and they ridiculed him" (New Revised Standard Version throughout). Jesus was talking to a group of Pharisees, and what Luke wants his readers to know about the Pharisees in connection with this passage is that the Pharisees were lovers of money. This is the context of the story. A group of Pharisees who were lovers of money were ridiculing Jesus because of what he was saying.

We have to go back to chapter 15, verse 1, to get the whole episode. Here we read: "Now all the tax collectors and sinners were coming near to listen to him. And the Pharisees and the scribes were grumbling and saying, 'This fellow welcomes sinners and eats with them.' So he told them this parable…"

Then Jesus proceeds to tell them three parables in a row: The Shepherd Who Rejoices Over Finding His Lost Sheep, The Woman Who Rejoices Over Finding Her Lost Coin, and The Father Who Rejoices Over Finding His Lost Son. Jesus tells these three parables specifically in response to the Pharisees and scribes who were disgruntled over the fact that he welcomes sinners and eats with them. These parables push God's grace toward sinners right up the Pharisees' and scribes' disgruntled noses.

Jesus wants them to know that "there is more joy in heaven over one sinner who repents than over ninety-nine righteous persons who need no repentance" (verse 7). The pointed remark is not lost on the Pharisees and scribes; they consider themselves righteous and not in need of repentance. Jesus (knowing they are not really righteous) is telling them that heaven is not singing their song.

Money vs. God

If the first two parables irritate the Pharisees and scribes, the third one, The Father Who Rejoices Over Finding His Lost Son (commonly known as the Prodigal Son) takes the cake. Here is a father who gives unbridled love and unconditional forgiveness to a son who dishonored him, wasted half his assets and dragged the family name through the mud. It was a scandalous story that trampled on any sense of common decency, dignity and honor. When Jesus finishes telling it, he turns to his disciples and addresses them with yet another story (Luke 16:1). But the Pharisees are still listening (verse 14).

The moral of this story, Jesus says, is that you cannot serve both money and God; you will find yourself devoted either to the one or to the other, not both (verse 13). If you love money, you will not love God. The Pharisees heard everything, but learned nothing. Instead of repenting so that there might be joy in heaven, they ridiculed Jesus. His words were utter foolishness to them, because they were lovers of money (verse 14).

Responding to their ridicule, Jesus says, "You are those who justify yourselves in the sight of others; but God knows your hearts; for what is prized by human beings is an abomination in the sight of God" (verse 15). He goes on to point out that the Law and the Prophets stand as witnesses that the kingdom of God has arrived and that everyone is urgently piling into it (verses 16-17). His implied message: "Because you prize the things of men, not the things of God, you are rejecting God's urgent summons to enter his kingdom, which can be done only through me."

The next statement (verse 18), which cites divorce and adultery, might at first appear to be completely out of context. More likely, it serves as a further declaration that the Law and the Prophets are in fact part and parcel with the kingdom of God, and that in rejecting the Messiah the Jewish religious leaders have "divorced" the Law and the Prophets, which witness to him, from the kingdom of God, and in so doing have rejected God (likened to adultery throughout the Old Testament; compare Jeremiah 3:6, etc.). Now, as the *coupe de grace* he tells the story of Lazarus and the Rich Man.

A tale of unbelief

There are three characters in the story, the rich man (representing the Pharisees who love money), the miserable beggar Lazarus (representing a class of people despised by the Pharisees), and Abraham (whose bosom or lap was a Jewish figure of comfort and peace in the afterlife).

And the point Jesus uses the story to make is the same point he has been making all along: You consider yourselves the high and mighty blessed of God, but the truth is you love money and hate God—that is why you are so rankled that I spend my time in fellowship with unvarnished sinners, this is why you despise your fellow human beings and will not humble yourselves and believe in me and find true riches.

But back to the story. The beggar dies. But then, without missing a beat, Jesus again pokes the Pharisees in the eye by saying, "... and was carried away by the angels to be with Abraham" (verse 22). This is, as usual with Jesus' stories, exactly the opposite of what the Pharisees expected would happen to a man like Lazarus. Such people were poor and diseased beggars because they were under God's curse, they assumed, and therefore it is only natural that such people go to be tormented in Hades when they die.

"Not so," says Jesus. "Your worldview is upside down. You know nothing of my Father's kingdom. Not only are you wrong about how my Father feels about the beggar, but you are wrong about how my Father feels about you." Jesus completes the turnabout by telling them that the rich man also died and was buried, but he, not the beggar, is the one who finds himself being tormented in Hades. And Jesus draws it out. From his torments in Hades, the rich man looked up and saw Abraham far off with none other than Lazarus by his side. He cries out, "Father Abraham, have mercy on me, and send Lazarus to dip the tip of his finger in water and cool my tongue; for I am in agony in these flames" (verses 23-24).

But Abraham tells him the way things stand. "All your life you loved riches and had no time for the likes of Lazarus. But I do have time for the likes of Lazarus, and now he is with me, and you have nothing." And then comes the out-of-context proof text: "Besides all this, between you and us a great chasm has been fixed, so that those who might want to pass from here to you cannot do so, and no one can cross from there to us" (Luke 16:26).

Have you ever wondered why anybody could possibly want to pass from "here to you?" It is obvious why someone might want to cross from "there to us," but from "here to you" makes no sense. Or does it? Abraham began his words to Lazarus by addressing him as "child," then points out to him that not even those who might want to get to him are able to because of the great chasm.

The Bridge across the chasm

There is one who crosses chasms for the sake of sinners. "For God so loved the world that he gave his only Son, so that everyone who believes in him may not perish but may have eternal life" (John 3:16). God gave his Son for sinners, not just for sinners like Lazarus, but for sinners like the rich man, too. But the rich man doesn't want the Son of God. The rich man wants what he always wanted—his own comfort at the expense of others, which is exactly the opposite of what the Son of God wants.

Jesus' condemnation of the unbelief of the Pharisees in this story concludes with the rich man arguing that if someone would warn his brothers, they would not come into the place where he was. "They have Moses and the Prophets; they should listen to them," Abraham tells him. (Remember Jesus' statements in verses 16-17? The Law and Prophets are nothing other than a testimony to him. See John 5:45-47 and Luke 24:44-47.)

"No, Father Abraham, but if someone goes to them from the dead, they will repent" (Luke 16:30). "He said to him, 'If they do not listen to Moses and the prophets, neither will they be convinced even if someone rises from the dead'" (verse 31). And they didn't. The Pharisees conspired with the scribes and the chief priests to have Jesus crucified, conspired to have soldiers lie about his resurrection (Matthew 27:62-66), and proceeded to persecute and kill those who became believers.

There is a bridge across the chasm, the bridge across all chasms. The bridge is Jesus. But the rich man (the Jewish religious leaders who constantly oppose Jesus) is not interested in putting his faith in Jesus. Permit me to paraphrase Abraham's reply to the rich man:

"Look, friend, you refuse to come to Christ, so there is no place left for you but right where you are. You won't even admit that you need forgiveness. You still want exactly what you always wanted—everybody else zipping around waiting on you hand and foot. You can't get over here because you won't go anyplace where you're no better than old Laz the bum. We can't get where you are to help you because you are precisely nowhere. You made your own chasm to separate yourself from who you are in Christ because you won't come to him to have life.

"You still think like you always thought—that you are something special and Laz here is a nobody, the dirt under your sandals. And now you're still so convinced you've got it all together that you can't even see that you've been the nobody all along and Laz the loser is the one who's "in like Flint" with me. Well, pal, you've still got just what you've always had—nothing, nothing that matters, anyway.

"What's that? Now you want Laz to run some errands to warn others like you? Are you kidding? They won't listen. They've got Moses and the Prophets who told them Messiah would come. If they won't listen to them, you think they're going to listen to Laz? Forget about it. What's that? If someone comes back from the dead they'll listen to him? Oh really? Well, guess what? That's just what Jesus did, came back from the dead, and yet there you are, over there in Nowhereland because you won't put your trust in him."

Even if you don't like my interpretation of this passage, you still have to admit one thing: it is bad business to base a doctrine on one verse alone, and especially on one in a story designed to make a different point altogether. This story is primarily about the refusal of the Jewish leaders to believe in Jesus and the willingness of others to do so, and secondarily about the reversal of common assumptions about riches being a sign of God's favor.

It is not there to paint us a portrait of heaven and hell. It is a parable of judgment against the unbelieving Israelite leadership and the unkind rich, using common Jewish imagery of the afterlife (Hades and "being with Abraham") as a literary backdrop to make the point. In other words, Jesus was not commenting on the validity of Jewish imagery of the afterlife; he was simply using that imagery as scenery for his story.

Jesus was not in the business of satisfying our itching curiosities about what heaven and hell must be like. He was in the business of filling us in on God's secrets (Romans 16:25;Ephesians 1:9, etc.), the mystery of the ages (Ephesians 3:4-5)—that in him, Christ, God has always been reconciling the world to himself (2 Corinthians 5:19). Our preoccupation with otherworldly geographical trivia leads us away from the very point missed by the rich man in the story: Believe in the One who came back from the dead.

LAZARUS AND THE RICH MAN

By Paul Kroll

Jesus told the story of Lazarus the beggar and the rich man to illustrate a point about having an authentic relationship with God. Some believe Jesus meant the parable as a satire of the Pharisees' belief that they were in a privileged position with God. In that context, the parable would be a statement about their love of privilege and wealth.

Luke's account implies the Pharisees loved the rich and riches, even though Pharisees were more likely to be of the tradesman class. When Jesus told his listeners that they could not serve both God and Mammon (Luke 16:13-14), the Pharisees scoffed. Luke says: "The Pharisees, who loved money, heard all this and were sneering at Jesus" (verse 14).

Luke's Gospel often portrays the rich in an uncomplimentary way and the poor as failing to find justice. The parable of Lazarus and the Rich Man is, in one sense, a commentary on justice rather than the nature of the afterlife. The story clearly implies that God's people do not necessarily have it easy in this life nor do they always get justice in this life.

The symbolism used in the story, such as the great gulf between the rich man and "Abraham's bosom," deals with the question of who are the true people of God and who aren't. The issue being that the unrepentant wicked will be lost and separated from God (by a "great chasm") while the righteous will enjoy a close relationship with God. It's not that there is a physical chasm, but in the parable, the physical separation represents the emotional breach in relationship that the rich man was choosing to be in.

"Abraham's bosom" was a metaphor used by Jews who lived in the time of Jesus to stand for the kingdom of God, the home of the people of God. The wicked and spiritually ignorant would be consigned to the place of torment and separation from God. Naturally, the Pharisees thought that Pharisees would be in "Abraham's bosom" and other people would be among the lost. We can surmise that Jesus told the story to shock the Pharisees into rethinking their view about their relationship with God (see verse 15).

The details of the story include metaphors, and these are not to be taken literally. Lazarus would not be literally sitting in "Abraham's bosom," as the King James translates the phrase. The rich man would not be talking if he was in the throes of an excruciating agony while burning in a fire and suffocating in the smoke. So we shouldn't take the details of the parable, such as bosom, chasm and fire, in a literal sense.

Let's now see what the story says. The rich man, after being raised from the dead, realizes the predicament he is in. (He is in hell and in torment.) Basically, as he did in his life, he considers only himself and his family, and not the poor. He wants his brothers saved from a similar fate to his own, but he seems unconcerned about anyone else.

The rich man also retains the same attitude toward Lazarus that he did in life. He wants Lazarus to be sent as a slave to bring the message to his brothers. The story also implies that the rich man thinks he has been unfairly treated. If only someone had given him the right information, he would not have found himself in this terrible predicament. Someone like the dead Lazarus springing to life in the presence of his brothers, he feels, would be dramatic enough to make the case to save his siblings.

But Abraham points to the Holy Scriptures of the Jewish people – to Moses and the prophets. If the rich man had listened to the admonitions in Scripture about loving his fellow human beings, he would not be in a situation of torment and alienated from God. The story concludes with Abraham pointing out that a miraculous event, such as a dead person being made alive, will not bring the necessary conviction. What is important is our internal conviction, desire and action to love God, which always translates into love for other human beings.

Originally, the story was leveled at the rich of Jesus' day (or those who thought riches and righteousness always went together), at those who were more concerned with money rather than showing mercy toward the poor. Good stewardship includes helping people who are less fortunate. This is an important issue to Luke, and one he comes back to on a regular basis. (See, for example, the following verses: Luke 12:13-34; 14:1-14; 16:1-15; 18:18-30.)

The story of Lazarus and the rich man was also a dramatic warning to the Jewish religious establishment. They would see Abraham, Isaac, Jacob, the prophets and people from all over the world in the kingdom of God, but they would be thrown out (Luke 13:28-30). Even this implies that people are not "thrown out" unless they are "in" to begin with. No doubt, Luke's Christian readers would have recognized in the Lazarus character a reference to Jesus as the one who had been rejected even though he had risen from the dead. As we know, the Jewish leaders of Jesus' day did not heed their Scriptures and refused to see Jesus as the one to whom the Scriptures pointed (John 5:39-47).

What can the parable tell us as Christians? For one thing, it shows us that God's people are not necessarily vindicated in this life nor do they always receive justice in the here and now. Lazarus continued to suffer till his dying day. The rich man was rich until his death. Jesus' gospel of liberty is about spiritual liberty and a relationship of love and faith with God now and immortality in the kingdom.

In the story, the situations of the beggar and the rich man are not reversed until the resurrection. Of course, the story does not tell us that Lazarus was righteous in human life or that the rich man was evil. The basis of Lazarus being in the kingdom is his relationship with God. Lazarus is pictured as a true child of Abraham, who is the "father of the faithful" in Scripture. This implies that the rich man had kept himself out because of his own faithlessness, which caused him to have a loveless relationship with his fellow human beings. The lesson from the parable is that in the end Christians win the victory through Christ. In the resurrection they enjoy immortality and an eternal relationship of love with God.

THE COMMA OF LUKE 23:43

Did Jesus Christ tell the thief on the cross that they would be together in Paradise that very day, or did he say on that day, that they would be together in Paradise? It has been argued that the Greek text is ambiguous on this point, and that the position of the comma (before or after the word "today") determines the sense of Christ's statement.

Of course, no one will doubt that commas were introduced into the manuscripts centuries after the authors of the New Testament books had died and that such commas are therefore not authoritative. And there is the question of context. No one can dispute the fact that Jesus and the criminal were dying on the cross, and that their death would be followed by a burial and, in Jesus' case, by a resurrection from the dead three days later.

It has been argued that, since the context does not allow the conclusion that anyone entered Paradise on that day, and since the position of the comma lacks authority, the punctuation "Today you shall be with me in paradise" would leave the reader with a discrepancy between what had been promised and what actually happened. On the other hand, the alternative punctuation ("Truly I say to you today, you will be with me in Paradise") has been endorsed as free from such problems since it is not stated when they would be in Paradise.

The presupposition behind the two possibilities is in the claim that the Greek text is ambiguous without the comma. Thus, one is obligated to go deeper into the matter to ascertain if that presupposition is legitimate.

Is the Greek text ambiguous?

The first point to note is that Jesus was communicating with the thief *verbally*. In any language, people converse without commas, semicolons, question marks or exclamation marks. In fact, writers employ such devices only because they believe that the spoken message is clearer and want to approximate it. It is not true, therefore, that what Jesus *said* was ambiguous. The introduction of the commas into the manuscripts (centuries later) is irrelevant.

One may be tempted to object by saying that it is the position of the *written* comma that reveals what Christ really said. This is precisely what is not true of the passage in question. The author of the Gospel was not present at the crucifixion to hear Christ's comment personally. Christ's comment was recorded from the *oral* tradition of the disciples. This leads us to the second point: that the oral tradition had preserved this comment in a particular form, with the *spoken* emphasis already built into it.

Commas have no syntactical value in New Testament Greek. If commas are later introduced by an editor, they would serve only to make the text easier to read — not to clarify the meaning. Commas, in any edition of the Greek New Testament, are intended only as a help to the reader, not as a means of safeguarding the correct understanding of a passage.

In view of the above details, the presupposition that the text of Luke 23:43 is ambiguous without the comma is not legitimate.

The self-explanatory verse

Luke 23:43 is self-explanatory, first, because of its context, and second, because of its syntactical structure.

First, the context includes the continuous tense *elege* (was saying) with reference to the comment of each thief. Neither simply "said" (made a one-time statement of) what he had in mind. The first man (v. 39) was engaging in continuous derision, while the other was approaching Christ (not once, but over a period of time) in sincere supplication (v. 42). The latter's plea was not a fleeting thought that had crossed his mind. It was a sincere and persistent request, obviously requiring all the energy he could muster in the circumstances.

One criminal's attitude and comments produced blasphemy, culminating in the thought "If you are the Christ, save yourself and us," while the other's produced a rebuke of the first man's wrong attitude and a penitent submission summed up in the thought, "Lord, remember me when you come into your kingdom."

The scene is dramatic, to say the least. It is not easy for a dying man to believe that he can be saved by the helpless individual being crucified next to him. The depth of his conviction becomes more real to us when we bring to mind that others had failed to believe in Jesus, even while he was energetically performing miracles in their midst! The thief's repentant request shows that he had already accepted Jesus Christ as the Messiah, even in a crucified state.

Second, the malefactor did not say, "when you come *into* your kingdom." He said, "when you come *in* (Greek *en*) your kingdom." On the surface, it appears to be a minor difference, but the meaning of this statement is "when you come *with* glory and power" — which he will do when he returns. The correct reading was missed by the King James translators, but the revisers noted it (see RSV — "when you come in your kingly power").

The Latin Vulgate rendering, "in regnum tuum" (to your kingdom) and the King James, "into thy kingdom," give the impression that the reference is to Christ's return to heaven after the resurrection — hence the common misunderstanding. No such meaning is entailed in the Greek text. The reading of the Latin Vulgate and that of the King James Version exceed the limits of the Greek text on this point. The malefactor's request was that he might be remembered, not on that day, but at the time when Christ would return in the power and glory of his kingdom.

Christ's reply

Christ's reply begins with the word "amen" (verily). Whenever this construction is chosen in the New Testament, it indicates that something emphatic is to follow.

For example, in Matthew 5:18, Christ said: "Amen I say unto you, Till heaven and earth pass, one jot or one tittle shall in no way pass from the law, till all be fulfilled." This construction enables Jesus to move to the diametrically opposite position. His audience had thought that he was doing away with the law. According to their thought, Christ's new statement would be false. For that reason, he began with the assuring tone of "amen" (verily). Christ's intent was to surprise his audience — just as we might do today by saying something like, "You may find this difficult to believe, but it is true, nevertheless."

Thus the word "amen" (verily) at the beginning of the first phrase (Verily I say unto you) announces that a surprising truth is about to be revealed, while the word "today," at the start of the next phrase (today you will be...), is the unexpected, complementary emphasis — the truth Christ had promised. In effect, Christ was saying, "It is not at all a case of my *remembering* you or that you need to wait for some *future* time! You will be *with me,* as of *today.*"

The reading "Verily I say unto you today" not only contains a redundancy ("I say" is in the *present tense already* — making "today" redundant), it destroys the natural force of these words.

The question of Paradise

Did Christ and the thief go to Paradise on that day? In order to answer the question, we need to be reminded that some Jews believed in the resurrection of the dead (Acts 23:6, 8). If a Pharisee were asked how the dead are raised (the very question that arose later in Corinth, cf. 1 Cor. 15:35), he would have said that, when righteous people die, they go to a special place where they await their resurrection. This place is called by various names. One name is "Paradise." Another is "the Bosom of Abraham."

Jewish tradition acknowledged all the elements used in Christ's parable. The poor man was carried by the angels to the Bosom of Abraham (cf. Luke 16:22 and *Ketubot* 104a). The Bosom of Abraham is mentioned in the writings of the intertestamental period (4 Maccabees 13:17) and in *Qiddusin* 72b. Most important, Abraham is "designated as he who receives…the penitent into Paradise" (Alfred Edersheim, *Life and Times of Jesus the Messiah,* II, p. 280; see also *'Erubin* 19a).

In Christ's parable of Lazarus and the rich man, it was Lazarus who found himself in the special place (the Bosom of Abraham). To say that a dead person was in that place was the same as saying that he was righteous, because only the righteous went to Paradise to wait with Abraham.

Of course, there is nothing in the parable of Lazarus and the rich man to indicate more than the fact that Jesus was using the language of the Jews to convey a thought to them — that, contrary to their expectations, it was the poor man that was righteous. One does not necessarily subscribe to a belief simply by using the language of the day. Otherwise we would not be able to make even the most common references — for example, to the days of the week (Sun-day, Moon-day, Mars-day, etc.). Similarly, the terms "lunatic," "Aphrodisiac," "enthusiast," etc., all contain claims educated people do not subscribe to; even so, they are freely used by all. Jesus also made use of the language of his day.

One should also keep in mind that this use of "Paradise" does not define all its appearances in the Bible. The same term is used for the Garden of Eden (Gen. 2:15 and 3:23, LXX), for the plains of Jordan (Gen. 13:10, LXX), for the third heaven (2 Cor. 12:2-4), and for God's kingdom (Rev. 2:7).

In the case of the thief on the cross, Jesus recognized the man's repentant attitude and his firm conviction that Jesus, although dying on the cross, was the prophesied Messiah. He heard the malefactor's plea for remembrance at the time when he, even as a companion in death, would return in power and glory as a King, and told the man that his request was *as good as done.* Obviously, the malefactor believed that he *could* be resurrected if Christ would only remember him. Therefore, Christ assured him of the surprising truth that, even on that very day, he would be counted among the righteous in Paradise, awaiting the resurrection with them.

Did Christ and the malefactor, then, go to Paradise on that day? We must say that, in light of the popular notion and the context explained above, they clearly did, even though they literally were in the grave. The language is picturesque. It is beautiful. Above all, it conveys the best possible news that the repentant criminal could have hoped to hear.

EXPLORE THE GOSPEL OF JOHN: "THAT THEY MIGHT HAVE LIFE"

By Jim Herst

Vital lessons from the Gospel of John

New Christians are often advised to begin their Bible reading with the Gospel according to John. Why? Because this book, more than any other, comprehensively explains Jesus' identity as the Son of God who came to earth in order to save the world from sin.

This truth is encapsulated in the most famous verse in the New Testament: "For God so loved the world that he gave his only Son, so that everyone who believes in him may not perish but have eternal life" (John 3:16).

John tells us that because Jesus is "God in the flesh" (fully divine yet fully human) he is able to reveal God to us clearly and accurately. So if we want to know what God is like, we only have to look at the life of Jesus of Nazareth who was, in the words of the apostle Paul, "the image of the invisible God.... For in him all the fullness of God was pleased to dwell" (Colossians 1: 15, 19).

To appreciate the true significance of John 3:16, let's analyze it within the context of the book as a whole. We will center our discussion around what could be called the "twin pillars" of John's theology: Present Judgment and Present Salvation. We'll quickly see that there is far more to the fourth Gospel than a sentimental call to "give your heart to the Lord."

Present judgment

John discusses the problem of sin more than any of the Gospel writers. In fact, he uses the word "sin" more than Matthew and Mark combined! This takes many Christians by surprise—probably because they don't usually associate John, "the apostle of love," with such an unlovely subject as sin.

But John makes it very clear that, unless sin is dealt with, human beings will perish eternally. The flip side of John 3:16 is that those who do not believe do not have everlasting life. We rightly cite this text to show that the ultimate demonstration of God's love is the provision he has made for the sins of humanity in the sacrifice of his only Son, Jesus the Christ. God forbid we should ever forget this central truth. But we must not overlook the fact that this love of God is aimed at saving us from a terrible fate. Those who believe are saved, but those who do not believe do not have everlasting life.

For John, the possibility of men and women perishing is very real indeed:

"Whoever believes in the Son has eternal life, but whoever rejects the Son will not see life, for God's wrath remains on him" (3:36). And Jesus himself warns: "If you do not believe that I am the one I claim to be, you will indeed die in your sins" (8:24).

In other words, unrepentant sinners exclude themselves from God's gift of life and bring his judgment upon themselves. And this judgment is a present one: "Whoever believes in him is not condemned, but whoever does not believe stands condemned already because he has not believed in the name of God's one and only begotten Son" (3:18).

True, there is a final judgment of Jesus Christ (John 5:27-29), but this judgment is not only a future reality, it is already in operation: "And this is the judgment, that the light [Jesus Christ] has come into the world" (3:18).

The problem is that some men and women love the darkness rather than the light. They prefer darkness (living in sin) over the light (living in Christ) and thus shut themselves up in darkness. This, to quote Martin Luther, is "man curved in on himself." In such a state, human beings are slaves of sin (John 8:34). Without God's salvation, they cannot break free.

For John, then, men and women divide according to their attitude to Jesus. Either you are for Christ and on the road to life, or you are against Christ and on the road to death. So monumental is this aspect of Christ's ministry that he can be said to have come into the world for the express purpose of judgment: "For judgment came I into this world, so that the blind will see and those who see will become blind" (9:39).

This does not mean that Christ's primary purpose was to condemn the world. On the contrary: "For God did not send his Son into the world to condemn the world, but to save the world through him" (3:17). John is simply making the point that, when the sun shines, shadows are inevitable. And when the light of Jesus Christ shines, those who hide in the shadows are shown up for what they really are: "This is the verdict: Light has come into the world, but men loved darkness instead of light because their deeds were evil" (3:19).

Present salvation

Sin is not the central doctrine of the Bible. God is. And God tells us that his salvation — deliverance from sin through Jesus Christ — is available to anyone who asks him for it. Early in his Gospel, John salutes "the Lamb of God who takes away the sin of the world" (1:29). This declaration of forgiveness is also not something that happens at some future judgment. Jesus himself tells us that it is a present possession of the believer: "I tell you the truth, whoever hears my words and believes him who sent me has eternal life and will not be condemned; he has crossed over from death to life" (5:24).

Note the present tense "has." We have eternal life and we have crossed over from death to life. John is not denying or diminishing our glorious future with God in a life beyond death; he is affirming that Christians also have a present possession of life that death cannot destroy. Time and again, John stresses that eternal life is a present possession of all who believe (1:12; 3:16, 36; 6:33, 40, 47). To put it another way, we are not saved because Christ will come. We are saved because he has come.

In addition, John reminds us that this life is not something that we can grab for ourselves. It is a divine gift: "My sheep listen to my voice; I know them and they follow me. I give them eternal life, and they shall never perish; no one can snatch them out of my hand" (10: 27-28; see also Romans 6:22 and Ephesians 2:8-9).

And more specifically than the other Gospels, John associates the giving of this gift with God the Father, God the Son and God the Holy Spirit.

First, the Holy Spirit convicts us of sin (16:8). Ordinarily, we human beings do not see ourselves as sinners. Only as the Spirit of God works with us do we begin to see ourselves for who we really are—as "enemies of God" (Romans 5:10). This same Spirit gives us life (John 6:33) and leads us into all truth (16:13).

Second, the Father also works with us by drawing us to his Son. Jesus said: "No one can come to me unless the Father who sent me draw him" (6:44). And he repeats it with emphasis: "No man can come unto me, except it be given to him by the Father" (6:65). We must not deceive ourselves into thinking that we can come to God any time we are good and ready. We cannot. Perception in biblical matters and a willingness to become a true disciple of Jesus are not natural attributes. They only come as a gift of God.

Third, the Son makes possible the gift of eternal life by his atoning death on the cross. Jesus said: "But I, when I am lifted up from the earth, will draw all men unto myself." This "lifting up" in John's Gospel is always a reference to Jesus being lifted up on the cross (3:14; 8:28; 12:32, 34). Jesus' death will draw men and women to himself. Note, once again, that the initiative here comes from God. It is not a matter of human beings simply deciding to come to Christ.

Perhaps a similar thing is implied in Jesus' words to Nathaniel: "You shall see heaven open, and the angels of God ascending and descending on the Son of Man" (1:51). Christ's words allude to the story of Jacob's ladder in Genesis 28:10-22 where a stone pillar at Bethel was the focal point of communication between heaven and earth.

In John's Gospel, the stone is replaced by the flesh and blood of Jesus Christ. There is now communion between heaven and earth through Jesus. Our Lord explains: "Whoever eats my flesh and drinks my blood has eternal life, and I will raise him up at the last day. For my flesh is real food and my blood is real drink. Whoever eats my flesh and drinks my blood remains in me, and I in him" (6:54-56).

Indeed, John's entire Gospel is concerned with the way in which God has brought us life through the sending of his beloved Son. John presents Jesus as the revelatory Word (Greek: *Logos*) of God, the unique and pre-existent Son of God who, in obedience to his Father, became a real human being to die sacrificially for the salvation of other human beings. In Christ's own words: "The thief comes only to steal and kill and destroy; I have come that they might have life, and have it to the full" (10:10-11).

As such, Jesus reveals the "truth." But this "truth" is no mere set of dry doctrinal propositions. Jesus himself is the truth (14:6). He is also "the bread of life" (6:35, 48; compare 6:41, 51); "the light of the world" (8:12); "the door" (10:7, 9); "the good shepherd" (10:11, 14); "the resurrection and the life" (11:25); and "the true vine" (15:1, 5). In short, Jesus was and is the ultimate reality of God's own person and character. This is why Jesus could boldly proclaim: "Anyone who has seen me has seen the Father" (14:9).

The core of the Gospel

Although John's Gospel is written in simple Greek, its plain words carry profound meaning. It contains theological concepts that are not easy to master in a short time. These concepts challenge even the most mature Christian. Yet, its reassurance of God's love for us can be understood by anyone. This fact is imbedded in the author's thesis statement: "Jesus did many other signs in the presence of his disciples, which are not written in this book. But these are written so that you may come to believe that Jesus is the Messiah, the Son of God, and that through believing, you may have life in his name" (John 20:30-31).

John highlights the Gospel — the good news that Jesus offers us eternal life here and now. We are invited to enter into a personal relationship with Jesus Christ, whom we can trust implicitly because he is the Son of God. Indeed, it is only through trusting Jesus that we can understand God's plan for us and carry out his will in our daily lives.

Yes, John "the beloved disciple" of Jesus has given us a powerfully spiritual portrait of our Lord and Master, the Eternal Son of God. He knew that love, and he wants his readers across the ages to know it too. But we must never confuse this love with a shallow sentimentality that sees God as nothing more than a hip-pocket psychotherapist we use to meet our "felt needs."

Love, as John sees it, is not an invitation to indulge in a life of indiscriminate sentimentality or superficial spirituality. He asks us, instead, to soberly consider two great truths of Scripture: First, we are sinners who have brought the death penalty upon ourselves. Second, God has forgiven us because his only begotten Son died in our place. Genuine repentance acknowledges both the sentence and the acquittal.

In response, John tells us that God demands nothing less than our wholehearted allegiance. This is why we must never allow an albeit sincere preacher to manipulate us into making a shallow "decision for Christ." God's calling is too important to be trivialized.

You can read the 21 chapters of John in a couple of hours. The gospel is perfect reading for new Christians, but it also repays the study of a lifetime. It has changed millions of people. It can change you!

Outline of John's Gospel

The Gospel of John has 21 chapters. By reading just one chapter per day, you can finish the entire book in just three weeks. The following outline will help you get a handle on the material. You might want to review it before plunging in to the actual text.

John opens with a beautifully written prologue (1:1-18) concerning the nature of what he calls "the Word" (Greek: *Logos*). Scholars who study the various forms of New Testament literature conclude that John has either reworked an early Christian hymn or composed one of his own against the backdrop of the Old Testament stories of creation (Genesis 1- 2: 3) and the giving of the law to Israel on Mt. Sinai (Exodus 19-20). "In the beginning" (John 1:1) is reminiscent of Genesis 1:1. "Was the Word" (John 1:1) brings to mind God speaking the various elements into their created order (for example, "Let there be light" in Genesis 1:3).

The prologue introduces many themes that the author expands on in the two main divisions of the book — divisions scholars commonly refer to as "the book of signs" and "the book of glory."

In "the book of signs" (1:19–12:50), Jesus reveals his divine nature through a series of miracles or signs. The first section (1:19-51) discusses the testimony of John the Baptist concerning the Messiah and shows how some of his disciples came to follow Jesus (1:35-51). Then comes the period of

Jesus' ministry, beginning and ending at Cana (2:1–4:54). The next section (5:1–10:42) is a series of passages that show how the Messiahship of Jesus was foreshadowed in the various Jewish Holy days: The Sabbath (5:1-47); Passover (6:1-71); Tabernacles (7:1–10:21); and Hanukkah (10:22-42).

In the final part of the book of signs (11:1–12:50), Jesus resurrects Lazarus from the dead (11:38-44). Ironically, this provokes hostility from the Jewish authorities and leads to Jesus' own death and resurrection.

In "the book of glory" (13:1–20:31), God glorifies Jesus through the crucifixion and resurrection. First, Jesus eats the "last supper" with his disciples (13:1-30). He then comforts them with an inspirational discourse that should be required reading for all Christians (13:31–17:26). The passion narrative comes next (18:1–19:42) followed by the dramatic appearances of the risen Christ (20:21).

Finally, the epilogue describes additional post-resurrection appearances of Jesus and provides a suitable transition to the ministry of the early church by explaining the roles of Peter and the beloved disciple (21:1-25).

JOHN 1: THE WORD MADE FLESH

By Joseph Tkach

John does not start "the story of Jesus" in the usual way. He says nothing about the way Jesus was born. Rather, he takes us back in time to "the beginning." In the beginning, he says, was "the Word." Modern readers may not know at first what this "Word" is, but it becomes clear in verse 14: "The Word became flesh and made his dwelling among us." The Word became a human being, a Jewish man named Jesus.

When John talks about "the Word," he is talking about a Person who existed in the beginning with God, and he was God (v. 1). He was not a created being; rather, it is through him that all created things were made (v. 3). The question that I'd like to comment on now is, Why does John tell us this? Why do we need to know that Jesus was originally a Person who was not only with God, but he was also God?

A great idea

By using the word *Word,* John was using a term that had rich meaning to Greek and Jewish philosophers. They also believed that God had created everything through his word, or his wisdom. Since God was a rational being, he always had a word with him. The "word" was his power to think — his rationality, his creativity.

John takes this idea and gives it a radical twist: The Word became flesh. Something in the realm of the perfect and the eternal became part of the imperfect and decaying world. That was a preposterous idea, people might have said. That did not fit their idea of what God was.

John may have agreed with them: This was quite unexpected. God did not act the way we thought he would. Indeed, as we read John's Gospel we will find that Jesus frequently did the unexpected. He was not acting the way that people expected a man of God to act — and that is part of the reason that he came, and part of the reason that John tells the story. We had wrong ideas about God, and Jesus came to set us straight.

Jesus did not just bring a message about God — he himself was the message. He showed us in the flesh what God is like. Shortly before Jesus was killed, Philip asked him, "Lord, show us the Father" (14:8). And Jesus answered: "Don't you know me, Philip, even after I have been among you for such a long time? Anyone who has seen me has seen the Father" (v. 9).

If you want to know what God is like, then study Jesus. Jesus shows us the love that God has for us; he freely gave his life to save others. When the Word humbled himself to become a flesh-and-blood human, it was a change

— something God had never done before — but it was not a change in God's nature. Rather, it was a demonstration of his unchanging nature — his unchanging faithfulness to us. It showed us the love that God has for us all the time.

The Greek philosophers imagined that God was so perfect that he would have nothing to do with messed-up human beings. Many Jews felt the same way — they emphasized God's holiness so much that they thought the people of God should have nothing to do with people who weren't careful about keeping the laws of holiness. They were right in saying that God was holy, but they had forgotten that his holiness includes love and mercy and his power includes tenderness.

Life and truth

As a disciple, John did not start off knowing that his teacher was eternally pre-existent. This awareness came to him slowly, and may be reflected in the words of the disciples. Peter said, "You are the Holy One of God" (6:69); Martha said, "You are the Christ, the Son of God" (11:27); and after the resurrection, Thomas said, "My Lord and my God!" (20:28).

John develops this theme throughout the Gospel, but he wants us as readers to know even from the beginning who Jesus is, so that we can watch the story unfold with a little more understanding. Jesus is "God the One and Only, who is at the Father's side" — and he "has made the Father known" (1:18).

This flesh-and-blood God had life, "and that life was the light of men" (v. 4). He was bringing eternal life, and his "light" reveals to us the way to eternal life. We can read the story knowing that this person is actually God in the flesh, showing us what God is like.

John the Baptist told people about Jesus, but most people could not accept what he said: "Look — the Lamb of God, who takes away the sin of the world!" (v. 29). But "the darkness" could not understand the light of the world. "The world did not recognize him … did not receive him" (vs. 10-11). But for those who did believe, John says, they became children of God, born not in the ordinary way, "but born of God" (v. 13).

"We have seen his glory," John says, and it does not consist of blazing fire and thundering voice. Rather, the glory of God that we see in Jesus is "grace and truth." In his words and in his works, Jesus shows us that truth is gracious. Some people want "truth" to be a weapon that beats other people down, but Jesus shows us that it lifts people up.

"The law was given through Moses," but the law could not give us eternal life. Here's what we really needed: "Grace and truth came through Jesus Christ" (v. 17). Yes, God gave the law, but the law could not reveal the true nature of God. God cannot be defined by a list of rules. He is revealed as a person who walked this earth as one of us, showed mercy to sinners, and died for others.

God did not have to do this, but the fact that he did shows how much he cares about us: "the compassionate and gracious God, slow to anger, abounding in love and faithfulness, maintaining love to thousands, and forgiving wickedness, rebellion and sin" (Exodus 34:6-7). This had been revealed to Moses, but it seems that the Israelites had forgotten it, so Jesus came to reveal it in the flesh.

Even today, after nearly 2,000 years of Christian teaching, many people — even many Christians — think that God is a stern Judge, but Jesus stepped in and thwarted God's plan to punish us. The truth is that the love and mercy we see in Jesus is exactly how God has always been. That's something worth thinking about.

JOHN 2: TURNING WATER INTO WINE

By Joseph Tkach

The Gospel of John tells an interesting story near the beginning of Jesus' ministry: He went to a wedding and turned water into wine. Several aspects of this story make it unusual:

- It seems like a minor miracle, more like a magician's trick than the work of a Messiah. It prevented a little embarrassment, but didn't really address human suffering the way that Jesus' healings did.

- It was a private miracle — done without the knowledge of the main beneficiary — and yet it was a sign that revealed Jesus' glory (v. 11).

- The literary function is puzzling. John knew of many more miracles than he had room to write about, and yet he chose this one to begin his book. How does it help achieve John's purpose — to help us believe that Jesus is the Christ? (John 20:30-31). How does it show that he is the Messiah, rather than a magician (as the Jewish Talmud later claimed him to be)?

A wedding in Cana

We can start by examining the story in closer detail. It begins with a wedding in Cana, a small village in Galilee. The location does not seem to be important — what is important is that it was a wedding. Jesus did his first messianic sign at a wedding festival.

Weddings were the biggest and most important celebrations among the Jewish people — the weeklong party signaled the social status of the new family in the community. Weddings were such joyous occasions that when people wanted to describe the blessings of the messianic age, they often used a wedding banquet as a metaphor. Jesus used the image of a wedding banquet to describe the kingdom of God in some of his parables.

Jesus often used miracles in the physical world to demonstrate spiritual truths. He healed people to show that he had the authority to forgive sin. He cursed a fig tree as a sign of coming judgment on the temple. He healed on the Sabbath to show his authority over the Sabbath. He raised people from the dead to show that he is the resurrection and the life. He fed thousands to show that he is the bread of life. And here, he provided abundant blessings for a wedding to show that he is the one who will provide the messianic banquet of the kingdom of God.

When the wine was gone, Mary told Jesus about it, and he said, "Why do you involve me?" (v. 4). What does that have to do with me? "My time has not yet come." And yet, even though it was not yet time, Jesus did something. John signals here that what Jesus is doing is somehow ahead of its time. The messianic banquet is not yet here, and yet Jesus did something. The messianic age was beginning, long before it would arrive in its fullness.

Mary expected him to do something, for she told the servants to do whatever Jesus said. Whether she expected a miracle, or a quick trip to the nearest wine market, we do not know.

Ceremonial water turned into wine

Now, it so happened that six stone water containers stood nearby, and they were not regular water jars, John tells us — they were the kind the Jews used for ceremonial washing. (For ceremonial cleansing, the Jews preferred water in stone containers rather than in clay pots.) They held more than 20 gallons of water each — far too heavy for picking up and pouring. That's a lot of water, just for ceremonial washing. This must have been at the largest estate in Cana.

This seems to be a significant part of the story — that Jesus was going to transform some water used in Jewish ceremonies. This symbolized a transformation in Judaism, even the fulfillment of ceremonial washings. Imagine what would happen if guests wanted to wash their hands again — they would go to the water pots and find every one of them filled with wine! There would be no water for their ritual. The spiritual cleansing of Jesus' blood superseded ritual washings. Jesus has fulfilled the rituals and replaced them with something much better—himself.

The servants filled the containers to the brim, John tells us (v. 7). How appropriate, for Jesus filled the rituals completely, rendering them obsolete. In the messianic age, no space is left for ritual washings.

The servants drew some wine out and took it to the master of ceremonies, who then told the bridegroom, "Everyone brings out the choice wine first and then the cheaper wine after the guests have had too much to drink; but you have saved the best till now" (v. 10).

Why do you suppose that John records these words? Was it advice for future banquets? Was it merely to show that Jesus makes good wine? No, I think it is reported because it has symbolic significance.

The Jews were like people who had been drinking wine (performing ritual washings) so long that they could not recognize when something better came along. When Mary said, "They have no more wine" (v. 3), it symbolized the fact that the Jews had no spiritual meaning left in their ceremonies. Jesus was bringing something new and something better.

Cleansing the temple

In keeping with this theme, John next tells us that Jesus drove merchants out of the temple courts. Commentators write pages about whether this temple-cleansing was the same as the one the other Gospels report at the end of Jesus' ministry, or whether it was an additional one at the beginning. In either case, John reports it here because of the significance that it symbolizes.

John again puts the story in the context of Judaism: "It was almost time for the Jewish Passover" (v. 13). And Jesus found people selling animals and changing money — animals for sin offerings fellowship offerings, and other sacrifices, and money that could be used to pay the temple taxes. So Jesus made a simple whip and drove them all out.

It is surprising that one man could drive all the merchants out. (Where are the temple police when you need them?) I suspect that the merchants knew that they should not be there, and that a lot of the common people didn't want them there either — Jesus was simply expressing what the people already felt, and the merchants knew they were outnumbered. Josephus describes other occasions when the Jewish leaders tried to change the way things were done in the temple, and the people raised such an outcry that they had to stop.

Jesus did not object to people selling animals for sacrifice, or changing money for temple offerings. He said nothing about how much they were charging. His complaint was simply their location: They were turning the house of God into a house of merchandise (v. 16). They had turned the religion into a moneymaking scheme.

So the Jewish leaders didn't arrest Jesus — they knew the people supported what he had done — but they did ask him what gave him the right to do this (v. 18). And Jesus said nothing about the inadequacies of the temple, but shifted the subject to something new: "Destroy this temple, and I will raise it again in three days" (v. 19). Jesus was talking about his own body, but the Jewish leaders did not know that. They no doubt considered it a ridiculous answer, but

still they did not arrest him.

Jesus' resurrection shows that he had the authority to cleanse the temple, and his words foreshadowed its destruction. When the leaders killed Jesus, they were also destroying the temple, for the death of Jesus brought all the sacrifices to obsolescence. And in three days Jesus was raised, and he built a new temple — his church.

And many people believed in Jesus, John tells us, because they saw his miraculous signs. (Note the plural word "signs." John 4:54 reports the "second" miraculous sign; this makes me think that the temple cleansing has been reported out of sequence because it is an advance indication of what the ministry of Jesus is about.)

Jesus was going to bring about the end of the temple sacrificial system and the end of the rituals of cleansing — and the Jewish leaders were unwittingly going to help him by attempting to destroy the body of Jesus. But in three days everything would be changed from water to wine — from lifeless ritual to the best spiritual drink of all.

Bringing it closer to home

What do these two episodes have to teach us today? First, Christians might well wonder if certain of our traditions have outlived their usefulness and blinded us to new developments in what Christ wants us to do. It might be the holidays that we keep, or the way in which we keep them. It might be the way that churches are organized and governed. It might be unnecessary restrictions on who can do what. It might be attitudes toward evangelism.

But we can do well to ask if our traditions have become as meaningless as water, and whether Christ wants to transform them into something more stimulating.

We can also ask about our attitudes about money. Has money become more important to us than our relationship with God? We can certainly ask this from a denominational perspective, or from a local church perspective as budget committees are being set up. And we can ask it from a personal perspective, whether we might be letting commerce take over time that should be used for the community and people of God. Do we allow shopping and banking to occupy space in our lives that ought to be devoted to worship? Both of these are worth thinking about.

JOHN 3: AN ODYSSEY OF FAITH

By Joseph Tkach

The Christian life is more than a simple path. It involves crises, transitions and surprises as well as victories and growth. Sometimes this never-ending odyssey with our Savior into eternal joy is a pleasant cruise, and sometimes it is a wild ride.

A new start for every person

Jesus taught that every person must have a fresh beginning. In John 3:3, Jesus told Nicodemus, "No one can see the kingdom of God unless he is born again." Nicodemus would hardly have been surprised at the idea that there would be a resurrection at the end of the age — many Jews already held that idea.

Jesus was talking about something more surprising — a new birth or a new start that enables a person to "enter the kingdom of God" (verse 5) *in this age*. He told the Pharisees, "The tax collectors and the prostitutes are entering the kingdom of God ahead of you" (Matthew 21:31). Even in this age, people are entering the kingdom of God, and they do it by accepting the good news that God offers his blessings on the basis of grace rather than law. But it takes a new start in life to experience the kingdom of God.

Nicodemus knew Jesus' statement could not be taken literally. "How can a man be born when he is old?... Surely he cannot enter a second time into his mother's womb to be born!" (verse 4).

So Jesus said it again, adding some words of explanation: "No one can enter the kingdom of God unless he is born of water and the Spirit. Flesh gives birth to flesh, but the Spirit gives birth to spirit" (verse 6).

For physical life, a person needs a physical birth. For spiritual life, a person needs a spiritual birth. Nicodemus, and Judaism in general, focused on the physical. They were concerned about purity laws, time and place, rules and rituals. Although they knew that God was Spirit, they expected his kingdom to be a physical kingdom like the kingdoms of this world, with geographic territory, agriculture and the enforcement of laws.

So Jesus chided Nicodemus for not understanding (verses 7, 10). The Pharisees (just like the Samaritans — see John 4:2124) were too concerned with physical aspects of worship. Jesus is saying that there is more to the kingdom of God than having better crops, tame animals and people keeping rules and rituals. God is concerned with the spirit of a person, a transformation of the spirit, and that requires a new start in life.

Spirit, like wind, cannot be seen, but its results can be seen (verse 8). The

Spirit changes people, and the change, although sometimes frustratingly slow, is evidence that the Spirit is working. We all need that kind of new start in life. As John 3 explains, it requires that we believe in Jesus, and trust that he gives us eternal life. When we put our faith in him, we are "born of the Spirit" — a new life has begun.

Believe in the Son

Jesus' death atoned for everyone on earth (1 John 2:2), but only those who *believe* can experience the kind of life that characterizes the age to come. That is why Jesus came: God loved the world so much that he gave up his only Son, "that whoever believes in him shall not perish but have eternal life" (verse 16).

God does not want to condemn us (verse 17). If we believe in Christ, we are saved; if we do not, we remain in condemnation, because our sins condemn us, and we have not accepted the only rescue that God offers (verse 18). The atoning sacrifice has already been given, but the benefits are not forced on people who don't want them.

The new life in Christ is a wonderful, yet sometimes frightening journey — an odyssey of faith filled with many ups and downs — always strengthened by the confidence that Jesus is with us, and that he will help us weather all the storms.

JESUS AND THE SAMARITAN WOMAN

Editor's note: This article an edited transcript of a small group discussion led by Dan Rogers.

Dan Rogers: Good morning. It's good to see all of you here today. We've had a nice time singing and worshipping together and good time of prayer. Now, it's time for us to get into God's word and talk about our message for today. As you know, we're going to be reading from John chapter 4 and the story of Jesus and the Samaritan woman. Before we actually get into the text, I thought it might be interesting just to talk about the background of Samaria and that part of the world and the Samaritan people so that we have a little bit of background to work with as we get in to the story.

Anybody here who wants to volunteer some information about Samaria or the Samaritans? What can you tell us about that country and the people who live there?

Female: They were hated by the Jews. I know that. Here, Jesus was walking through it.

Dan: Okay.

Female: That's interesting.

Dan: There was some kind of antipathy between the Samaritans and the Jewish people. Anybody know what that's all about? Why? They're neighbors. How come they don't like each other? Anybody remember?

Female: Different religion.

Dan: Yeah. How so? How was it different?

Female: They worshipped at different places.

Dan: Aha. Did they worship a different god?

Female: Yes.

Dan: Did they think they worshiped a different god?

Female: No. They thought they …

Dan: The Jews thought they worshiped a different god, but the Samaritans thought they worshipped the same god as the Jews but as Barbara said, they did it in the wrong places, and the Jewish religion, in the Old Testament, was very place-conscious. Jerusalem was God's headquarters on earth and how dare they not worship in Jerusalem and worship somewhere else? Anybody know where they liked to worship? Anybody can remember?

Dan: We could figure it's probably going to be on the top of a mountain.

Female: Yeah.

Dan: What mountain was it? Anybody remember?

Female: No.

Dan: Okay. Mount Gerizim. You knew that, didn't you?

Female: We knew that.

Dan: They built a temple on the top of Mount Gerizim and they worshipped their god who they thought was the God of Israel. They almost considered themselves Israelites, which was a real insult to the Jews because it was like they were lying about their national identity, claiming to be the true people of God, claiming to worship, and doing it in a false place and in a false way with false priests. The Jews hated this defilement, as they saw it, of the true religion which they had and yet the Samaritans, sometimes, could not understand this because they thought they were worshipping the same god as the Jews did.

But then, during the Maccabean period just prior to the birth of Jesus by a couple of hundred years, John Hyrcanus led an armed force of Jews up Mount Gerizim and destroyed their temple which was an affront to the Jews, but now this became a very horrible thing in the life of the Samaritans. The Samaritans never got over the Jews coming up and destroying their temple. For years afterwards, they continue to go up Mount Gerizim and to worship in the rubble of the temple that the Jews had destroyed.

Over the centuries, this animosity have been building and reached a fever pitch. Everybody know where Samaria is?

Female: Real close to Israel.

Dan: Israel, to the Jews, to Judea. I have a little map here and if you can see it, it might be helpful just to give you an illustration. If you can see that there is Galilee in the north and there is ... Samaria is in the middle and down here is Judea. You can see that you have Galilee to the north, and who came from Galilee?

Female: Jesus.

Dan: Jesus and... 11 of his 12 disciples came from Galilee, and then there's Samaria.

Female: In between.

Dan: Judea is to the south of Samaria and Galilee is just to the north and you notice the Sea of Galilee and the Jordan River flowing along there and sort of dividing the land from what they call the Transjordan.

Dan: If you were going to go from Jerusalem down here, it would appear you had to go through Samaria but wait ... Jews don't like Samaritans and the Samaritans don't like the Jews, so what do you think that the Jewish people going north and south from Galilee to Jerusalem would tend to do?

Female: Go around it.

Dan: They would tend to go around it and it was an easy trip. They just had to cross the Jordan River, go up that side, and then cross back over into Galilee, and they preferred that, lest they encounter any Samaritans and touch any unclean Samaritan or some Samaritan thing that had been touched. It was typical to go around Samaria to get from Galilee to Judea and Judea to Galilee, kind of an interesting little detour that they had to take.

We have some pictures here too on the TV screen. You might want to look at this area. This is in the late 1800s. This is what the site of what's called Jacob's Well in Samaria looked like. You might notice that it's in the side of a hill, and we don't typically think of having to go into a cave-like area to get to a well, but that's what it looked like in the 1800s, and then we have a more modern picture. As you notice, they've turned it into tourist attraction and built a wall around it and now, people can file in and it's labeled in three languages there, Jacob's Well. Both Jewish scholars, Muslim scholars, and Christian scholars do agree that this was Jacob's Well that's spoken of here in John chapter 4. It's pretty good archeological evidence for that.

I think we have one more picture. This is what it looks like inside. Can you see the bucket? Of course, it has been touristified to make it a shrine worthy of visiting, but it gives you an idea of where it was, and it's still there to this day. You can actually go to Jacob's Well and visit.

All right. We got some pictures to give us a little bit of background, a little bit of geography. Now, let's go to our text at John chapter 4. We read here that "the Pharisees heard that Jesus was gaining and baptizing more disciples than John." This is not good news for the Pharisees. The Pharisees thought they controlled the territory outside of the temple. If you want to know the religious marketplace of the day, the Sadducees controlled the temple. The Pharisees had everything else.

Now, here's this what we would call wild card, John the Baptist. He is not exactly an Essene but he kind of looks like one. He is not a Pharisee. He is not a Sadducee and he is getting followers. This is marketplace competition.

Now, John is gone, but of all things, there's another guy coming on the scene who is taking away people after him, and that's Jesus. He is getting "more disciples than John. Although in fact, it was not Jesus who baptized but his disciples. When the Lord learned of this, he left Judea and went back once more to Galilee."

You remember our little map there where everything is? Now, notice verse 4. "Now, he *had* to go through Samaria." What do you think John means, he *had* to go through Samaria? Did he have to go through Samaria?

No. Most Jews did not want to go through Samaria and went around it.

Could John mean something more?

Female: He was led to go through Samaria.

Dan: He felt led, felt a compulsion, felt a need. This gives you the sense of what? A mission?

Female: Yes.

Dan: The wonderful thing about reading the fourth Gospel is the writer, John, loves to use double entendres and two and three and four layers of meanings in so much of what he says. We always have to read beyond what appears on the surface when we read John. "He had to go through Samaria. He came to a town in Samaria called Sychar near the plot of ground Jacob had given to his son, Joseph. Jacob's Well was there and Jesus, tired as he was from the journey, sat down by the well and it was about the sixth hour." Anybody got the time in your translation?

Female: Noon time.

Female: Lunch.

Dan: What do you make of this "Jesus was tired from the journey?"

Female: Been walking a long time.

Female: It was hot.

Female: He needed something to drink?

Dan: What do you think John is telling us about the nature of Jesus?

Female: He's very human.

Female: He too gets tired.

Dan: He got tired? Yeah, he wanted to rest and he was thirsty.

Female: He needed food and drink.

Dan: It's noon time. Verse 7: "When a Samaritan woman came to draw water, Jesus said to her, 'Will you give me a drink?'"

Okay. It's noon time and we have a Samaritan woman coming out from the city of Sychar. The well was outside of the city, so she has to come out of the city, walk out to this area where we saw the well located, go in there with her pitcher or bucket or whatever she had, her rope and all of that and draw water. Does anything strike you as unusual about this scenario of the Samaritan woman coming out at noon time to draw water?

Female: That seems an odd time to draw water. You would either do that in the morning or at night when it's not so hot.

Dan: Right.

Female: To come out in the middle of the day seems out of place.

Dan: Right. Do you notice anyone else coming out?

Female: She's by herself.

Female: No friends.

Dan: If you read the Old Testament, as Suzie indicates, there are many examples of women coming out for water in the stories as you read the Old Testament and they always come out at morning or in evening. Never at noon.

Why else might a woman not want to come out to a well outside of the city by herself?

Female: Safety.

Female: Robbers.

Dan: Who would typically stop by wells during the middle of the day?

Female: Strangers.

Female: People passing through.

Dan: Travelers, right. Probably caravans, and who knows who they are and what they're up to, so it would be kind of a dangerous time for a woman to come outside of the city walls by herself in the heat of the day to draw water. There's something strange going on here, and as Barbara suggested, she does not seem to have any friends. She has to come out by herself all alone—an unusual situation.

Male: It could be she's avoiding other people.

Dan: Maybe she doesn't want to be with them, right? "Jesus says to her, 'Will you give me a drink?' His disciples had gone away into the town to buy food." Every time I read that verse, I think of kind of the jokes that go like, "How many disciples does it take to buy lunch?"

Male: All of them.

Dan: What's with that? Would it take 11 disciples to go into town and buy lunch? What do you think is going on here?

Female: He sent them all.

Female: It was the plan.

Dan: Yeah. He sent them to buy lunch. I don't think you needed 11 to go into town to buy lunch. That would be a pretty big lunch for 11 people to have to carry. Do you think Jesus had something in mind here?

It looks like this was planned. He had to go through Samaria. He stayed by the well and sent them all away so that he could be alone and, "aah!" Surprise, here comes the Samaritan woman. We don't know the background. We don't know how Jesus knew all this, whether he was led of the Spirit or whether he had word that this happened or how. All we know is the story, so we have to take it at face value.

Let's see what we can glean from it. Jesus said, "Will you give me a drink?" Then, in verse 9, the Samaritan woman said to him, "You're a Jew. I'm a Samaritan woman. How can you ask me for a drink?" Then John, for the benefit of his writers who don't know history, said, "For Jews do not associate with Samaritans." Something very unusual is going on here. What do you make of Jesus asking her, "Will you give me a drink?" What do you think is happening here? What's going on? Why would he do this?

Female: A Jew would never address a woman and never address a Samaritan.

Dan: Right.

Female: He was showing acceptance of her which was ...

Dan: Yes. Even though he asked her a favor, he was showing that he accepted her equal to himself.

Female: So weird. He is breaking down some major walls here.

Dan: That's very strange. Some major barriers of religion, of genderism, of classism and all those isms are being dramatically broken by Jesus. She gathers that he is Jew, we read that in the text. How do think she figured out he was a Jew?

Female: The way he dressed.

Dan: Yeah. Without even hearing him speak, but then when he said, "Will you ..." "Mhmmm ... I recognize that accent." It's Galilean if you ask me.

You must be a Jew, but I think the way he dressed and he was probably dressed somewhat like the rabbis of his day. Here you have someone who possibly is not only a Jew, not only a male, but possibly a rabbi, and he is talking to a Samaritan woman. This is earth-shattering. This is just not done.

She even almost mildly rebukes him for his nerve. How dare you speak to me?

Female: Don't you know you'd be contaminated? You may be hurt.

Dan: Verse 10: Jesus answered her, "If you knew the gift of God and who it is that asked you for a drink, you would have asked him, and he would have given you living water." What do you make of some of these statements? We've got the gift of God, we got living water. What do you think these things are talking about here? Let's start with the gift of God. What do you think that might be? "If you knew the gift of God ..."

Female: Jesus.

Female: If you knew who is talking to you and what I can offer you, you would beg me for the living water.

Female: He is being very plain in one sense with her because he hasn't talked to others in this way before.

Dan: In the book of John, he hasn't even talked to his disciples this way. He's talking to her in a more open way than he did with anyone that he met, at least, in the book of John to this point. Is there anything called the gift of

God in the New Testament you can think of other than Jesus?

Female: The Spirit, the Holy Spirit.

Dan: If you knew the gift of God, that Spirit. If the Spirit worked with you, if you just know the gift of God and know he's with you and who it is that asked you, the Son of God ... Whoa! He's getting into a Trinitarian theology here.

Talking or hinting about the Spirit, hinting about who he is, assuming that she knows some God in heaven who unbeknownst to her is the Father but he is really working with her in a Trinitarian way which he has talked to no one else about, at least at this point, his ministry throughout the Gospels.

Female: He must have known that she's very receptive in her circumstances, of coming at noon and that she was a candidate to be very open with.

Dan: What made her a good open candidate?

Female: He knew her heart. Just her brokenness probably.

Female: No friends and ...

Dan: Coming out alone at dangerous time of the day.

Female: She was vulnerable.

Female: Felt very empty.

Dan: What do you think of her, let's say, intelligence and understanding?

Female: I think she was curious already and obviously was wondering about him and she was almost seeking an answer from him.

Dan: The first thing she does to him when he says, "Give me a drink of water," is to do what?

Male: Ask him a question.

Dan: What do we call people today who ask questions about Jesus?

Female: Seekers, learners.

Dan: She was, "Hey, wait a minute. I want to know more here. This is interesting. Tell me what's going on." She was indeed somewhat receptive. He said, "If you knew the gift of God and who it is that asked you for a drink, you would have asked him and he would have given you living water." What is living water? What does that expression mean?

Female: Water that will make you live forever.

Dan: That's how he's going to interpret it, as water that will make you live forever but let's say if you were just ... took him at face value, do you know what they would mean by living water in that day?

Female: It would be fresh water.

Dan: Fresh water because it's alive and not dead like the Dead Sea but not full of salt but living water. Where did living water usually come from?

Female: Springs?

Dan: Springs, yeah, flowing water from … but wait a minute – this is not a spring. This is not flowing water. This is a well. He says, "I asked you for a drink out of the well but if you ask me, I would give you living water, flowing water." Rushing water, not just sitting-still water at the bottom of this well.

"Sir," very respectful. "Sir," the woman said. "You have nothing to draw with and the well is deep. Where can you get this living water?" What? You're going to go down to the very base of the well and find out if there's anything running in from outside somewhere? You don't even have a bucket. You don't even have a rope. How are you going to do this? "Are you greater than our father, Jacob, who gave us the well and drank from it himself as did also his sons and his flocks and herds?" What do you find interesting about that statement?

Female: She's very feisty.

Female: She really thinks that he might be. she's hoping that he might be.

Dan: She's engaging with him as an equal, isn't she? "You may be a rabbi, but I know a thing or two."

Female: Right, because she's saying that she knows something about her ancestor Jacob. She knows a little bit about the … maybe she even knows something about living water what he is referring to.

Dan: She could have been tongue-in-cheek saying, "I get your message but I don't understand how you're using it." Yeah.

What do you think of this, "Our father, Jacob?"

Female: That's probably who she thought was the most important person at that period of time.

Dan: Does anyone know where the Samaritans actually came from who were living in Samaria at that time of Jesus, their national origin or their regional origin? Do you know where they originated from?

The northern tribe of Israel was taken captive in about 722, 721 BC by the Assyrians. The Assyrians brought in people from some of their inhabited lands to replace the northern kingdom of Israel that they've taken. They didn't take all of them. They only took a small portion (relatively, probably) away, but they did replace them with others, and then there was intermarriage between the northern tribes of Israel that remained and all of these, let me call them Macedonians as a generalism of where they came from, that were replacing them. You got kind of a mixed breed. You know how the Jews feel about mixed breeds?

Dan: That's bad.

Dan: What does she say?

Female: She's giving a common link.

Dan: She's saying we're related to Jacob.

Dan: If you were a Jew, who would you have said your father was?

Female: Abraham.

Dan: Is that interesting? The Jews say our father, Abraham. The Samaritans say, our father, Jacob.

A little difference in theological views here. Are you greater than Jacob? After all, Jacob is the greatest of all the patriarchs from their estimation. Jesus answered, "Everyone who drinks this water will be thirsty again, but whoever drinks the water I give him, will never thirst. Indeed, the water I give him will become in him a spring of water welling up to eternal life."

What a statement! What is he saying to her? How do you interpret that statement? What do you think it meant to her?

Female: Life.

Dan: What kind of life?

Female: Good.

Dan: Good life, the best life.

Female: Fresh and clean.

Male: Eternal life.

Dan: Had Jesus offered anyone else that you know of in the Gospels at this time in his ministry eternal life?

Female: No. I don't think so.

Female: He talks about it gushing, so it's a lot. It's not like he's going to just give her a little portion of it but a lot of … the whole amount.

Dan: There's a power there. There is a force in the sense of a spring of water welling up from the source, and flowing out and up to… the source will give you eternal life. I am impressed at the theology that Jesus is laying on this Samaritan woman. This is pretty deep and evidently, he feels she can process it.

I'm also amazed at how he … if you noticed, he leads her step by step and he began by saying, "Will you give me a drink of water?" That one question, based on her response, he then went a little further. Then based on her response, he went a little further and now, he's going, "You can have eternal life, if you will."

Female: Yes. Exciting.

Dan: At verse 15, the woman said to him, "Sir, give me this water so that I won't get thirsty and have to keep coming here to draw water." She's interested, isn't she? "Okay. You're offering, I'm buying."

Female: She sounds excited.

Dan: "I don't know exactly fully what you're talking about, but it sounds good to me. I want it." What's the reason she gives for wanting this water so that she will never thirst?

Female: She doesn't like her life.

Dan: What makes you think that?

Female: She doesn't want to come there ever again.

Dan: There's something about coming to the well that she doesn't like.

Female: By herself in the heat of the day.

Female: It could be her business.

Dan: It could be something, the way … something going on in her life.

Dan: It could be her business. It could be something going on in her life. We don't know yet. Of course we do, because we've read the end of the story, but we don't know yet what it is, but she's not happy.

She wants some changes. She wants to change her life. This is really quite remarkable. Jesus has not dealt with anyone like this. Of all people, the first one he deals with is a Samaritan and a woman. The 12 are "out to lunch." [laughter]

So he says to her in verse 16, "Go call your husband and come back." She says, "I have no husband." Jesus seems to have known that.

That always reminds me of asking the children, "Did you eat that cookie?" You know that they did, so why do you ask them?

Female: See what they'll say.

Dan: I think he asked her just to see what she would say, and she said, "I have no husband." Jesus said to her, "You were right when you say you have no husband." He didn't say, "I know you're a whore."

Dan: What did he do? What approach did he take with this woman?

Female: Very gentle.

Female: Respectful.

Dan: He complimented her, didn't he? Because she told the truth. She didn't lie to him. She didn't try to deceive him. She could have, but she was just honest and forthright and said, "Yeah. I am who I am and I don't have a husband." Jesus said, "You're right."

Female: She made herself very vulnerable to someone who was giving her hope perhaps. He held something that she wanted that sounded interesting. It was giving her hope. She was being very forthright.

Dan: You get the feeling that her life had hit bottom. She's, "I got nothing to lose. You got some living water? I'll go for whatever it is. I don't fully understand but I'll tell you, where I am, I'll take whatever you have to offer."

Female: It seems like that … just from reading and I know it probably was a lot harder than it seems, drawing water and going out in the middle of the day, but that could not have been the end of the story. Just that she was this desperate to get out of that particular job. It seemed like there was layers underneath that she really wanted to get out of.

Dan: Yeah. Her whole way of life, perhaps. She wants to leave.

Jesus said to her, "You're right when you say you have no husband. The fact is, you have had five husbands." The interesting thing here is that he said she had five husbands.

Female: In that culture, you had to have a protector. You had to have a husband.

Female: Somehow, she had five husbands.

Dan: Yeah. We don't know what happened to these five husbands, do we?

Female: No.

Dan: Do you think all five died?

Female: It doesn't sound like it and why not?

Dan: Unless she's a more dangerous woman than ... but she had five husbands.

Female: She may have had abusive husbands.

Dan: She may have had abusive husbands and so we're assuming perhaps she had had five husbands. Maybe she was divorced. In Jewish law, how many times were you allowed to divorce?

Female: Once.

Dan: Actually more. They allowed three. None was the ideal. One, you were kind of "errrr." Three, that's the limit. She had had five.

Male: I don't know what Samaritan law was. I have no record of it but ...

Female: Three, five ... five men put her away maybe.

Dan: Yeah. That's what I was going to ask next. Could a woman put away a man?

Female: No. Rejected.

Dan: Five men had put her away.

Female: Rejection.

Dan: Who was it awhile ago? I think it was it Pat who said she was feisty.

Dan: A strong woman. A strong-willed woman, which was probably not very favorable in her culture.

Dan: Five men had put her away.

Dan: Do you think it was because she was strong willed? There could have been other reasons, various reasons.

Dan: We don't know what they all were, but five men ...

Female: She seems very intelligent too, so maybe that was intimidating to the men.

Female: She seems like she had some sort of education. She does talk about as if she is aware of Jacob, of what's going on.

Female: She understands where he is from, so she doesn't sound uneducated, and he is engaging her as if she understands what ... And perhaps that was intimidating to five husbands.

Female: That they were supposed to be very quiet.

Dan: I'll share a comment, this man is giving me water and saying, "What are you talking about?" Immediately, she spars with him.

Now, it tells us something about her nature. Here in verse 18, Jesus says, "The fact is you have had five husbands." Evidently five legitimate, legal arrangements, and the man you now have is not your husband, an illegal, immoral arrangement. What did he say to her? "You adulterer, you harlot, you whore?" What did he say?

Female: He said, "You spoke the truth. You were honest about this."

Dan: He did not put her down. He did not rebuke her. He did not criticize her. He complimented her for her forthrightness and her honesty. She again speaks to him with respect at verse 19. "Sir," the woman said. "I can see that you are a prophet." What do you make of that statement? She said, "I see you are a prophet."

Male: He knew stuff that he couldn't have known.

Dan: He sees things that other people don't. He obviously is an intelligent man versed in knowledge of his day.

Female: She sees that he's a rabbi. She doesn't see a Jew. He's probably …

Dan: Probably a rabbi, a teacher, a Jew, yeah, and he is not a Pharisee or Sadducee who she may be familiar with, but he stands outside of them like a prophet. Sort of like John the Baptist type of prophet, but it's interesting to note that in the Samaritan religion, they were looking for one sent from God who would be the descendant of (of course) Jacob, who would come and free their people and they did not call him the Messiah. They called him, the Prophet.

They were looking for not just a prophet but The Prophet, but I think that we can see here that Jesus is already leading her to think in a certain direction about just who he might be and he's already offered her eternal life. Wow!

Female: She must have been really surprised too that he didn't condemn her. She must have been so surprised by his response. I can only imagine her bracing for the rebuke that was to come when it was obvious that she had five husbands and was living with a guy now. His response I think triggered some of that respect that she seems to display in the ways she talks to him because she's probably floored.

Dan: Yeah. I think so. She's now very respectful, calling him a prophet and I think she's deeply touched. This is moving her emotionally.

Female: She was probably ready to put up her defenses if he had come back.

Dan: Probably used to it, don't you think? Daily ... yeah.

Female: Yeah. She's got gloves on.

Dan: She was ready, but his approach was totally different from what she was used to or expected. She says to him, "Our fathers worshipped on this mountain. [That would be Mount Gerizim.] But you Jews claim that the place where we must worship is in Jerusalem." There is a key difference.

If you worship in the wrong place, you can't be God's people. The place is what's important, and that's what divided them primarily. Jesus declared,

> Believe me, woman. A time is coming when you will worship the Father neither on this mountain nor in Jerusalem. You Samaritans worship what you do not know. We worship what we do know, for salvation is from the Jews. Yet a time is coming and now has come when the true worshippers will worship the Father in spirit and truth for they are the kind of worshippers the Father seeks. God the Spirit and his worshippers must worship him in spirit and in truth.

Wow! What a message! "A time is coming," he said to her, when who is going to worship the Father?

Female: All people. It says ... yeah.

Dan: But in particular?

Female: The Samaritans.

Dan: The Samaritan woman, first of all, and the Samaritans secondarily. There is a time coming when you – that seems to me a prediction.

Female: He's very personal to her right now.

Dan: Yeah. When you, the woman, you the Samaritans, you're going to worship.

Dan: Who are you going to worship?

Female: The Father.

Dan: Anything about that strike you as unusual?

Female: Because it was Jacob that they worshipped? ...

Dan: Yeah. I wonder what she thought he meant when he said, "You will worship the Father." He might be right she might tell. He means Jacob.

Female: Or maybe he means Abraham since he is Jewish.

Dan: Or maybe he means Abraham. How many people did Jesus teach about the Father in his ministry?

Female: His disciples?

Dan: Very few—and I don't think [it included] the disciples. They haven't heard about the Father. He is telling her about the Father, maybe before anyone else hears. He is revealing the Father to her and saying that, "You are going to worship the Father." To worship him, probably you ought to know who he is. Again, we get back to (in my estimation) some very heavily Trinitarian theological utterances here by Jesus to the Samaritan woman, of all people, but neither on this mountain nor in Jerusalem. What does that mean? You're going to worship the Father.

Female: A place …

Female: The place is not important here.

Dan: Yeah. The place would not be important any longer. "You Samaritans worship what you do not know." They didn't know the Father. They honored Jacob, looking for a prophet. They were a little bit confused. "We worship what we do know." At least we Jews have some things right.

What do you think he means, "salvation is from the Jews?"

Female: He was born Jewish. He is the Son of God.

Dan: The Messiah comes from Judah. One of the reasons the Maccabeans (who freed the Judeans from the Syrian armies and so forth) and they were very pleased throughout the Seleucid reign and all of that), but as much as Judas Maccabaeus and the Maccabean family did, the Judeans never really quite fully accepted them. You know why? They weren't of David.

You got to be of David. Salvation is of the Jews and in particular of the line of David, if you're going to be the Messiah, so they were looking to Jacob and they were looking for a prophet and Jesus is saying, "No. Salvation is from the Jews." A son of David, from the tribe of Judah. [Jesus may have said that, but John likes that phrase a lot, and he uses it quite frequently.]

"A time is coming and now has come when the true worshippers…" What do you think he means by true worshippers?

Female: For me, what stands out, he didn't call them the Jews or the Samaritans. He just calls them the worshippers so …

Dan: That's a very good observation.

Female: … taken away the … basically, the background of the person.

Dan: It's irrelevant whether you're a Jew or Samaritan.

Female: Your identity now is the worshippers.

Dan: It's not the location. It's not your national identity. It's who you worship.

Female: It's not your gender.

Dan: It's who you worship and you come to know him. The true worshippers will worship the Father in spirit and truth. What do you make of the triad? The true worshippers will worship the Father in the spirit ...

Female: And in truth.

Dan: ... and truth, and who is the truth?

Female: Jesus.

Dan: Jesus is the truth. We've got worshipping the Father and the Spirit through the truth. "For they are the kind of worshippers the Father seeks." Anything strike you as interesting about that statement there?

Female: He doesn't seek the ones that just give lip service or to him, goes to the temple and they think they're the worshippers.

Dan: He's still looking for people like the Samaritan woman of all people who are authentic, who are open, right?

Dan: Anything else?

Female: That have the spirit of God in them and are using it.

Female: It sounds like he's still seeking and he's looking.

Dan: Who's doing the seeking?

Female: The Father.

Dan: Anything interesting about that? Wouldn't we expect that in most religious circles that you must seek God ...

Dan: ... and yet Jesus says, "You're not seeking God. God is seeking you."

Female: Jesus went to seek her.

Dan: Aha. He sought her out. God is seeking for people like you.

Female: He knew her and he understood her.

Dan: Wow. I'm not a Jew. I'm a woman.

Female: I'm a sinner.

Dan: Exactly. God is seeking true worshippers like you.

Female: I think it's interesting too it says here a couple of times "in spirit and in truth," connecting those two together, that spirit and truth, they go together, they are inseparable. It seems that he did it two times here.

Dan: Right. As he says, "God is spirit and his worshippers must worship in spirit and in truth. The only way to the Father is in the Spirit through the truth, the Son." Any other worship that is not Trinitarian, I would say you're missing the boat.

I am amazed at how Trinitarian his teaching is to this woman... While as you know that disciples who are still down at McDonald's buying lunch while this deep Trinitarian theological discussion is going on out by the well.

Female: He didn't do it there, instead of with her, so they couldn't add their two cents.

Dan: What do you think would have happened, that Barbara raises an interesting point?

Female: They couldn't believe that he was talking to her, first of all. They would make her feel that she was condemned. They couldn't help themselves, but Jesus came not to condemn.

Dan: They probably would have been judgmental. They would have judged both Jesus and her. They would have tried to stop him. They would have sent her away. He knew he had to get rid of them in order to do …

They were not yet ready for the level of discussion that he was having with this woman. Verse 25, the woman said, "I know that Messiah [and John helpfully adds for us Greek speakers] called Christ, I know that Messiah is coming. When he comes, he will explain everything to us."

Female: Here she says, "So, she must have known something."

Dan: She knows about the Messiah.

Female: She knew about the Messiah which is a little unusual for a Samaritan.

Dan: She's probably familiar with the Jewish customs, evidently, so she is educated, well-read, well-versed. Now, Jesus, I think, has led her thinking and has shifted it away from Samaritan by saying, "Salvation is of the Jews," she has come back and connected the dot and saying, "I know the Messiah… I know he will come," and what does she say her understanding of the Messiah is?

Female: He will proclaim all things.

Dan: Right. He will explain everything to us.

Female: She's probably very happy about saying this. This is probably something that's always been inside of her. She knew that the Messiah was going to come someday to rescue and now she could verbalize it because she's happy, she's excited. The woman said, "I know that the Messiah is coming," and she didn't have any Samaritans denying her of that or anybody else.

Dan: Yeah, that's a pretty straightforward statement, "I know …"

Female: She just let it come out. It's there. It's hidden. Now, it's out.

Dan: Then, Jesus declared, "I who speak to you, am he." How many people has he revealed himself as the Messiah to? You can read the whole of book of Mark and they call it the Messianic Secret because he never tells anybody who he is, and this Samaritan woman meeting her for the first time, he says, "Hey, I'm the Messiah."

Female: Wow.

Dan: Now, for some comic diversion, the disciples return. "Just then, his disciples returned and were surprised to find him talking with a woman. [That's just not right. This is improper.] No one asked, 'What do you want?' or 'Why are you talking with her?'" What do you think the scene must have been like?

Female: They couldn't believe it.

Dan: I've almost imagined them nudging, "You ask him." "No, I'm not going to ask him. You ask him." "Peter will ask him." "No, I've had enough trouble. I'm not asking him."

Female: I think the body language probably revealed everything, though. They didn't need to say anything. When you have that kind of shock and surprise, most people can't hide that. They probably were already revealing their true feelings about it without having to say anything.

Dan: Non-verbal expression said it all.

Female: Our children's Bible says, "What do you want *from* her?" That's what he said …

Dan: Ohhh, that's not a nice thing to say.

Female: I know. That's what this says. I know. You'll never know. Maybe they knew.

Dan: That maybe what they were thinking …

Female: Maybe they knew that was her business and …

Dan: They thought that she was a woman of ill repute.

Dan: They just said … You know what? It reminds me of this Sergeant Schultz on *Hogan's Heroes,* "I see nothing. I know nothing. I'm going to pretend like I don't see this. Don't anybody say anything." They were shocked indeed.

Female: They probably were worried about their reputation too if this is leaking out to the public …

Female: … that our Master is talking to her …

Female: What are people going to think of us?

Female: … and how does this reflect upon us?

Female: He will lose his credibility.

Dan: Definitely. This is a major scandal.

Dan: Verse 28: "Then leaving her water jar, the woman went back to the town." What does that indicate?

Female: She was excited.

Dan: Excited. She forgot she came out to get water. That's not important.

Interesting, that water is not important anymore — I found the Living Water.

Female: She didn't really let the disciples deflate her feeling that she just experienced with Jesus. She just, "Oh, I'm out of here, to tell everybody."

Dan: Does she keep her mouth shut?

Female: No.

Dan: No, but she said to the people, "Come! See a man who told me everything I ever did." What do you think that may indicate?

Female: That he could possibly be the Messiah.

Dan: Right. Do you think her fellow citizens of Sychar knew a lot of the things she had done?

Female: Yes.

Dan: They knew, and this man told her everything she had ever done and showed her nothing but love and respect. How had the city folks treated her?

Female: She was fetching water in the middle of the day ...

Dan: By herself. You get the feeling she was kind of ostracized, marginalized by the city because probably they knew everything she had ever done, and yet Jesus knew everything she had ever done and treated her with respect and offered her eternal life.

Female: She was happy. She had a different attitude if somebody that wasn't repentant or ... you told what they did then, "Oh no, I didn't do that." I may be very mad and angry ... But instead she was very excited.

Dan: She's very honest about it and excited. Yeah. Some people call her the first evangelist. If evangelism is indeed an overflow response, this is what we see here. This woman was filled with this spirit. In a sense, she was overflowing with good news and couldn't wait to share it, even with people who didn't particularly like her or respect her. She couldn't help herself. She is so filled and so excited she has to tell people about Jesus. Indeed, in the Gospel of John, she is the first evangelist and she is a Samaritan and a woman.

The 12 are still standing around the well.

She says, "Come and see a man who told me everything I ever did. Could this be the Christ?" I think she thinks it is, but I believe she asked that question to get their interest. "Come and see him. What do you think? What do you think? This could be..." In other words, if I say he's the Christ, you're going to say, "Nah." You come and decide for yourself and see if this is not the Messiah.

Male: Why does she say Christ and not Prophet?

Dan: Yes, isn't that interesting. It's a good point. Why?

Male: Because hey weren't looking for the Christ.

Dan: No. This would have been a shock. I thought he went to the Jewish folk.

Female: And he's here.

Dan: He's here, the Jewish Messiah is here, in Sychar in Samaria? I've got to see this for myself. I think that's a good point. Got their curiosity up. "I have to see what's going on here. This doesn't make any sense to anything I know about what's supposed to be happening religiously."

Female: I think, to me, what strikes me here is she must have really been filled with the love of Jesus at this moment because instead of the response of, "Oh, I just had this great exciting experience, but I am who I am and nobody is going to believe me. Nobody is going to ... They're going to laugh at me. They might kick me out even further." She didn't have any of this response. She was filled with confidence and love to share this good news, which to me seems would be very supernatural. This is the love of Jesus that filled her. This is not a natural response.

Dan: Her eyes appear to be open and her ears appear to be hearing at this point and she's really connecting with Jesus. We find verse 38, "the people came out of the town, made their way toward him." Meanwhile ...

Male: Back at the ranch.

Dan: ... back at the ranch, Jesus' ever deeply, spiritual disciples, are urging, "Rabbi, eat something. Eat! Eat! It's lunch time." He said to them, "I have food to eat that you know nothing about." Then the disciples said to each other, "Could someone have brought him some food when we weren't looking? We were in town. Where did he get food?"

Female: They were talking to themselves too. They still didn't ask him any question.

Dan: Yeah. I think they were smart enough not to ask. Verse 34, "My food," said Jesus, "Is to do the will of him who sent me and to finish his work." Hmm.... finish his work. Whose work do you think the Samaritan woman was?

Female: His.

Dan: Yeah, the work of the Father and the Son through the Spirit.

"Do you not say four months more and then the harvest?" What does that mean? Anybody know what, agriculturally, that refers to? Four months to the harvest.

Female: You plant and then you wait for the harvest to be ready to reap. He's saying, "I plant ..." It's almost like he's saying, "I've planted the seed and the harvest is already ready." There's no waiting here.

Dan: Yeah. That's interesting. What I've read about the agriculture in Palestine is that when the rains come from like November to March and the soil is tillable and you till the soil and then you plant the grain (usually the barley and the wheat), and then you do nothing. You've done all you can do. You just wait and God has to do the rest.

I'm struck by that analogy of cultivating, planting, and then waiting for God to bring the harvest and do the work. Normally, in the agricultural cycle of things, that took four months. Indeed, they would cultivate, plant and say "four months to the harvest, four months to the harvest," and sit back and do nothing.

Female: Hope.

> Dan: "Do you not say four months more and then a harvest? I tell you, open your eyes and look at the fields. They are ripe for harvest. Even now, the reaper draws his wages, even now he harvests the crop for eternal life so that the sower and the reaper may be glad together. [Interesting.] Thus the saying, one sows and another reaps is true. I sent you to reap what you have not worked for. Others have done the hard work and you have reaped the benefits of their labor."

What do you think is going on there? "Open your eyes and look at the fields. They are ripe for harvest."

Female: Maybe he's teaching the disciples that the harvest may look different than what they might have expected. It might be in the form of a woman, a sinner— that might be the harvest, where the disciples would not have looked at her as somebody to bring to Jesus. They probably would have tried to shield him from her and get her away, and he's turning things around and says, "No. My harvest looks very different. You need to look around. It's ready."

Dan: Right.

Female: Then, the time too.

Dan: Yeah. I imagine the setting something like … I don't know there was. I imagine it this way, that Jesus is speaking and the disciples are on one side and have their backs to the city. Who's coming out of the city?

Female: All the people.

Dan: All the people are coming out of the city and the disciples are just standing there with their backs to it and Jesus was going, "Hmmm… the harvest is here and the fields are ripe and here comes the harvest."

The disciples are going, "What's he talking about?" Then, you can imagine the look when they turned around and saw the whole city coming out. I wonder if they even got his words then, but he told them, it's a process. Isn't that interesting? There is cultivating, there is sowing, and there is reaping. Not necessarily one person does it all, but it's all a part of what God does, but it's people participating with him in various phases as he works with the people.

Verse 39,

> Many of the Samaritans from that town believed in him because of the woman's testimony, "He told me everything I ever did." When the Samaritans came to him, they urged him to stay with them and he stayed two days. Because of his words, many more became believers. They said to the woman, "We no longer believe just because of what you said. Now, we have heard for ourselves and we know that this man really is the Savior of the world.

According to John, the first group of people to say this …

Female: Are Samaritans.

Dan: … are Samaritans, of all things.

Male: Yeah, a little village.

Dan: Who would have thought in a little village led by an evangelistic female? What conclusions does anybody draw? What really stands out in this story to you? Something that really strikes you?

Female: The harvest is there. It's finding it. It's looking around and seeing it.

Female: He helps you see it too, because he says, "It's here. It's coming."

Female: And do not cut. They're saying that, "They can't know Christ. They're not good enough. They haven't done all the right things."

Female: To look beyond.

Dan: They're people of another religion, of another country.

Female: It's not a matter being good.

Dan: How should we preach to them? They won't get it.

Dan: Hmmm … maybe they will better than some who've grown up in Christianity. Anyone else?

Female: It's the manner of his love and their background. She was prepared for this time and place and he had her in mind.

Dan: The least, the last, and the lost …

Female: Yeah. He knew exactly what she did.

Dan: … are the ones that Jesus tends to go to first and they tend to be the first to receive him, the most open.

Dan: It's a remarkable story that tells us many things about God's love for all people, and there's goodness and there's God working in the lives of all people in all countries, all nations, all ethnic groups, all religions or no religion at all. God is still there loving those people and working with them. It's quite a story, Jesus and the Samaritan woman. Let's conclude with a closing hymn and a final prayer.

LIVING WATER

By Joseph Tkach

In the developed world, we don't really need to pray, "Give us this day our daily bread." Our supermarkets have great variety from which to choose. It is the same with water. Millions of people in the poorer parts of the world must pray, "Give us this day our daily water"—and then walk several miles to get it. We, on the other hand, are spoiled for choice. In the Western world, bottled water is a multi-billion dollar business. My local supermarket offers at least 12 varieties, each promising to be superior to the others. Some people argue that none of them is actually better than plain old tap water, which is one hundred times less expensive. Maybe that's true. I don't know.

Though I am not an expert on water, Jesus was. He not only turned water into wine, he walked on it. And in the beginning, he created it. You will remember the account in John's Gospel, where Jesus met the Samaritan woman who was drawing water from a well. He told her he could supply her with a never-ending supply of what he called "living water." This water was so superior that whoever drank it would never be thirsty again.

Clean drinking water was scarce in Jesus' day, so the woman naturally asked him how she could get this exceptional water. The phrase "living water" usually meant moving, flowing water. The woman knew there was no flowing water nearby. The only water available locally was in that well. Jesus was using a play on words. He explained, "Everyone who drinks this water will be thirsty again, but whoever drinks the water I give them will never thirst. Indeed, the water I give them will become in them a spring of water welling up to eternal life" (John 4:13-14). This was a great metaphor, since water is essential to life. Just as the physical body needs water to continue living, so does the spirit.

When we become physically thirsty, water satisfies us. However, we are not just physical creatures. We are made in God's image and we have a spiritual appetite, whether we recognize it or not. We can become hungry and thirsty spiritually for a restored and right relationship with God. Jesus explained that he was the source of the "spiritual water" that can quench the thirst of the spirit. By drinking the living water, one can live and never thirst again.

The woman was astonished, not only by his extraordinary offer. In fact, she may not have fully understood it at the time. What astonished her was that Jesus spoke to her in the first place. She was a Gentile, a woman, and had a somewhat dubious reputation. She was used to being shunned by her own people. A Jewish man should have gone to great lengths to avoid her. Nevertheless, Jesus accepted her and offered hope and encouragement.

This story teaches us that Jesus offers his forgiveness to everyone. No matter how many sins one has committed, Jesus offers new life—and he offers it to all humanity. By reaching out to an outcast Samaritan woman, Jesus showed that his kingdom is for everyone from every nation, every tribe and every culture.

Our denomination is greatly blessed to be truly "international"—not just in word but in fact. I am humbled that the Holy Spirit sees us as a "safe place" to bring people looking for grace and truth. We did not go seeking several thousand members in Mozambique. They were looking for a "well" to satisfy their thirst for truly knowing and worshiping God. Right now, their need is physical as well as spiritual and so we will do what we can to help them. However, let's not forget our own backyard. Physical food and drink is not the critical need for most Western nations. But they are spiritually undernourished and in desperate need of wholesome spiritual food and clean living water.

When Jesus spoke to the Samaritan woman at the well, he opened up a whole new perspective to his ministry. His disciples were shocked to find him talking to "that kind of woman" (John 4:27). But they eventually came to understand that Jesus had a ministry to all the world—not to just a select few.

We are privileged to participate in that ministry today. Think about it next time you see the array of rather expensive "superior" bottled waters on your supermarket shelf. Remember, the best water of all is free. You just have to know where it comes from.

JOHN 4: TRUE WORSHIP

By Joseph Tkach

Jews and Samaritans simply didn't get along. The trouble went way back, five centuries or so, to the days of the Jewish leader Zerubbabel. Some Samaritans offered to help the Jews rebuild their temple, and Zerubbabel rebuffed them. The Samaritans responded by complaining to the king of Persia, and the work stopped (Ezra 4).

Later, when the Jews were rebuilding the walls of Jerusalem, the governor of Samaria threatened to take military action against the Jews. The Samaritans eventually built their own temple on Mt. Gerizim, and in 128 B.C., the Jews destroyed it. Although their religions were both based on the laws of Moses, they were bitter enemies.

Jesus enters Samaria

But Jesus was not shackled by the squabbles of the past. Although most Jews avoided Samaria, Jesus walked right into it, taking his disciples with him. He was tired, so he sat down at a well near the city of Sychar, and sent his disciples into town to buy some groceries (John 4:38). Along came a Samaritan woman, and Jesus talked to her. She was surprised that he would talk to a Samaritan; his disciples were surprised that he would talk to a woman (verses 9, 27).

Jesus shows us a simple way of dealing with people who have different religious beliefs, people who are from a different ethnic group, people who are traditional enemies: just treat them like normal human beings. Don't ignore them, don't avoid them, don't insult them. But Jesus had something much more profound than that to say.

He began in the simplest possible way: He asked the woman for a drink. He was thirsty, but he had nothing to draw water with — but she did. He had a need, she had a means of fulfilling it, so he asked her for help. She was surprised that a Jew would actually drink from a Samaritan water pot — most Jews considered such a vessel ritually unclean. And then Jesus said: I have something a lot better than water, if you want it. I am willing to ask you for a drink of water — are you willing to ask me for something that's better? (verses 7-10).

Jesus was using a play on words — the phrase "living water" usually meant moving water, flowing water. The woman knew quite well that the only water in Sychar was in that well, and there was no flowing water nearby. So she asked Jesus what he was talking about. He said he was talking about something that would lead to eternal life (verses 11-14). He was talking about religious ideas — but would the woman be willing to listen to spiritual truth from a religious enemy? Would she drink Jewish waters?

The woman asked for the living water, and Jesus invited her to get her husband. He already knew that she didn't have one, but he asked anyway — possibly to show that he had spiritual authority. He was the vessel from which she could receive the living water. The woman got the message: "I can see that you are a prophet" (verse 19). If Jesus knew the facts about her unusual marital status, then he probably knew spiritual truths, as well.

True worship

After learning that Jesus was a prophet, the woman brought up the age-old controversy between Samaritans and Jews about the proper place to worship: We worship here, but you Jews say that people have to go to Jerusalem (verse 20). Jesus responded: The day will soon come when that won't be relevant. It won't matter whether people look to Mt. Gerizim or Jerusalem — or any other location. The hour is already here when people will worship God in spirit and truth (verses 2124).

Has Jesus suddenly jumped to a different subject? Maybe not — the Gospel of John gives us some clues about what he meant: "The words I have spoken to you are *spirit* and they are life" (John 6:63). "I am the way and the *truth* and the life" (John 14:16). True worship means listening to the words of Jesus, and coming to God through him. Worship does not depend on place or time or ethnic group — it depends on our attitude to God as shown in our attitude to his Son, Jesus Christ. True worship comes along with the living water.

Jesus was revealing a profound spiritual truth to this stranger — a truth just as profound as what he had discussed with one of Israel's religious leaders (John 3). But the woman was not quite sure what to make of it, and she said, When the Messiah comes, he'll tell us what's right (verse 25).

Jesus responded, I am he — probably his most direct claim to be the Messiah — and yes, what I am telling you is right. The woman left her water jar behind and went back to town to tell everyone about Jesus, and she convinced them to check it out for themselves, and many of them believed. They believed not just because of the woman's testimony, but because they listened to Jesus himself (verses 39-41).

Worship today

Sometimes people today get too opinionated about worship — true worship has to involve a certain day of the week, a certain type of song, a certain posture or some other detail. But I think that Jesus' answer to the

Samaritan woman covers it well: The time will come when you will worship God neither this way nor that, because God is not to be found in earthly places, rotations of the earth, cultural music or human gestures.

God is spirit, and our relationship with him is a spiritual one. We live in time and space, and we use time and space in our worship, but those details are not the meaning of worship. Rather, our worship centers in Jesus, and in our relationship with him. He is the source of living waters that we need for eternal life. We need to admit our thirst, and ask him for a drink. Or to use metaphors from the book of Revelation, we need to admit that we are poor, blind and naked, and ask Jesus for spiritual wealth, sight and clothing. We worship in spirit and truth when we look to him for what we need.

In marriage, different people express love in different ways, and some forms of expression are appropriate in public, and some are not. This is true of worship, too. We express our adoration in different ways, and some ways are more appropriate in private than in public. Certain activities, though they may seem worshipful to one person, may appear disrespectful or distracting to another person. When we worship together, we do not want our activities to put other people off. At the same time, believers who are more formal need to be tolerant of a little diversity. True worship is not defined by external matters, but by our attitude toward Jesus Christ.

When it comes to worship, though there will always be room for improvement and maturity, may we continue to learn from Jesus not only about what worship really is, but also the way we interact with people who think about it differently than we do.

JOHN 6: 'LET NOTHING BE WASTED'

By Joseph Tkach

Jesus saw a large crowd coming toward him, and he asked Philip, "Where will we buy enough bread for all these people?"

Jesus already knew what he was going to do, but he asked the question because he wanted Philip to think about it and learn something from it (John 6:5-6, my paraphrase, throughout). John included this story so that we could think about it and learn something from it, too.

Spiritual significance

Let's fast-forward into the story so we can see what Jesus already knew would happen. He miraculously fed the large crowd, and they later asked Jesus to prove that he was the Messiah (v. 30). Jesus told them, "My Father gives you the true bread from heaven—bread that gives life to the world."

"Well then," they said, "give us some of this bread" (v. 34). Their response was like the Samaritan woman at the well: When Jesus said that he had water that would give eternal life, she said, "Give me some" (John 4:15), and eventually Jesus said that he was talking about himself.

And in John 6, Jesus also reveals that he is talking about himself: "I am the bread of life. Whoever comes to me will never go hungry, and whoever believes in me will never be thirsty" (v. 35). Jesus is the bread who came down from heaven to give life to the world. Just as bread is nourishment for our physical lives, Jesus is the source of spiritual life and energy.

The miracle of feeding the large crowd pointed toward a spiritual truth, and that is why Jesus did it, and that is why he wanted Philip to think about it, and that is why John tells us the story. Jesus did many miracles that John did not include in his book, but John includes certain ones to help us have faith in Jesus (20:30-31) — not just believe that Jesus did certain things in the past, but that we would trust him with our eternal future. The miracles are signs pointing us toward Jesus' spiritual significance.

Let's look at the story again.

It was almost Passover, John tells us (v. 3). Bread was an important feature of the Passover season, but Jesus is revealing that salvation does not come from physical bread, but from Jesus himself. Jesus asked Philip, "Where are we going to buy bread for these people?" And Philip answered, "It would take (roughly) five thousand dollars to buy enough bread for this crowd!"

Andrew did not speculate about the price, but he must have been good with kids. He had already befriended a boy and learned that he was carrying a little extra food. "This boy has five small loaves and two dried fish, but that's not near enough, is it?" Perhaps he was hoping that the crowd included a few more boys who had the foresight to bring lunch.

"That's good enough," Jesus said. "Have everybody sit down." So everybody did. Jesus thanked God for the food, and gave everyone as much food as they wanted (v. 11). It was quite a crowd — larger than many towns are today — and the people began to talk among themselves, "Surely this is the Prophet" (v. 14).

They thought that Jesus was the leader Moses had predicted (Deut. 18:15-19)—and yet, ironically, they were not willing to listen to him. They wanted to make him a king by force — forcing him into their idea of what a Messiah should be — rather than letting Jesus do what God sent him to do.

When everyone had enough to eat, Jesus told the disciples: "Gather the pieces that are left over. Let nothing be wasted" (John 6:12). Doesn't this strike you as a little odd? Why would Jesus want to gather all the leftovers? Why not let the people keep the extra? Or let it be a bonanza for the birds and chipmunks?

The disciples picked up 12 baskets full of leftovers, John tells us — but then he says nothing about what they did with all those half-eaten loaves. I think there's something going on behind the scenes. What is there in the spiritual realm that Jesus does not want to go to waste? I think that John gives us a clue later in the chapter.

Walking on water

The disciples took a boat back home — but they left Jesus stranded there, without any other boat to pick him up (vs. 17, 22). John does not indicate that anything was out of the ordinary with this, so I conclude that the disciples often left Jesus alone, presumably because Jesus wanted to be left alone sometimes. He needed some time on his own for prayer, no doubt. (As an aside, I might point out that this is also true for pastors today — they need some time to themselves, even though there will always be people who want more of their time.)

As far as I know, Jesus was not in a hurry. He could have walked back to town on the roads that went around the lake. Or he could have waited for a boat, like the other people did (v. 23). But he walked on the water, apparently to make a spiritual point.

In Matthew, the spiritual point is faith, but John says nothing about Peter walking on water or sinking and being saved by Jesus. What John tells us is that when the disciples took Jesus into the boat, "immediately the boat reached the shore where they were heading" (v. 21). This is the feature of the story that John wants us to take note of.

If Jesus could do teleporting, why did he need to walk on water? Why not just zap to wherever you want to go? What's the point? You might have a better idea, but here's mine: The story tells us that Jesus is not limited by physical circumstances, and as soon as we accept Jesus, we are spiritually at our destination. It may not look like it, but Jesus is not limited by physical appearances. Spiritually, the reality is set; it has been done.

The bread of life

The people searched Jesus out again, looking for another free lunch, and Jesus encouraged them to look for spiritual food instead: "Do not look for food that spoils, but for food that endures to eternal life" (vs. 24-27). "The Son of Man will give you this food," Jesus said, but instead of asking for this gift, they asked what they should do (v. 28). They were asking for works instead of grace.

"What does God want us to do?" they asked, wanting to meet the requirements of the messianic age. Jesus told them: "God wants you to believe in the person he sent" (v. 29). The messianic age has already begun, so don't try to work your way into the kingdom — just trust Jesus, and you'll be in. Just take that one step, and you'll be there!

Could it really be that easy?, the people wondered. They asked for evidence — as if feeding 5,000 people had not been enough! "What miraculous sign will you do that we might believe you?" As an example of a miracle they might be willing to believe, and in keeping with the Passover season, they mentioned a miracle of bread associated with the Exodus — Moses gave them manna (bread from heaven) to eat. Some Jews thought that God would provide manna in the messianic age, too.

But Jesus said that the real bread from heaven doesn't just feed the Israelites — it gives life to the world! (v. 33). "Give it to us," they said, probably wanting to examine it to see if it met their qualifications. Jesus replied that he was the bread from heaven, the source of eternal life for the world.

The people had seen Jesus perform signs, and they still did not believe in him (vs. 33-36), because he did not meet their qualifications for a messiah. Why did some believe, and others did not? Jesus explained it as the work of the Father: "Everyone the Father gives me will come to me." He repeats this idea in verses 44 and 65: "No one can come to me unless the Father draws him ... unless the Father has enabled him."

Once the Father does that, what does Jesus do? He tells us his role when he says, "I will never drive them away" (v. 37). Perhaps they can leave on their own, but Jesus will never push them away. Jesus wants to do the will of the Father, and the Father's will is that Jesus will lose none of the people the Father has given him (v. 39). He does not let anyone go to waste.

Since Jesus does not lose anyone, he promises to raise them up at the last day (v. 39). This is repeated in verses 40, 44 and 54. Jesus stresses that the person who believes in him has eternal life (vs. 40, 47).

Eating his flesh?

Jesus also says that people who eat his flesh and drink his blood have eternal life (vs. 51, 53-56). Just as he was not referring to the stuff made from wheat when he called himself the true bread, he was not referring to muscle tissue when he spoke of eating his flesh.

Some of the Jews wondered, "How can this man give us his flesh to eat?" (v. 52), but in the Gospel of John, it is often a mistake to take Jesus' words in a literal sense. For example, Nicodemus asked, How can people enter their mothers' wombs and be born again? (3:4). Similarly, the Samaritan woman said, Give me some of this living water so I won't have to come back to this well (4:15).

They pushed the literal meaning, but the story shows that Jesus meant something spiritual. Here in chapter 6, Jesus said, "The flesh counts for nothing; the words I have spoken to you are spirit and they are life" (v. 63). Jesus is not making a point about his muscle tissue — he is talking about his teachings.

And his disciples seem to get the point. When Jesus asks them if they want to go away, Peter answers: "Lord, to whom shall we go? You have the words of eternal life" (v. 68). Peter was not worried about having access to the flesh of Jesus — he focused on the words of Jesus. The consistent message of the New Testament is that salvation is experienced through faith, not special food and drink.

From heaven

Jesus repeats one more point several times in this chapter: that he is from heaven (vs. 33, 38, 41, 42, 46, 50, 51, 58, 62). The reason that people should believe in Jesus is because he has come down from heaven. He is absolutely trustworthy, because he does not just have a message from heaven, but he *himself* is from heaven.

The Jewish leaders did not like this teaching (v. 41), and some of Jesus' disciples could not accept it, either (v. 66) — even after Jesus made it clear that he was not talking about his literal flesh, but rather his words themselves were the source of eternal life. They were troubled that Jesus claimed to be from heaven — and therefore more than human.

But Peter knew that he had nowhere else to go, for only Jesus had the words of eternal life (v. 68). Why did he know that only Jesus had these words? Because only Jesus is "the Holy One of God" (v. 69). *That* is the reason his words are trustworthy; that is the reason his words are spirit and life. We believe in Jesus not just because of what he says, but because of who he is. We do not accept him because of his words — we accept his words because of who he is.

Since Jesus is the Holy One of God, we can trust him to do what he says he will do: He will not lose anyone, but will raise us all at the last day (v. 39). Even the crumbs will be gathered, so that nothing goes to waste. That's the Father's will, and that's something worth thinking about.

JOHN 9: A BLINDING LIGHT

By Joseph Tkach

"I am the light of the world," said Jesus. "I have come into this world so that the blind will see" (John 9:5, 39). And to demonstrate it, he healed a man who had been born blind. He came to help people see, to help them understand something about God's love for them.

But Jesus also said that he came to bring blindness: "I have come into this world so that...those who see will become blind" (John 9:39). This is a hard saying — it is easy to understand a physician who came to heal the sick, but it is hard to understand a physician who came to make healthy people sick.

Whose fault is it?

Let's review the story in John 9. As Jesus and the disciples walked through Jerusalem, they saw a blind man. Somehow they knew that the man had been blind from birth, and the disciples used the opportunity to ask Jesus a theological question that had puzzled them: Whose fault is this, they asked, did the man sin before he was born, or is he being punished because his parents sinned? Problems like this, they assumed, are the result of sin, but who sinned?

Neither answer seemed right, and Jesus agreed. "Neither this man nor his parents sinned," Jesus said, "but this happened so that the work of God might be displayed in his life" (v. 3). Did God cause the man to be blind just so that Jesus could do a miracle? I don't think that is what Jesus is driving at.

Jesus seems to be talking about the result rather than the purpose or cause. The man was born blind, and it doesn't do him or anyone else any good for us to speculate about whose sin caused it. The man does not need a discussion about the causes of evil — he needs his sight, and Jesus said that the result of his condition is that "the work of God" would be seen in him. And by that, I think that Jesus was talking about more than a miracle.

"As long as it is day," Jesus said, "we must do the work of him who sent me." A modern proverb that is roughly equivalent is, "Make hay while the sun shines" — or work while you can, because, as Jesus warns, a time will come when you can't: "Night is coming, when no one can work." When will that be, we might wonder. When will it not be possible to do the work of God?

Jesus continued, "While I am in the world, I am the light of the world" (v. 5). As long as he is here, it is daytime — but a time would come when he would go away and the work would stop. Fortunately for us, that "night" did not last long, for Jesus was raised from the dead and now works in and through his people. (We also need to work while we can, because a time will come for each of us when we can do no more.)

Blind obedience

To illustrate what he meant by being a light to the world, Jesus spit on the ground, made a little mud, put it on the eyes of the blind man and told him to go wash in the Pool of Siloam. It's hard to know from this account how much the man knew about Jesus. He knew his name, but may not have known much more than that. But he went to the Pool of Siloam anyway, and he was healed. It would have been interesting to see his reaction, but all we are told is that he went home (v. 7).

Now, why did Jesus heal the man in such an unusual way? If he just wanted to display a miracle, he would have healed him instantly. He could have said to his disciples, I can give spiritual sight just like this: snap! But the disciples did not see a miracle — all they saw was that Jesus put mud on somebody's face and then told him to go wash it off.

John never does tell us how they reacted when they eventually found out. So the story that John is telling here is not so much about the miracle — it is about how the man learns who Jesus is, and how he reacts when he does. This is the far more important work of God that is being demonstrated in this man's life.

The news got around, and the man told people that "the man they call Jesus" had healed him (v. 11). Then the Pharisees, the self-appointed judges of all spiritual truth, started to investigate this supernatural event. Some of them had already concluded that Jesus couldn't be from God because he worked on the Sabbath. (Even God had to keep their rules, apparently.)

Others were more open-minded, saying that sinners (at least the sinners they knew) couldn't do miracles like that (v. 16). So they asked the formerly blind man what he thought. "He is a prophet," the man replied. He is like Elijah, sent by God with a message.

The Jews, or at least some of them, didn't seem to like that answer, so they searched for a way to discredit the miracle. They asked his parents about it, and the parents verified the facts: He was born blind, but now he can see, but we don't know who did it. They didn't offer an opinion on whether Jesus was from God, because they were afraid of being expelled from the synagogue (v. 22).

I feel sorry for the parents. They had probably lived for years with the accusation that their son was blind because they had sinned. They needed the synagogue because faithful attendance was the only way they could show they were good people after all. Even though their son could now see, they were not willing to risk expulsion — and John probably includes this because it was precisely the situation that some of his readers faced. After Jerusalem was destroyed in A.D. 70, the Jewish leaders regrouped and began demanding more conformity; they did not allow people to attend synagogue if they had any forbidden beliefs about a messiah.

John has set before us several types of people: 1) Some who have already made up their minds that Jesus is ungodly. 2) Some who are puzzled by Jesus but still try to discredit him. 3) Some who refuse to say, and probably don't even want to find out because they are afraid of the consequences. 4) The man who viewed Jesus as good, and was willing to learn more.

Growing in faith

The Jewish leaders went back to the healed man and asked him again, and he told them again. "We know this man is a sinner," they said (v. 24). I'm not sure about that, the man replied, but I know for sure that I've been healed. He must have been a little exasperated with their attitude, for he asked, "I have told you already and you did not listen. Why do you want to hear it again? Do you want to become his disciples, too?" (v. 27).

The leaders were offended by this idea, so they responded with insults, drawing a line in the sand: "You are this fellow's disciple! We are disciples of Moses!" — and you can't be a disciple of both. John knew his readers needed to hear that, too. Don't worry about getting kicked out of the synagogue, he seems to say. You should have left it long ago, anyway.

The man became bolder, saying, You don't even know whether this man is from God, but he opened my eyes, and God doesn't listen to sinners! "He listens to the godly man who does his will" (v. 31). In other words, Jesus is a godly man who is doing the will of God. "If this man were not from God, he could do nothing." That's the central question that runs throughout the Gospel of John: Is Jesus from God? The man declared that Jesus is from God.

The Jewish leaders became angry at this layman who tried to teach them theology, and they expelled him from the synagogue. They didn't want him telling his story to more people.

Jesus heard about it and went looking for the man. "When he found him, he said, 'Do you believe in the Son of Man?'" (v. 35). Here Jesus seems to be using the "Son of Man" as a messianic title, perhaps derived from Daniel's vision of "one like a son of man" who was given supreme authority (Dan. 7:13-14). "Who is he, sir?" the man asked. "Tell me so that I may believe in him." If you say I am supposed to believe in somebody, then I will.

Jesus revealed himself to be the Son of Man, and the man worshipped him (v. 38). Just as he could see physically, he could also see spiritually, and in this way he displayed the work of God in his life.

Judgment

Jesus now gives another theological lesson: "For judgment I have come into this world, so that the blind will see and those who see will become blind." Jesus is the category by which all humanity will be judged. If people accept him, then God accepts them. But if they reject him, they are rejected. In other words, when a person refuses light, they have only darkness. Jesus is claiming to be the way, the truth and the life. Here he says he is the light, the one who enables people to see.

Some people refuse to see. Some are afraid, because Jesus nullifies their badges of righteousness. And when they turn away from Jesus, from the only true Light, they go further into darkness. In this story, the leaders of the synagogue would rather be blind than to admit that they had been wrong.

Some Pharisees asked, "Are we blind too?" And Jesus explained his parable: "If you were blind, you would not be guilty of sin; but now that you claim you can see, your guilt remains" (v. 41). When he said, "Those who see will become blind," he was not talking about people who really had spiritual insight. Rather, he was talking about people who only *thought* their insight was spiritual light, when it really was only darkness. They claimed to know spiritual truth, but when the Truth was right in front of them, they would not see it. Jesus did not *make* them blind, but he showed that they were blind.

People are judged by the way they respond to Jesus. If they admit their ignorance and are willing to be taught, they are not counted guilty. But if they claim to see, yet reject the only true Light, then they are guilty.

When you look at Jesus, what do you see?

JOHN 10: WHICH VOICE DO YOU HEAR?

By Joseph Tkach

Jesus told a parable and, as usual, the people did not understand him. So he explained it: "I am the gate for the sheep" (John 10:7). In this parable, the sheep are God's people, and they are entering a safe place, a sheep pen, representing salvation. We enter salvation through Jesus.

"I am the good shepherd," Jesus continued, and "the sheep follow the shepherd because they know his voice. But they will never follow a stranger; in fact, they will run away from him because they do not recognize a stranger's voice" (vs. 11, 4-5). God's people hear the voice of Jesus and recognize it, but they stay clear of other voices.

The voices we hear

If Jesus has the voice of salvation, what are the other voices (the "strangers") that might call for our attention? In the first century, it might have been the Pharisees, who were trying to lead God's people. And it would have included the Dead Sea Scroll commune, who had their own path to pleasing God. The Herodians offered another approach to life: do whatever it takes to stay on good terms with the Roman government.

In our own day, various groups offer different paths to salvation: Muslims, Hindus, New Agers and others offer people different paths — even different ideas of salvation. For some, salvation is physical pleasure; for others it is the absence of feeling. Some focus on the afterlife, others on life right now. "Come to my sheep pen," they might be calling. "You'll be safe here."

But these voices do not sound like Jesus. They do not have the message of grace from the God who loves us. Instead, they usually offer a message of "Do this and try harder." Jesus says that we need a radical change, and just working harder will not be effective. Humans cannot save themselves — we can be saved only because God himself came into our world, suffered the pain of our corruption himself, and not only paid the ultimate penalty, but also lived the perfect life in our place.

Some versions of Christianity fall away from grace, and begin to preach works — good works, usually, but works nevertheless. There are conservative do-gooders and liberal do-gooders. Some people have the right words for Jesus (Lord and Savior, Son of God) but subtly drown out his voice by preaching about works as the key to salvation.

Such a message turns into a message about family values (which are very good) with a little Jesus thrown in for spice. Or it turns into political action, with a little Jesus thrown in for credibility. Some have even turned Jesus into merely a good teacher, a good example who encourages us to try harder and do more.

"Come into this sheep pen," they might say. "This will give your life more meaning" — and it does, since it gives a semblance of purpose in life, which is more satisfying than selfishness. But it still falls short of the gospel of Jesus Christ, because in the message of "do good and try harder," people always fall short. Jesus says, "Come into my sheep pen, where the burden is light and there is no condemnation" (Matt. 11:30; Rom. 8:1). Do we hear his voice, or are we attracted to the gospel of good works?

God made us to do good works (Eph. 2:10), but he also made us to find our meaning and purpose in Jesus Christ. We were made through him, by him and *for* him (Col. 1:16), and we will never be fully satisfied until we find our meaning and purpose in him.

Thieves and robbers

If people try to get to the sheep pen in any way other than Christ, they are thieves and robbers, Jesus says (John 10:1). They are trying to get something in an unlawful way — they are trying to give life meaning without the Creator of life.

They may mean well. Maybe they don't understand who Jesus is and what he is offering. Maybe Jesus' grace insults their ability to work hard and direct their lives on their own. Maybe they think grace sounds too easy, too cheap. Whatever the reason, if they try to achieve life's purpose in any other way, through any other gate, they will fail.

The people who offer other paths to salvation generally mean well. They honestly believe that they have a better way — and their way probably is better than what they had before. But it falls far short of what Jesus offers: full and unconditional pardon. They offer different sheep pens, and invite people to come in.

Many of us have tried those sheep pens. Some have tried Islam, some have tried Hinduism, some have tried liberalism and some of us have tried legalism. "My sheep hear my voice," Jesus says, but by that he does not mean that our response is automatic. Rather, he is encouraging us to hear him, to listen for him, to respond to him instead of the counterfeits. We need to train our ear so that we hear him better, so that we recognize a false gospel for what it is: a thief and a robber that will short-change our happiness.

The other gospels do not intend to maim and kill, but that's what they end up doing. They offer something attractive, something good, but it's just not good enough. It's not Jesus, it's not grace, it's not finding our meaning in Christ.

Many voices can lead us away from Christ. If we have drifted away from Christ, what voices are we listening to? Are we so consumed by business, sports, television, partying, politics, sex, alcohol or other diversions that we have little or no time left for Jesus? Such things, when they crowd Jesus out, become thieves and robbers. They take our time, maybe even the rest of our life, but they will not give us life.

The shepherd who gives his life

"I am the good shepherd," Jesus said. "The good shepherd lays down his life for the sheep. The hired hand is not the shepherd who owns the sheep. So when he sees the wolf coming, he abandons the sheep and runs away" (vs. 11-12). All the other shepherds will let you down. Only Jesus died and rose for you. Only he deserves your full allegiance. Do you hear his voice?

JOHN 10:10 – THE ABUNDANT LIFE

By Paul Kroll

Many preachers quote John 10:10 as support for the idea that Christianity leads to physical prosperity and "every good thing." The verse has been used as a description of the Christian life, the normative pattern of life that Christians can expect because of God's blessings.

Other scriptures, including the salutation of 3 John 2, "I wish above all things that you prosper and be in good health," are also used to teach that Christians are promised health and wealth if they have enough faith. However, the New Testament usually emphasizes a radically different result of following Christ. We are told that we will be persecuted, that Christ's message is divisive, that we will need to take up our cross and follow him, that the normative expectation for Christian is *suffering*. Job promotions, new cars, and throwing away crutches are not among the fringe benefits offered by Jesus Christ.

3 John 2 appears as a part of the introductory comments of the letter, and it was meant specifically for a man named Gaius. It was simply part of the polite way to begin a letter in those days, and similar greetings are found in other ancient writings. One manual of letter writing explains that this is the appropriate was to begin a letter. Someone today might begin a letter by saying, "I hope that this letter finds you in good health." It is not meant as a promise. Likewise, 3 John 2 should not be used as a promise that God applies to all his people. This scripture does not guarantee that Gaius, or any other Christians, will be rich or that they will never suffer from sickness or disease.

And in order to understand what John 10:10 means, we need to look at its context. Chapter 10 of John's Gospel develops the biblical theme of sheep and the shepherd. The shepherd is accessible to the sheep. Strangers do not have a personal relationship with the flock, but the good shepherd does. Verse 10 draws the contrast between Jesus and false shepherds, the thieves who come to kill, steal and destroy.

John 20:31 describes the purpose of this Gospel. Speaking of the miracles and signs, John says, "But these are written that you may believe that Jesus is the Christ, the Son of God, and that by believing you may have life in his name." *The New International Commentary on the New Testament* comments,

Life is one of John's characteristic concepts. He uses the term 36 times, whereas no other New Testament writing has it more than 17 times (this is Revelation; next comes Romans with 14 times, and 1 John 13 times). Thus in this one writing there occur more than a quarter of all the New Testament references to life. "Life" in John characteristically refers to eternal life (see on 3:15), the gift of God through His Son. Here, however, the term must be taken in its broadest sense. It is only because there is life in the **Logos** that there is life in anything on earth at all." (John, page 82).

The Expositor's Bible Commentary says this about John 10:10:

Jesus' main purpose was the salvation (health) of the sheep, which he defined as free access to pasture and fullness of life. Under his protection and by his gift they can experience the best life can offer. In the context of John's emphasis on eternal life, this statement takes on new significance. Jesus can give a whole new meaning to living because he provides full satisfaction and perfect guidance.

Barclay's *Daily Study Bible* adds,

Jesus claims that he came that men might have life and might have it more abundantly. The Greek phrase used for *having it more abundantly means to have a superabundance of a thing*. To be a follower of Jesus, to know who he is and what he means, is to have a superabundance of life. A Roman soldier came to Julius Caesar with a request for permission to commit suicide. He was a wretched dispirited creature with no vitality. Caesar looked at him. "Man," he said, "were you ever really alive?" When we try to live our own lives, life is a dull, dispirited thing. When we walk with Jesus, there comes a new vitality, a superabundance of life. It is only when we live with Christ that life becomes really worth living and we begin to live in the real sense of the word.

In its volume on John, the *Tyndale New Testament Commentaries* summarizes the passage that leads up to John 10:10:

Those who are really "His own" listen to His voice. They recognize that He has been sent from God, and are ready to follow Him as the good Shepherd, who by His sacrificial love rescues His flock from evil and death, and leads them into the best of all pasturage where they can enjoy a richer and a fuller life (9,10). He does not offer them an extension of physical life nor an increase of material possessions, but the possibility, nay the certainty, of a life lived at a higher level in obedience to God's will and reflecting His glory.

In summary, John 10:10 should not be used as though it gives some promise of an improved physical life for the Christian. Such a view, in light of the context, is shallow, and it overlooks the profound truth of the passage. The passage promises superior, superabundant spiritual life, life empowered by the indwelling of Jesus Christ. Because Christians "have" Jesus Christ, because he lives within them, they have the riches of the superabundant life. This is what Paul meant when he said he counted all things loss, that he might win Christ. John 10:10 promises a spiritual dimension to life, not physical abundance. A focus on the physical trivializes the profound depth of John 10:10.

JOHN 11: 'LAZARUS, COME OUT'

By Joseph Tkach

Most of us know the story: Jesus raised Lazarus from the dead. It was a tremendous miracle, showing that Jesus has the power to raise us from the dead, too. But there is more to the story than that, and John includes some details that may have deeper meaning for us today. I pray that I do not do injustice to the story as I share some of my thoughts with you.

Notice the way that John tells the story: Lazarus was not just a random resident of Judea — he was the brother of Martha and Mary, the Mary who loved Jesus so much that she poured perfume on his feet. "The sisters sent word to Jesus, 'Lord, the one you love is sick'" (John 11:1-3). To me, that sounds like a request for help, but Jesus did not come.

Delay with purpose

Does it ever seem to you like the Lord is slow to respond? It surely did for Mary and Martha, but the delay does not mean that Jesus doesn't like us. Rather, it means that he has a different plan in mind, because he can see something that we cannot.

As it turns out, Lazarus was probably already dead by the time the messengers reached Jesus. Nevertheless, Jesus said that the sickness would not end in death. Was he mistaken? No, because Jesus could see beyond death, and he knew that in this case, death was not the end of the story. He knew that the purpose was to bring more glory to God and his Son (v. 4). Nevertheless, he let his disciples think that Lazarus would not die. There's a lesson there for us, too, for we do not always understand what Jesus really meant.

Two days later, Jesus surprised his disciples by suggesting that they return to Judea. They did not understand why Jesus would want to go back into the danger zone, so Jesus responded with a cryptic comment about walking in the light, and the coming of darkness (vs. 9-10), and then telling them that he had to go wake Lazarus up.

The disciples were apparently used to the mysterious nature of some of Jesus' comments, and they had a round-about way of getting more information: They pointed out that the literal meaning didn't make sense. If he's asleep, then he'll wake up by himself, so why do we need to risk our lives to go?

Jesus explained, "Lazarus is dead" (v. 14). But he also said, I'm glad I wasn't there. Why? "So that you may believe" (v. 15). Jesus would do a miracle that would be more astonishing than if he had merely prevented a sick man from dying. But the miracle was not just in raising Lazarus back to life — it was also the knowledge that Jesus had of what was going on perhaps 20 miles away, and the knowledge of what would happen to him in the near future.

He had light that they could not see — and this light told him of his own death in Judea, and of his own resurrection. He was in complete control of the events. He could have avoided arrest if he wanted to; he could have stopped the proceedings with a simple word, but he did not. He chose to do what he did because that's what he had come for.

The man who gave life to the dead would also give his own life for the people, for he had power over death, even his own death. He became mortal so that he could die, and what looked on the surface to be a tragedy was actually for our salvation. I don't want to imply that every tragedy that happens to us is actually planned by God, or is good, but I do believe that God is able to bring good out of evil, and he sees realities that we cannot.

He sees beyond death, and his mastery of events is just as good today as it was back then — but it is often just as invisible to us as it was to his disciples in John 11. We cannot see the bigger picture, and sometimes we stumble in the darkness. We have to trust God to work it out in the way that he knows is best. Sometimes we are eventually allowed to see how it works out for good, but often we just have to take his word for it.

Martha's faith

Jesus and his disciples went to Bethany and learned that Lazarus had been in the tomb for four days. The eulogies had been given and the funeral was long over, and the doctor finally shows up! Martha said, perhaps with a little exasperation and hurt, "Lord, if you had been here, my brother would not have died" (v. 22). We called for you several days ago, and if you had come then, then Lazarus would still be alive.

But Martha has a glimmer of hope — a little bit of light: "But I know that even now God will give you whatever you ask" (v. 23). Maybe she felt that it would be a little too bold for ask for a resurrection, but she hints at something.

"Lazarus will live again," Jesus said, and Martha responded, "Yes, I know that (but I was hoping for something a little sooner)." Jesus said: "That's good, but did you know that I am the resurrection and the life? If you believe in me, you will never die. Can you believe that?"

And Martha, in one of the most outstanding statements of faith in the entire Bible, said: "Yes, I believe that. You are the Son of God" (v. 27). Life and resurrection can be found only in Christ — but can we, today, believe what Jesus said? Do we really believe that "whoever lives and believes in me will never die?" I wish we all could better understand that, but I do know for sure that in the resurrection, we will be given a life that will never end.

In this age, we all die, just like Lazarus did, and Jesus will have to "wake us up." We die, but that is not the end of the story for us, just as it was not the end of the story for Lazarus.

Martha went to get Mary, and Mary came to Jesus weeping. Jesus wept, too. Why did he weep when he already knew that Lazarus would live again? Why did John report this, when John also knew that joy was just around the corner? I don't know — I don't always understand why I weep, even at happy occasions.

It's OK to weep at a funeral, even if we know that the person will be resurrected into immortal life. Jesus promised that we will never die, and yet death still happens. It is still an enemy, still something in this world that is not the way it's supposed to be in eternity. Even if eternal joy is just around the corner, sometimes we have times of great sadness, even though Jesus loves us. When we weep, Jesus weeps with us. He can see our sadness in this age just as well as he can see the joys of the future.

He stinks

"Roll away the stone," Jesus said, and Martha objected, "There's going to be a bad smell, because he's been dead for four days." Is there anything in your life that stinks, anything that you don't want Jesus to expose by "rolling back the stone"? There is probably something like that in everyone's life, something we'd rather keep buried, but sometimes Jesus has other plans, for he knows things that we do not, and we just have to trust him.

So they rolled back the stone, and Jesus prayed, and then he called out, "Lazarus, come out!" "The dead man came out," John reports — but he was no longer dead. He was wrapped up like a dead man, but he was walking. "Take off the grave clothes," Jesus said, "and let him go" (vs. 43-44).

Jesus calls out to spiritually dead people, today, too, and some of them hear his voice and walk out of their graves — they come out of the stench, they come out of the self-centered way of thinking that leads to death. And what do they need? They need someone to help them unwrap the grave clothes, to get rid of the old ways of thinking that so easily cling to us.

That's one of the functions of the church. We help roll back the stone, even though there may be a stench, and we help the people who are responding to Jesus' call. Do you hear Jesus calling you to himself? It's time to walk out of your "grave." Do you know someone Jesus is calling? It's time to help roll back their stone.

PALM SUNDAY

By Joseph Tkach

Early in its history, the Christian church, desiring to worship Jesus by focusing on the great saving events of his death and resurrection, formed a tradition of celebrating in the spring what became known as "Holy Week."

Palm Sunday commemorates Jesus' entry into Jerusalem amidst a huge demonstration of support by the common people. No doubt, most of them were thinking that Jesus would declare himself a Messiah in the tradition of the Maccabees, who had temporarily restored some of the Jewish nation's glory nearly two centuries earlier. Even some of Jesus' disciples thought that Jesus was the warrior-king who would deliver them from Roman oppression (John 12:17-18). But Jesus' entry into Jerusalem was far from the "triumphant" entry of a conquering military general riding astride a white war horse. We know some of the details from Luke 19 and John 12.

Jesus entered Jerusalem from the humble town of Bethany, riding on a donkey. Bethany was about two miles from Jerusalem, just off the road from Jericho. There would have been some houses and trading stalls along the road leading into the city. So when the people heard he was coming, they lined the road to greet him. They threw their coats and cloaks in his path, as well as the branches of the trees.

The palm branch was a traditional symbol of Israel, so waving it was like waving the Jewish national flag. They waved palm fronds in the air shouting "Hosanna," which in Hebrew means "God saves" and "Blessed is the king of Israel!" (John 12:13, quoting Psalm 118:25-26). This is how people in the first century greeted a visiting king—they would go out to meet him, praise him and then escort him into the city. These people were welcoming Jesus as their king.

At that time of year, since the Passover festival was only a week away, there would also have been many sightseers and pilgrims in the area. Many would have heard about Jesus the great teacher, miracle-worker and, perhaps, the one who would lead them to freedom from Roman oppression. They may have remembered Zechariah's prophecy: "Rejoice greatly, Daughter Zion! Shout, Daughter Jerusalem! See, your king comes to you, righteous and victorious, lowly and riding on a donkey, on a colt, the foal of a donkey" (Zechariah 9:9).

No wonder everyone greeted Jesus so enthusiastically!

Well, not everyone. The religious leaders, who had an interest in maintaining the status quo, saw him as a threat. "'See, this is getting us nowhere. Look how the whole world has gone after him!' they said to one another" (John 12:19). The atmosphere in Jerusalem was always tense during the religious festivals. The political leaders feared the gathering crowds could result in demonstrations and protests that could easily get out of hand. The religious leaders, such as the Pharisees, feared the same since they did not want to give their Roman overlords an excuse to crack down.

Some of these words that the crowd sang and shouted in praise were also chanted in the temple during the Passover festival. But these people were praising him for the wrong reason. They thought he had come to liberate them from Rome, and thus missed the real point of these scriptures. The Messiah had come to liberate them and all of humanity, from a much greater oppression—the absolute tyranny of evil in the human heart and society and from alienation from God.

It was an understandable mistake, given the situation at the time. It is a mistake many still make today. They see in Jesus someone who can help them fulfill their agenda. Today we know of some appalling examples, like the malevolent sectarian militias in Africa who attach the word "Christian" to their cause, while committing crimes against humanity. Most of us would never go to these extremes. But we all can make the mistake of that Palm Sunday crowd—using the name of Jesus to advance our personal projects and agendas, while calling it "God's work."

We do well to remember that Jesus said, "They worship me in vain; their teachings are merely human rules" (Matthew 15:9). It is so easy to shift the focus away from Jesus and onto ourselves. Some people still approach the Lord's Supper with a sense of foreboding. They strive to "examine themselves" to see if they are "worthy" to receive the bread and wine.

Can you see how this shifts the focus away from Jesus and onto ourselves? It can lead us to think in terms of what we have done, and cause us to focus on our attempts to either condemn or justify ourselves on that basis. But Jesus told us to partake of the Lord's Supper in memory of what he had done for us (Luke 22:19). Through his self-giving, Jesus delivered us from the delusional prison of self-justification, freeing us both to receive and to extend God's forgiveness.

The apostle Paul referred to the events of this important season as having primary importance in salvation history: "For what I received I passed on to you as of first importance: that Christ died for our sins according to the Scriptures, that he was buried, that he was raised on the third day according to the Scriptures, and that he appeared to Peter, and then to the Twelve" (1 Corinthians 15:3-5).

These central events of the gospel, which began to unfold on the road into Jerusalem on Palm Sunday, did not just change the history of one small nation. They altered forever the destiny of everyone who has ever lived. That is something to celebrate!

RIGHT WORDS, BUT THE WRONG REASON – A STUDY OF JOHN 12:12-19

By Michael Morrison

Each year, one week before Easter, Christian churches observe Palm Sunday, commemorating the day Jesus rode into Jerusalem on a donkey while the people waved palm branches and shouted praise. The people were right to praise Jesus, but they were doing it for the wrong reason.

Praise to the king!

John tells us that Jesus was in Bethany six days before the Passover (John 12:1). The next day, Jesus started walking to Jerusalem, and many people found out about it. "The great crowd that had come for the festival heard that Jesus was on his way to Jerusalem. They took palm branches and went out to meet him, shouting,

"Hosanna!" [a Hebrew word meaning "save!"]

"Blessed is he who comes in the name of the Lord!"

"Blessed is the king of Israel!" (John 12:13, quoting Psalm 118:25-26; NIV 2011 used in this chapter).

This is the way people in the first century greeted a visiting king—they would go out to meet him, praise him, and escort him into the city. These people were welcoming Jesus as a king. They were eager for Judea to have its own king, independent of Rome.

But the Romans did not want anyone to be king over Israel without their permission, and this parade for Jesus implied disloyalty to Rome. When the people waved palms, they were waving a Jewish national symbol. When Judea eventually did rebel against Rome, they put images of date palms on the coins. Palm trees represented a free and independent Judea.

Jesus knew that he was coming into the city toward his death, and that this same crowd would soon call for his crucifixion. Right now, the crowds cheered because they thought that Jesus would be a military hero, but he was not; they were badly mistaken about who Jesus was—and yet correct in their praise.

Seated on a donkey

Jesus did something else that may have added to the crowd's excitement: He "found a young donkey and sat on it, as it is written: 'Do not be afraid, Daughter Zion; see, your king is coming, seated on a donkey's colt'" (John 12:14-15, quoting Zechariah 9:9).

Some of the people probably knew from Zechariah that the promised

Jewish king would ride a donkey. But none of them, not even the disciples, really understood what Jesus was doing. "At first his disciples did not understand all this. Only after Jesus was glorified did they realize that these things had been written about him and that these things had been done to him" (John 12:16).

The disciples were probably thinking just like the crowd. Although Jesus had told his disciples that he was going to be killed, they did not understand it. Perhaps they thought it was a riddle, and they hadn't yet figured out the hidden meaning. But they understood it later—they understood that Jesus really was a king, and that he fulfilled the messianic prophecies, but that his kingdom was very different from anything they expected; it was "not of this world" (John 18:36).

But at this moment, the crowds and the disciples were excited because they thought Jesus might be the king who would deliver them from Rome (John 12:17-18).

Jesus could have gathered quite a large following if he had wanted to—and this terrified the Jewish leaders. They knew what Rome did to populist uprisings, and they definitely didn't want that. "So the Pharisees said to one another, 'See, this is getting us nowhere. Look how the whole world has gone after him!'" (verse 19).

They also spoke the right words, but for the wrong reason.

The Greeks had a word for it: *eulogeo*

We get the English word "eulogy" from the Greek word *eulogeō;* it comes from root words meaning "to speak well of." In eulogies, we speak well of people; we praise them.

The New Testament uses *eulogeō* 41 times; the Greek Old Testament uses it more than 500 times, usually with the meaning to praise or to bless. James 3:9 says that we eulogize God—we praise or speak well of him.

When Jesus eulogized his disciples (Luke 24:51), he was *giving* a blessing. To bless a person means "to ask God to bestow divine favor on … . In a number of languages the closest equivalent of to 'bless' is 'to pray to God on behalf of' or 'to ask God to do something good for'" (Johannes Louw and Eugene Nida, *Greek-English Lexicon of the New Testament Based on Semantic Domains,* I: 442).

In Ephesians 1:3, Paul says that God has already blessed us, already done good to us. When the people called Jesus "blessed" (John 12:13), they were saying that God had already been good to him.

When Jesus blessed bread (for example, Luke 24:30), he was asking God to further his good purpose through that bread.

JOHN 13: FOOTWASHING:
A TRADITION OF SERVICE

By Joseph Tkach

Jesus, the evening he was betrayed, "poured water into a basin and began to wash his disciples' feet, drying them with the towel that was wrapped around him" (John 13:5).

"When he had finished washing their feet, he put on his clothes and returned to his place. 'Do you understand what I have done for you?' he asked them…. 'Now that I, your Lord and Teacher, have washed your feet, you also should wash one another's feet'" (vs. 12, 14).

In the days of dusty roads and open-toed sandals, feet often became dirty, and it was the job of the lowest servants to wash the guests' feet. But Jesus set an example of service by doing this job himself, despite the protests from Peter.

What did Jesus teach?

Jesus said, "I have set you an example that you should do as I have done for you" (v. 15). We must ask, then, just what did Jesus do?

1. He got up from the meal,
2. took off his outer clothing,
3. wrapped a towel around his waist,
4. poured water into a basin,
5. washed the 12 disciples' feet, and
6. dried them with his towel.

If we look at this list, we will realize that Christians generally skip most of what Jesus did. We do not wash feet during a meal, take off our suit jackets or wrap towels around our waists. We do not pour water into a basin, or wash feet, or dry them with our own towel.

Most Christians do not literally wash one another's feet. Some churches do have an annual footwashing service, but if they do, people usually wash two feet that are already clean. Jesus washed 24 feet that really needed to be washed. Jesus performed a service that really needed to be done.

Did our Lord instruct his disciples to "wash one another's feet" (v. 14)? Yes. Then why don't we have any evidence that the apostles actually did it? They didn't do it the evening Jesus commanded it, and we see nothing about it in Matthew, Mark, Luke, Acts, the epistles or in early church history.

The closest thing we find to it in the New Testament is 1 Timothy 5:10, which is about the qualifications of widows who may be put on a list of widows working for and supported by the church (we don't do that anymore, do we?). One of the qualifications is that she must be "well known for her good deeds, such as…washing the feet of the saints." Here, footwashing is a notable act of service, not something that all Christian women are expected to do on a regular basis.

Apparently the apostles understood Jesus to be talking about real service, not a ritual. When Jesus said, wash one another's feet, he meant, serve one another. He simply used a specific example as a figure of speech representing all types of service. (The Gospel of John has many such figures of speech that should not be taken literally.) Jesus is saying that we should humble ourselves and be willing to do even menial tasks for one another.

Symbol of service

I am not saying that it is wrong for Christians to wash one another's feet. But we do not turn the figure of speech into a literal requirement.

The Bible was written in a specific culture, and its instructions are sometimes phrased with specific customs. Paul tells us to greet one another with a holy kiss, and footwashing is even more tied to culture than kissing is. It is based on foot travel, dusty roads and open-toed sandals. In Jesus' day, footwashing was a normal part of a formal banquet. Now it is not. It is no longer part of customary formality, and it is no longer viewed as an honor or service.

We obey the intent of Paul's command not by kissing, but by greeting one another with affection. We obey the intent of Jesus' command not by washing our guests' feet, but by helping them in other ways. There is no need to insist on taking one command literally and adapting the other to modern customs. Both may be adapted so that we obey the intent.

When we serve one another throughout the year, helping one another in our real needs, we are obeying the spirit of the law of Christ. We are "washing feet" when we give believers rides to church, when we help them move furniture, when we bring a meal for the sick, when we clean house for the bereaved. We wash feet when we encourage the depressed, are patient with the angry, spend time with the lonely.

There are a thousand ways to "wash the feet of the saints." Sometimes it might even involve washing their feet — even cutting their toenails and helping them with cleanliness. Real service for genuine needs is far more important than a sanitized ritual. As Paul wrote: "You, my brothers, were called to be free. But do not use your freedom to indulge the sinful nature; rather, serve one another in love" (Gal. 5:13).

JOHN 14: "IN HIS NAME"

By Joseph Tkach

"Whatever you ask in my name," Jesus said, "I will do it" (John 14:13). Some people seem to think that Jesus is giving us a blank check — we can ask for anything at all, and he will sign his name to it and pass it along to the Father, and it will be done — guaranteed.

We all know that this doesn't work — and it's a good thing it doesn't! Some people pray for rain at the same time as their neighbors pray for sunshine. The home seller prays for a high price, the home buyer prays for a low one.

If God had to answer every request he was given in the name of Jesus, the world would be chaotic, driven by the whims of well-meaning but foolish people. Even if humans could all agree, we simply don't have the wisdom to be telling God how to run the universe.

So what did Jesus mean?

Whatever we ask

"I tell you the truth," Jesus said, "my Father will give you whatever you ask in my name.... Ask and you will receive, and your joy will be complete" (John 16:23-24). Does this mean that we fill out the request form, and Jesus signs it and sends it to his dad? "Hey, Dad, I've got a buddy here who wants a million dollars. How about doing it as a favor for me?"

No, that is not the way it works. Jesus is not a middleman who stamps his signature on our request, pretending that our request is really his. He says: "I am *not* saying that I will ask the Father on your behalf. No, the Father himself loves you" (verses 26-27). We have permission to go to the Father directly, because God loves us just as much as he loves his own Son. (Does that thought astonish you as much as it does me?)

Hebrews tells us that Jesus gives us permission to go to God directly. We do not need a middleman. So what does it mean to ask in the name of Jesus?

Let's imagine that we are in an ancient palace. The king is sitting on his throne, his prince at his right hand, dozens of guards at attention, hundreds of loyal servants waiting for orders so that every decree will be carried out immediately.

And now imagine that we go into the palace, and the guards immediately make way for us, knowing that we have permission to approach the king. They swing aside, snap to attention and give us the royal treatment. We walk into the throne room, bow before the king, bow before the prince, and then tell the king: "In the name of the prince, I ask you for a better job and a nicer home."

Maybe my palace protocol is a little rusty, but it seems a little odd for me to speak "in the name of the prince" when the prince is sitting right there. Maybe this is not what it means to ask "in the name of Jesus."

More than pronunciation

Some people think that Jesus was talking about pronouncing his name in a certain way. They believe we have to get his name right — like a secret password — before the request will get through the heavenly filters. But when ancient peoples talked about someone's "name," they were not worried about the right pronunciation — they were referring to a person's status or importance.

We can see that in the book of Hebrews. It begins by telling us that Jesus has inherited a better name than the angels have. The name in that context seems to be "Son," but the precise word isn't really important — the point being made is that Jesus is superior to the angels. He has a higher status, a greater glory.

When we talk about the superior name of Jesus, we are really talking about his superior importance. When we pray in the name of Jesus, we are not dealing with a special word — we are dealing with a special person. When we pray in his name, we are praying according to the way that he is — according to his nature. Our praise and requests should be something that fits his character.

Let's use another analogy. Suppose that a police officer says, "Stop in the name of the law" — it means that the officer has the force of law behind the command. But suppose that same officer asks for a bribe: "Give me $20,000 cash in the name of the law." Using the words "in the name of the law" does not automatically give the officer legal support, does it? When the officer says "in the name of the law," he is supposed to be acting within the rules of the law.

In the same way, when we use Jesus' name, we are not obligating him to support our own whims and desires. Rather, we are saying that we are already in accord with what he wants. We are saying something that he has authorized us to say.

Rather than forcing him to conform to our wishes, "in his name" means exactly the opposite: We are conforming to his wishes, we are acting within his will. When we speak on his behalf, we need to make sure that we are saying something that he would agree with.

When we say "in Jesus' name," we are conforming to the words of the

Lord's prayer: Let your will be done on earth as it is in heaven. Let it be done in my life. If my request is not according to your will, then feel free to change it to what it needs to be. "In Jesus' name" is our affirmation that, as best we know, our request is within his will.

Let your requests be known

However, if we have to pray according to God's will, what's the point of praying? Isn't he going to do his will whether we ask for it or not? Doesn't it go without saying that if we ask God to do what he already wants to, that he will do it?

But God is the one who is telling us to pray. In his wisdom, God has decided to do certain things only in answer to prayer. Sometimes this is so that we will learn, in the process of prayer, what his will is, and whether our request is for selfish purposes. We don't always understand what God's will is, and praying can sometimes help us come to a better understanding.

But I suspect that on many things, God's will is not set in stone. God may not have decided, for example, which person we should marry — but he has already decided how we should treat the person we marry. He requires that we choose the person, and choose each day how we will interact with that person. Prayer can help us here, too.

Prayer changes us — but it also affects what God does. Since he has decided to do certain things only in answer to prayer, he decides what to do based in part on what we do, on what we need in the situations we have chosen, and on what we ask him to do. He has the power to carry it out, the compassion to help us in our needs, and the wisdom to know what is really best for us.

"In everything," Paul says, "by prayer and petition, with thanksgiving, present your requests to God" (Philippians 4:6). Whatever is on your heart, whatever it is that you want, ask God for it.

Jesus has given us the authority to ask — but it is a request, not a command. We can trust God to answer in the best possible way, at the best possible time. But whatever we do (prayer included), we are to do it for the glory of God (1 Corinthians 10:31). When we do that, we can be confident that we are praying in Jesus' name.

JOHN 19: CROWNED WITH THORNS

By Joseph Tkach

When Jesus was on trial for his life, the soldiers twisted thorns into a makeshift crown and jammed it on his head (John 19:2). They hung a purple robe on him and ridiculed him, saying, "Hail, King of the Jews," while they punched and kicked him.

The soldiers did it to amuse themselves, but the Gospels include this as a significant part of Jesus' trial. I suspect that they include it because it has an ironic truth — Jesus is the king, and yet his rule would be preceded by rejection, ridicule and suffering. He has a crown of thorns because he is the ruler of a world filled with pain, and as the king of this corrupt world, he established his right to rule by experiencing pain himself. He was crowned (given authority) with thorns (only through great pain).

Meaning for us, too

The crown of thorns has meaning for our lives, too — it is not just part of a movie scene in which we are overwhelmed with the suffering that Jesus went through to be our Savior. Jesus said that if we want to follow him, we must take up our cross each day — and he could just as easily have said that we must experience a crown of thorns. We are joined to Jesus in the crucible of suffering.

The crown of thorns has meaning for Jesus, and it has meaning for every individual who follows Jesus. As Genesis describes it, Adam and Eve rejected God and chose to experience for themselves evil as well as good.

There is nothing wrong with knowing the difference between good and evil — but there is much wrong with experiencing evil, because that is a path of thorns, a path of suffering. When Jesus came proclaiming the arrival of the kingdom God, it is no surprise that humanity, still alienated from God, rejected him and expressed it with thorns and death.

Jesus embraced that rejection — accepted the crown of thorns — as part of his bitter cup of enduring what humans endure, so that he could open the door for us to escape with him from this world of tears. In this world, governments jam thorns on the citizens. And in this world, Jesus suffered whatever they wanted to do

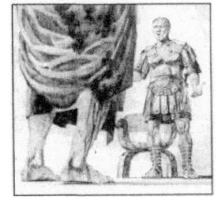

with him so that he could redeem us all from this world of ungodliness and thorns.

The world to come will be ruled by the human who has overcome the way of thorns — and those who give their allegiance to him will take their place in the government of his new creation.

We all experience our crowns of thorns. We all have our crosses to bear. We all live in this fallen world and take part in its pain and sorrow. But the crown of thorns and the cross of death have met their match in Jesus, who bids: "Come to me, all you who are weary and burdened, and I will give you rest. Take my yoke upon you and learn from me, for I am gentle and humble in heart, and you will find rest for your souls. For my yoke is easy and my burden is light" (Matthew 11:28-30).

CAN YOU BELIEVE IT?
A STUDY OF JOHN 20:18-29

By Michael Morrison

Jesus died on a cross. So have many other people. But only one came back to life—Jesus. The early church announced the resurrection of Jesus, and it has been a key teaching of Christianity ever since.

But some people find it hard to believe. There must be some sort of mistake—either a mistake in the diagnosis of death or a mistake in thinking that the person is alive again.

Jesus knows that it's hard to believe—an incident with Thomas illustrates this and has a lesson for us as well.

In John 20, we are told that some disciples found that Jesus was no longer in his tomb. He soon appeared to Mary, and she told the other disciples about it. But one woman's word was not enough to convince them.

The disciples see Jesus (verses 19-20)

"On the evening of that first day of the week, when the disciples were together, with the doors locked for fear of the Jewish leaders, Jesus came and stood among them and said, 'Peace be with you!'" (NIV 2011). We do not know exactly how Jesus got into the room on that Sunday evening, but John implies that it was in some supernatural way. Jesus could still do miracles.

He greeted them with peace, and "after he said this, he showed them his hands and side." Apparently there were still holes in his hands and a spear wound in the side—although the wounds caused by scourging were presumably gone.

"The disciples were overjoyed when they saw the Lord." They believed.

Authorized to preach (verses 21-23)

Jesus repeated his greeting and then added, "As the Father has sent me, I am sending you." This is John's version of the Great Commission. Just as Jesus was sent to earth with a mission, so now this mission is given to the disciples.

Jesus had promised that he would not abandon the disciples— he would come to them in the form of "another advocate...the Spirit of

439

truth" (John 14:16-18). Jesus fulfilled that promise: "And with that he breathed on them and said, 'Receive the Holy Spirit.'"

Some scholars think that Jesus was reissuing the promise and that it was not fulfilled until 50 days later, on the day of Pentecost (Acts 2). Others say the disciples received the Spirit at this time, and the Spirit came again in a visible way on the day of Pentecost. We do not need to resolve that question now, but we see here that Jesus was not a ghost, vision, or apparition—he was a living, breathing human being with a real body.

Jesus described the results of their mission: "If you forgive anyone's sins, their sins are forgiven; if you do not forgive them, they are not forgiven." Does this mean that God may want to forgive someone but will be thwarted by disciples who are not quite so gracious? No, Jesus is not giving the disciples the power to control what God can or cannot do.

Rather, he is speaking about what people *experience*. The context is the mission of the disciples: preaching the gospel. When the disciples preach forgiveness, people will experience forgiveness. When the disciples don't preach it, people will not have the joy of knowing they are forgiven. Jesus wants the disciples to announce forgiveness to all the people God forgives (and that, as we find out elsewhere in the Bible, includes everyone).

Thomas believes (verses 24-29)

However, one disciple was absent from the Sunday evening gathering. "Thomas (also known as Didymus), one of the Twelve, was not with the disciples when Jesus came. So the other disciples told him, 'We have seen the Lord!'"

But he was skeptical. He said, "Unless I see the nail marks in his hands and put my finger where the nails were, and put my hand into his side, I will not believe." He wanted not just to see, but also to touch.

Jesus gave him what he wanted: "A week later his disciples were in the house again, and Thomas was with them. Though the doors were locked, Jesus came and stood among them and said, 'Peace be with you!'

"Then he said to Thomas, 'Put your finger here; see my hands. Reach out your hand and put it into my side. Stop doubting and believe.'" Jesus not only appeared—he knew what Thomas had said a week earlier.

We do not know whether Thomas touched Jesus, but he responded with faith. "Thomas said to him, 'My Lord and my God!'" Earlier, Thomas had called Jesus Lord (John 14:5); now he calls him God. As John tells us in the opening verse, "The Word was God" (John 1:1). John wants Thomas's response to be ours as well, that we accept Jesus as our Lord and our God.

Jesus himself moves the discussion to future believers, including us: "Then Jesus told him, 'Because you have seen me, you have believed; blessed are those who have not seen and yet have believed.'"

ABOUT THE CONTRIBUTORS

J. Michael Feazell, D.Min., formerly vice president of Grace Communion International, wrote most of the articles on Mark as a series in *Christian Odyssey* magazine.

Michael Morrison, PhD, is Professor of New Testament at Grace Communion Seminary. He is also the editor of this volume. He wrote most of his articles as columns in *Christian Odyssey* magazine.

Joseph Tkach, D.Min., was President of Grace Communion International; he is now retired. Most of the articles on John were first published in *Christian Odyssey*.

Other articles were written by personnel working for Grace Communion International. Timothy Finlay went on to earn a doctorate in Old Testament studies at Claremont Graduate School. He now teaches at Azusa Pacific Seminary and Grace Communion Seminary.

Most of the artwork was done by Ken Tunell while he was employed by Grace Communion International.

ABOUT THE PUBLISHER...

Grace Communion International is a Christian denomination with about 30,000 members, worshiping in about 550 congregations in almost 70 nations and territories. We began in 1934 and our main office is in North Carolina. In the United States, we are members of the National Association of Evangelicals and similar organizations in other nations. We welcome you to visit our website at www.gci.org.

If you want to know more about the gospel of Jesus Christ, we offer help. First, we offer weekly worship services in hundreds of congregations worldwide. Perhaps you'd like to visit us. A typical worship service includes songs of praise, a message based on the Bible, and opportunity to meet people who have found Jesus Christ to be the answer to their spiritual quest. We try to be friendly, but without putting you on the spot. We do not expect visitors to give offerings – there's no obligation. You are a guest.

To find a congregation, write to one of our offices, phone us or visit our website. If we do not have a congregation near you, we encourage you to find another Christian church that teaches the gospel of grace.

We also offer personal counsel. If you have questions about the Bible, salvation or Christian living, we are happy to talk. If you want to discuss faith, baptism or other matters, a pastor near you can discuss these on the phone or set up an appointment for a longer discussion. We are convinced that Jesus offers what people need most, and we are happy to share the good news of what he has done for all humanity. We like to help people find new life in Christ, and to grow in that life. Come and see why we believe it's the best news there could be!

Our work is funded by members of the church who donate part of their income to support the gospel. Jesus told his disciples to share the good news, and that is what we strive to do in our writings, our worship services, and our day-to-day lives.

If this book has helped you and you want to pay some expenses, all donations are gratefully welcomed, and in several nations, are tax-deductible. If you can't afford to give anything, don't worry about it. It is our gift to you. To donate online, go to https://www.gci.org/online-giving/.

Thank you for letting us share what we value most – Jesus Christ. The good news is too good to keep it to ourselves.

See our website for hundreds of articles, locations of our churches, addresses in various nations, audio and video messages, and much more.

www.gci.org
Grace Communion International
3120 Whitehall Park Dr.
Charlotte, NC 28273
800-423-4444

You're Included...

Dr. J. Michael Feazell talks to leading Trinitarian theologians about the good news that God loves you, wants you, and includes you in Jesus Christ. Most programs are about 28 minutes long. Our guests have included:

Ray Anderson, Fuller Theological Seminary

Douglas A. Campbell, Duke Divinity School

Gordon Fee, Regent College

Jeannine Graham, George Fox University

Trevor Hart, University of St. Andrews

George Hunsinger, Princeton Theological Seminary

C. Baxter Kruger, Perichoresis

Jeff McSwain, Reality Ministries

Paul Louis Metzger, Multnomah University

Paul Molnar, St. John's University

Cherith Fee Nordling, Antioch Leadership Network

Andrew Root, Luther Seminary

Alan Torrance, University of St. Andrews

Robert T. Walker, Edinburgh University

N.T. Wright, University of St. Andrews

William P. Young, author of *The Shack*

Programs are free for viewing and downloading at https://learn.gcs.edu/course/view.php?id=58

**GRACE COMMUNION
SEMINARY**

GRACE COMMUNION SEMINARY

Ministry based on the life and love of the Father, Son, and Spirit

Grace Communion Seminary serves the needs of people engaged in Christian service who want to grow deeper in relationship with our Triune God and to be able to more effectively serve in the church. We offer three degrees: Master of Pastoral Studies, Master of Theological Studies, and Master of Divinity.

Why study at Grace Communion Seminary?

- Worship: to love God with all your mind.
- Service: to help others apply truth to life.
- Practical: a balanced range of useful topics for ministry.
- Trinitarian theology: a survey of Bible, theology and ministry with the merits of a Trinitarian perspective. We begin with the question, "Who is God?" Then, "Who are we in relationship to God?" In this context, "How then do we live and serve?"
- Part-time study: designed to help people who are already serving in local congregations. There is no need to leave your current ministry. Full-time students are also welcome.
- Flexibility: take your choice of courses or pursue a degree.
- Affordable, accredited study: Everything can be done online.

For more information, go to www.gcs.edu.

Grace Communion Seminary is accredited by the Distance Education Accrediting Commission, www.deac.org. The Accrediting Commission is listed by the U.S. Department of Education as a nationally recognized accrediting agency.